Thomas T Bouve, Boston Society of Natural History

Historical Sketch of the Boston Society of Natural History

with a notice of the Linnaean Society which preceded it

Thomas T Bouve, Boston Society of Natural History

Historical Sketch of the Boston Society of Natural History
with a notice of the Linnaean Society which preceded it

ISBN/EAN: 9783337095956

Printed in Europe, USA, Canada, Australia, Japan

Cover: Foto ©ninafisch / pixelio.de

More available books at **www.hansebooks.com**

ANNIVERSARY MEMOIRS

OF THE

BOSTON SOCIETY OF NATURAL HISTORY

PUBLISHED IN CELEBRATION OF THE

𝔉iftieth 𝔄nniversary of the Society's 𝔉oundation.

1830-1880

BOSTON:
PUBLISHED BY THE SOCIETY.
1880.

PUBLISHING COMMITTEE.

SAMUEL H. SCUDDER,   EDWARD BURGESS,
SAMUEL L. ABBOT,   ALPHEUS HYATT,
J. A. ALLEN.

PRESS OF A. A. KINGMAN.
BOSTON SOCIETY OF NATURAL HISTORY.
BERKELEY ST.

TABLE OF CONTENTS.

SOCIETY ANNALS.

List of the Present Officers of the Society. (1 page.)

Prefatory Note, with extracts from the minutes of the annual meeting, May 5th, 1880. (3 pages.)

Historical Sketch of the Boston Society of Natural History, with a notice of the Linnaean Society of New England which preceded it; including biographical notices of all the Society's prominent past members, officers and benefactors. By THOMAS T. BOUVÉ. (250 pages, six floor plans, view of the Museum, and portraits of Benjamin D. Greene, George B. Emerson, Amos Binney, John C. Warren, Jeffries Wyman, Thomas T. Bouvé, Augustus A. Gould, D. Humphreys Storer and William J. Walker.)

SCIENTIFIC PAPERS.

N. S. SHALER. *Propositions concerning the Classification of Lavas considered with reference to the Circumstances of their Extrusion.* (15 pages.)

ALPHEUS HYATT. *Genesis and Evolution of the species of Planorbis at Steinheim.* (114 pages, ten plates on nine sheets, one plate of sections; map and two sections in text.)

SAMUEL H. SCUDDER. *The Devonian Insects of New Brunswick; with a note on the Geological Relations of the Fossil Insects from the Devonian of New Brunswick*, by Principal J. W. Dawson, LL.D., F.R.S., etc. (41 pages, one plate.)

W. G. FARLOW. *The Gymnosporangia (Cedar-apples) of the United States.* (38 pages, two plates.)

THEODORE LYMAN. *A new Structural Feature, hitherto unknown among Echinodermata, found in Deep-Sea Ophiurans.* (12 pages, two plates.)

W. K. BROOKS. *The Development of the Squid, Loligo Pealii Lesueur.* (22 pages, three plates.)

A. S. PACKARD, JR. *The Anatomy, Histology and Embryology of Limulus Polyphemus.* (45 pages, seven plates.)

EDWARD BURGESS. *Contributions to the Anatomy of the Milk-Weed Butterfly, Danais Archippus Fabr.* (16 pages, two plates; one cut in text.)

SAMUEL F. CLARKE. *The Development of a Double-headed Vertebrate.* (6 pages, one plate.)

CHARLES SEDGWICK MINOT. *Studies on the Tongue of Reptiles and Birds.* (20 pages, one plate; six cuts in text.)

EDWARD S. MORSE. *On the Identity of the Ascending Process of the Astragalus in Birds with the Intermedium.* (10 pages, one plate; twelve cuts in text.)

LUCIEN CARR. *The Crania of New England Indians.* (10 pages, two plates.)

WILLIAM JAMES. *The Feeling of Effort.* (32 pages.)

LIST OF THE PRESENT OFFICERS OF THE SOCIETY.

President.
SAMUEL H. SCUDDER.

Vice-Presidents.
JOHN CUMMINGS,   FREDERICK W. PUTNAM.

Custodian.
ALPHEUS HYATT.

Honorary Secretary.
SAMUEL L. ABBOT.

Secretary.
EDWARD BURGESS.

Treasurer.
CHARLES W. SCUDDER.

Librarian.
EDWARD BURGESS.

Committees on Departments of the Museum.

MINERALS.
THOMAS T. BOUVÉ,
R. H. RICHARDS,
M. E. WADSWORTH.

GEOLOGY.
WILLIAM H. NILES,
G. FREDERIC WRIGHT.

PALAEONTOLOGY.
THOMAS T. BOUVÉ,
N. S. SHALER.

BOTANY.
JOHN CUMMINGS,
CHARLES J. SPRAGUE,
J. AMORY LOWELL.

MICROSCOPY.
SAMUEL WELLS,
R. C. GREENLEAF,
B. JOY JEFFRIES.

COMPARATIVE ANATOMY.
THOMAS DWIGHT,
W. F. WHITNEY.

RADIATES, CRUSTACEANS AND WORMS.
H. A. HAGEN,
ALEXANDER AGASSIZ.

MOLLUSKS.
EDWARD S. MORSE,
J. HENRY BLAKE.

INSECTS.
SAMUEL H. SCUDDER,
EDWARD BURGESS,
A. S. PACKARD, JR.

FISHES AND REPTILES.
F. W. PUTNAM,
THEODORE LYMAN,
S. W. GARMAN.

BIRDS.
J. A. ALLEN,
SAMUEL CABOT.

MAMMALS.
J. A. ALLEN,
E. L. MARK,
GEORGE L. GOODALE.

PREFATORY NOTE.

THE BOSTON SOCIETY OF NATURAL HISTORY, founded in 1830 by a few earnest men, has this year celebrated its fiftieth anniversary. Its growth during this period has been so considerable, it has gained for itself so firm a hold upon the esteem of our citizens, and its relations to the higher education of the people have been so significant, that it has been thought fitting to signalize this anniversary by the issue of a special volume of scientific papers, preceded by a detailed history of the Society, the preparation of which was entrusted to the President. Included in the history will be found the proceedings of the jubilee meeting, held on the twenty-eighth of April last. At the annual meeting, held a few days later, the President, Thomas T. Bouvé, Esq., declined a reëlection; having been an officer of the Society for nearly forty years and its President for ten years, no man living is so thoroughly identified as he with its life and interests during the most eventful period of its history; and it is therefore fitting that this statement should be followed by the tribute paid at the annual meeting to his untiring devotion to the interests of the Society, not only during his Presidency, but for nearly the whole period of its existence.

BOSTON, Dec. 15, 1880.   PUBLISHING COMMITTEE.

Extract from the minutes of the Annual Meeting, May 5, 1880.

Mr. S. H. Scudder, on assuming the presidential chair, discussed the mission of the Society, closing his remarks with the following words: At a previous meeting I have already expressed my sincere regret that we can no longer be led in this work by the President whose devotion we have been only too pleased to acknowledge by our ballots for ten years past; but as long as his life is spared to us we shall have his sympathy and wise advice,

(v)

and we may be sure that in all the work the Society undertakes, it will have no stronger friend than he.

Mr. John Cummings thereupon offered the following vote:—

"In consideration of the fact that Mr. Bouvé has declined to be a candidate for the first office of this Society, the members desire to express their grateful acknowledgment of the long and valuable service he has rendered as President, and their cordial thanks for his arduous labors, unremitted devotion, prudent and successful administration; nor can they part from him in this official capacity without the additional expression of their warm personal esteem."

No one ever associated with Mr. Bouvé, added Mr. Cummings, who did not feel himself drawn to him by the strongest and tenderest ties. In his own experience he had never met a man with so much devotion to any cause as Mr. Bouvé had shown for the welfare of the Society.

Mr. Cummings's remarks were warmly applauded and the motion was seconded by Prof. A. Hyatt, who said, in respect to Mr. Bouvé's administration, that although from the first the present policy of the Society had met the severest criticism and sometimes disapprobation from the intimate friends and advisers of the President, he had yet been able to keep his judgment unwarped and to consider those ideas, which were new to him, purely on their own merits. It is not too much to say that the Society's aims, which we have heard so highly praised in this anniversary year, could not have been so developed without Mr. Bouvé's constant support. The feelings expressed by Mr. Cummings will be echoed in the heart of every officer of the Society, for we have always found our President full of kindness and consideration, as well as just and sound in judgment.

Mr. F. W. Putnam said he could not allow this opportunity to pass without a few words, which at best would be but a feeble expression of his feelings; for in addition to a long and cherished friendship that every year had strengthened, his official ties to Mr. Bouvé were double, and both were broken by his resignation, since, as might not be remembered by all present, the President of the Society was *ex-officio* a member of the board of trustees of the Peabody Museum at Cambridge; and while, as Curator of that Museum, he welcomed his friend, the new President of the Society, he was very sorry to lose one who had been so long connected with the Museum and had ever been ready to give his kindly aid in furtherance of its objects.

Prof. W. H. Niles spoke of the large amount of work in the care and arrangement of the collections which Mr. Bouvé had accomplished during the term of his presidency. Most of this has been done after the business duties of the day, and how frequently he has remained until called home by some one, none but his family know. When alterations in the building were going on, he habitually inspected the entire premises after all others had gone, to see that all was left in safety. The Society has steadily progressed in its usefulness and scientific position during the administration of Mr. Bouvé, and he now leaves the presidential chair with nothing to regret, and with the esteem and friendship of every member. Day by day, and year after year, he has brought here a large heart, full of geniality and goodness, and has been in himself a source of happiness to those who have known him as President. It would be a pleasure to reciprocate, in some small measure at least, his long-continued kindness, and this could be best done by each member's trying to make the Society so pleasant for Mr. Bouvé, that, as a source of his future happiness, it should be second only to his home and his family. In conclusion, Mr. Niles said he did not doubt that each member present would like to express in some special way his personal respect and honor for him who was the dear friend of all and one of the best benefactors the Society ever had; and he hoped they might do so by rising as they voted for the adoption of the resolution proposed by Mr. Cummings.

The Chair accordingly called for a standing vote and the resolution was unanimously adopted.

HISTORICAL SKETCH

OF THE

BOSTON SOCIETY OF NATURAL HISTORY;

WITH

A NOTICE OF THE LINNÆAN SOCIETY,

WHICH PRECEDED IT.

By THOMAS T. BOUVÉ.

BOSTON:
PUBLISHED BY THE SOCIETY.
1880.

TO

CHARLES JAMES SPRAGUE and JAMES CLARKE WHITE,

Companions with me for years in laborious work upon the collections of the Society,
these pages are dedicated,
with the great respect and kind regards of
THE AUTHOR.

HISTORICAL SKETCH OF THE BOSTON SOCIETY OF NATURAL HISTORY: WITH A NOTICE OF THE LINNÆAN SOCIETY, WHICH PRECEDED IT. BY THOMAS T. BOUVÉ.

No history of our Society can well be given without some brief account of the attempts previous to its formation to interest the public in the study of Natural History. Before any organized efforts were made to this end but few publications even had appeared on the subject, and these are cited from remarks made by Dr. A. A. Gould in a sketch of the Linnæan Society, which appeared in the Proceedings of the Boston Society of Natural History in 1863.[1] The most valuable of them was one by the Rev. Manassah Cutler, entitled "Account of some of the Vegetable Productions naturally growing in this part of America, botanically arranged." Another was a pamphlet published by the celebrated Dr. Benj. Waterhouse, who seems to have brought with him from Holland "some general notions of Systematic Natural History." The pamphlet was entitled, "Heads of a Course of Lectures on Natural History," Cambridge, 1810, in which he distributes the lower animals under the heads of Ornithology, Amphibiology, Ichthyology, Insects and Vermes; which latter he mentioned as "outskirts of Animated Nature extending to the confines of the vegetable world." In a note he said he would "extend, contract or omit parts of his programme to suit his audience." As Dr. Gould quaintly remarks, it does not appear whether he ever had any audience at all. In addition to these publications some articles of a practical character were written by Prof. W. D. Peck, who occupied the Chair of Natural History at Harvard College from 1805 to 1822. They appeared in agricultural papers, and the most important of them purported to give a natural history of the slug worm and the canker worm. Dr. Gould, in referring to the Professor's work at Cambridge, says, "He gave such instruction as was demanded, which was very little." Harris's Natural History of the Bible, Mather's Magnalia, Thacher's Dispensatory, with some treatises on the medicinal properties of herbs, and a few other papers of little importance, complete the publications referred to.

THE LINNÆAN SOCIETY.

The time at length arrived for an organized effort to excite some interest on the part of the public in natural science, and the men were not wanting. On the 8th of December, 1814, there met at the house of Dr. Jacob Bigelow, a number of gentlemen, then prominent in the community, some of whom afterwards became eminent in their several professions, if not in natural science. They were, besides Dr. Bigelow, Wm. S. Shaw, Octavius Pickering, Dr. Walter Channing, Ezekiel D. Cushing, La Fayette Perkins, Dr. Geo. Hayward, Nathaniel Tucker, J. Freeman Dana, John W. Webster, and

[1] Vol. IX, 335.

Dr. John Ware. Dr. Channing was chosen Chairman, and Dr. Bigelow Secretary, and a committee, composed of Dr. Bigelow, Mr. Pickering, and Dr. Hayward, was appointed to draft a Constitution for the Society, which they called the New England Society for the Promotion of Natural History. Two days after they met again by adjournment, and the Constitution reported by the Committee was read, discussed, and adopted. Among its provisions are some which may interest readers of the present day.

The 1st article provides that the Society shall consist of Immediate, Associate, Honorary, and Corresponding Members.

The 2d, that the officers shall consist of a President chosen from the Honorary or Immediate Members; Vice President, Corresponding Secretary, Recording Secretary, Treasurer, and Cabinet Keeper, who shall be chosen from the Immediate Members.

The 11th, that there shall be a meeting once a week.

The 12th, that any Immediate Member who shall unnecessarily be absent three times successively, shall forfeit his membership.

The 14th, that all specimens placed in the Museum shall be the property of the Society, and that no others shall have a place, except by express vote.

The 17th, that no person shall be chosen an Immediate Member except by unanimous vote of all present; other members may be elected by a two-thirds vote, but none without nomination at a previous meeting.

The 18th, that there shall be a Standing Committee of five members, chosen annually, to provide a suitable room for the collection, employ one or more persons for service, and draw on the treasurer for payment of the expenses thereby incurred, under such restrictions as the Society may from time to time make.

The 19th, that each Immediate Member shall pay $5 annually.

The 20th, that every Immediate Member absent from a stated meeting without excuse, shall be fined fifty cents.

Such articles have been quoted of the Constitution adopted as tend to show the animus of the members. Who can say that they were not thoroughly in earnest?

In subsequent proceedings of the Society it appears that fines were collected, undoubtedly for absence without excuse; but there is no recorded instance of a member forfeiting his membership by unnecessary absence.

It is not easy to understand the principle or the policy which dictated the selection in all cases of persons on whom was conferred Honorary, Corresponding or Associate Membership. In numerous cases individuals were elected to the former who cannot be supposed to have manifested much interest in natural science, and who too were residents of Boston. They were distinguished perhaps as Doctors of Divinity, or as Doctors of Medicine, but neither then nor afterwards were known as Naturalists. Among the Corresponding Members are found the names of several residing in the immediate vicinity of Boston, as Cambridge and Charlestown; which seems singular, for the perils of a ferriage across the Charles, which at an earlier date might have made these ports appear distant, were no longer to be incurred; good bridges then as now uniting the populations. But this is not all, some of the Corresponding Members were citizens of Boston itself.

From the records it seems that the number of Immediate Members at first, or soon after the formation of the Society, was about 20; of the Honorary, 19; of the Corresponding, 68, and of the Associate, 24. It is not clear what privileges these last had as members of the Society, except the implied one that they were not subject to assessment.

In the list of the early Corresponding Members, it is pleasant to find the name of Dr. William J. Walker, to whose great bounty the Boston Society of Natural History is indebted for its present standing among the leading scientific societies of the world, if not for its very existence; for there is much reason for the opinion that had the Society continued dependent on the voluntary labors of its members as would necessarily have been the case without his help, it would have met the fate of the majority of the societies of natural history, which have been formed under apparently favorable auspices, have flourished for a time, and then faded out of existence. But more of this when his large benefactions to the Boston Society of Natural History are mentioned in the course of this history.

It may be a matter of interest to the reader to have presented here some of the names of members connected with the Society, particularly of such as afterwards distinguished themselves in their several callings, or at a subsequent period became active members of the Boston Society of Natural History. Among them may be found: —

As Immediate Members:

Dr. Jacob Bigelow.	Francis C. Gray.	Dr. John Randall.
Dr. Walter Channing.	Dr. Geo. Hayward.	Dr. John Ware.
Benj. A. Gould.	Octavius Pickering.	Dr. John W. Webster.

As Honorary Members:

Hon. John Davis.	Rev. James Freeman.	Rev. John Prince.
Hon. John Lowell.	Prof. Wm. D. Peck.	Rev. J. Lathrop.
Hon. Christopher Gore.	Rev. Manasseh Cutler.	Rev. J. T. Kirkland.
Dr. John Jeffries.	Dr. John Warren.	

As Corresponding Members:

Nathaniel Bowditch.	Prof. Benj. Silliman.	S. G. Perkins.
Josiah Quincy.	Robert Hare.	Dr. E. Hale.
Dr. W. J. Walker.	Prof. Parker Cleaveland.	Thomas H. Perkins.
	Benjamin Pierce.	

As Associate Members:

Joseph Tilden.	Rev. Wm. Ellery Channing.	Dr. Geo. C. Shattuck.
Dr. J. C. Warren.	Wm. Minot.	Rev. Edward Everett.
Dr. James Jackson.	Richard Sullivan.	Nathan Hale.
	Francis Boott.	

The first officers elected were
John Davis, LL.D., *President*.
Wm. S. Shaw, *Vice-President*.
Jacob Bigelow, *Corresponding Secretary*.
George Hayward, *Recording Secretary*.
Octavius Pickering, *Treasurer*.
John W. Webster, *Cabinet-Keeper*.

On December 29th, in accordance with a vote previously passed, the several members having specimens to present to the Society towards the formation of a museum brought them forward, and it is recorded that a considerable collection was made.

At a meeting held January 14th it appears that much dissatisfaction was expressed at the name of the Society, and it was therefore voted that each member should propose in writing at the next meeting such name as he judged the most suitable. When the Society again met, on the 21st of January, 1815, the members, after due consideration, unanimously

Voted, That the Society shall be called the Linnæan Society of New England.

To understand the spirit and do justice to the labors of the active members of this Society, let us look a little into their proceedings of the first year. February 4th it was voted that each member shall, if possible, prepare some animal in the course of the week and present it to the Society at the next meeting. In the record of a following meeting it is stated that a considerable number of animals were presented to the Society, all of which had been prepared by the members in the course of the week. Whether these animals were of the dimensions of elephants or mice is not stated. At the same meeting the Recording Secretary was requested to draw up some popular directions for the preservation of specimens in Natural History, to be given to masters of vessels and others, and to report at the next meeting; and at the next meeting a circular letter was presented containing such directions. This was ordered to be printed.

The subjects brought before the members did not always pertain to natural history. At a meeting on March 4th a paper by the Hon. John Lowell was read, "On the resemblance between certain customs of the modern Italians and ancient Romans." It was voted to copy it into the common place book of the Society.

Besides the weekly meeting it was decided to hold once a quarter a general meeting, to which should be invited the Honorary, Corresponding and Associate Members, and at each such quarterly meeting a paper by some person appointed at the preceding meeting should be read on some subject connected with the pursuits of the Society. The first of these quarterly meetings was held on the 21st of June, and Judge Davis delivered what the record of that date states to have been "an elegant address on the advantages of natural history and the objects of the institution."

At the regular meeting held a few days afterwards, Dr. Randall, as the text expresses it, was unanimously chosen to *perform* at the next quarterly meeting. It was also voted that on the next Wednesday, the 28th of June, the day appointed by the Constitution for the Annual Meeting, the Society should dine together at Richards' in Brookline. In accordance with this vote, the Immediate Members met at Brookline and after transacting the business of electing officers for the year, they dined together, the record states, in company with the Hon. John Lowell and Hon. Josiah Quincy. This combination of scientific pursuits with feasting is not mentioned as a peculiarity of the members of this pioneer society, and even in later days it has not been found disagreeable or unprofitable. In some degree these Annual Meetings partook of the character of what has been more recently called in some of our societies "Field Days", for they were held at some selected place in the country, and a portion of the day was employed in obtaining specimens. Thus, at the first meeting, it is mentioned that "after dinner the members divided themselves into several parties for the purpose of making an excursion in search of specimens in the several branches of natural history." Towards evening it is further said: "they returned to town after having passed a delightful day."

Presentations of objects of natural history are frequently mentioned as having been made to the Society during the year, and sometimes those of other character, as for instance a likeness of Mr. Roscoe, of Liverpool, presented by Mr. Francis Boott. In June, the Society was the recipient of two living tigers, presented by Capt. Stewart, of the United States frigate Constitution. Whether it was more fortunate in receiving or losing them, it is now impossible to say; certain it is, they were by some means lost, and a Mr. Savage was held accountable; for in February, 1818, the record states that "a settlement was effected with Mr. Savage for the loss of the Brazilian tigers, which were presented to the Society by Capt. Stewart of the Navy," and it subsequently appears that the treasurer was authorized to pay out of the money received from Mr. Savage, rent due by the Society.

At the second Quarterly Meeting of the year, held in September, Dr. Randall read an interesting paper on the history and medical properties of the native plant *Triosteum perfoliatum*.

In October, the Museum was arranged into several departments, and members were allotted to take charge of them, as follows:

First division of Minerals.	Dr. Randall.	Amphibia	Mr. Gould.
Second " " "	Dr. Channing.	First division of Insects	Mr. Pickering.
Third " " "	Mr. Dana, Sen.	Second " " "	Mr. Dana, Jr.
Plants	Mr. Tucker.	Third " " "	Mr. Codman.
Mammalia	Dr. Bigelow.	Shells	Mr. Gray.
Birds	Dr. Cushing.	Zoophytes, &c.	Dr. Hayward.
Fishes	Dr. Ware.		

In November, a paper was read by Dr. Goodwin of Sandwich, on tadpoles found there

In December, Dr. Channing was requested to make up, from the duplicates, a box of minerals, and send to France, for exchange, and the Vice President·was requested to use his exertions to procure a moose for the Society. Professor Cleaveland of Bowdoin College, a distinguished mineralogist, had been invited to deliver the quarterly address in December, but unable to visit Boston, was obliged to decline, and no address was delivered.

It has been thought well in view of the lesson to be derived from the experience of this Society, to give at some length an account of the proceedings of this first year of its existence with the intention of being more brief in mention of subsequent proceedings. Enough is known of the character and ability of the members of the Society, and enough has been shown of their devoted zeal in its service, to satisfy all that if ultimate success did not crown their efforts, the fault was not so much in them, as in the fact, that more was undertaken for accomplishment through voluntary labor, than can ever be expected from men however zealous, who are engaged in professional or business life.

The second year of the Linnæan Society was marked by the same manifestation of zeal on the part of the members as was shown during the first. From the assessment of the members enough was raised to pay for some professional labor, and an artist, so called, was hired, who probably could mount specimens; as in January, a committee was appointed to procure animals, that he might find employment in preparing them. In February the room in which the cabinet was kept being unsatisfactory, one was hired over Boylston Hall, where the collection was placed, and where meetings were subsequently held. The Museum of the Society was opened to the public every Saturday afternoon.

In all the months of this year valuable donations of specimens were received. Among others specified may be mentioned a living bear, presented by Commodore Chauncy of the navy; a miscellaneous collection of objects of natural history from Bowdoin College; a valuable collection of birds from Africa; besides cases of insects, handsome minerals and beautiful shells and corals, from other donors.

The meetings were well attended, and there appeared throughout the year no loss of interest on the part of the members. The annual meeting was held at Fresh Pond Hotel, Cambridge, and the attendance was general on the part of the members. Judge Davis presided, and the day being pleasant, all found great enjoyment in excursions and in amusements until dinner, which they partook of together, returning to town in the evening.

In August Dr. Bigelow gave an interesting account of an expedition, undertaken by himself, and the other members of the Society, for the purpose of visiting the White Mountains in New Hampshire. Being equipped, as he states, with proper instruments, the height of the mountains was ascertained more accurately than it ever had been. His estimate of the height is not mentioned. Particular attention, the record states, was given to the mineral, animal, and vegetable specimens that were found in the mountains, and the whole paper abounded with curious facts and ingenious observations. All who in subsequent years had the pleasure of intercourse with Dr. Bigelow, need not be assured of the interesting character of the paper presented by him to those who were favored by hearing it. It would, undoubtedly, be read with great interest now, notwithstanding the general knowledge prevailing relative to the region mentioned.

The Society increased in numbers during the year, and there appeared no loss of interest on the part of the members. Save a few lines found in the report of one of the meetings in September, everything denoted great prosperity. But these few lines are enough to suggest to those of a later day, conversant with the history of natural history societies, the probable decay at a not distant time, of that zeal and interest so marked at this period. They may be found in the report of a committee appointed to obtain from the Legislature an act of incorporation. This report declares it inexpedient to petition at present, provided our expenses can be defrayed until we are united with the Athenæum. This is the first expression in the records implying what, alas, the history of most natural history societies shows to be inevitable when sustained only by the voluntary labors and assessments of members, and dependent on the uncertain contributions of friends; lack of adequate means for the care and preservation of the rapidly augmenting collections and consequent disaffection. We shall later see, that notwithstanding the strenuous exertions of the members, and abundant success in collecting specimens, an increasing uneasiness manifested in a disposition to unite with another society and thus sacrifice its own identity; or, failing this, to dispose of its collections in a way that would not have been considered for a moment at an earlier period.

The time, however, has not arrived to dwell upon anything not agreeable in the record of the devoted workers of the Society. The Recording Secretary appears to have been quite elated at the progress made, for he writes in October: The zeal and activity of the members seem to be unabated, and if the collection continues to increase for a few years in the same proportion, it will surpass every establishment of the kind in the United States, and almost rival those of Europe.

The close of the year shows no less activity. In December a valuable paper was read by Dr. John Ware. Large and valuable specimens were set up under the superintendence of the committees, and arrangements were made, as the record states, for labelling all the birds, beasts and fishes belonging to the cabinet. A committee was also appointed to see what could be done in relation to furnishing permanent apartments for the collection of the Society, which implies, probably, that it had increased to a size rendering more room necessary for its accommodation.

1817. Judging by the records of this year's doings alone, it might be thought that all was well with the Society, and that its continued existence and progress were secure. Donations continued to pour in, many of a very valuable character. Among them may be noticed a fine American elk, which is mentioned as one of the most interesting and valuable animals which our country affords. There seems certainly to have been no fears of calamity, for in the early part of the year a fine specimen of a female moose, from Maine, was purchased, and the hope is expressed that another year a male may be obtained, together with a reindeer, which the Secretary states will make complete the collection of the deer of the United States. Arrangements were also made with Capt. Waterman to procure specimens of natural history from the coast of Africa.

The annual meeting was held at Brookline, where the members, as usual, sat down to dinner. Valuable papers were presented, one on the mineralogy and geology of Cambridge and its vicinity, by Mr. S. L. Dana, Jr., containing, it is stated, "unquestionably more accurate information on the subjects upon which it treats than has ever before been communicated;" one on the luminous appearance of the sea, translated from the Transactions of the Swedish Academy by Judge Davis; and one on the medical properties of *Phytolacca decandra*, by Dr. Hayward.

It is distinctly mentioned by the Secretary, in June, that the usual business of collecting and preserving specimens had been regularly attended to.

On the 18th of June, Dr. Channing delivered an address. At a previous meeting of the Society it had been voted to call a public meeting of the members, each of whom should have the privilege of inviting others to be present on this occasion, which was made one of great interest, many of the leading men of the state and city being present. Among them, the Governor, Lieutenant Governor, Council, members of the Senate, and many ladies. The whole company were surprised at the size of the collection, and highly pleased with its general order and neatness.

At twelve o'clock the address was given, which was upon the importance of literature and science, particularly to the people of New England. The claims of the Society to the patronage of the public were urged with great force and ingenuity. A sketch of the progress of the institution from its first foundation was given, and statements made showing the rapid growth of the cabinet.

The interest excited by this meeting gave the Society reason to believe that the importance of its work was fully appreciated, and that the public already felt disposed to protect and patronize it. It is sad to think how soon the hopes excited by the feeling manifested at this meeting were doomed to fade away.

Soon after this meeting, wonderful stories were circulated concerning a strange marine animal, said to have been seen in the harbor of Gloucester, and a special meeting of the Society was called for the purpose of taking measures to obtain information. Judge Davis, Dr. Bigelow, and Mr. Gray, were constituted a committee to write to, and have depositions taken of, all who had seen the animal. The committee reported, in September, that they had no doubt of the existence of an animal of extraordinary appearance and enormous dimensions, as there were many credible witnesses. They expressed the hope of getting more information soon. In October, a very full report was made upon what was now designated as the sea serpent, and an account was also given of a small one, probably, the record says, of a "spawn," that had been taken at the water's edge. The committee were of the opinion that these animals were of a genus wholly unknown to naturalists, and they designated them under the name of Scoliophis, from the singular curvatures of the spine, by which they possessed a vertical motion. To this they added the specific name Atlanticus.[1]

It is a subject of great regret, the Secretary wrote, that all the efforts that were made to take the great serpent proved wholly ineffectual, notwithstanding the zeal and activity of his pursuers.

1818. We have thus far traced the history of this Society from its formation, have dwelt upon the evidences of its rapid progress, and have had brought before us accounts of its great acquisitions, through which it had become possessed of a collection which, in the language of its Secretary, seemed likely to surpass any one of like character in this country and even rival the great collections of Europe. Henceforth we shall find evidence of declining vigor on the part of the Society as such, notwithstanding great struggles on the part of many of its members to sustain it and give it renewed activity; we shall see the interest in its meetings rapidly wane, and its valuable cabinet becoming ruined for the want of proper care; we shall see that even the hope for continued existence is giving place to utter despair, foreboding dissolution.

In January a committee was appointed to make propositions to the trustees of the Athenæum for a union of the two institutions, and if this could not be effected, to report what measures should be taken for the preservation of the cabinet.

Meetings were held in the succeeding months, but not with so much regularity as heretofore. At one of the meetings a valuable paper was read by Dr. J. W. Webster on the mineralogical character of the Island of St. Nicholas, which he had lately visited. This seems to have been the only paper brought forward during the year. The Immediate Members made an excursion up the Middlesex Canal, upon invitation of Mr. J. L. Sullivan, and they dined together at Woburn, — their last dinner as a society.

---

[1] Report of a Committee of the Linnæan Society of New England relative to a large marine animal, supposed to be a Serpent, seen near Cape Ann, Mass. Boston, 1817. 8vo. 52 pp. See remarks by Dr. Jeffries Wyman, Proc. Bost. Soc. Nat. Hist., IX, 245.

1819. During this year the meetings were not held with any regularity. Attempts were made to take charge of and preserve the specimens, but without success, and the members had the mortification of seeing a museum going to decay that had cost them so much labor and expense; but it seemed inevitable. They were mostly engaged in professional pursuits, and of course could not give their personal services to the preservation of the collection; and the funds of the society were not sufficient to hire any one permanently.

1820. Things remained in this condition until March, 1820, when a meeting was called for the purpose of considering the expediency of disposing of the collection.

It was then voted, that if one hundred dollars per year could be obtained for ten years, the members would renew their efforts to preserve the institution.

In April it was reported that enough had been subscribed, and more, for the preservation of the collection. This seemed for a time to revive hope and inspire interest. Amendments were made to the Constitution, and a committee was appointed to attend to the preservation of the collection. A number of new members were elected.

In May, committees were chosen to examine and report upon the state of each department of the collection, and they were expected to attend at the hall of the museum every Saturday, from 3 to 6 o'clock. A committee was also appointed to petition the legislature for an act of incorporation; evidence certainly of renewed hope.

The Society became incorporated, and the first meeting under the act was held in June. Dr. Jacob Bigelow was elected President.

In August a specimen of a seal and several minerals were presented, and in October there were many minerals added to the collection. In December a movement was made towards the formation of a library, and in the following March (1821) rules and regulations were adopted for it. Notwithstanding, however, these signs of activity on the part of the Society, the records afford sufficient evidence of declining interest. The meetings were not well attended. Immediate Members resigned as such, and were made Associate Members, mainly for the reason that they could not attend to the duties of the former.

1822. In the early part of this year there yet appeared no evidence of yielding to the inevitable, and specimens, among them the bones of a camel, were received for the cabinet with satisfaction and thanks. In August, however, we find that a committee had been appointed to consider upon the future disposal of the cabinet, which reported:

"That it appears, by the resignation and non-attendance of members, that it has become burdensome to individuals of the Society to support its meetings and collections as they have hitherto done; that it is expedient, therefore, to suspend its meetings and give up the room of the Society, and place the collection, or such part of it as can be preserved, in some place where it will occasion no further expense to the Society or its contributors; that a committee be appointed to remove it from its present location and place it in the hands of any other person or persons who will afford suitable rooms for its reception, the preference being always given to a scientific corporate body; that the present funds of the Society be devoted to removing, securing and enlarging the collection, at the discretion of the committee."

This committee was made permanent, with directions to appoint a Secretary, and to call a meeting of the Society on the application of three members.

The expression that the funds of the Society be devoted to enlarging as well as securing the collection denotes the existence of a vague hope at least of renovation.

The election of officers was made, as in former years.

1823. In March of this year a meeting was called by the Society, and the committee appointed in August of the previous year relative to the collection reported, that they had offered the whole of it to the Boston Athenæum, upon condition that suitable rooms should be provided for its reception and preservation, but that the Trustees had declined to accept it; that they had subsequently offered it to the Corporation of Harvard College or to the Board of Visitors of the Massachusetts Professorship of Natural History, who jointly accepted the offer, agreeing to erect a building for the collection and to grant to the members of the Society free access to the collection and to the Botanic Garden.

This report after consideration was acted upon by a vote that the conditions on which the Corporation of Harvard College and the Board of Visitors of the Massachusetts Professorship of Natural History, propose to accept the cabinet of this Society, be acceded to; and the committee were requested to make the transfer. This was done, and the balance of cash in the hands of the Treasurer, $264.29, was also included in the transfer.

A vote was finally passed that all subscriptions and assessments not collected be cancelled. Thus came to an end the Linnæan Society so far as exertion for the furtherance of the objects of its existence was concerned. It yet remained a corporate body, and years after, upon the formation of the Boston Society of Natural History, it was once more called together by its Secretary for the purpose of recovering if possible from Harvard College such part of the collection as yet remained worth removing, in order to present it to the new society. This reclamation was made on the ground that the College had failed entirely to comply with the conditions made at the time of the transfer; no building having been erected, and proper care not having been given for its preservation as a collection for promoting the study of natural history. In the sketch which follows of the doings of the Boston Society of Natural History, it will be found that very little of the really extensive and valuable collection of the Linnæan Society came into its possession, though all that remained of it was given up by the College. It had gone to ruin for want of care, as hundreds of earlier collections had before it, and as hundreds will hereafter, if the views which the history of the Linnæan Society are calculated to inculcate do not prevail in their aims and purposes.

That these views may be presented and dwelt upon has been the motive of giving so full an account of the doings of this Society, as its experience so well illustrates their truth. As stated in an earlier page, if success did not crown the efforts made by the members to build up a permanent institution, the fault was not so much in them, as in the fact that they undertook more than it was possible for men engaged in professional or business life to accomplish, however zealous and devoted they might be. The views referred to and which it is thought desirable to inculcate, may be given in a few paragraphs. They are not new, for the same ideas may be found expressed in an address delivered before the Linnæan Society of London, in 1867, by its President, George Bentham, F.R.S., and also in an article by Dr. H. A. Hagen, published in the American Naturalist (Volume x, pp. 80 and 135). They are as follows:

No society organized for the pursuit of the study of natural history should undertake to form a large museum, unless it is endowed with means fully adequate for the constant care and preservation of its collections, either through support of the government, or from funded property that will yield income sufficient for such purpose. Large collections require enormous expense for preservation from destructive agencies, in the necessary supplies of jars, bottles, alcohol, and other articles absolutely required for use; and for the payment of competent curators; as experience demonstrates that none others than those who are paid for their services can be relied on to permanently do the work, without which, sooner or later, all there is destructible in a collection will certainly go to ruin. In the early period of an institution founded by voluntary effort and designed to be so sustained, the members, zealous and active, may for a time, and while the collection is not great, manage to arrange the specimens received, and keep them from destruction by care, but as the museum increases, this becomes onerous to them, and finally impossible. Its impending destruction discourages the members, and the society itself, unable to bear the necessary expense of preserving what they look upon as an important element of existence, is finally dissolved. A society of natural history not supported by government, and inadequately endowed, should never undertake to make more than a very limited collection of specimens, and these should be confined to such as illustrate the natural history of the immediate neighborhood, with perhaps a few others, typical specimens only, of forms found in distant regions. Where more than this is attempted by any society, continued existence and progress can only be predicted in case it possesses ample means to employ steadily a sufficient number of capable men to take charge of its museum, and exert a careful watchfulness over the specimens. No society can long exist that depends upon voluntary continuous labor on the part of its members, or on the voluntary subscriptions of its friends.

Nor is the collection of an immense number of specimens in every department of natural history a desirable thing for the general student. It is far more important that there shall be an epitome collection so arranged as to give elementary instruction to visitors who seek knowledge and to whom a great multitude of specimens might be confusing. Of course there is no objection to the largest collection of known species where there are abundant means to obtain and care for them, but an arrangement of such should always be preceded by a proper synoptical series; the latter for the instruction of the general student, the former for the use of advanced naturalists who need such collections for comparison. A large collection has the effect of attracting great attention, and the wondering thousands who are drawn by its exhibition to visit it daily or weekly, enjoy an innocent pleasure that is well worth providing for in all large communities, especially as the influence may often go far beyond gratifying curiosity. The collection of species local to the neighborhood, should perhaps be the aim of every society, as a knowledge of all the forms of life met in our daily walks is very desirable.

Perhaps the experience of no society better illustrates the truth of some of these remarks than that of the Linnæan Society. It was formed by men of more than ordinary ability, and in a community ready and willing to aid it by voluntary contributions. Its members were hard workers, and freely gave much time to its interests. But it had no funded wealth and could not look to government for support. It flourished greatly for a considerable period and only showed signs of weakness when its rapidly increasing collections, garnered from every quarter of the globe, called for continuous labor and large expenditure of money. Engaged as the members were in professional or business occupations, they could not give the former, and they became tired of soliciting subscriptions to meet the latter. The result was inevitable.

THE BOSTON SOCIETY OF NATURAL HISTORY.

In passing from the consideration of the doings, the experience and the dissolution of the Linnæan Society to a review of the history of the Boston Society of Natural History, the question naturally arises in the mind whether the new Society started under any better auspices, financially or otherwise, than the old, and if not, whether its aims and objects were so different as to render it less liable to ultimately meet with the same fate.

A careful reading of its records fails to show that pecuniarily it was any better provided with means in the early period of its existence, or that its aims and objects or its proposed methods of action were in the least different from those of its unfortunate predecessor. This is especially noticeable, as among its earliest members are found the names of several who had been active in the Linnæan Society.

As will be seen further on, the Society was at first dependent entirely on the annual assessment of its members; yet it proceeded at once to collect specimens for its museum without discrimination, thus involving itself in the same kind of expenditure for their arrangement and preservation. That it finally succeeded in establishing itself on a firm foundation will be seen to have been the result of fortunate circumstances that could not have been foreseen, much less depended upon, and without which success would probably have been impossible.

The first meeting of such persons as favored the formation of a new society was held at the house of Dr. Walter Channing, February 9th, 1830. Dr. Channing was made Chairman, and Mr. Simon E. Greene, Secretary. A committee was appointed to recommend at a future day such measures as it should judge advisable for the formation of the Society, and for creating an interest on the part of the public in its objects.

Dr. George Hayward, Dr. John Ware, Mr. Edward Brooks, Dr. Amos Binney and Mr. Geo. B. Emerson, composed the committee. It does not appear whether other persons were present than the seven named, as the number that met is not mentioned. Of those whose names appear, three were active members of the Linnæan Society, viz.: Dr. Walter Channing, Dr. Hayward, and Dr. Ware. There were two other original members of the new Society who had been active in the Linnæan, viz.: John Davis, LL.D., and Mr. Henry Codman.

At a meeting subsequently held, the date of which is not given, the committee made a report, which was adopted and a vote was passed, "That a Society on the plan proposed, be now formed," and this was followed by the appointment of a committee to wait upon persons favorable to the objects of the Society and obtain their signatures; with authority to call another meeting as soon as a sufficient number had subscribed.

Such a meeting was called together on the 28th of April, and was held at the room of the Trustees of the Athenæum at 7 1-2 o'clock P. M. Dr. Channing was chosen Moderator, and Theophilus Parsons, Secretary. The names of the subscribers were read, and a sketch of rules and by-laws for the government of the Society presented for consideration. It was then

Voted, That the name of the Society shall be *The Boston Society of Natural History*.

Then followed discussion on the rules proposed, and finally a committee was appointed to draft a constitution and code of by-laws and to report at the next meeting. Dr. Binney, Dr. Hayward and Simon E. Greene were made this committee.

Thus was formed this Society, destined to become one of the leading institutions of the kind in the world, into whose museum thousands would gather weekly for observation and instruction, and whose publications would be known and valued in every civilized community.

The next meeting was held on May 6th, and the constitution and by-laws which had been proposed, after due consideration and with some amendments, were adopted. An adjournment for one week followed. On reassembling at the appointed time the members proceeded to vote for officers and the following named persons were chosen to fill the positions designated:

    Thomas Nuttall, *President.*
    Geo. Hayward, *First Vice-President.*
    John Ware, *Second Vice-President.*
    Gamaliel Bradford, *Corresponding Secretary.*
    Theophilus Parsons, *Recording Secretary.*
    Simon E. Greene, *Treasurer.*
    Seth Bass, *Librarian.*

    CURATORS:

Francis C. Gray,	Edward Brooks,	Amos Binney, Jr.,
Geo. B. Emerson,	Walter Channing,	Benj. D. Greene.
Joseph W. McKean,	Francis Alger,	

A committee was then appointed to make enquiries relative to the collection of the late Linnæan Society, which had been presented to Harvard College upon certain conditions which had not been complied with, and to learn whether the whole or any part of it could be obtained for the cabinet of this Society. No farther meeting is recorded until August 9, though the adopted by-laws required that one should be held on the first Thursday of every month. At this meeting it was announced that Dr. Nuttall had declined to accept the office of President, whereupon the members present proceeded to fill the vacancy, and Benj. D. Greene was unanimously elected. Thus was completed the organization of the Society, and we find that the Council, now composed of all the officers, proceeded at once to take active measures for the furtherance of its objects. The next day after the election of Mr. Greene, it held a meeting and appointed a committee to arrange for a course of lectures, to designate the lecturers, and to decide upon their compensation; also one to procure rooms for the use of the Society. At the next meeting of the Council a week later, the committee on lectures reported in favor of a course of sixteen to be given besides an introductory lecture, and that tickets of admission be put at $3 each,

$5 for a gentleman and lady, and $2 for each person additional. The subjects proposed and the number of lectures to be devoted to each were as follows:

Two on a general account of the Mineral Kingdom and Geology, particularly as connected with animal and vegetable remains; four on Anatomy and Physiology of the Vegetable Kingdom, with general account of the characters, relations, and uses of plants and their distribution; two on Anatomy and Physiology of the Animal Kingdom, and of the principles upon which its scientific arrangement is founded, etc.; two on the Mammalia; two on birds; one on Reptiles and Fishes; two on Insects; one on Invertebrate Animals.

Subsequently the Committee reported that they had decided upon the compensation for the lectures, and fixed it at $20 for each. The persons selected to deliver the lectures, and who accepted the invitations, were Dr. George Hayward, Mr. Thos. Nuttall, Dr. Gamaliel Bradford, Dr. John Ware, Dr. Walter Channing, Dr. J. V. C. Smith and Dr. D. Humphreys Storer. The introductory lecture was free to the public. This course of lectures was commenced on the third Tuesday of October, and they were continued weekly. Where they were delivered, and by whom the introductory one was given, does not appear in the records.

These lectures yielded a net profit of $174.58. Besides this course, there was another given under the auspices of the Society, before the close of the lecture season, by Mr. Nuttall, on Botany. This yielded $170, $100 of which was paid the lecturer and $5.50 for expenses; the balance, $64.50 going into the treasury.

It will be recollected that in the sketch given of the closing proceedings of the Linnæan Society, it was stated that as the Trustees of Harvard College had failed to comply with the conditions binding upon them in accepting the collection of that Society, reclamation had been made with the purpose of presenting whatever might yet be of value to the Boston Society of Natural History. This had been done at the instance of several members of the latter society who had likewise been members of the former, and who reasonably felt aggrieved at the want of care shown for the collection by its possessors. One of these, Dr. Hale, remarked that "he felt it to be his duty as an officer of the Linnæan Society, to express the opinion that something effectual should be done; that he would take the opportunity to again assert that Harvard University had forfeited all her right to the possession of the cabinet of the Linnæan Society. The members of that Society were not so faithless to the cause they had espoused as to desert it. When few in numbers and burdened with heavy assessments, they had relinquished their rich collection to the Corporation of said University, that body having passed at a formal meeting a vote to erect a suitable building to preserve the collection, for the benefit of students in natural history. That agreement had not been complied with, no building had been erected, and the specimens were scarcely to be found. Justice to the members of the Linnæan Society compelled him to make these observations." It seems now but right to give here the remarks of one whose statement can be taken as authentic concerning the whole matter, as it furnishes more succinctly than anything else found, a full justification of the course taken in presenting the valuable collections of the Linnæan Society to the College. Provision was made as far as was possible for its preservation, in placing it where it was thought it would be of great service to students in Natural History.

The result of the application which was made to obtain for the Society whatever might be left of value may be given in the few words taken from the record of the Annual Meeting of the Society in May, 1832, which are as follows: "In the course of the year, an order was obtained from the President of Harvard College for the surrender of such articles as might remain of the old Linnæan Society, in pursuance of which a quantity of refuse matter was sent to the Society's room, but nothing of any considerable value was obtained."

Early action was taken to render the monthly meetings interesting, first, by referring specimens presented to such Curators as were the most interested in the department to which they belonged, to report upon at the next meeting. This added much interest to the proceedings, and led to better attendance. At that time, so little was known of many of the objects now familiar to all in the collections of natural history, that many which would now be received without remark, because of their well known character, excited not only much interest, but considerable discussion. It was at a time when a convoluted mass of chalcedony might have been seen in the Boston Museum, labelled petrified kidney, when at the store of a dealer in curiosities, within a stone's throw of the hall of the Society, fossil corals were exposed for sale as petrified flagroot, when Ammonites upon being discovered in the rocks were heralded in the papers as coiled snakes, sometimes mentioned as being as large as cart-wheels, and exciting wonder in proportion to their size. The writer well remembers receiving notice of a remarkable "petrified bug" in a museum at New Orleans, and upon its being procured and sent to him, finding it to be an excellent specimen of a Trilobite, originally, no doubt from the Trenton limestone of New York.

Soon after the organization of the Society a room was hired for its use in the Athenæum building in Pearl street. Here its collections were deposited and here the meetings, after the first two, were held until more suitable accommodations were obtained three years afterwards. The early meetings took place in the evening, but subsequently for several years in the afternoon, sometimes at 3 and sometimes at 3½ o'clock. They were held once a month until August, 1833, but after this time twice a month.

In January, 1831, measures were taken to procure an act of incorporation for the Society, and in the same month, in view of the great lack of books on Natural History, it was *Voted*—That this Society considers a library of works essential to its success; and funds were appropriated to purchase the best elementary books in the different branches of natural history.

A Committee of the Council was also appointed at this time to apply to the Governor and his Council requesting that the gentleman making a Geological Survey of the State might furnish the Society with a suite of geological specimens. No further reference is made to this matter, and the request does not appear to have been favorably considered, as no such collection ever became the property of the Society. The State Collection itself, was, however, deposited for several years in the Society's rooms.

A singular provision to obtain information was made in February, 1831, by a vote passed, which was in substance as follows:

That a blank book be provided and placed on the table in which may be written queries on subjects of natural history by any member and such answers as may be given; unless the latter may be of considerable length, when they may be put on file.

March 18, 1831. A special meeting of the Society was held to accept the Act of Incorporation, and to organize under it, which was done. The Constitution and By-laws were re-adopted, the only change made being that of providing that the Annual Meetings of the Society be held on the first Wednesday of May each year, and that stated meetings be held on the first Wednesday of every month. The same officers were elected the preceding year, excepting that Dr. Storer was chosen to fill the place of Theophilus Parsons who had resigned, and J. S. Copley Greene was chosen Curator in the place of B. D. Greene elected President.

May 4, 1831. In accordance with the provisions of the Constitution as re-adopted in March, the first Annual Meeting, so called, of the Society, was held on this day. As an account of the receipts and expenditures during the period from its organization to this time may interest the present generation of members, the items are recorded and given in full.

RECEIPTS:	Admission of 75 Members	$375.00	
	Tickets sold for Lectures	600.22	$975.22
EXPENDITURES:	Compensation of Lectures	340.00	
	Fuel, Lights, Advertising and Printing Tickets for Lectures	86.20	
	Rent of Society Rooms	125.00	
	Fuel and attendance Society Rooms	7.00	
	Cabinets $170, and Chairs $14.77	184.77	
	Other small bills	57.07	$800.64
	Leaving at disposal of the Society		$174.58

The Society proceeded to the choice of officers for the year, and the following named gentlemen were elected:

Dr. Benj. D. Greene, *President.*
Dr. George Hayward, *First Vice-President.*
Dr. John Ware, *Second Vice-President.*
Dr. Gamaliel Bradford, *Corresponding Secretary.*
Dr. D. Humphreys Storer, *Recording Secretary.*
Simon E. Greene, *Treasurer.*
Dr. Seth Bass, *Librarian.*

CURATORS:

Francis C. Gray,	Dr. Joseph W. McKean,	Dr. Joshua B. Flint,
Dr. Amos Binney, Jr.,	Rev. J. S. Copley Greene,	Dr. Augustus A. Gould.
George B. Emerson,	Francis Alger,	

To avoid frequent repetition the names of those elected each year will not be mentioned hereafter, except in a summary of the past officers of the Society at the end of this sketch. The election at this time being the first under the act of incorporation, this list of those chosen is given in full.

A letter was received at this time from Professor Edward Hitchcock, then engaged in making a Geological Survey of the State, requesting the aid of members of the Society in furnishing lists of the animals of Massachusetts, to be published with his report. The following were appointed by the Council to serve as requested: Thos. Nuttall and Simon E. Greene, on Ornithology; Drs. John Ware and Joshua B. Flint, Mammalia; Dr. J. V. C. Smith, on Ichthyology; Drs. Bass, Storer, and Binney, on Mollusca; Drs. Harris and Gould on Entomology; Dr. B. D. Greene, on Zoophytes. They were to submit their reports to the Society.

In July, 1831, the Committee on lectures reported that it was expedient to have fifteen, and the following gentlemen were invited to deliver them: Dr. George Hayward, the 2d, 3d and 4th, on the natural history of man; Dr. Joshua B. Flint, the 5th and 6th, on quadrupeds; Simon E. Greene, the 7th and 8th, on birds; Dr. McKean, the 9th and 10th on reptiles; Dr. D. Humphreys Storer, the 11th and 12th, on shells; Dr. Thaddeus W. Harris, the 13th, 14th and 15th, on insects. Mr. Francis C. Gray was afterwards appointed to give the introductory one.

This course of lectures was given the ensuing season, but no record is found of the result. That it was pecuniarily unsuccessful is, however, clear from a statement made when the question of another series came up in the following February, to the purport that the failure was disheartening.

In February, 1832, a proposal was received from Mr. Savage of the Savings Bank, for leasing a room in the building to be erected for that institution on Tremont street. This led to the appointment of a committee to confer with him, and finally to an arrangement by which the hall of the third story was engaged for the use of the Society.

In February also, the committee on lectures reported that a course for the next season was absolutely necessary for the prosperity of the Society. They advised that seventeen should be given, and that Mr. Edward Everett be asked to deliver the introductory one; that the price of tickets should be $2 for the single one, and $1 for each additional; that the lecturers be requested to deliver them gratuitously; and that the whole arrangement for the course be to the important one of increasing the finances of the Society. The committee were instructed to engage Temple Hall for the lectures, and to make all necessary arrangements for their delivery.

At a subsequent meeting of the Society, doubts were expressed relative to the success financially, of the proposed course for 1832-33, and apparently to ensure this it was voted to put the tickets at $1. Whatever the effect of this reduction may have been, it is certain, from the Treasurer's report of the next year, that financially, the course was an exceedingly successful one, as it yielded a net profit of $720 to the Society.

In March of this year, the committee on publication reported that it was expedient to publish a Journal, but nothing appears to have been done towards carrying the recommendation into effect, until sometime after. The report of the committee shows, however, the feeling at this period relative to such publication. There seems to have been for a considerable time an arrangement with the proprietors of Silliman's Journal, by which some of the papers read before the Society and some of its proceedings appeared in that periodical.

At the annual meeting of May, 1832, the report upon the collection in the different departments stated that donations were withheld from the Society awaiting its having proper accommodations for their preservation and exhibition.

At the election of officers the following changes were made : Dr. John Ware was chosen first Vice President, in place of Dr. George Hayward, resigned ; Mr. Francis C. Gray was chosen second Vice President, in place of Dr. John Ware. Dr. Amos Binney, Jr., was chosen Treasurer, in place of Mr. Simon E. Greene, resigned ; Mr. Charles Amory was chosen Librarian, in place of Dr. Seth Bass, resigned. Dr. Winslow Lewis, Messrs. William B. Fowle, Clement Durgin, Dr. George W. Otis, were chosen Curators, in place of Mr. F. C. Gray, Dr. Amos Binney, Jr., Rev. J. S. Copley Greene, and Dr. Joshua B. Flint.

As in the sketch of the Linnæan Society the earlier proceedings were more fully described, so in the account of this Society they are given in greater detail than will be possible to accord to the subsequent records, consistently with proper limits. It has seemed well to dwell somewhat at length upon early transactions, in order that the reader may better understand the character and scope of the work undertaken by the first members, and the better appreciate their earnestness and devotion. To do full justice to their merits, it would be necessary to understand the great difficulty of procuring any information upon many of the objects sent to the Society. It was sometimes impossible to make out their character, and often found indispensable to await the reception of works on natural history before any adequate idea could be expressed concerning them. Mr. Samuel H. Scudder, in a brief sketch of the history of the Society, given some years since, quotes what seems particularly appropriate to repeat here. One of the original members recalling, in after years, the success of their undertaking, wrote thus of the difficulties encountered :

"At the time of the establishment of the Society there was not, I believe, in New England an institution devoted to the study of natural history. There was not a college in New England, excepting Yale, where philosophical geology of the modern school was taught. There was not a work extant by a New England author which presumed to grasp the geological structure of any portion of our territory of greater extent than a county. There was not in existence a bare catalogue, to say nothing of a general history, of the animals of Massachusetts, of any class. There was not within our borders a single museum of natural history founded according to the requirements and based upon the system of modern science, nor a single journal advocating exclusively its interests.

"We were dependent chiefly upon books and authors foreign to New England for our knowledge of our own zoology. There was no one among us who had anything like a general knowledge of the birds which fly about us, of the fishes which fill our waters, or of the lower tribes of animals that swarm both in air and in sea.

"Some few individuals there were, distinguished by high attainments in particular branches, and who formed honorable exceptions to the indifference which prevailed ; but there was no concentration of opinions or of knowledge, and no means of knowing how much or how little was known. The laborer in natural history worked alone, without aid or encouragement from others engaged in the same pursuits, and without the approbation of the public mind, which regarded them as busy triflers."

In August of this year Dr. Martin Gay reported in reference to some objects which he had been requested to give an account of, that it was impossible to do so, because of the want of necessary books.

In October the Council held a meeting for the especial object of arranging the Hall, which the Society was to occupy, for the Cabinet.

In December, recognizing the importance of a permanent fund, it was voted in Council assembled—That all money received from Patrons and Life Members should be invested in bank stock for the purpose of creating one.

Probably the most important event of the year was the election to membership of Mr. Ambrose S. Courtis, whose subsequent benefactions were a great aid to the Society when, by reason of increased expenditure it had become considerably in debt, and when its efficiency seemed likely to be much impaired, to say the least, for the want of means to carry on its work.

In March, 1833, the hall engaged for the Society over the Savings Bank in Tremont Street, being represented as ready or nearly ready for occupancy, a committee was appointed to remove articles to it, and in May following this committee reported that the cabinet had been transferred and would be arranged as soon as circumstances would admit. It was announced at the same time that the Historical Society had voted to deposit its collection of Natural History in the cabinet of this Society.

Arrangements were made early in the year for a course of lectures in the winter of 1833 and 1834, and the committee having this business in charge, reported that Audubon would deliver the introductory one, that the Rev. Dr. Greenwood would give two; Dr. Harris, three; Dr. Gould, one; Dr. Otis, one; F. C. Gray, one; and Dr. C. T. Jackson, two. It was subsequently stated that as Mr. Gray had declined to serve, Dr. Bradford had been substituted in his place, and that he would give two lectures. The committee considered it expedient to pay $15 for each lecture.

Dr. J. V. C. Smith, an active member of the Society, who had devoted much time to the study of fishes, and had made quite a large collection of them, offered to sell all that he possessed at a very low price, and a committee appointed for the purpose of considering the subject, having reported in favor of securing them for the cabinet, they were purchased for the sum of $100. The collection was contained mainly in 141 glass vessels, many having several specimens, and was generally in good condition. Besides the contents of the bottles, there were several dried preparations.

At the Annual election of officers in May, Mr. Chas. K. Dillaway was chosen Librarian in place of Mr. Charles Amory, resigned, and Dr. Chas. T. Jackson, Curator, in place of Mr. Clement Durgin, resigned.

The president, B. D. Greene, at one of the meetings of the Council of the Society this year, expressed a strong desire that a fund of $5000 might be raised, the interest of which should be devoted to paying the rent bills incurred by the Society. He wished that we might feel independent, and thought with such provision against indebtedness there would need be no doubt of success. He then pledged himself ready to furnish $500 for this object. Mr. Charles Amory likewise pledged himself to raise $400. Nothing further seems to have been done towards the creation of such fund.

Pending the arrangement of the cabinet in the new hall, and the necessary preparation for its use, meetings were not held in June or July of this year.

The first meeting in the new hall was held on Aug. 7. The cabinet of the Society, increased by the collection purchased of Dr. J. V. C. Smith, had been fully arranged during the summer months. The magnificent collection of shells belonging to Dr. Amos Binney, Jr., and of minerals belonging to Dr. Chas. T. Jackson had also been deposited with the cabinet of the Society, and put on exhibition.

Surrounded by such evidences of prosperity, the members might well feel gratified at what had been accomplished in the past, and reasonably hopeful for the future. They were rejoiced too, by the accession of a large number of specimens to the several departments of the Museum, that had long awaited a fitting place for their reception.

Before adjourning, it was voted that hereafter meetings be held twice, instead of once a month, as heretofore. Accordingly on the 21st of August the second meeting for the month was held, and a large number of members were present. At this meeting an address was delivered before the Society by the Rev. F. W. P. Greenwood, commemorative of the opening of their new hall. This very admirable address was published in full in the first volume of the Journal of the Society. As the first paragraph undoubtedly expresses fully the feeling pervading the minds of all the members, it is quoted here.

"With good cause, gentlemen, may we congratulate each other at this meeting, on our condition and prospects as a Society. This spacious and delightfully situated apartment; these neat and well contrived cases and tables, already exhibiting treasures, the lustre of which is more pleasant to the eyes of science than the shining of silver and gold; this convenient furniture; these ample accommodations—are all indubitable evidences of our improved, established, and promising state. Everything wears a congratulatory aspect. Our countenances are full of animation. Even the mute representatives from the several kingdoms of Nature, which here in new order surround us, seem to participate in our pleasure, and, rejoicing in their deliverance from the damp and obscure region in which they have been hidden, to bid us welcome to upper air, and the comforts of our present abode." Another quotation from the address of Dr. Greenwood will find an appropriate place in this history, before its conclusion.

It may be well to note, as showing the comprehensive ideas relative to the work of the Society, that a committee at this meeting was appointed at Dr. J. V. C. Smith's desire, to consult with him upon the expediency of forming a zoological garden. Nothing of course could come from this under the circumstances of the period, and the consummation of such a wish seems now but a remote possibility of the future.

Action was taken at a meeting of the council in October of this year, which shows that as yet the public were not admitted to view the Society's treasures, as a record states that a vote was passed to allow those who purchased tickets to the lectures the privilege of visiting the Society's cabinet one day each week.

Early this year a committee was appointed to inspect the rock specimens and minerals collected by Dr. Hitchcock in making the survey of the State, and, if thought best, to petition the Legislature to allow them to be deposited with the collection of the Society. This was done, and for many years following the whole State collection arranged in proper order was on exhibition with that of the Society.

1834. In February, a very triumphant vindication, by the Rev. John Bachman, of the accuracy of the observations and truthfulness of the statements of the honored and beloved Audubon, written against attacks made upon his veracity which appeared in Loudon's Magazine, was read before the Society, and subsequently published in the first volume of the Journal. It excited great interest at the time and was regarded as fully conclusive.

At the annual meeting in May, the Curators reported that the collection contained of Mammalia, 14 perfect ligamentary skeletons, 34 crania, 15 pairs horns and many teeth; of Reptiles, 16 Chelonia, 60 Ophidia, 52 Saurians; of Birds, 40 species; of Corals, 30 species; of Fishes, about 100 species, well preserved; of Insects, about 4000 species, of which 2000 were numbered per catalogue; of Shells, 1000 to 2000 species; of Plants, about 800 specimens, nearly all from the neighborhood. Of the Insects it stated that the collection would soon surpass all in America.

Before the election of officers, an alteration in the Constitution and By-laws proposed at a previous meeting was made, by which the office of Cabinet Keeper was created. His duties were defined to be the general charge of the rooms of the Society, that the contents be kept in the best order, that he should select a competent person as a porter, who should be under his immediate control, and that when convenient he should attend personally at the rooms upon days of public exhibition.

Upon balloting, Rev. F. W. P. Greenwood was chosen Second Vice-President in place of Francis C. Gray, resigned; Dr. Amos Binney, Jr., Corresponding Secretary, in place of Dr. Gamaliel Bradford; Epes S. Dixwell, Treasurer, in place of Dr. A. Binney, Jr.; Dr. J. B. S. Jackson, Curator, in place of Francis Alger, resigned; Estes Howe, Cabinet Keeper.

In October, the committee on lectures for the season reported that Professor Hitchcock of Amherst, Rev. F. W. P. Greenwood, and Dr. Flint, had been chosen to deliver them, and they advised that $20 be paid for each lecture. This programme was probably carried out as there is no mention to the contrary. In November, Dr. Ware suggested applying to the Legislature for a grant in aid of the objects of the Society, and a committee was appointed to ask it. The result of this was a subsidy of three hundred dollars per annum, for five years, granted by the State, payment of which commenced in 1845.

1835. At the first meeting of the Society in January, the members were cheered by the announcement that one of their number who was in Europe, Mr. Ambrose S. Courtis, had provided in a will made by him that the Society should receive certain sums for specific purposes amounting in all to $15,000, and that to ensure the reception of a part of it soon, he had forwarded an order for the immediate payment of $2000. This amount was received by the Society. It is painful to add, considering the Society's financial condition, that this whole sum was lost by the failure of a bank in which it was deposited. There were conditions annexed to the benefaction of Mr. Courtis, which were not entirely satisfactory, and a committee was appointed to correspond with him and suggest some modification of them.

Up to this time the meetings of the Council had not been held regularly, but only as occasion seemed to require. It was now, January 7th, voted that they be holden twice each month, immediately after the regular meetings of the Society.

At the annual meeting in May, it was reported that besides the $2000 cash before mentioned, a note payable in five years for a like amount had been received from Mr. Courtis.

It was also reported that the usual success did not attend the lectures of the last season, the expenses having exceeded the receipts, $177.05. The first "*annual*" so called, issued by the Society, embracing the address delivered by the Rev. F. W. P. Greenwood, upon opening of the new hall; Remarks in defence of the Author of the Birds of America, by the Rev. John Bachman; Description of a Gibbon, by Winslow Lewis, M. D.; Cicindelae of Massachusetts, by Augustus A. Gould, M. D.; and observations on a shell in the cabinet of the Society, supposed to be identical with the Murex aruanus of Linnaeus, by Dr. Amos Binney, Jr., was reported to have paid for itself the first year. These papers compose part first of the first volume of the Journal of the Society.

At this meeting the Annual Address was delivered by Dr. Walter Channing. It is thus spoken of in the record. " Dr. Channing laid the Society under great obligation by an exceedingly well-timed and interesting address. The objects and progress of the Society, its wants, its claims upon the members and the community at large, the reasons why it should live and flourish; all these considerations were dwelt upon with an earnestness and enthusiasm which could not but produce a corresponding impulse in the minds of his hearers."

The thanks of the Society were voted to Dr. Channing, and he was requested to deposit a copy of his discourse with its papers, for the use of the members.

In a revision of the proceedings of the Society published some years later than this period, the statement is distinctly made that this address of Dr. Channing, which was highly commended by those who heard it, was printed, but a copy has been sought in vain. Unfortunately the manuscript itself cannot be found in the archives of the Society, which is the more to be regretted as it is supposed to have embraced matter connected with its early history, that would have been interesting to present in these pages.

The only changes made in the officers this year were as follows: Dr. N. B. Shurtleff was chosen Cabinet Keeper, in place of Estes Howe, resigned; Dr. Thaddeus W. Harris, Mr. J. E. Teschemacher, and Dr. Martin Gay, were elected Curators in place of Mr. William B. Fowle, Dr. George W. Otis and Dr. Joseph W. McKean.

In June of this year the curators agreed among themselves to each take charge of separate divisions of the cabinet. The curatorships were not assigned to special departments until three years later.

A solar microscope was received this year from Europe, the gift of Mr. Ambrose S. Courtis, who purchased it for presentation to the Society. This was put on exhibition for its benefit, the members only being admitted gratis. In October the exhibition having ceased to be remunerative was closed. In August, the committee on lectures reported that they had been disappointed in every way, and had not been able to obtain a single lecturer. At a subsequent meeting, Dr. Gould expressed his unwillingness that the lectures should be entirely omitted, and offered himself to give a course on Botany in the Spring. The offer was accepted and a committee appointed to make the necessary arrangements.

1836. In April of this year, considerable discussion took place relative to the means of paying the debts of the Society, and it was unanimously voted at a Council Meeting to expend the money received from the State towards this end.

At a meeting this month it was announced that no one had accepted an invitation to deliver the annual address, and it was therefore voted to omit it and have the report of the Curators substituted.

The Annual Meeting was held May 4, the Rev. F. W. P. Greenwood in the chair.

From the Treasurer's report at this time, the liabilities of the Society were shown to be $1476.76 with a cash balance of only $56.69 in his hands, and but $227 due it from members, much of which might not be realized. The Courtis Fund was stated to be intact and amounting to $2057, invested in Fulton and Granite Bank stocks.

The officers of the previous year were re-elected, with the following exceptions: Rev. F. W. P. Greenwood was chosen first Vice President, in place of Dr. John Ware, resigned; Dr. Walter Channing, second Vice President, in place of Rev. F. W. P. Greenwood; Dr. Martin Gay, Recording Secretary, in place of Dr. D. Humphreys Storer; Dr. D. Humphreys Storer, Curator, in place of Dr. Martin Gay. The thanks of the Society were presented to Dr. Storer, the late Secretary, for the great zeal, accuracy and fidelity which he had manifested in its behalf since the establishment of the institution.

The Cabinet of the Society had been enriched by the addition of the skeleton of an elephant that had died in a menagerie. The bones were stored and bleached in the house of Mr. James Blake, and a vote of thanks was passed to him for his great kindness in allowing this, and for the care shown by him in their preservation. To the skill and labor of Dr. Shurtleff the Society was indebted for putting them together and forming the perfect skeleton.

The Committee on lectures reported in August that it was not expedient to have a course of lectures during the coming season.

At a meeting held Dec. 7, Mr. Epes S. Dixwell resigned the office of Treasurer, and Mr. Ezra Weston was elected to fill the vacancy thus created.

1837. The Legislature of the State was invited to visit the rooms of the Society.

In February of this year, a letter having been written to the Legislature recommending a re-survey of the State, and that a collection of the plants and animals should be made under the charge of the Boston Society of Natural History, a Committee was appointed by the Society to meet a Committee of the House, to whose consideration the subject had been given.

In April, the Legislature authorised the Geological Survey by Prof. Hitchcock, and the following persons were commissioned subsequently to report upon the Botany and Zoology of the State: George B. Emerson, President Boston Society of Natural History Chester Dewey, Professor of Botany in the Berkshire Medical Institute; Ebenezer Emmons, M. D., Professor of Natural History in Williams College; Rev. William B. O. Peabody, of

Springfield; Thaddeus W. Harris, M. D., Librarian Harvard University; D. H. Storer, M. D., Curator of Boston Society of Natural History; Augustus A. Gould, M. D., Curator of Boston Society of Natural History.

These gentlemen met, and it was arranged among them that Professor Emmons should undertake to report upon Mammalia; Rev. Mr. Peabody, upon the Birds; Dr. Storer, upon Fishes and Reptiles; Dr. Harris upon Insects, Dr. Gould, upon Mollusca, Crustacea, and Radiata; Professor Dewey, upon the Herbaceous Plants; and Mr. Emerson upon the Trees and Shrubs.

The Reports presented to the Legislature were published in 1839–1846.

It will be remembered that in January, 1835, the announcement was made to the members that Mr. Ambrose S. Courtis had provided in a will that the Society should receive certain sums for specific purposes, amounting to $15,000, and that prepayment had been directed by him of $2,000 of that amount. A copy of the will had been forwarded to him for examination by the Society, and a committee on its part had been appointed to suggest some modifications of its provisions.

It is not known whether the matter received his attention. Possibly his change of residence from place to place delayed the reception by him of the communication of the committee until increasing illness prevented consideration of it. Intelligence of his death was received a few months after. What is known of this early benefactor of the Society is but meagre. It will however be read with grateful interest,

Mr. Ambrose Stacy Courtis, for that was his full name, was born in Marblehead, Mass., on March 1, 1798. He received only a common school education, but early acquired a taste for literature and science, which often manifested itself in his subsequent life. Upon leaving school he entered a country store of his native place, and there was accustomed to devote all the spare time he had to classical and scientific studies. He afterwards came to Boston, and entered into partnership with Mr. Samuel Johnson, the firm being Johnson & Courtis. The business was that of wholesale dry goods.

While actively engaged in that occupation, he kept up his interest in other pursuits, devoting much spare time, as when at Marblehead, in reading works upon his favorite pursuits. He accumulated property, but his health became impaired. In 1834, he retired from the firm of which he was a member, and travelled in Europe, hoping to regain his strength. In this he was disappointed, and he finally died in Greece, August 27, 1836. His remains were brought home and buried at Mount Auburn.

On a tablet in the vestibule of the Museum, may be found the following inscription:

TO

AMBROSE S. COURTIS
MERCHANT OF BOSTON
WHOSE GENEROUS BEQUEST IN 1838 WAS
FOR TWENTY-FIVE YEARS ITS CHIEF SUPPORT
THE BOSTON SOCIETY OF NATURAL HISTORY
ON THE FIFTIETH ANNIVERSARY OF ITS FOUNDATION
APRIL 28 1880
GRATEFULLY INSCRIBES THIS TABLET

There seems to have been some anxiety on the part of the Society relative to the will of Mr. Courtis. In February of this year, at a meeting of the Council, extracts were read and considered, and finally a committee was appointed to take charge of the matter with power to take legal measures if necessary to protect the Society's interests.

At the Annual Meeting in May, the Rev. Hubbard Winslow delivered an address on the relation of natural science to revealed religion, which was subsequently published by the Society. It is spoken of in the records as an ingenious, eloquent and fervid address.

The Treasurer's report at this meeting shows the Society had on hand but $180.17, whilst it owed a note for $677 with 10 months interest.

No money had been expended on the library during the year, and the need of a fund for the purchase of books which were indispensable for progress was strongly felt. Dr. Storer reported upon the state of the collections, giving a very elaborate account of the condition of every department, with notice of the many valuable additions made to it during the year.

The most important acquisition was that of the great collection of insects purchased of Professor Hentz, the entomologist, then residing in Florence, Alabama. This was the fruit of seventeen years labor in this field of study, and was undoubtedly one of the best collections extant. Professor Hentz was very desirous that the whole collection should be possessed by some society of similar character to our own, rather than that it should be sold abroad. He had previously offered it to Harvard College, together with his entomological books, for $1600, but the offer had been declined. Professor T. W. Harris, then Curator of the Entomological department of the Society, interested himself in obtaining subscriptions in its behalf, and after much exertion, obtained in this way enough to secure the collection, and also such portion of the library of Professor Hentz as was most needed for our Society. The insects alone cost $550, the books $200, and other incidental expenses, $39, making in all $789.

The principal donors to the fund were Dr. B. D. Greene, Dr. James Jackson, Dr. George C. Shattuck, Hon. Francis C. Gray, Hon. Jonathan Phillips, Dr. John Randall, the Hon. David Henshaw and an anonymous person who gave $250 of the amount.

The collection contained, by the count of Dr. Harris after arrival, 14,126 specimens, of which 12,811 were American, and 1315 foreign. There had been much delay in responses to the application for subscriptions, and Dr. Harris was annoyed in consequence. In mentioning the great accession to the cabinet at the annual meeting, he expresses himself thus: "I congratulate the society in the acquisition it has received, and although the tediously protracted negotiation has caused me much anxiety and vexation, and the small and lingering success which has attended my efforts in your behalf has subjected me to severe mortification and disappointment, I cannot but feel happy at the result. It is my hope that we shall have here in entomology, as well as in other departments, a standard collection, rich in genera and species, as complete as possible in the productions of our own country, arranged and with the names affixed to every described species. Our museum then will be useful, not only to ourselves, but to all others who may wish to refer to well authenticated specimens, to remove their doubts or confirm their conjectures."

The reception and the magnitude of this collection has been particularly dwelt upon, because of what will follow, in due time respecting its fate. It is necessary that there should be a proper appreciation of the value of this as well as of other important collections subsequently allowed to perish, in order that lessons may be derived from experience such as it is so well calculated to teach.

Previous to the election of officers, the highly respected and much beloved President, Benjamin D. Greene, tendered his resignation, greatly to the regret of all. The following changes were made : Mr. George B. Emerson was chosen President, in the place of Dr. B. D. Greene, resigned ; Dr. Amos Binney, 2d Vice President, in place of Dr. Walter Channing, resigned; Mr. Epes S. Dixwell, Corresponding Secretary, in place of Dr. Amos Binney ; Dr. T. M. Brewer, Cabinet Keeper, in place of Dr. N. B. Shurtleff; Dr. N. B. Shurtleff, Curator, in place of Mr. George B. Emerson.

In August of this year, Louis Agassiz was elected an Honorary Member, and in November, Jeffries Wyman was elected a resident member of the Society. These admissions are particularly mentioned, because of the great influence these gentlemen afterwards exerted upon its welfare.

As showing the financial trouble of the Society, it may be mentioned that at a meeting of the Council in November, it was reported that the rent of the hall, $150, was due in two days, and that there were only $50 on hand to meet the call. It was voted that the treasurer make the best arrangement in his power with Mr. Savage, respecting it.

The Committee to whom the subject of lectures was intrusted, reported that several members of the Society had pledged themselves to bring forward at times such exercises upon the subject of natural history as they thought would be interesting to the public, and recommended that the members should have the privilege of attending these, and of introducing members of their families and strangers who might be in the city. The recommendation was adopted.

This seems to have led not exactly to what was suggested, but to the admission of ladies of the members' families and such others as they chose to invite, to the regular meetings; for at the next one, held Dec. 20, the record states that the occasion being the first on which ladies had been invited, the President, Mr. Emerson, addressed the Society upon the subject of this invitation. He explained the objects of the Society somewhat at length, and said much to interest the audience in the study of natural history. He spoke of the many pleasures and benefits to be derived from some knowledge of Nature as shown in her works and operations, and concluded with some account of the advantage we have over the ancients in our more extended knowledge of these subjects.

The admission of ladies seems to have had for a time considerable influence upon the attendance, as the number of members reported as present at this and succeeding meetings was much larger than had been usual. There was a gradual falling off however, but how soon ladies ceased to attend is not mentioned in the reports of subsequent meetings.

1838. In January, the Council voted: That notice be given by written card posted up in the State House, that the Museum will be open every Wednesday, between 12 and 2 o'clock, for visits from the public, and that the members of the Legislature be invited to examine it at those times.

By the advice of the Council, an alteration was made in the By-laws by which each Curator should have his particular department allotted him at the time of his election; he to have the privilege of selecting from among the members of the Society a person to assist him in arranging and labelling the specimens.

The Annual Address was delivered this year by Dr. Chas. T. Jackson, and was a very interesting and lucid discourse upon the various influences of the study of Natural History of Man, both in an individual and a social capacity.

At the election of officers the following changes were made: Dr. Augustus A. Gould was chosen Recording Secretary in place of Dr. Martin Gay; Dr. Jeffries Wyman, Cabinet Keeper, in place of Dr. Thos. M. Brewer.

The Curators were for the first time elected for special departments; the following were chosen:

Dr. N. B. Shurtleff, for Comparative Anatomy; Dr. Thos. M. Brewer, Birds; Dr. D. Humphreys Storer, Reptiles and Fish; Dr. Thaddeus W. Harris, Insects; Mr. J. E. Teschemacher, Botany; Dr. Chas. T. Jackson, Mineralogy and Geology, State Collection; Dr. Martin Gay, Mineralogy and Geology, Society's Collection.

1839. In January, 1839, the Legislature was formally invited to visit the collection during the hours when it was open to the public.

Since occupying the hall in Tremont street, the library of the Society had been placed in cases much needed for portions of the cabinet, and the librarian having made a proposition to receive it into his room in Tremont Row, where the books could be kept together, and where access could be had to them at all times, and at all hours of every day; it was voted to accept the offer of the librarian, and that unoccupied cases in the attic over the hall be made use of by him for the reception of the books in his room.

The necessity for more room for the increasing collection had become so great, that many claims were at once presented by the curators of several departments for the space about to be vacated by removal of the library, and it became necessary to appoint a committee with power to assign it as they thought expedient.

At the Annual Meeting this year, the Treasurer reported receipts amounting to $1337.18, and payments $1167.51, leaving on hand $169.67, with debts outstanding to the amount of $1001.96.

The Report on the Cabinet stated that out of one hundred and twenty species of Massachusetts Fishes ninety were in the collection, and of the Reptiles every described species; all in good condition. The Annual Address was delivered by Rev. John L. Russell, on the pursuit and delight of the Study of Nature.

At the election the changes made in the officers were as follows: Dr. Jeffries Wyman, chosen Recording Secretary, in place of Dr. Augustus A. Gould; Mr. John James Dixwell, Treasurer, in place of Mr. Ezra Weston; Dr. Samuel Cabot, Jr., Cabinet Keeper in place of Dr. Jeffries Wyman; Dr. Jeffries Wyman, Curator of Mammals, in place of Dr. Winslow Lewis; Mr. Thomas J. Whittemore, Curator of Mollusks (office not previously filled).

In June, at a meeting of the Council, it was voted that the Committee to whom was referred the affairs relating to the will of the late Ambrose S. Courtis, be authorized to complete the negotiations with the heirs of said Courtis on such terms as they may deem expedient, and to receive all money accruing therefrom, to be deposited in some bank for safe keeping.

Before the close of the year, a settlement was made with the heirs of Mr. Courtis, by which they were to be released from all obligations, upon the payment of $10,250. For some reason not given, $10,000 were finally received.

In October, Dr. Samuel Cabot resigned the office of Cabinet Keeper, and Mr. William I. Bowditch was elected to the position, but as he preferred a month later to have another substituted in his place, Dr. Samuel L. Abbot was chosen to succeed him.

In November, a report was made upon the disposition of the money from the Courtis bequest, and the members, feeling now that they could reasonably expend something towards meeting wants long felt: *Voted,* to procure such books as were most needed for the library. They also appointed a committee to make an estimate of the cost of mounting the Birds of Massachusetts in first rate order.

In December, the librarian proposed that the meetings through the winter should be held once a week at his room opposite the hall, provided he should be made a life member, and the expenses of the lights and fuel be paid for by the Society. This offer was accepted, and the meetings were accordingly held there.

It is pleasant to notice in looking over the proceedings of the Society, that it was enabled sometimes to aid others in scientific measures to serve the public, as it has often done in more recent periods. At one time we find Prof. Hitchcock appealing to it for information concerning soils; at another the specimens of the Cabinet were solicited by Prof. Silliman for use in illustrating his great course of lectures before the Lowell Institute. It is unnecessary to add that these calls were cheerfully met.

1840. In February, of this year, the Society was saddened by the death of one of its original founders and most interested members, Mr. Simon E. Greene. This gentleman was a business man of great activity. In early years he was an officer in one of the city banks, but afterwards, and until the close of his life, was a broker in whom the utmost confidence was placed. All of his contemporaries represent him as a man high minded and honorable in all his dealings, and of much public spirit. He was a nephew of Gen. Simon Elliott, and from him derived his name. In the formation of the Society he was not only one of the original members, but was the secretary of the first meeting of gentlemen favorable to the formation of a society for the study of natural history, which was held at Dr. Walter Channing's house. He was afterwards appointed, with Dr. Amos Binney, Jr., to call upon such persons as it was thought would like to be associated in the project and obtain their signatures. At the first election of officers for the new Society, Mr. Greene was chosen Treasurer, which office he held for two years, when he resigned, receiving the thanks of the Society for the services rendered by him. At a meeting held February 12, the President feelingly alluded to the loss the Society had sustained, stating that Mr. Greene had a great love for the study of nature, more particularly for the departments of Ornithology and Botany; that he had ever shown himself one of the firmest friends of the Society, ready to assist and co-operate with others in times of need, and on all occasions manifesting a strong interest in its prosperity and usefulness. The following resolutions, offered by the President, were unanimously adopted:

"*Resolved*, that in the death of our late valued and honored associate, Simon Elliott Greene, we, members of this Society, feel that we have lost a firm, liberal, and enlightened friend.

" That we cherish fondly in our hearts the memory of his many virtues as a generous friend, an honorable merchant, a perfectly upright and honest man; and that while we mourn over our loss, we deeply sympathize with those whose bereavement, from their nearer connection with our friend, is still more heavy than ours."

Mr. Greene, though bearing the same family name, was not connected by ties of relationship with the President. His means were limited, but he manifested his continued interest in the Society by a bequest of five hundred dollars in money, a fine collection of about twelve hundred species of shells, and several works on natural history.

In April of this year the meetings were resumed in the hall of the Society, and were continued weekly, as through the winter, until the Annual Meeting in May, after which they were held twice a month.

At the Annual Meeting held May 6, Dr. C. T. Jackson, who presented the Reports of the Curators, after referring to the additions made to the Cabinet during the year, made some pleasant remarks relative to the Society, of which a few lines may be appropriately quoted: " We have now shown to the world that a Society of Natural History can be supported in Boston, and trust that the time is not far distant when the public generally will feel that the establishment of such a Society has contributed not a little to the general weal. Our hall is already crowded with visitors at such times as we throw open the doors for general admission, and there cannot be a doubt respecting the beneficial influence which is exerted by this institution upon the minds of its young visitors. Many a student in science will look back with gratitude to those objects in your collection that first attracted his attention to the delightful walks of Natural History."

The only change made in the officers of the Society at the election was in Mr. Marshall S. Scudder being chosen Curator of Birds, in place of Dr. Thomas M. Brewer, who resigned.

The Curatorships of Comparative Anatomy and Mammals were united at this time, and Dr. Nathaniel B. Shurtleff, who had held that of the former, was chosen to fill that of the combined departments. Dr. Jeffries Wyman, who had been Curator of Mammals, retired.

Let us now review briefly the history of the Society during the first ten years of its existence, touching upon some general points not hitherto presented. It will be well to do this at the close of each decade, as thus perhaps a better idea may be conveyed, not only of the progress of the institution during each period in material prosperity, but of the change in thought relative to its proper mission as an educational institution, and the means necessary for the accomplishment of its aims and purposes.

Some statements have been made in the notices of the Annual Meetings, of the Treasurer's reports showing excess of expenditure over receipts, and the fact of an accumulating debt which threatened seriously the welfare of the Society, notwithstanding the annual subsidy of $300 received from the State, and which was granted for five years. The Treasurer's Report for the year ending May, 1840, will show the financial condition of the Society, at the end of the ten years of its existence.

Its receipts for the year were as follows:

From the previous treasurer	$150 00	
Dividend on one share Granite Bank stock	18 00	
Annual and last grant from the State	300 00	
Annual assessments and entrance fees	504 00	
Borrowed from the Courtis Fund in order to pay off indebtedness of the Society	800 00	
		$1,772 00

Payments as follows:—

Notes held against the Society and interest	$767 17	
Rent and taxes due for rooms prior to the past year	271 96	
Amounts due incurred prior to year	51 25	
Whole debt paid		1,090 38
Books added to library	$25 72	
Rent and taxes of Society's apartments	280 51	
Printing and advertising	32 77	
Miscellaneous expenses of cabinet	10 00	
Current expenses of the cabinet	89 42	
Entomological cabinet	50 00	
Care and attendance on the room, fuel, &c.	90 47	
Expense altering shell-cabinet	63 00	
Commissions collecting fees, &c.	27 05	
		668 94
		$1,759 32
Cash balance in treasury		12 68
		$1,772 00

This account has been given in full, in order to exhibit more clearly the economy exercised in managing the affairs of the Society, necessary if the Society was to be saved from the burden of a debt that could not be borne, yet destructive afterwards to portions of the collection of very great value, from that want of expenditure requisite to the proper care and preservation of perishable objects.

The Society had struggled with debt during the greater part of its existence, and was for the first time free from its harrassing claims. This, however, was only brought about by borrowing from the fund which it desired to hold sacred for special purposes; that received from the heirs of Ambrose S. Courtis, $10,000. The claim that "we had now shown to the world that a Society of Natural History could be supported in Boston," having the aims and objects of the one existing, and relying on voluntary labor and voluntary contributions for the furtherance of its objects, is not sustained by the condition of affairs at this time, for it may well be asked how long the Society could have gone on with an increasing debt consequent upon increasing expenditure not to be avoided, if the bequest of Mr. Courtis had not relieved it from embarrassment; especially when it will be seen that with the additional means thus acquired, the best portion of its rich collections went to ruin for want of that necessary care which only paid service can be relied upon to render, and which could not be afforded.

The income from the Courtis fund was a great help, and a great encouragement. It enabled the Society to go on with its work in a manner that secured for it public approbation, of great service to it later when its increasing collections called for more room for their exhibition, and made an appeal for help necessary. It was not enough to enable it to adequately protect its perishable treasures. A much larger income was indispensable, but experience had not yet demonstrated this fully.

Sometime during this year, though no record is made of it, the Council agreed to appropriate the income of the Courtis Fund one-third to the Library, one-third to publications, and one-third to the Cabinet.

It may be interesting to the members of the present time to know something of the attendance of members in the early days of its activity.

The following table will show the highest and lowest number present, together with the average attendance each year.

Year.	Highest No. present at any meeting.	Lowest No. any meeting.	Average attendance.	Year.	Highest No. present at any meeting.	Lowest No. any meeting.	Average attendance.
1831	22	7	18	1836	50	6	14
1832	26	11	17	1837	40	6	12
1833	26	8	13	1838	40	8	19
1834	45	10	26	1839	35	9	14
1835	70	6	21	1840	61	8	12

An increasing interest seems to have been felt in the meetings during the year ending May, 1834, as the average attendance is shown to be double that of the one previous. This was due in part at least to the removal of the Cabinet to the new hall in Tremont Street, over the Savings Bank, where subsequently the meetings were mostly held. The average afterwards fell off and became small in the years ending in May, 1836 and 1837, when it again increased considerably, as during the year ending May, 1838, there was an attendance of over 50 per cent. more than during the two previous years. This is likely to have been the temporary effect of ladies being permitted to accompany the members. There is no record of this permission being withdrawn, and the probability is that too few continued to feel such interest as to lead to the custom of their attendance becoming permanent. In the years following nothing is said of their presence and the average number of members at the meetings again fell off.

Respecting the increase of the Cabinet up to this period it may be said that there were but few meetings held when specimens were not brought forward and presented. Sometimes these donations were of great value, and deserve special mention.

At one meeting, Park Benjamin presented ninety-two beautifully preserved bird-skins and a box of insects, from Demerara. Joseph Coolidge, forty-five bird-skins, with corals and other objects from Bombay. John James Dixwell, one hundred and thirty-three specimens of bird-skins, in perfect order, with many fishes, from the vicinity of Calcutta. J. N. Reynolds, a magnificent collection of between four and five hundred bird-skins; a large collection of botanical specimens; boxes of minerals, organic remains, and of insects; a large and valuable collection of shells; skulls, fruits, and fishes, all from South America, the Islands of the Pacific, and the South Shetland Islands. Dr. James Jackson, a valuable Herbarium. Mr. J. S. Copley Greene, also, a valuable Herbarium. Dr. F. W. Cragin, of Surinam, magnificent donations of zoological and botanical specimens.

Dr. D. Humphreys Storer was continually bringing forward specimens for the cabinet. At one time he presented seventy specimens all carefully put up by him, in glass bottles and labelled. To his generosity mainly was due the fact, that out of one hundred and twenty species of Massachusetts fishes then known, ninety were in the collection, and every described reptile of the State, with one exception. Alas, that through the want of proper care in after years, nearly all these should have been destroyed! Of this more will be said hereafter.

It would require pages to specify all the donors who enriched the cabinet by their contributions; suffice it, therefore, to mention the names of some who were particular benefactors in this way, viz., Doctors Augustus A. Gould, Amos Binney, Jr., Winslow Lewis, John Flint, B. D. Greene, C. T. Jackson, J. V. C. Smith, G. C. Shattuck; Rev. F. W. P. Greenwood; Messrs. Joseph P. Couthouy, William B. Fowle, Estes Howe, Edward Tuckerman, Jr., Simon E. Greene; Commodore Downes, of the United States Navy; Messrs. George W. Pratt, George James Sprague, J. W. Mighels, H. T. Parker, and C. J. F. Binney.

It is impossible to state the number of specimens in all the departments of the cabinet. There were of fishes three hundred and forty-four species, of which there were, as has before been stated, ninety of Massachusetts waters alone, out of one hundred and twenty known. Of birds, there were of mounted specimens about seventy-five, and of bird-skins not mounted, about four hundred. There had been a much larger number of the latter, but the collection had suffered from the attacks of insects.

Of Reptiles no statement can be made excepting that already given, that the collection contained every known Massachusetts species excepting one, and that had only once been found within our limits. In the Mazological department there were 23 specimens. In that of Comparative Anatomy many, but the number is not given.

Of Mollusks there were over 3000 species in the collection, but whether these embraced the private collection of Dr. Amos Binney, is not certain. At this time he had already proffered to give the whole of his to the Society, provided other gentlemen having collections would allow, a committee to select from those species not possessed by him or the Society. This was complied with afterwards, so that all in the cabinet at the time soon became the property of the Society, with a great number in addition.

The Entomological department was very rich, embracing as it did the great collection purchased of Heutz, but the whole number of species and specimens cannot be stated.

Of the Herbarium there is no mention of the magnitude at this time, but it contained the valuable donations of plants made by Dr. Jas. Jackson and by J. S. Copley Greene.

Already the collections of the Society were beyond the ability of the curators to find proper space for in the exhibition cases, and it was necessary to put away many in drawers out of view.

The Library as well as the Cabinet had constantly received donations during the ten years past, but as yet was very deficient in works necessary for students in every department. It consisted at this time of 660 volumes, besides numerous pamphlets. But little money had been expended for books, as the financial condition of the Society had not warranted it. The largest donors to this department were Judge Davis, who in 1837 presented a great number of valuable works; and Col. Thomas H. Perkins, who in the last year of the decade presented a magnificent copy of Audubon's work on the birds of America. Other donors to the library of valuable books were Drs. D. H. Storer, John Ware, Amos Binney, Jr., Joseph W. McKean, B. D. Greene, and Messrs. E. Tuckerman, Jr., Edward Warren, Henry Codman, Isaac McLellan, John Lowell, Jr., and Joseph Coolidge.

Addresses were delivered before the Society at its annual meetings, first in 1835, and afterwards in 1837, 1838, 1839, and 1840, as already mentioned. Several of these were published.

At this time the first two volumes of the Journal of the Society and the contents of a large portion of the third had been published. All the papers were communications that had been made at meetings of the Society, and were of such character as to establish for it a high scientific reputation, both at home and abroad. It served greatly towards obtaining the works of foreign societies through exchange.

Communications of important character were made at almost all the meetings, and often interesting discussions followed concerning the matter presented in them. The members who took the most conspicuous part in the proceedings during the first five years, were Dr. C. T. Jackson, Dr. D. H. Storer, Dr. A. A. Gould, Mr. George B. Emerson, Mr. C. C. Emerson, Mr. Epes S. Dixwell, Dr. J. V. C. Smith, Dr. J. B. S. Jackson, Dr. Walter Channing, and Rev. F. W. P. Greenwood, though many others participated. During the later five years may be mentioned as the most frequent contributors to the interest of the meetings by their communications, Drs. C. T. Jackson, Augustus A. Gould, D. Humphreys Storer, Thomas M. Brewer, Martin Gay, Thaddeus W. Harris, Amos Binney, Rev. F. W. P. Greenwood, Professors Jeffries Wyman and C. B. Adams, and Messrs. J. E. Teschemacher, Edward Tuckerman, Jr., George B. Emerson and Epes S. Dixwell.

The Council of the Society, consisting under the Constitution of the officers elected by it, and whose duty it was to control the expenditure of the money, select lecturers and decide upon the subjects to be treated upon by them; designate what books should be purchased for the library; nominate Honorary and Corresponding Members; attend to the publication of the Journal; and to transact any other business not inconsistent with the Constitution and By-laws; met in the early days only as specially called together, but subsequently, after the regular meetings of the Society.

For the furtherance of its objects, Committees were annually chosen on the Finances, on Lectures, on Publications, and on Honorary and Corresponding Members. Those who were active on these Committees previous to this period were Drs. Harris, Binney, Gould, C. T. Jackson, Lewis, Storer, the Rev. Mr. Greenwood, and Messrs. Emerson, Dillaway, J. J. Dixwell, Epes S. Dixwell, and S. E. Greene.

DECADE II. MAY, 1840–MAY, 1850.

We now enter upon the second decade of the existence of the Society, with the gratifying fact of its freedom from debt, and its possession of a funded property sufficient at least with due economy to sustain its life and enable it to do much in furtherance of its objects; but not enough to furnish the means necessary for the proper care and preservation of its increasing collections, as will be seen hereafter. At the first meeting after the annual one, there came to hand a large donation of very valuable specimens from Dr. Thomas S. Savage, a missionary at Cape Palmas, West Africa, mostly of just the character which afterwards suffered greatly from lack of care, viz., insects and reptiles.

In June of this year, an official communication was received from the heirs of Mr. Simon E. Greene, announcing the bequest before mentioned, of five hundred dollars, and of some works on natural history.

In November, the lease of the hall occupied by the Society was renewed for three years, and also an arrangement similar to that of the previous year was made with the Librarian, by which the meetings through the winter were held at his room in Tremont Row, in the evenings, once a week until Dec. 30th, and twice a month afterwards.

The Society had again an opportunity of making a part of its Cabinet serviceable to the public otherwise than by exhibition within its own halls, by granting permission to Prof. Wyman to use specimens from it, in illustrating his course of lectures before the Lowell Institute on Comparative Anatomy, given this season.

1841. Early this year, the usual invitation was extended to the Legislature to visit the Museum. On such occasions the Curators made it their business to be present, in order that such visits might be the more agreeable and instructive.

An attempt to render the meetings more interesting was made at this time by forming committees on the several departments of natural history, who should be held responsible for the presentation of communications.

As showing a strong feeling against the absorption of the Courtis Fund in the expenditures of the Society, action taken in February of this year is noticed. It will be remembered that in order to liquidate outstanding debts before the last annual meeting, a sum of eight hundred dollars had been borrowed from this fund, and four notes of two hundred dollars each, on interest, had been given by the Treasurer to the Trustees of that fund.

The Society now voted to apply the five hundred dollars, received by the bequest of Mr. Simon E. Greene, and the proceeds of a sale to be made of the one share yet held of the Granite Bank stock, to pay the first three notes; and that the fourth note should be paid out of any surplus in the hands of the Treasurer, during the current year.

For the first time in the history of the Society, we find the Council appropriating any amount of money for the use of the several departments of the Museum. The income from the Courtis Fund now enabled the Curators to expend something, though little, towards the purchase and preservation of specimens. We accordingly learn that $50 were appropriated for the department of Ornithology, $30 for that of Comparative Anatomy, and $25 for that of Botany. Moderate sums have ever since been asked for by the Curators, as required in the several departments, and these have been granted when the state of the finances would justify the expenditure.

It will be remembered that Dr. Amos Binney, Jr., had proffered his whole collection of shells to the society, upon the condition that other gentlemen possessing cabinets should open them to a committee, who should be allowed to select from them such species as would serve towards completing the collection of the Society. At the annual meeting in May of this year, the Curator of the Conchological department reported that from the cabinets of Messrs. Dixwell, Greenwood, Emerson, Storer, Emmons and Warren, about six hundred species had been selected, most of which were new to the collection. He also reported that by the bequest of the late Simon E. Greene, his entire collection of about 1200 species had come into the Society's possession. The Curator, after referring to the accession of Dr. Binney's collection and that of Mr. Simon E. Greene, with the additions made from compliance with the conditions of Dr. Binney's gift, and by the donations received from various other parties, spoke of the cabinet of shells as standing foremost of all the public collections of the New World. By the reports of the other Curators for the year, it appeared that the donations to their departments had not been very important, except to that of Entomology. The additions to the Library were numerous and valuable, some being received from the bequest of Mr. Simon E. Greene and others from purchase by means of the money received from the Courtis fund.

The Treasurer reported the entire receipts for the year $1837.41; the entire expenditures $1715.32; leaving a cash balance of $122.09 applicable to the purposes for which the income of the Courtis Fund had been specially appropriated, viz., the increase of the cabinet, the increase of the library and the publication of the Society's Journal.

After the reading of the several reports, the President congratulated the Society on the evidence furnished by them of its prosperous condition. He remarked that "the constant circulation of the volumes proves the usefulness of the library and the increasing taste for study and investigation on those subjects for the pursuit of which we are associated. The state of the treasury shows the gratifying fact that the Society is out of debt and with a considerable income annually applicable to its purposes. During the past year there have been twenty-five meetings, at which seventy-five reports, written and oral, were made, including the whole range of subjects embraced by the Society. Besides these, twelve other written communications of interest, with letters received, have occupied the time of the meetings, and afforded us the gratification of reflecting that we have not been quite idle in the work we have undertaken to do."

The following changes took place among the officers of the Society — Rev. Dr. Greenwood having declined to serve longer on account of ill health, Dr. Amos Binney, Jr., was elected First Vice-President in his place, and Dr. Charles T. Jackson succeeded Dr. Binney as Second Vice-President; Dr. Frederick A. Eddy was chosen Recording Secretary; Dr. A. A. Gould, Curator of Conchology; Thomas Bulfinch, Curator of Mineralogy and Geology (State Collection); S. L. Abbot, Jr., Curator of Ornithology, and Thomas T. Bouvé, Cabinet Keeper.

The Society then listened to an interesting and instructive address from Mr. Teschemacher upon the progress of Natural Science. This was subsequently published.

Nothing of unusual interest occurred during the summer and fall months. When the season became too cold for meetings in the hall, the members met by invitation at the President's house in the evening, until February; after which they assembled at the room of the Librarian, 7½ Tremont Row, until spring.

1842. In April of this year a committee was chosen to make arrangements for the reception of the Association of American Geologists and Naturalists in the hall of the Society, where their approaching meetings were to be held by invitation of the Society. These meetings, the first in Boston, took place during the week commencing April 25th and ending on Saturday the 30th. The most eminent scientific men of the country were present, including Profs. William B. and Henry D. Rogers, Dr. Samuel G. Morton, Prof. Hitchcock, Prof. Benjamin Silliman, Dr. James D. Dana and Prof. Locke. Mr. Lyell the distinguished geologist, afterwards Sir Charles Lyell, was also present. The meetings were of great scientific interest and importance, and several of the members, also members of the Association, took an active part in the proceedings and discussions, among others Dr. C. T. Jackson and Capt. Joseph P. Couthouy.

The Association before adjourning passed a vote of thanks to the Boston Society of Natural History for the use of the hall, and for the kind attention shown by its individual members.

Previous to and in anticipation of the meeting of the Association, the Society had voted to hold a special meeting on the 27th of the month, in order to invite the members of that body to hear the Annual Address which was to be delivered by one of their number, Dr. Samuel G. Morton, the celebrated ethnologist. This meeting so held, was largely attended by the members of the Society and by those of the Association. The President first gave a brief history of the doings of the Society the past year. This was followed by the address, which was upon the distinctive characteristics of the aboriginal race of America, and was extremely interesting and instructive. It was published by the Society in its Journal, Vol. IV, p. 190, and in pamphlet, 8vo., 1842.

The yearly reports of the Curators were not always of such character as to give particular information concerning the extent of the collections, sometimes being limited to a statement of donations received, with remarks upon condition, etc. When presented in detail, it seems well to embody their substance here, in order that comparisons may be made hereafter if desirable. Some of the reports made at the annual meeting in May, 1842, are therefore dwelt upon at length. They were all quite encouraging.

In the Ichthyological department the whole number of species was given as 450, of which 390 were from the Western Hemisphere, and 60 from the Eastern. Of the Massachusetts species alone, there were now 108, an increase of 7 during the year.

Of the mineral Cabinet it was stated by the Curator that he had rearranged the collection, and that there were 610 specimens on the shelves, which probably comprised all worthy of exhibition.

The Curator of Entomology reported the enriching of this department by the addition of eighty species of African beetles presented by Rev. Dr. Savage.

The Curator of Conchology reported the continued prosperity of the department under his charge. During no former year had a greater amount of labor been bestowed upon it, or more important accessions made. Six hundred and fifty species had been added and entered in the catalogue, and nearly a thousand names had been ascertained, and the labels applied. There were now in all 3900 species, not including duplicates, all of which had come into the possession of the Society by donation. Of the whole number, 1722 species had been contributed by Dr. Binney, 1197 by Captain Joseph P. Couthouy, 104 by Commodore Downes of the Navy, 95 by Mr. Dixwell, 54 by Mr. George B. Emerson, 85 by Mr. T. J. Whittemore, 43 by Mr. George Brown, 44 by the Rev. Dr. Greenwood, 29 by Mr. John Warren, 33 by Mr. Stephen Emmons, 41 by Dr. Storer, 155 by Dr. Gould, and many had come from the bequest of Simon E. Greene. The want of room and the want of books on the subject were complained of, the members being almost wholly dependent upon the splendid library of Dr. Binney for information. This, however, was liberally open to the use of all who sought knowledge.

The Curator of the State Collection of Geology reported the addition to it of 1100 specimens collected by Professor Hitchcock on his resurvey of the State, making, with the previous collection, 2646, besides the series of soils numbering 227.

The Curator of Botany reported the addition of 1194 species, mostly foreign, to the department under his charge. No account of the whole collection was given.

The Curator of Ornithology reported the whole number of birds in the collection as 540, very few being duplicates; 120 of these were mounted, of which 106, including 75 species, were of Massachusetts. Forty-three specimens were received during the year, the donors being Capt. Joseph P. Couthouy, Judge Amos of Bengal, Messrs. Teschemacher, H. Bryant, Lewis Ashmun, Charles Mayo, and Dr. J. P. Kirtland.

The Curator of Comparative Anatomy reported some additions to his department, but stated that the large skeletons were in bad condition from exposure to dust.

The Librarian reported the condition of the library as prosperous; 140 volumes, including 38 pamphlets, having been added during the year, presented by various individuals.

The Treasurer reported the whole receipts during the year, including balance at commencement, $1350.29; whole amount expended, $1213.36, leaving a balance of $136.93.

The changes among the officers this year were, that Dr. Martin Gay was chosen Curator of Minerals, Mr. T. T. Bouvé of Geology, Mr. T. Bulfinch, Recording Secretary, and Dr. Henry Bryant, Cabinet Keeper.

In May of this year the Diploma now in use by the Society was first adopted.

In June, it is recorded that Dr. Jeffries Wyman was made a delegate to represent the Society at a meeting of the British Association, soon to be held at Manchester, England.

In September, there appears to have been some apprehension as to the safety of portions of the collection, as Dr. Wyman was requested to devote such of his leisure as he could command for the ensuing year, to its preservation and increase, and $200 were appropriated for the purpose.

In December, the Council of the Society having learned "that a proposal had been made to take from their authors the notes, journals, and observations made by some of the corps of the late Exploring Expedition, and to place them in the hands of others for publication," and recognizing the injustice of such proceeding as well as the many other objections thereto, thought fit to remonstrate against it, which they emphatically did, by passing votes expressive of their views on the subject, copies of which were sent to the Hon. Secretary of the Navy, and to Hon. Robert C. Winthrop, the representative of this district in Congress.

1843. In the early part of this year ten members of the Society subscribed to Audubon's work on the Quadrupeds of the United States for presentation to the Society. They were George B. Emerson, N. I. Bowditch, Amos Binney, Jr., George C. Shattuck, Jr., J. Amory Lowell, George Parkman, William Sturgis, F. C. Gray, John James Dixwell and Amos A. Lawrence.

On May 3d, in the absence of many members who were attending the meeting of the Association of Geologists and Naturalists at Albany, it was voted to postpone the business of this meeting, the annual one, to the 17th inst. On that date, therefore, it was transacted. The Curators' reports were generally very gratifying. Dr. Cragin of Surinam had again enriched the cabinet by donations to the several departments of Comparative Anatomy, Herpetology, Ornithology, and Ichthyology, and as usual in former years frequent contributions to them all had been made by the members.

The Curator of Ornithology mentioned that the collection had increased during the year to 753 specimens mounted and unmounted, of which 172, comprising 131 species, were natives of Massachusetts.

The Curator of the department of Geology as disconnected with that of Mineralogy, made his first report. The whole collection was stated to consist of about 1000 specimens, 400 of which had been received by donations during the year, 200 of these being Silurian, 50 Carboniferous, 25 New Red Sandstone, nearly 500 Tertiary and 50 of unstratified rocks, lavas, etc. The remainder were undetermined. It should be borne in mind that this department of Geology embraced the fossils of the several formations at this time, that of Palaeontology not being made a separate one until years later.

The Librarian stated the increase of books during the year to have been 105 volumes and 55 pamphlets, making the whole collection 1071 volumes and 250 pamphlets, independent of the publications of the Society.

The Treasurer reported expenditures exceeding receipts in the general account showing a deficit of $258.45, but of the Courtis Fund income he reported excess of receipts over expenditures $303.53.

The annual address was delivered by Dr. Jeffries Wyman, and was a learned and interesting discourse on the progress of science during the past year.

Mr. George B. Emerson, who had served the Society with great fidelity as President for six years, having declined a re-election, Dr. Amos Binney was unanimously elected in his place. The Corresponding Secretary who had likewise held this office for six years, also resigned, and Dr. A. A. Gould was elected to fill the vacancy. Dr. Charles T. Jackson was chosen First Vice-President, and Dr. D. Humphreys Storer, Second Vice-President. Other changes were in Jeffries Wyman being elected Curator of Reptiles and Fishes, and A. E. Belknap, Curator of Conchology.

On the 2d day of August of this year, there passed from earth one of the best of men; one whom all who knew, loved and revered. This man was the Rev. F. W. P. Greenwood. It is a joy to dwell on such a character, and it was a privilege of the early members of the Society to have associated with them one so much loved and respected, and whose tastes led to his zealous coöperation with them in advancing its interests until health and strength no longer permitted active exertion.

Dr. Greenwood was not one of the original members of the Society, but he was early connected with it and ever afterwards participated largely in its work. He became second Vice President in 1834 and first Vice President in 1836, holding the latter position until May 1841, when by reason of failing health he resigned. As Vice President he was frequently called upon to preside at the meetings of the Society, and he often by communications or otherwise, took part in the proceedings. In 1833 he delivered an address before it upon the opening of its new hall in Tremont street. This was published in the Journal of the Society and formed its first article. This address has been before referred to; but some remarks in it bearing upon the importance of a collection of local species merit attention. He said: "It should be our object to attend particularly to the formation or completion of such collections as may give a good idea of the natural features of our own country and of our own section of our country. If I were traveling in Spain or Persia, I should desire especially to examine some depository of the natural productions of Spain or Persia. If I were traveling in our western states I should prefer seeing a museum well stocked with their own curiosities to one well stocked with all curiosities but their own. And so, too, I presume a traveler in New England will first of all desire to see those objects which illustrate the natural history of New England. For our own instruction and gratification, indeed, and for the advancement of natural science amongst us, we shall gladly collect from every quarter and every coast and corner of the globe; from every sea and lake and river, whatever can be furnished for our purposes; and yet, for our sakes too, we shall least of all choose to be ignorant of the beings and things with which Providence has surrounded our own dwellings, of the plants which spring from our native soil, the birds which fly in our own heavens, and whatsoever passeth through the paths of our own seas."

We pass on to the Annual meeting of 1844, which was held on the 1st of May. The President in presenting the reports of the Curators for the year took occasion to make some remarks upon the early history, progress and present condition of the Society, and then forcibly stating the pressing want of larger accommodations for the collections and for the library, appealed to the public for aid in supplying them.

The Reports then given, though generally satisfactory as to the condition of the specimens in the several departments, presented exceptions which were but too suggestive of what would inevitably follow under the system of reliance wholly upon voluntary care and labor.

The Curator of Entomology reported that the collection had been infested to an alarming extent by Anthreni, and great injury done; that in order to better preserve the specimens he had been obliged to take a portion of them into his own keeping away from the Hall, and resort to active measures to destroy the pest that was making such ravages. Nothing, he said, but the utmost vigilance on his part enabled him to keep the collection from destruction, and he urged that provision should be made for such glazed cases as would effectually exclude the enemy.

The Curator of Comparative Anatomy reported that by subjecting the specimens under his care to over 180° of heat in the steam oven of the Society, they had been freed from insects, and by the free use of poisonous washes future ravages prevented.

The Curator of Ornithology likewise reported that specimens in his department had been attacked, but that by baking those infected, the collection was now in good condition.

Thus it will be perceived that in three of the important departments of the Museum the collections had been seriously attacked and much injury done. Up to this period no harm had come to the Ichthyological collection, which the Curator reported in good order.

The only reports that specified to what extent the collection had been increased, were those of Ornithology and Geology. The mounted birds were given as 233, of which 195, comprising 151 species, are found in Massachusetts. Of unmounted skins the number given was 592, making in all 825 specimens.

The number of specimens in the Geological Collection was given as upwards of 1000, of which about one half were Tertiary, the remainder being of the older formations. Quite a number of these were yet undetermined, and the Curator stated would have to remain so, until the Library should be better furnished with works on the subject of Palaeontology.

The most important addition to the Cabinet of the Society, during the year, was that made to the department of Herpetology by Dr. Cragin of Surinam. From him twenty-three jars were received, containing nearly one hundred specimens of Saurian, Ophidian, and Batrachian reptiles, all in an excellent state of preservation. The Curator deplored the necessity of storing these out of sight for want of room to put them on exhibition.

The officers elected were the same as chosen the year previous, except that Dr. A. A. Gould was made Curator of Conchology; Dr. S. Cabot, Jr., of Ornithology; and Dr. H. J. Bigelow, Cabinet Keeper.

The Annual Address was delivered by Professor Asa Gray, and gave an account of the recent progress and present state of Vegetable Physiology. It was exceedingly interesting and instructive, and was listened to by a numerous and highly cultivated audience with marked attention.

In June of this year, the first notice was taken of the bad condition of the Buttonwoods in New England, which had always been, until within a short time, one of our healthiest and most beautiful trees. At the suggestion of Dr. J. B. S. Jackson, the Rev. John L. Russell was appointed a Committee to investigate the cause of the injury to them. Mr. Russell, whose attention had already been given to the subject, communicated the result of his observations at a meeting in August. His views appear in the Proceedings of the Society of that date. He ascribed the evil to the young wood being winter-killed, remarking that well ripened wood was always essential to vigorous health in perennial vegetation, and that for several years no such young wood had been seen. He thought that the great vigor in the larger limbs would eventually enable the trees to survive until favorable circumstances facilitated the ripening of the young wood, though doubtless some would perish. The views then given of the cause of the trouble have been sustained by experience, and are here briefly expressed because the subject has by no means lost its interest in the minds of those who admire stately and vigorous growth, such as was exhibited in the Buttonwoods of our neighborhood forty years ago.

1845. As showing the means sometimes adopted to obtain specimens for its collections, it may be mentioned that early this year the Society appropriated $25, and various members individually subscribed a considerable amount in aid of an expedition to Florida, for such a purpose, to be undertaken by Mr. John Bartlett.

It had been for some time apparent that the accommodations afforded by the Hall of the Society were entirely inadequate for the proper care and arrangement of the increasing collections.

At the Annual Meeting in May, several of the Curators complained bitterly of this, and it became manifest to all that some measures should be adopted towards obtaining more room to meet this requirement. The Curator of Ornithology stated that less than one third of the specimens in his department were mounted, for the want of room to place them in, that the cases in which the unmounted specimens were placed were so accessible to moths and other destructive insects that the collection had suffered considerably, and there was consequently not much encouragement for him or others to make exertion for its increase, until assured that the labor would not be thrown away. Others of the Curators expressed themselves in like manner.

In the President's review of the doings of the Society during the past year, he likewise remarked upon the necessity for more room, saying that the time had now come when the crowded state of the collections and limited accommodations for meetings made it necessary to take earnest measures for the erection of a suitable building for the Society.

The present is a propitious time, he said, to commence an energetic movement for the accomplishment of this great object.

The members all feeling the necessity for decisive action, it was

Voted: That in the opinion of this Society, the time has now arrived when a strenuous effort should be made to raise sufficient funds to ensure the prosperity and permanence of the institution.

Voted: That a Committee be appointed to act personally or through others, to be selected by them, to solicit subscriptions for the purpose of erecting a building for the use of this Society.

Drs. Amos Binney, Jr., C. T. Jackson, D. H. Storer, and A. A. Gould, were elected to compose this Committee.

The Curators' Reports did not mention generally the extent to which the collections had increased. That of the Treasurer showed, independently of the Courtis fund, an excess of expenditure over the income of $142.88, which added to excess of former years, $327.22, made an amount of debt due to the Courtis fund of $470.10.

The income from the Courtis fund showed a balance of cash on hand of $421.88, with $470.10 due from the General Fund. The understanding that the income from this fund should be equally divided between the Library, Publication expenses and the Cabinet, had not been complied with, in fact it seldom if ever was; the general expenses of the Society being too great to admit of such compliance. The publications, moreover, frequently required too much to allow the others a fair share. During this year they had over $300 of the $618.66 received, whilst the Library had obtained only $28.55, and the Cabinet nothing.

Among the pleasant events of the year just closed, may be mentioned two of considerable importance; one was the bequest of $2000 from a gentleman then recently deceased, John Parker, Esq., a merchant of the city, and the other a donation of more than fifty volumes to the Library by Dr. Francis Boott of London.

One means of obtaining many books much wanted by the Society has not been yet referred to. At the time of the generous donation of the great work of Audubon, by Col. Thos. H. Perkins, there was already a copy in the library which had been acquired through the subscription of a number of the members. After the reception of the last copy, the consent of the donors of the first was asked and readily obtained, to its disposal by the Society in exchange for other works. A Committee was therefore appointed by the Council to effect such exchange. Messrs. Little & Brown, who had always manifested a very friendly feeling in behalf of the Society, purchased the work, agreeing to allow $625.00, and to deliver in return for it such books as might be ordered from time to time through the Committee. As the works received in exchange were to be such as related to Ornithology only, it was several years before the negotiation was completed; the Committee for this purpose meanwhile being annually reappointed.

Mr. John James Dixwell, who had served the Society as its Treasurer for six years, resigned at this meeting, and a vote was passed expressing sincere regret at his retirement, and thanks for the acceptable manner with which he had filled the office for so long a period. Patrick T. Jackson, Jr., Esq., was chosen to succeed him. The only other change among the officers was that Edward Tuckerman, Esq. succeeded Dr. A. A. Gould as Curator of Conchology.

The Annual Address was by Prof. Charles Brooks, and was entitled "The history of Philosophical Zoology from the earliest times to the present day."

In July of this year the Society had again the gratification of serving the cause of Science by a loan of several of its specimens from the collection of the Radiata to Dr. Dana, who was preparing his great work on the Corals of the U. S. Exploring Expedition.

In this year, too, the Society was enabled, by the publication of a report made by Prof. Jeffries Wyman at one of its meetings upon what purported to be the skeleton of a Sea Serpent, to do great service to the community by saving it from continued deception. There had been placed on exhibition in New York some fossil remains, consisting of a great number of vertebrae arranged in such a way as to give them the appearance of having belonged to a single individual. These, with what purported to be the head, measured in length about one hundred and fourteen feet. There were also teeth, ribs and paddles. The character of the remains was not understood by the exhibitor, Dr. Koch, and no obstacle was put in the way of as thorough an examination as could be made without separating the parts which had been, to a greater or less degree, cemented together. The name of *Hydrarchus Sillimani* had been given to this so-called sea-serpent, and its exhibition of course attracted large crowds of visitors. The full description of the bones, as read by Dr. Wyman, may be found in the published proceedings of the Society. Suffice it here to state that the vertebrae were shown to belong, not to one individual, but probably to many of different ages, that so far as they could be studied they did not present any of the characters of an ophidian reptile; and that some at least of what purported to be bones, or portions of the bones of the paddles, were not bones at all, but casts of the cavities of a camerated shell. The teeth Dr. Wyman claimed to be those, not of a reptile, but of a warm blooded mammiferous animal, probably a Cetacean.

This report did honor to the Society, and added much to the reputation of Dr. Wyman. It soon became well known that the bones were not those of a Reptile, but of a Cetacean belonging to a genus to which Prof. Owen had given the name of Zeuglodon. They were found in the Tertiary deposits of Alabama and belonged undoubtedly to many individuals. Vertebrae and other bones of this animal may be now seen in the collection of the Society.

It may be well to state, as the annual reports of the Curators do not always give particulars desired relative to the collections, that during this year the Museum was visited by Prof. Lewis R. Gibbes of South Carolina, and that he carefully studied the Crustaceans in its cabinet and made a full catalogue of them. This represents that there were 58 genera and 91 species, some of them rare and until recently undescribed.

1846. But little happened during this year that would interest the general reader. From the reports of the Curators it appeared that a gratifying increase was made to the several departments of the Museum, and from that of the Librarian that there had been added 143 volumes to the Library, mostly obtained by purchase. No very considerable donations were mentioned. Great complaints of lack of room for useful exhibition of the specimens in the Museum were made.

The Treasurer reported a balance in his hands belonging to general fund of $20.72 and a balance of income from permanent fund of $148.01. The permanent fund now amounted to $12,000.

The only change in officers was the election of Dr. John Bacon, Jr., to succeed Edward Tuckerman, Esq., as Curator of Conchology.

1847. The advent of Agassiz among us, was, as Mr. George B. Emerson afterwards characterized it, a most important event to all engaged in the study of natural history in our country. It was not alone that he possessed information most desirable for our education in science, and great ability to impart it, but largely because of a personal influence that he extended over all who came in contact with him. His noble mien, his personal beauty, his genial manner and expressive features, the earnestness with which he spoke whenever he sought to interest others in the pursuits he loved; all conspired to impress every one who approached him not only with admiration for himself, but with the great importance of the science he taught. It is to show what were the feelings of the members of the Society regarding him and his teaching, that this notice of him is given in this place, together with the action of the Society at a meeting held Feb. 3, 1847. He had but recently arrived, and had just completed his first course of lectures before the Lowell Institute. At the meeting referred to, Dr. D. Humphreys Storer submitted the following resolutions, which were unanimously adopted:

"*Resolved,* That this Society present to Professor Agassiz their heartfelt thanks for the gratification and instruction received by its members during his late course of lectures on the Plan of Creation.

"They would assure him that his lectures have given an impetus to the study of natural history such as has never before been felt in this community; and which, while they have excited the curiosity and called forth the admiration of the public, have more than realized the most sanguine expectations of this Scientific Society.

"While as a body we would thus tender our acknowledgement to the liberal naturalist and enlightened philosopher, we beg him to accept our individual esteem and friendship."

These resolutions not only received the signatures of all present, but of the members generally, who subsequently visited the library, all gladly availing themselves of the opportunity to sign them.

In March of this year the Society received the sad intelligence of the death of its highly respected President, Dr. Amos Binney. A special meeting was called on the 24th of this month to take such action as the feelings of the members should dictate. After remarks by the Vice President, Dr. C. T. Jackson, upon the melancholy event that had brought the members together, Dr. Storer moved the following resolution:—

"*Resolved*, That the unexpected tidings of the death of our much valued friend, Amos Binney, Esq., late President of this Society, fills us with inexpressible sorrow. To us, we feel that his loss is irreparable. The founder of this Society, he was ever its steady, devoted, true friend; constantly evincing his interest by suggesting new plans for its advancement; constantly proving his sincerity by his endeavors to perfect them. To his encouragement, decision and perseverance we owe, in no slight degree, our present prosperous condition. With full hearts, we would acknowledge our obligations, while we gratefully cherish his memory."

Prof. Asa Gray offered the following resolution:—

"*Resolved*, That the Council be requested to prepare, or cause to be prepared by such members of the Society as they may designate for that purpose, a sketch of the life, the scientific labors and the services of our late lamented President, to be read before the Society and published in its Journal, or in such other manner as the Society may direct."

These resolutions were unanimously adopted.

At a subsequent meeting of the Council Dr. Augustus A. Gould was appointed to prepare the memoir asked for. This was done, being made introductory, however, to the publication of Dr. Binney's work on the Terrestrial Mollusks of the United States. From this memoir are taken many facts here presented concerning the subject of it. Dr. Binney was born in Boston, October 18th, 1803. He received his early education at the Derby Academy in Hingham, and afterwards entered Brown University, from which he graduated in 1821. Subsequently he studied medicine with Dr. George C. Shattuck of this city, and attended medical lectures at Dartmouth College. At this time his health failed and he was obliged in consequence to give up his studies, and by the advice of his medical friends to travel extensively over this country and Europe. Whilst abroad he visited England, France, Italy and Germany, giving his attention to the hospitals and to the great collections of science and art. In December, 1825, he returned home much improved in health. He again devoted himself to professional study, and took the Degree of Doctor in Medicine at Harvard University in 1826. The practice of his profession, however, he did not find congenial to his tastes, and thinking it would not be so favorable for his health as mercantile pursuits, he abandoned it, and engaged in trade and subsequently in mining operations.

While so employed he never lost his interest in scientific studies, which indeed absorbed a large part of the leisure time that could be spared from business. After suffering from some vicissitudes of fortune, and having finally obtained a competence, he determined to devote his life especially to science and art, intending "after his own family" to make the Boston Society of Natural History and the Boston Athenaeum, the objects of his solicitude and bounty. His anticipations were not realized. His health again declined, and encouraged by his former experience he sought to regain it by a sea voyage and a sojourn in Europe. His intentions were, if health permitted, to make himself acquainted with the scientific collections of the old world, and to select while there, a. fine library of such scientific works as would be of service not only to himself but to others engaged in like pursuits. He left home in October, 1846, was not improved by the voyage, and after suffering much from disease both in France and Italy, finally died at Rome, February 18, 1847. His remains, in obedience to his wishes, were brought home for burial at Mount Auburn. As the memoir states, "Dr. Binney in person was above the middle stature, erect, robust and well formed. His complexion was dark, with very dark hair and eyes. His features were full and well formed. His dress was scrupulously neat, his manners were dignified and bespoke the gentleman. His voice was deep toned, full and melodious, and his enunciation was remarkably distinct. In his opinions he was decided but not obstinate. He was elegant and refined in his tastes, and passionately fond of the fine arts. He was most happy in his domestic relations, an excellent father, unspeakably anxious to train up his children, both by example and precept, in all their duties to God and Man." An extract from his Journal quoted in the Memoir expresses well his feelings relating to his children. "May they," he wrote, "especially imbibe principles of honor and religion, and may it be their high aim to acquire and deserve the name of the Christian gentleman. May it be said of my house, not that all the sons were brave and the daughters virtuous, but that all the sons were upright and honorable, and all the daughters good."

The part taken by Dr. Binney in the formation of the Society, and his active zeal for its interests manifested ever afterwards, have been shown but inadequately in the pages of this history. To do full justice to the memory of all to whom it owed its origin, and who nurtured it in its infancy, would require volumes where but brief chapters can be given. He was, as has been stated, of that small number of persons who first met at the house of Dr. Walter Channing on February 9, 1830, to consider the question of forming a Society of Natural History.

He felt a great interest in the Journal of the Society and contributed several papers which appeared in its columns. To the Museum he presented specimens of great value, not only for his favorite department of Conchology, but for any of them as opportunity favored. It will be borne in mind by readers, that he offered upon condition that other gentlemen opened their cabinets to a committee of the Society to select from them species not in his own, his whole collection of more than twelve hundred. The condition having been complied with, the Society was enriched through his generosity to the extent of about two thousand species. The first large donation of fossils and of minerals was made by him and the number of specimens aggregated about five hundred. Of mounted American birds he also presented many. He had a large and valuable library of books on scientific subjects, and these were always at the service of all who required them for investigation.

Up to the time when again forced by disease to relinquish his labors, he continued to manifest the same zeal in behalf of the Society as had always been shown by him from its formation. His last work for it was in a strenuous effort to obtain subscriptions from the public that would enable it to possess a building suitable for its increasing collections, and he had well nigh succeeded before incapacitated from further exertion.

The Society could have met, apparently, no greater loss than that incurred by the death of Dr. Binney. This was felt deeply by its members, as his intentions to devote time and means largely to its service were well known to them.

But they did not mourn his loss merely as that of one from whom, had he lived, the Society might have received continued benefits, but because they felt in common with all who knew him intimately, that a helpful companion, a good citizen, and an upright man had passed away, one possessing all the traits that constitute the character which he prayed might be the high aim of his children to acquire, that of a Christian gentleman.

In April, Dr. Samuel Cabot, in behalf of a Committee to whom had been allotted the duty of seeking for the Society a suitable edifice for its purposes, reported that the building in Mason Street known as the Massachusetts Medical College was for sale at a reasonable price, and that after a thorough examination, they judged it capable of being adapted perfectly to the wants of the Society. They therefore recommended its purchase, and that the necessary alterations be made.

After some discussion a vote passed unanimously that the Committee have authority to purchase the property and make the proposed alterations.

The Annual Meeting was held on the first Wednesday of May and the reports of the Curators were presented, but on motion being made, the reading of them was postponed until the next meeting, when the annual address would be delivered. The officers of the Society were elected, John Collins Warren, M. D., being chosen President. The only other change from those of the previous year, was that Dr. S. Kneeland, Jr., was made cabinet keeper.

The reports of the Curators were read at the next meeting. The specimens of the several departments, excepting that of Entomology, of which no report was made, were represented to be now in safe condition, though not much increased in number. Those of the Ornithological department were two-thirds of them stowed away carefully in the garret, sealed up, for want of more suitable accommodations. To preserve them from the Dermestes, which had attacked them seriously in spite of previous precautions, they had been immersed in corrosive sublimate. Twenty-seven or twenty-eight specimens had been received from that indefatigable friend of the Society, Dr. Cragin of Surinam.

As was remarked at the meeting, it must not be inferred from the reports of the Curators, that there was any less interest felt in the collections than formerly. It had been necessary to refuse specimens for want of room to accommodate them and it had not been possible to arrange properly those already belonging to the Society.

The Vice President, Dr. Storer, made some very appropriate remarks upon the late President, Dr. Binney, and addressing his successor, warmly welcomed him to the seat he was now occupying, pledging the hearty co-operation of his brother members and himself in aiding him to advance the interests of the Society.

The President, Dr. Warren, expressed the gratification felt by him at the honor conferred in his election, and at the kind welcome given him.

An address by Dr. Augustus A. Gould, followed, and was principally upon the life, character and labors of the late President, Amos Binney. He closed by congratulating the Society upon the prospect that the next annual meeting would be held in a new edifice, more suitable for its purposes.

From the Treasurer's report for the year it was shown that the whole receipts on general account had been $499.22, and the expenditures $499.26, leaving a balance due the Treasurer of four cents. The Courtis fund account exhibited receipts including balance of previous year, $555.51, and expenditures $358.26, showing a balance on hand of $197.25.

There was a special meeting, later in May, at the house of the President, to take further measures relative to the proposed new building. It would seem from the action taken that the purchase had not been consummated, probably awaiting the subscription of a sufficient amount to warrant it, as votes were passed directing the Treasurer to collect the moneys already subscribed for the purpose; that the Building Committee be requested to continue their efforts to increase the subscription; and that they be authorized to conclude the purchase of the Medical College.

From the subsequent records of the year there is little or nothing to be learned of further action relative to the acquisition of the building it was proposed to purchase; yet before its close it had come into the possession of the Society, and such alterations had been made as were necessary to adapt it for the use of the museum and library.

1848. On the fifth of January, 1848, the Society met in the new building, and a large number of members were present. The President congratulated the Society on the agreeable circumstances under which the first meeting of the year was held; spoke of the difficulties under which it had labored from restricted accommodations and narrow means; and ended with expressing the hope, that with increased means of usefulness, it would not permit the achievements of its maturity to contrast unfavorably with those of its youth.

The movement inaugurated by the late President to raise an amount of money by an appeal to the public sufficient to enable the Society to possess a building of its own, had been quite successful, the sum of $28,600 having been contributed for the purpose by eighty-six individuals. The following resolutions were introduced by Dr. Storer at this meeting:—

"*Resolved*, That the heartfelt thanks of this Society be presented to those gentlemen whose munificence has enabled us to call this temple our own.

"*Resolved*, That we will endeavor to prove our sense of obligation by a renewed devotion to the cause of science.

"*Resolved*, That we deeply feel the kindness and liberality of George M. Dexter and Edward C. Cabot, Esqs., in advising and aiding in the architectural arrangements of our building; and most especially do we feel indebted to N. B. Shurtleff, M.D., for the skill he has exhibited in adapting, and the zeal and fidelity with which he has for months superintended the advancing work."

At the next meeting, held January 19th, a vote was passed thanking Dr. Storer, Dr. Cabot and their associates for the earnestness and perseverance shown by them in raising funds towards the purchase of the new building and its adaptation to the use of the Society, and at a meeting in February a special vote of thanks to Dr. Shurtleff was passed for the great care taken, for the time given, and for the taste and skill exhibited by him in providing for the accommodation of the Society and its collections.

At the annual meeting in May the Treasurer reported that the whole amount received

From general sources was		$1288.96
From Courtis fund		1103.56
From subscribers to building		26999.75
Total received		$29392.27

That the whole amount expended was

For general purposes	$1300.35
From Courtis fund	450.73
Towards new building	20000.00
For repairs and alterations	7257.63
Total expended	$29008.71
Leaving a balance of cash	$383.56

There yet remained due,—

On the building	$3000.00
Interest	425.00
To architects and others	1295.00
	$4720.00
Towards liquidation of this, subscribers to the building yet owe	1720.00
Leaving an amount to be provided for of	$3000.00

The Librarian reported that during the year there had been received 120 volumes, and 102 pamphlets and parts of volumes, most of them donations. Of the works received, twelve volumes had been selected from the library of the late Hon. Judge Davis, in accordance with a provision in his will; Audubon's Quadrupeds of America had been presented by subscribers to that work; and other valuable publications had been the gift of Alcide D'Orbigny, and Drs. Kneeland, Shurtleff and Bacon. The whole number of volumes in the library now numbered 1260, and of pamphlets and parts of volumes there were 120.

The Curator of Mineralogy reported that of the specimens in his department eight hundred only were thought worthy of a place on the shelves of the new building, where they had been deposited and classified. Mr. Francis Alger had presented eighty valuable specimens to the collection, and others, costing fifty dollars, had been procured by subscription.

The Curator of Ornithology reported that there had been presented eighty birds by various persons during the year, and that he was ready to give from his own collection one hundred more, as soon as funds could be had to mount them. A valuable collection of eggs had been received. The donors to this department during the year, were Major Townsend, Messrs. G. M. Dexter, E. C. Cabot, W. Sohier, Robbins and Ogden, and Drs. Shurtleff, Read, Abbot and Bethune.

The Curator of Ichthyology reported that the collection of this department was not in good condition, owing to the losses produced by the ravages of insects and the means used to eradicate them. To Capt. N. E. Atwood the Society was indebted for several fine specimens, two of which were of genera new to the waters of Massachusetts.

The Reports upon other departments were too meagre of information to call for notice here.

The same board of officers was elected, except that Dr. S. L. Abbot was chosen Recording Secretary, Waldo I. Burnett Curator of Entomology, W. O. Ayres of Ichthyology, Dr. Jeffries Wyman of Herpetology, and Dr. Wm. Reed of Conchology.

The annual address was delivered by Dr. D. Humphreys Storer, and was a very interesting historical sketch of the origin and growth of the Society up to that period. Dr. Storer availed himself of the opportunity to acknowledge the indebtedness of the Society to its numerous friends and benefactors, who at all times had been ready with a liberal hand to supply its wants and promote its interests, until by a crowning act of munificence it had been furnished with a building in every respect suited to its wants. He urged with great earnestness upon the members the duty of making redoubled efforts in the cause of science.

This address, of which the record gives the above account, was listened to with great attention by a crowded audience. The thanks of the Society were voted to Dr. Storer for it, and he was asked to furnish a copy for publication. It is to be regretted that he neither did this nor preserved the original manuscript, as there was undoubtedly much in it of historical value.

From the time that the Society took possession of its new apartments there was an increased interest shown on the part of the members, both in attendance upon its meetings and in work upon the collections. The room of meeting, that of the Library,[1] was a cosy one, and in the afternoons some of the Curators were generally to be found there engaged in the examination and study of specimens, or arranging them on tablets. Here the Curator of Botany might often, for years, have been found at work upon the Herbarium, and the Curator of Geology, then embracing Palaeontology, striving in vain perhaps to obtain some knowledge of fossils, of which little could be learned, for want of the necessary books.

1849. At the annual meeting this year, the figures given, showing the extent of the collections, are repeated here. Several of the Curators as usual, omit a statement. The department of Mineralogy had been increased by the addition of 542 specimens, making the whole number now about 1450. Of those received, about 200 had been presented by Francis Alger, the remainder by several donors. The collection of insects was reported as containing 14,000 specimens comprising about 4,000 species. J. M. Bethune, Esq., had presented 540 species from the vicinity of Boston, and Dr. T. W. Harris 670 species. Great pains had been taken to exclude Dermestes and Anthreni, and to repair the ravages already made by them. The collection of birds had been increased by several donations, and now numbered somewhat over a thousand specimens, effectually secured against the attacks of insects.

The department of Ichthyology had received donations from Dr. D. Humphreys

---

[1] The use of the Library room was sometimes granted to members of the Society who wished to lecture. Mr. Desor was thus permitted to occupy it two evenings in a week, for a course delivered by him in the fall of 1848.

Storer, Mrs. Binney, Dr. H. B. Storer and others. The collection contained 360 species, all reported in good condition.

The Library now contained 1320 volumes, and 213 pamphlets.

The Treasurer's account showed a balance of cash in his hands of $124.98, and an amount of $1100 due from subscribers to the Building, debts to the amount of about $4500.

The changes among the officers this year, were in C. C. Sheafe being chosen Cabinet Keeper; Francis Alger being made Curator of Mineralogy, and Dr. S. Kneeland, Jr., of Comparative Anatomy.

This year a proposition was made by an Association called "A Republican Institution" to deposit the books possessed by it in our library, and to grant for the use of the Society one half of a fund belonging to the Institution, of over $2500, for the purchase of such works upon Natural History as the Society might select, with the understanding that the other half should be expended upon works of History, Biography, Geography, Politics and Finance; and that the whole, together with other books now owned by them, should be placed in our library on deposit; provided that the members of the Association should have the same privileges in the use of the Society's library, as the members of the Society. This proposition was accepted, and the sum of $1300 was placed in the hands of the Treasurer for purchase of books on natural history.

Another event very gratifying to the members occurred this year. This was the munificent donation of two thousand dollars, made by Mr. Jonathan Phillips of Boston. By this most timely and helpful act, the Treasurer was enabled to pay the debts of the Society, and to have the satisfaction of reporting it free from all encumbrances.

Most heartily the Council passed a vote of thanks, which was conveyed to Mr. Phillips in a letter signed by the President and Secretary of the Society.

1850. In the early part of this year the Society was called upon to mourn the loss of one of the original members of the Society, Dr. Martin Gay. He was a man of learning, and ardently devoted to science and art; of strict integrity, and of singular purity of life and thought. Perhaps the writer of these pages can give no better idea of him than by repeating from the records of the Society, the words in which he gave utterance to his feelings upon the announcement of the sad event.

"With Dr. Gay I was indeed most intimate, and I express, therefore, what I know, when I claim for him a degree of virtue, a nobleness of purpose, an exaltation of character, far beyond what is generally found in man. Conscientious to a great degree, every deed performed by him, every judgment given, first received the sanction of the highest sentiments of his soul; and, long as I have known him, I never heard him express an impure thought. Loving God, and loving man, his desire was to enlarge his own being that he might the better serve both. Too great by nature and culture to confine his regard to those of a class, or a sect, all who sought his friendship and were worthy, found in him ready sympathy. The bickerings and the jealousies that trouble smaller men, never reached him; but yet he was always ready to advocate manfully the cause that appeared to him just. Without guile, transparent to all whose motives were kindred to his own, he inspired and enjoyed the confidence of the community. His attainments were of a high order. Love of the beautiful in nature and art, and in spirit, was a ruling trait of his character. A fine scene, a good painting, or a noble action, would alike kindle his enthusiastic admiration. In truth we have lost from amongst us a presence which sanctified communion by its purity; a wisdom which was more than that of this world; and a loving soul which we trust has found acceptance in the land of the pure and the holy. God help us, that we may be as ready as was our brother, to bid adieu to present scenes of action, when we are summoned hence to be no more here forever."

All that was thus expressed before the Society of the character of Dr. Gay was recognized as being true of him by his associates in the medical profession, and in other Societies of which he was a member; and by a large number of friends, among whom he was respected and beloved. Dr. Gay was born in Boston, Feb. 16, 1803, and received his education at Harvard College, being a member of the class of 1823. His attainments as a chemist were of a high order. Judge Shaw, in a tribute to his memory before the Academy of Arts and Sciences, of which he was a valued member, spoke of him as an adept in medical jurisprudence, and as having a peculiar faculty of rendering scientific principles and processes intelligible to a jury.

From annual reports of the Curators of the Museum, May 1, 1850, and of the other officers of the Society, may be learned, so far as these give particulars, statements of the conditions of the several departments, and what progress had been made during the two decades now passed in the history of the Society. Unfortunately they are too brief to be entirely satisfactory.

The Ornithological department is mentioned as in good condition, free from insects, and as improved by the substitution of many good, in place of bad specimens. The whole number reported in the Cabinet was given as 1207. In the Geological department but little change was reported as having occurred through the year. It may be stated, therefore, that the collection at this time consisted of about 1000 specimens desirable for exhibition, and about 500 duplicates. The Curator of Ichthyology reported the collection in his department to be in good condition, but gave no figures. As there were reported at the previous annual meeting, 360 species, and a large number of donations had been received during the year, there were probably about 400 species.

The Curator of Entomology reported that there had been no material increase in his department, and stated that he thought it more an object to take care of and to systematically arrange what specimens were already in the Cabinet, than to add to their number. It may be presumed from this that there were about as many specimens in the Cabinet as mentioned the previous year, viz: 14,000, comprising about 4000 species.

The Curator of Comparative Anatomy reported many valuable additions, among others the entire skeleton of the Manatee, then the only one in the country; with the stuffed skin also. This had been obtained and presented by the President. A fine skeleton of a male moose had likewise been presented by him and had been beautifully mounted by Dr. Shurtleff. The number of specimens was not reported in this department, and as this had been the case for several years, no statement as to how many there were can be made.

The Curator of Mineralogy reported the accession of about 100 specimens to his department during the year, but made no mention of the entire number belonging to it. Adding those received since the previous annual meeting to those then reported in the

Cabinet, and we have about 1550 specimens as comprising the whole collection at this time.

The Curator of Herpetology made no report beyond stating that the collection was in about the same condition as it had been for some time. The number of specimens cannot be stated, as the reports for several previous years are too meagre in detail. It will be remembered, however, that every species of reptile belonging to Massachusetts, with possibly one exception, was reported in a previous year as in this department, in good condition.

The Librarian reported the whole number of books in the Library as 3500, including about 300 deposited, these being the property of "A Republican Institution."

The Treasurer reported a balance due him on general account of $746.19. This occurred from causes not likely to happen again, arising from the removal, such as adding iron shutters to the building. As there was a balance at the same time to the credit of the Courtis fund account of $983.88, the Society could not be regarded as in debt. The Treasurer was afterwards authorised to pay himself out of the income of that fund. Mr. J. Elliot Cabot was chosen Corresponding Secretary at this meeting, and Dr. N. B. Shurtleff, Treasurer. The other officers were re-elected for the ensuing year.

Notwithstanding the favorable character of the Reports of the Curators at the annual meeting, upon the condition of the collections under their charge, there must have been indications of evil; as at the meeting of the Council held after that of the Society, a Committee of three was appointed to check the ravages of insects, with power to notify the various Curators of their presence in the specimens under their charge, and if need be to adopt measures themselves to free the cases from them. This implies not only the opinion that harm was likely to result from insects, but some question whether the Curators could be relied upon to free the collections from them.

The annual address was not delivered until June 5. It was by the Rev. Zadock Thompson, of Burlington, Vermont, upon the natural history of that state, and was a very interesting and instructive discourse.

There were some facts mentioned by Mr. Teschemacher at the annual meeting which, considering the great excitement following the recent discovery of gold in California and the consequent results, were certainly surprising. These were, that in a work printed in London in 1818, Phillips' Lectures on Mineralogy, it is distinctly stated that gold is found in large lumps deposited a few inches below the surface of the soil throughout an extensive district bordering on the sea; that Mr. Ellis, thirty years ago (about 1820) obtained from this region a mass of native gold mixed with quartz; and that in 1839 Mr. Alfred Robinson sent to Boston from California $10,000 worth of gold in large lumps. It seems strange in view of such evidence of the existence of gold in large quantities in the soil of California, that no action was taken to obtain it, and that the finding of it by Mr. Sutter in 1847 should have been regarded as a new discovery. Phillips probably had learned from Spanish priests what he stated.

In November Mr. Wm. Read, who had served the Society for over two years as Curator of Conchology, resigned, and in December Mr. William Stimpson was elected to this office.

In reaching the end of the second decade of the existence of the Society, some mention will now be made of what has not been before presented, respecting the attendance of members at the meetings.

In the year ending May, 1841, the average number was about 11. For the year 1842, 12, for the year 1843, 10, for the year 1844, 11, for the year 1845, 11, for the year 1846, 9, for the year 1847, 11, for the year 1848, 18, for the year 1849, 18, for the year 1850, 25.

It should be borne in mind that meetings were held then in the summer months as well as at other seasons of the year, when very many of the members would be likely to be away from the city. The average attendance from this cause, was unavoidably less than it would have been if meetings had been omitted in the hot season. There were, however, very rarely more than from fifteen to twenty present until the building in Mason street was occupied by the Society. The average attendance then increased very much, as the figures show, and during the last year mentioned it had more than doubled that of any one of the first seven, and it was not uncommon to have present over thirty members. This increased attendance arose largely from the interest added to the proceedings by the presence of such distinguished men as Agassiz, Desor, Wm. B. Rogers and others, who took an active part in them. Those whose names appear the most frequently as making communications at the meetings during the first five years of the decade are Drs. Gould, Storer, Wyman, Cabot, S. L. Abbot, C. T. Jackson, J. B. S. Jackson, Binney, and Messrs. Teschemacher, Emerson and Bouvé; during the last five years Drs. Gould, Wyman, C. T. Jackson, Storer, Kneeland, J. B. S. Jackson, Burnett, Bacon and Cabot; Profs. Agassiz and Rogers; Messrs. Teschemacher, Desor, J. D. Whitney, Ayres, Alger and Bouvé.

Addresses were made at the Annual Meetings of 1841, 1842, 1843, 1844, 1845, 1847, 1848, and 1850.

Donations were made to the several departments frequently, but to less extent than during the first ten years. The collection of Herpetology was enriched by many specimens from Dr. F. W. Cragin of Surinam; that of Ornithology by many from Dr. Cragin also, and by some from Dr. G. A. Bethune; that of Entomology by insects from Dr. Savage of Cape Palmas; that of Mineralogy by about 200 fine specimens from Francis Alger; that of Comparative Anatomy by many anatomical preparations from Dr. Jeffries Wyman; and that of Icthyology by fishes from J. G. Anthony of Cincinnati, Dr. F. W. Cragin of Surinam, and Capt. N. E. Atwood of Provincetown.

The American Board of Commissioners for Foreign Missions presented many shells and plants, and Dr. Morton, Rev. Mr. Bachman, Mr. Audubon and many others, presented books.

The increase of the Library during the ten years had been from about 600 volumes to upwards of 3000.

The financial condition of the Society was not much better than at the commencement of the decade. The income derived from assessments and from the funded property had sufficed for its ordinary expenditures, and there remained a small balance of cash in the Treasury. Yet its means remained far from adequate to provide for the necessary care and preservation of its collections.

In 1841, the Society commenced publishing its Proceedings, and the first two volumes with a large part of the third, had been issued before the annual meeting of 1850.

The Journal of the Society was issued with some degree of regularity, gaining for it much reputation both at home and abroad, by the character of its articles. At the time of the annual meeting in 1850, five volumes had been published, all of them containing papers of great value, many of them elaborate treatises upon the natural productions of our own State, of which may be mentioned those on the Fishes and Reptiles of Massachusetts, by Dr. Storer; on the Lichens of New England, by Edward Tuckerman, Jr.; on the Mosses of Massachusetts, by John Lewis Russell; on the Shells of Massachusetts, by Dr. Augustus A. Gould and by Joseph P. Couthony; and on the Coleoptera of Maine and Massachusetts, by Dr. J. W. Randall.

The members of the Standing Committees of the Council during the ten years past, should be mentioned here, as on them devolved a great part of the business of the Society other than that performed in the Museum.

They were the Presidents, Geo. B. Emerson and Amos Binney, Jr.; the Librarian, Charles K. Dillaway; the Treasurers, John Jas. Dixwell and Patrick T. Jackson, Jr.; with Drs. Harris, Storer, Gould, Bacon, Kneeland, Abbot, Cabot, Wyman, Shurtleff, and Messrs. Epes S. Dixwell and Thos. Bulfinch.

Dr. Storer served on two of these Committees, viz., those of Publication and the Library during the whole period, and several of the others a great part of the time.

DECADE III.   MAY 1850 – MAY 1860.

1850. In June, a letter was received from the President of the Society, stating that he had procured through the American Minister at the Court of St. James, a donation from the Hon. East India Company of a complete suite of casts from the fossils of the Himalaya Mountains. These were received in the following November, and were placed in the Cabinet of the Society. There were in all forty-one specimens, mostly of Mammalia. The collection was found to be peculiarly rich in Pachydermata, especially mastodons and elephants. Of reptiles there were casts of several bones of a gigantic turtle. Upon motion made, the thanks of the Society were passed to the Hon. East India Company for the very valuable donation made by them, and also to the Hon. Abbot Lawrence, and to Sir John Richardson, for their kind offices in aiding the President to secure it.

1851. In January of this year, two very remarkable Indian children, a boy and a girl, dwarfs, were exhibited in Boston and other cities of the United States, under the name of the Aztec children. They were quite small, of nearly the same size, and having much vivacity, drew the attention of crowds to visit them. As it was claimed that they belonged to a race of similar beings found in Central America, they became objects of scientific examination. Dr. J. Mason Warren, after studying their characteristics, read a paper in which were presented his conclusions respecting them, viz.:

1. That these children are possessed of a very low degree of mental and physical organization, but are not idiots of the lowest grade.

2. That they probably originated from parents belonging to some of the mixed Indian tribes.

3. That they do not belong to a race of dwarfs, because history teaches the truth of the doctrine of Geoffroy St. Hilaire, that dwarfs cannot perpetuate their kind.

These children were subsequently brought before the Society, and being placed upon the table, the members sitting around, amused all by their interesting and lively movements. There was nothing disagreeable in their appearance or manners.

The views of Dr. Warren were fully corroborated by a letter received from Mr. E. G. Squier, respecting their origin.

At the annual meeting the usual reports were made, the several departments being represented as in good condition. That of Ornithology had received valuable donations from Mrs. G. H. Shaw, Dr. Henry Bryant, Mr. J. C. Leighton, Mr. Theodore Lyman and others; that of Geology from the Hon. East India Co., Dr. C. T. Jackson, Messrs. Moses H. Perley and Alexander Vattemare; that of Ichthyology from Mr. Horatio R. Storer, Dr. Henry Bryant, and Dr. Samuel Kneeland, Jr.

The Report upon the department of Comparative Anatomy was unusually full, embracing what had not before been presented for several years. From it is learned that there were in the collection at this time, 73 complete skeletons, 17 human skulls, and 143 of animals, including birds; 85 jars of specimens in alcohol; and 25 stuffed skins.

The Treasurer reported the total receipts during year, $2218.59, expenditures, $1714.54, leaving a balance of $504.05 in his hands.

The Librarian reported the addition to the library of 353 volumes, and 130 pamphlets, and that the whole number of volumes in the Library was 2569, including 59 copies of the Society's Journal, and 28 of the Proceedings; unbound volumes 1280, including 80 Legislative reports on the natural history of the State; and about 500 pamphlets or parts of volumes. The number of volumes in circulation during the year was 500.

The only change made at the annual election, was in the choice of Horatio R. Storer as Curator of Herpetology in place of Prof. Jeffries Wyman.

1852. The Reports of the Curators at the annual meeting in 1852, were brief, and excepting that upon the Crustacea and Radiata, presented but little of interest. The collection of that department was represented to have suffered very seriously from the attacks of insects. Almost all the specimens of Crustacea had been mutilated, limbs detached, and in some cases lost. Many very valuable species had been entirely destroyed. Of the Radiata the soft parts had been completely consumed.

The Treasurer reported a balance of $754.56 in his hands. The Librarian, alluding to the fact that the Smithsonian Institution at Washington had made such arrangements as to enable the Society hereafter to transmit abroad, and to receive from foreign Societies, publications at little expense, recommended a more liberal exchange of our Journal and Proceedings, for the works of such Societies.

Before the election of officers, final action had been taken upon a proposed amendment to the Constitution, by which the number of Curators was no longer limited. In July of the previous year, Dr. Thomas M. Brewer had been placed in charge of the nests and eggs of birds, and Mr. W. O. Ayres of the Crustacea and Radiata of the Society, and at this election these gentlemen were made Curators of the two departments respectively.

There had been in Feb. 1841, a department established, embracing the collections of Crustacea and Radiata, and Dr. Amos Binney, Jr., had had charge of it for several months, when it appears to have been discontinued. Other changes at the election were as follows:

Mr. Charles Stodder succeeded Mr. Chas. C. Sheafe as Cabinet keeper. Mr. Charles J. Sprague was chosen Curator of Botany in place of Mr. Jas. E. Teschemacher, and Dr. Silas Durkee, who had been the previous July elected Curator of Ichthyology in room of Mr. W. O. Ayres, was rechosen for this position.

At a meeting of the Council in November of this year, Dr. Storer, as a Sub-committee of the Boston Society for Medical Improvement, chosen to aid Dr. C. E. Brown-Séquard in his arrangements for delivering a course of lectures on Physiology, submitted a proposition that the Society be advised to allow the use of the library room for such lectures. He spoke of the high scientific character of Dr. Brown-Séquard and hoped that favorable action might be taken upon the proposition. Dr. Storer mentioned that the lectures would be illustrated by vivisections, and that these being very repugnant to his feelings he could not witness them, but yet on account of the addition to human knowledge which might result, he should favor the proposed action of the Council. Strong opposition was manifested by a number of the members of the Council, particularly Dr. Kneeland, Mr. Bouvé, Mr. Dillaway and Dr. Abbot. The subject was finally disposed of by a vote declining to lay the matter before the Society, on the ground that there was a restriction in the deed of their estate forbidding the use of their building for anatomical purposes.

1853. In February of this year the Society took action in favor of the prosecution of a geological survey of Oregon and Nebraska, by passing strong resolutions and transmitting them to Congress, recommending the necessary appropriations.

At the annual meeting the Curator of Botany reported great improvement in the collection during the year. The previous May only a small proportion of the specimens had been systematically arranged. Large bundles of plants from France, Italy, the Vosges mountains, the Cape of Good Hope, Florida and Kentucky, were in the same condition as when received. These had all been examined and provided with sheets of paper during the year.

There had also been valuable donations, one from the Historical Society, of a large number of plants procured many years ago by the Hon. Thos. H. Perkins. A package of New England plants collected by the late William Oakes, particularly rich in White Mountain specimens, had been purchased by the Society. The Curator had obtained over a hundred specimens of plants growing in the Botanic Garden, Cambridge, through the kindness of Prof. Gray, many of them being new and unpublished species from Texas and New Mexico. The entire Herbarium had been revised and sheets provided for all the plants. The genera had been placed in manilla paper and arranged upon the shelves according to Endlicher's Genera Plantarum. The Herbarium contained representatives of 1300 genera and five or six thousand species. The Curator remarked that not being able himself to collect specimens away from the immediate neighborhood, he would be glad to receive the assistance of those who could, particularly in obtaining New England species.

The report of the Curator of Botany was noticeable as showing an immense amount of work done in one year upon the Herbarium; work, too, that was not only desirable in order to make the collection useful, but absolutely necessary to prevent its destruction. It was the first of a series of years during which Mr. Charles J. Sprague devoted almost all his leisure afternoons and holidays to bringing order out of disorder, with the view of making available many thousand species before inaccessible to examination, and of preserving the plants and increasing the collection.

The report of the Treasurer exhibited a balance of $1102.69 in his hands, including that belonging to the Courtis fund.

Upon the election of officers Dr. J. B. S. Jackson was chosen Curator of Crustacea and Radiata, in place of Mr. W. O. Ayres, and Mr. T. J. Whittemore, Curator of Conchology, in place of Mr. William Stimpson.

At this meeting a motion was made by Mr. Bouvé and adopted, that a committee be appointed to take measures, if decided expedient by them, for the purchase of the collection of Ornithichnites, so called, belonging to the estate of the late Mr. Marsh, of Greenfield.

The committee, consisting of Mr. James M. Barnard, Mr. Francis Alger, Dr. Brewer and Mr. Bouvé, feeling the great importance of securing for the Society the collection soon to be disposed of at auction, obtained by subscription a considerable sum towards its purchase, and detailed two of their number, Mr. Alger and Mr. Bouvé, to be present at the sale. They attended and bought a large part of the whole for about $1400. Thus the Society became the possessor of several of the large and valuable slabs covered with footprints, which now adorn the entrance hall of the Museum, and of many other specimens contained in the Cabinet. One of these, Prof. Hitchcock of Amherst College pronounced the best and largest slab of fossil footprints ever found, or that in his opinion ever would be found.

The President had prepared an address for the annual meeting, but was prevented by ill health from delivering it. It was, however, subsequently printed and distributed. In it was given an account of the early efforts made in Boston to encourage the study of natural history, which finally culminated in the formation of the Boston Society of Natural History. As there had been no previous annual address since 1850, a statement was appended giving an account of the proceedings of the Society during the three years since that date.

In November, by invitation, President Hitchcock of Amherst College addressed the Society, giving some of the results of his examinations in the Connecticut Valley. His remarks were replete with interest and instruction, and were followed by some on the same subject by Prof. Henry D. Rogers. The views presented may be found in the published Proceedings.

In December of this year, the death of Mr. James E. Teschemacher, long an active and very useful member of the Society, was announced, and the President was requested to draw up such resolutions in reference to this event, as should be judged proper by him. In accordance with this request, he presented at the next succeeding meeting, a notice of his life and writings, much of which is given here as follows:—

"Our Society has experienced a great loss in the death of Mr. Teschemacher, one of its most valuable members, and we must turn aside a moment from the path of science to pay a tribute to his memory. This gentleman, who joined our Society in the year 1835, and has since that time been an able associate in our labors, and a large contributor to the advancement of science in our country, has suddenly terminated his mortal career at the age of sixty-three, from a disease of the heart."

These remarks were followed by resolutions, one of which expresses "That a record be made in our transactions of the high estimation in which we hold the private qualities and scientific labors of Mr. Teschemacher, as manifested in his excellent papers on botany, mineralogy, some departments of geology, and particularly in his able and practical investigations of the carboniferous formations. We also regard his productions in the composition and improvement of soils, as a valuable and permanent contribution to the agriculture of the country."

A brief notice of Mr. Teschemacher was then read, and is here given.

"James Engelbert Teschemacher, of Hanoverian extraction on the paternal side, was born in Nottingham, England, on the 11th of June, 1790. At the age of fourteen he commenced his commercial career in a mercantile foreign house of eminence in London, where he evinced application and business talents of a high order; and amid the extensive transactions of mercantile life, in which during a long series of years, he was engaged, his fine comprehensive mind ever remained unshackled by any of the less elevating habits sometimes contracted in commercial pursuits. At an early period of his life he imbibed a taste for studying out of Nature's beautiful book, thus acquiring that purity and love of truth, so constantly pervading all his thoughts and writings. In the year 1830, Mr. Teschemacher accepted the offer of a partnership in a house of considerable standing in Havana, and proceeded to Cuba with highly advantageous prospects, but these faded on his approach, and he returned to England. After a short time, he made up his mind to repair to the United States with his family, reaching New York Feb. 7, 1832. He finally settled in Boston, where during the space of twenty-two years he was unremitting in his exertions for his family. Of his untiring zeal and devotion to science, we need not speak; his hours of leisure, it may naturally be inferred, were few, but those few were employed (apparently as a recreation) in the severe branches of study which frequently form the labor of a life, even with those who make science their occupation. Truly may he be said to have improved the talents committed to his charge."

To what was said of Mr. Teschemacher at the meeting, may be added that he was engaged daily in active business through all the years of his connection with the Society, but yet found time to do considerable work for it while Curator of Botany. In order to secure time for this, he was accustomed to visit the rooms of the Society, after an early breakfast, and stay until business required his presence perhaps an hour later. The published Proceedings of the Society attest to his interest in the meetings, and the character of the communications made by him to the value of his observations, and to the extent of his scientific knowledge. He was an excellent mineralogist, a good botanist, and a very accurate observer in both fields. One could not very well be a more careful and painstaking investigator. Had he been able to devote more time to scientific pursuits, he would undoubtedly have accomplished much more than he did in this direction, as he lacked neither ability, industry nor perseverance.

Besides papers to be found in the printed Proceedings of the Society and in its Journal, several addresses by him were published. One before the Society at its annual meeting in 1841, one before the Horticultural Society, and one before the Harvard Natural History Society.

1854. A vote passed by the Society in March of this year, shows that the members were already indulging the hope of yet better accommodations than those of the structure so recently purchased and adapted for their use. A thousand dollars having been received from the estate of the late Hon. Thos. H. Perkins, subscribed by him towards the building now occupied by the Society, but not so appropriated, it was ordered that this sum be invested by the Treasurer as a commencement of a fund to be called the Building Fund, and that the income from it be annually added to the principal.

The Society had an opportunity at this time to perform a graceful act in helping their unfortunate brethren of the Portland Society of Natural History, which had lately lost the whole of its valuable collection by fire. A vote was passed, that a complete set of the Journal of the Society be presented to the Portland Society, and another, that a series of duplicate shells belonging to this Society, be presented to the Portland Society, whenever they are prepared to select and receive them.

It is sad to know that by a second great fire a few years afterwards, the recipients of these donations again lost their entire collection.

At the annual meeting the Reports of the Curators were quite satisfactory, though the donations through the year were not numerous.

The Botanical department had received some additions of value from Prof. Asa Gray, Mr. B. F. Kendall and the Curator. These, with others obtained by exchange, had added about 800 specimens to the collection.

The department of Oölogy was reported as now having about 240 specimens of eggs, belonging to 165 species.

The department of Geology had been enriched by the splendid collection of the Footmarks of Animals upon the Red Sandstone of the Connecticut Valley, obtained by purchase, and by the donation to it of a series of Silurian fossils.

The Curator of Herpetology reported that this department now contained about 480 specimens, of which 50 were Chelonians, 227 Serpents, 122 Saurians, and 81 Batrachians.

The Librarian reported a considerable increase of bound volumes and pamphlets. Among the most valuable works presented to the Society was the splendid one by Geoffroy St. Hilaire and Cuvier, entitled "Histoire Naturelle des Mammifères," three volumes finely bound, from the Hon. Francis C. Gray.

Upon the election of officers for the ensuing year, Dr. Samuel L. Abbot was chosen Corresponding Secretary in place of Mr. J. Elliot Cabot; Dr. Benj. S. Shaw, Recording Secretary, in place of Dr. Samuel L. Abbot; Dr. Henry Bryant, Curator of Ornithology, in place of Dr. Samuel Cabot, Jr.; Dr. Jeffries Wyman, Curator of Herpetology, in place of Dr. Horatio R. Storer.

This year the Society lost one of its most useful and active members, and science one of its most ardent votaries, in the death of Dr. Waldo Irving Burnett. To characterize his ability as wonderful, and his achievements as extraordinary, is to speak moderately of one who in the short life allotted him had manifested such knowledge, and accomplished so much in scientific research. To express all concerning him that his memory deserves, would require too much space for this volume; but the reader who may desire to learn more than is here presented, will find a full and delightful tribute to his worth and services, prepared at the request of the Society, by Dr. Jeffries Wyman, and published in the fifth volume of its Proceedings. What follows is but a brief abstract of this paper.

Waldo Irving Burnett was born in Southboro', Mass., July 12, 1828. He early manifested a strong love of study, and became so much absorbed in that of insect life as to cause a fear on the part of his father, who was a distinguished physician, that his health would suffer, and he was therefore subjected to some restraint. The passion for investigation was, however, too strong to be more than temporarily checked. His mental activity was remarkable, enabling him to master all the studies of the academy where he was placed, with ease. In mathematics he became so efficient as to lead the teacher to confess that he was no longer able to instruct him. Later he became familiar with the French, Spanish and German languages, and had made progress in the Swedish.

At sixteen years of age he manifested a strong inclination to learn the nature of things, and became interested in all that claimed to give an explanation of the phenomena witnessed about him. He had, young as he was, commenced the study of medicine with his father, accompanying him on professional visits and being present at examinations of bodies after death. His father died when he was of the age mentioned, and he afterwards studied with Dr. Joseph Sargent of Worcester, in the Tremont Medical School of Boston, and in the Massachusetts General Hospital. He did not receive a collegiate education.

In 1849, at the age of twenty-one, he graduated in medicine, and soon after visited Europe, where he spent much of his time in attention to natural history and microscopic observations. There the symptoms of disease manifested themselves, and he returned to the United States with the hope that the climate of the more southern portion would be beneficial. For several years he was obliged by increasing illness to pass his winters in the South, but wherever he was he kept incessantly at work, accomplishing more than it would be possible for many well men to do, in investigation with the microscope; in writing the results of his investigations; and in giving lectures on microscopic anatomy.

While a medical student he became an active member of our Society, and soon after Curator of Entomology. He also was admitted at the early age of twenty-three to the American Academy of Arts and Sciences.

His communications to different scientific bodies and journals, considering the circumstances of his waning health and frequent travel, were astonishingly numerous and manifested a degree of activity, mental and bodily, that few could exert. Many of these communications may be found in the Journal and in the Proceedings of the Society.

To a speculative and inquiring mind like that of Dr. Burnett's, there would of necessity arise questions of perplexing character involved in the problem of life, and doubts did arise of a disturbing nature, which however, were afterwards replaced by a settled and firm conviction, that if there was much to live for, and no man valued life more, there was still more to die for. He passed away on July 1, shortly before he completed his twenty-sixth year.

Resolutions, expressive of the great loss the Society had sustained by his death, and of condolence with his family, were passed by the Society.

At a meeting of the Council in November, the Cabinet keeper exhibited several cases of insects destroyed by the pests that finally caused the great loss of nearly all the valuable collection.

1855. In the doings of the annual meeting this year, we find some evidence to show that the lack of proper accommodation for specimens was already felt in the building so joyously taken possession of scarcely eight years before. It was not entirely from want of sufficient room, but partly from the fact that there was more need of air and sunlight for the best good of the Museum. The Curator of Comparative Anatomy mentioned that the collections in his department had been injured by dampness in the cases. This evil he ascribed to the external circumstances of the building, for which there seemed no remedy so long as it should be screened from the light and heat of the sun, and from free ventilation.

The Curator of Ornithology reported some donations to his department, the principal of which were 41 specimens from Dr. F. J. Bumstead, 11 from Mr. C. J. F. Binney, 10 from Mr. E. Samuels and 8 from Mr. Thure Kumlein. He mentioned that he had commenced a catalogue of the specimens, but from the limited number of the books of reference feared he would not be able to perfect it.

The Curator of Oölogy reported that the collection now contained 209 ascertained species, 16 of which had been added during the year.

The Curator of Botany stated that the collection under his charge was in excellent condition and that several hundred species of native and foreign plants had been added to the collection during the year, some of the most valuable of which came from I. A. Lapham, Esq., of Wisconsin, and from Prof. Gray.

Several of the Curators made no reports.

The Librarian gave the whole number of books now possessed by the Society, as about 3500. He complained that books were frequently taken away from the library in his absence, sometimes without entering them in the record book, and though these were generally returned, there had been some loss. He did not know where to look for the property. He also stated that since the erection of the new theatre next to our building, the room had become dark and damp, uncomfortable to those occupying it, and injurious to the books. He thought if there was no prospect of having a new building, the interests of the Society would require better accommodations for its books, and for those using them. Some alterations were subsequently made by placing windows where none were before, which considerably improved the room.

The Treasurer reported receipts from all sources, $1,950.39; expenditures $1,652.18, leaving a cash balance in his hands of $298.21.

At the election of officers, Dr. Jeffries Wyman was chosen Curator of Comparative Anatomy and Mammals, in place of Dr. Samuel Kneeland, Jr.; Dr. J. P. Reynolds, Curator of Crustacea and Radiata, in place of Dr. J. B. S. Jackson; Dr. J. Nelson Borland, Curator of Herpetology, in place of Dr. Jeffries Wyman; and Dr. H. K. Oliver, Jr., Curator of Entomology, in place of Dr. Waldo I. Burnett, deceased.

At a meeting of the Council there was an appropriation made of $100 for a Card Catalogue of the books and pamphlets, none having been provided previously.

In the death of Mr. James Brown, which occurred in March of this year, the Society lost one of its best friends and patrons, one to whose memory is due some notice of his life and character. He was born in Acton, Mass., in 1800, and when a young man was poor, but highly respected for his industry and fidelity. He began business as a publisher of books in Cambridge, but not long afterwards became an active partner in the firm of Little & Brown, in Boston, a house which soon became well known all over the country for its publications, and for its high character. The business was very successful, and by it Mr. Brown became possessed of considerable wealth, through which he was enabled to gratify his taste, and to contribute much to the welfare of others. He keenly enjoyed the beautiful in Nature, and became much interested in the study of Ornithology, in which department of natural history he possessed a valuable library.

He bequeathed to the Society this library, or the most valuable part of it, and through this bequest it became the owner of the works most wanted, which could not otherwise perhaps, have been obtained, their cost being probably not less than $2000. Mr. Dillaway, the librarian, made some remarks when announcing this valuable accession to the library, and of which part are here given. He said, " This is not the first time we have been indebted to the liberality of Mr. Brown. On many occasions his purse and his influence have been freely offered in aid of our efforts for the promotion of natural science. In the list of our patrons, numbering eighty of the most liberal and public spirited citizens of Boston, his name now stands among the first. As my acquaintance with him has been a long one, commencing at a time when his whole property could not have purchased one of the volumes he has bequeathed to us—when industry, integrity and a generous heart were all his capital, and reaching to a period when he was able and willing to give his thousands to the promotion of literary, scientific and charitable objects, I may be permitted to express a belief that Boston has lost a citizen of whom she had good reason to be proud, and our Society a valued friend, whose memory we shall ever hold in honor."

The Society appointed a committee to prepare resolutions suitable for the occasion, which were presented and adopted at a subsequent meeting. A vote of thanks was also passed to Mrs. Brown, for her generous donation of a portrait of the distinguished Naturalist, Thos. Nuttall.

1856. In February of this year, it was announced that the Society had lost by death, two of its oldest and most highly esteemed members, Dr. Thaddeus W. Harris of Cambridge, and the Rev. Zadock Thompson of Burlington, Vt. Their services to the Society and to science generally merit notice in these pages, and this will be given by reporting the action taken at the meetings following the announcement.

Prof. Jeffries Wyman, in behalf of a Committee appointed to prepare resolutions expressive of the loss the Society had sustained in the death of their late member, Dr. Thaddeus William Harris of Cambridge, offered the following, which were unanimously adopted:—

"*Resolved*, That the members of the Boston Society of Natural History have learned with deep regret, the death of their late associate, Dr. Thaddeus William Harris. That in his death, the Society has lost one of its earliest and most respected members, science a faithful and zealous student as well as a conscientious observer, the results of whose labors have eminently contributed to the extension of the knowledge of natural history; and have reflected dignity and honor upon American science.

"*Resolved*, That the members of this Society sympathize with his family in the loss they have sustained in his death."

Prof. Wyman in presenting the resolutions, referred to Dr. Harris's wide reputation as a naturalist at home and abroad, and to his scientific labors. He spoke of his researches as chiefly confined to entomology, though he had an extensive knowledge of other departments of natural history, especially botany. As an entomologist he ranked among those, comparatively few in number, who with a strong knowledge of classification, combined the faculty of correctly observing and accurately recording the habits of insects. His very valuable report to the Legislature of Massachusetts on Insects injurious to Vegetation, is an admirable testimonial of his industry and patience, his powers of observation, and his happy manner of portraying the subject of his thoughts. At the time of his death he was engaged in an investigation of the origin of some of the cultivated plants, and their subsequent distribution by human agency over the world.

In relation to the Rev. Zadock Thompson, Prof. Wm. B. Rogers addressed the meeting, speaking of him as a thorough and persevering worker in geology, and as possessing a large amount of accurate practical knowledge on the subject.

Dr. Samuel Kneeland read a sketch of Mr. Thompson's life, of which the following is an abstract. He was born in Bridgewater, Vt., in 1796, and at an early period showed a strong propensity for observing facts in natural science, and for mathematical applications. He graduated at the University of Vermont in 1823, and afterwards was occasionally occupied as a teacher. His chief labors were those of independent investigations into the resources of his native state. He wrote the History of Vermont, and thereby became extensively and honorably known. In 1853 he was appointed State Naturalist, making it his duty to study its physical geography, geology, mineralogy, botany and zoology. On this work he entered with zeal, and had far advanced towards its completion, when his labors were closed by death.

Mr. Thompson delivered the annual address before the Boston Society of Natural History, in June, 1850, on the Geology of Vermont. He made several communications to the Society, and through his instrumentality many specimens were added to the Cabinet.

In view of these facts it seemed proper that the Society should take special notice of his death. Dr. Kneeland, therefore after his remarks, moved the following resolution, which was unanimously adopted:

"*Resolved:* That in the death of the Rev. Zadock Thompson, the Boston Society of Natural History has lost a valued friend, a distinguished member, and a sincere and truthful co-worker in the various departments of natural science."

It is certainly not a little singular that the next event to be dwelt upon here is the death of the venerable President of the Society, which occurred on the 4th of May. Upon the 5th, a special meeting of the Society was called to take measures appropriate to the occasion, and a committee was appointed to prepare resolutions. It was also voted to attend the funeral of the late President, and to meet at the rooms of the Society for that purpose, on the morning of the 7th inst.

At the annual meeting, May 7th, Dr. Chas. T. Jackson, Vice-President, in the Chair, Dr. D. H. Storer, on behalf of the committee appointed to prepare a series of resolutions expressive of the deep sense of regret which the Society experienced in its recent bereavement, read the following report, which together with the resolutions, was adopted.

Mr. President and Gentlemen: —We are again called upon to mourn; we meet here to sympathize in our common sorrow. Science has lost a true friend; her votaries, we would reverently bow to the stroke, while we deeply feel and gratefully acknowledge the goodness which so long averted the blow. He, who for the nine years has presided over this institution with paternal solicitude—who has performed every duty devolving upon him with the greatest cheerfulness, with unsurpassed fidelity—who with the enthusiasm of youth, would not allow the most inclement night of the last most inclement season to prevent his attendance at your meetings—but who was ever here to encourage you by his presence to increased exertion—has accomplished his work. He has left us forever.

He needs no fulsome eulogy. His claims upon the respectful and lasting remembrance of his professional brethren have already, elsewhere, been most eloquently portrayed. The debt we owe his memory can never be repaid; but, as naturalists, that debt we should recognize.

Upon the death of Dr. Amos Binney, our much loved President, Dr. Warren was selected to succeed him. From the day of his appointment his interest never flagged, but increased with his advancing years.

His first great desire was to see our valuable collection displayed in a more safe and commodious building—to accomplish which his efforts were indefatigable. A large portion of the means required to purchase our present accommodations, was procured directly by him, and but for the influence he was enabled to exert in his social relations, we could hardly have succeeded in our attempt.

Dr. Warren's labors were principally directed to the great object of exciting and keeping alive a taste for natural history, by constantly presenting its wonders to such minds as he thought susceptible of being thus influenced.

He delighted to gather around him those whose tastes were congenial—to enjoy with such the beauties of his country seat—to extend its hospitalities. How many of us have been made the happier by his yearly festival!

He has, however, done more than this. Three years since he prepared an address, which was published, presenting a history of the Society from its foundation. He became exceedingly interested in palæontology—he exerted himself to assist in procuring the magnificent slabs, containing the ornithichnites from the Connecticut River, which ornament our vestibule. He also made a most valuable private collection of these footprints, and two years ago described some of the most striking of them in a small volume, with the title, "Remarks on some Fossil Impressions in the Sandstone Rocks of Connecticut River." At a great expense he purchased the most perfect skeleton of the *Mastodon giganteus* now known to exist; and his elaborate work upon that subject will ever remain a monument to his zeal, his industry, his munificence.

Just previous to his decease, he had prepared a paper on the animal of the Argonauta, all the available species of which genus he had collected, described and figured. This memoir he had completed, the last page of manuscript having been corrected by him within a week of his death.

This was his last labor—his dying legacy to science. Let us cherish his memory; and upon this occasion, upon this altar, renew our devotion.

John C. Warren

In compliance with the duty devolving upon us, we would present the following resolutions:

Resolved, That in the sudden bereavement which has befallen our Society, we would not suppress the grief so deeply felt. For the long-continued, unwearied interest manifested by our late President in our prosperity; for the readiness, the liberality with which he seconded every effort for our advancement; for the uniform courtesy with which he presided over our assemblages, and the kind-heartedness often evinced there; for his anxious desire to see around him a band of brothers engaged in the same ennobling pursuits, actuated by the same spirit, aiming at the same end, we shall ever with gratitude remember him.

Resolved, That some member of the Society be appointed to prepare a biographical sketch of our late President, to be presented to the Society at a future meeting.

Resolved, That our deep sympathy be extended to his afflicted family.

Prof. Jeffries Wyman was chosen in conformity with the recommendation of the committee, to prepare a biographical memoir of the late President. The Society then adjourned, out of respect to the memory of the deceased.

Dr. Wyman, in accordance with the wishes of the Society, prepared a very full biographical memoir of Dr. Warren, which was read by him at the meeting of Dec. 17, and which may be found in the published Proceedings, Volume VI. A list of Dr. Warren's scientific writings is appended.

At the adjourned annual meeting held May 21st, the Curator of Ornithology called attention to a magnificent donation of birds from the Government Museum of Natural History, at Victoria. Among them were one hundred species or more, not previously in the Museum. Other valuable donations had also been received from Dr. Samuel Kneeland, Jr., Mr. Geo. S. Shaw of Cambridge, and Mr. E. Samuels.

The Botanical department had received from Prof. Asa Gray several hundred South European plants.

The Geological Cabinet had been the recipient of a fine series of Eocene shells from the Paris basin, presented by Geo. B. Emerson, Esq.

The Curator of Comparative Anatomy mentioned several valuable donations from Dr. J. V. C. Smith, Geo. B. Emerson, Esq., and Dr. S. Kneeland, Jr. He called attention to the fact that specimens under his charge were injured from year to year, in consequence of the increased dampness and other unsuitable conditions of the building.

The Librarian reported that a card catalogue had been prepared for the use of the Library.

The officers for the ensuing year were then elected, with the exception of the President.

Dr. John Bacon was chosen Curator of Mineralogy, in place of Mr. Francis Alger; Dr. Samuel Kneeland, Jr., Curator of Ichthyology, in place of Dr. Silas Durkee; and Dr. Silas Durkee, Curator of Entomology, in place of Dr. H. K. Oliver, Jr.

A Committee consisting of Dr. A. A. Gould, Prof. Jeffries Wyman, Dr. Samuel Cabot, Dr. N. B. Shurtleff, and Mr. C. J. Sprague were appointed to nominate a candidate for the office of President. This committee at the next meeting were further instructed to report the names of two or more persons as candidates.

At a meeting held on the 18th of June, the Committee on nomination made a report which is not given in the records.

The Society proceeded to vote, and upon collecting the ballots it was found that Prof. Jeffries Wyman was unanimously elected President. With his usual modesty he hesitated to accept the position tendered, doubting his ability to serve the Society satisfactorily as President. This led to an emphatic expression of feeling on the part of the members in favor of his accepting the office. He still hesitated, and finally begged the Society to give him time for consideration, which was granted.

At the next meeting, July 2d, Prof. Wyman announced his acceptance of the office of President, and entered upon its duties.

The first and the only excursion that the Society ever made as such, took place this year. A committee was appointed to consider the subject of summer excursions, of which Mr. Bouvé was chairman. In behalf of the committee he reported in favor of the plan, and proposed that the first one should be made to Hingham and the neighboring country. It was voted to assemble on board the Hingham Steamboat at 9 A. M., on Wednesday, July 23d, and it was understood that the Committee would make arrangements for proper conveyances at Hingham when the company should arrive.

Accordingly the Society met on board the boat at the time appointed. The day was beautiful and everything conspired to make it an agreeable and instructive one to the members. Upon landing at Hingham they were conveyed to Nantasket Beach in carriages, stopping on the way to examine a colony of night herons in the woods, and many trunks of submerged trees buried in salt water peat, which had become exposed by excavations. This gave rise to much conversation upon the breaking away of the barrier which had formerly kept the ocean back from this tract of land, and the consequent destruction of the forest. The next interesting locality was the site of an Indian cemetery near Nastasket Beach. Here the President, who had previously with his brother and Mr. Francis Boyd, had an opportunity of examining some of the graves, gave an account of what had been found there, which was quite interesting. Mr. Boyd, who resided near, invited the members to his house, where he showed them such relics as were in his possession from the cemetery, and also regaled them with a generous entertainment. After riding on the beach, the carriages were sent round to the Cohasset shore, and the members, wandering along the margin of the sea and climbing over the rocks, collected such specimens of shells, fish and marine plants as they met with, listening meanwhile to the remarks of such as were conversant with the objects found. Dr. David F. Weinland particularly called attention to the ovaries of the whiting, in which were eggs in process of embryonic development.

Upon again resuming seats in the carriages, a pleasant drive along the ridge road followed, with a stop to view the great trap dyke which there protrudes through the granite rock. Here remarks were made upon the dyke and the enclosing rock, by Dr. Jackson, Mr. Alger and Mr. Bouvé.

After a further very interesting drive, the company arrived at the house of Mr. Bouvé at about 3 P. M., where they examined his mineralogical cabinet, listening to some explanations respecting the specimens, made by Dr. C. T. Jackson and himself.

Dinner followed; this having been partaken of with much hilarity, the members separated, some going into the woods to collect specimens, while the larger portion assembled under a grove near the house to listen to some scientific remarks upon what had been seen during the morning, and other matters. This proved to be a very interesting gathering. Prof. Wyman gave an account of the horse shoe (Limulus), and the way in which it casts its shell. Mr. Francis Alger spoke upon the great Beryl formation in Grafton, N. H., and Dr. Jackson, upon the geology of the hill where the Beryls are found. Dr. Jackson then gave an account of trap dykes, as illustrated by what had been seen by them in the course of the excursion on the coast. Dr. Weinland gave an account of the reproduction of parasitic animals, and Mr. Charles J. Sprague exhibited and talked upon a parasitic fungus growing upon the body of a beetle.

Informal, but interesting and instructive conversation followed. The members then passed votes of thanks to those who had been instrumental in enabling them to pass the day so agreeably, and proceeded to take cars for Boston from the station only a few hundred feet distant.

Of course it has not been possible to make any reference to the many valuable papers brought forward and read at the meetings of the Society. To have mentioned even briefly the most important of them would have required that volumes should have been devoted to this historical sketch, where only pages are given. Moreover these may all be found in the Journal, or the printed Proceedings of the Society. When, however, an important discovery is mentioned as having been made in our immediate neighborhood, it seems well not to omit notice of it.

Of this character certainly was the discovery of Trilobites in the slates of Braintree, scarcely a dozen miles from Boston. This was announced by Prof. Wm. B. Rogers, in August of this year, and specimens were exhibited. This afforded the first satisfactory evidence yet presented of the geological age of the stratified rocks of eastern Massachusetts.

A letter was received in November from Mrs. M. A. Binney, tendering a portion of the library of the late Dr. Amos Binney for deposit with the books of the Society, upon certain conditions not objectionable. It was voted to receive them, and present the thanks of the Society to Mrs. Binney for the kind interest manifested by her in making the proposal. The number of works thus deposited were 353, and the number of volumes, including pamphlets, 1145. This accession to the library was of very great service to the members, the works deposited being many of them of great value for investigation, and not otherwise to be had by them.

1857. Early this year the Society lost from among its corresponding members no less than three, distinguished for their scientific attainments, viz.: Prof. J. W. Bailey, of West Point; William C. Redfield of New York, and Prof. Michael Tuomey of Alabama. Resolutions expressive of the great loss that science had sustained by their death, were passed by the Society, introduced by remarks concerning their lives and labors. From Prof. Bailey a bequest was received of great value, consisting of his microscopic collection, and of a collection of Algae, with a great deal of material for microscopic research. Also a great many works upon microscopy, botany and histology. These embraced Ehrenberg's Mikrogeologie, Lindley and Hutton's Fossil Flora, and others of great value. The bequest was upon the condition that the collection should be kept in cases by themselves, and that the sons of Prof. Bailey should have such access to them for study or examination, as might be consistent with the rules of the Society.

At the annual meeting, the reports of the Treasurer, Librarian and Curators were presented, and the substance of them is here briefly given.

The Report of the Treasurer was very unsatisfactory, showing an amount due him of $1726, largely arising from the fact that collections from members of the annual assessments had not been made, as they should have been. The Trustees of the Courtis fund held about $400, which would lessen the indebtedness to $1326, and it was thought that $900 might be realized from members who owed much more than this, but some of whom had not been called upon for several years. This would still leave an amount due the Treasurer of $436. The Auditing Committee expressed the opinion that much money was lost to the Society by lack of promptness and want of system in collecting, and strongly advised that all the members should be annually called upon during some one month, for their assessments. They suggested too the importance of the utmost economy in expenditure, considering the unsatisfactory financial position of the Society.

The Librarian's report was more exhilarating, stating as it did, that not less than 1500 volumes had been added to the collection during the year. Of these over 1000 had been deposited by the widow of the late Dr. Amos Binney, in accordance with what she believed to be his wish, viz.: for the use of members of the Society and others, who may resort to its library for scientific investigations, and to be subject to the same regulations as are the books of the Society. This collection is very rich in scientific works, and there is scarcely a department of science not represented.

The Library had also received, as before mentioned, through the bequest of the late Prof. J. W. Bailey, in addition to his valuable microscopical collection, a very valuable library of microscopic and botanical works, numbering in all eighty-four volumes, and one hundred and fifty pamphlets.

The whole number of books in possession of the Society including those deposited, was stated as follows:

	Bound Vols.	Pamphlets and Parts
Belonging to the Society, not including the bequest of Prof. Bailey,	3,000	300
Bequest of Prof. Bailey,	84	150
Deposited by "A Republican Institution,"	767	
Deposited by Mrs. Binney,	1012	
Total,	4863	450

The Curator of Mineralogy reported his department as indebted to Dr. S. Kneeland, Jr., Mr. N. H. Bishop, Mr. Wm. Haley, and Rev. S. Adams for specimens received from them during the year.

The Curator of Geology reported the additions to the collection under his charge as few and of little value, compared with those received in previous years.

The Curator of Entomology, in referring to the destruction in past years of specimens in the collection, stated that there yet remained many uninjured, and entitled to care and attention. These had been subjected to a heat of about 200 degrees, and the drawers containing them had had a constant supply of camphor.

Specimens of value had been received from Mr. Samuels, collected by him in California, and one beautiful Neuropterous insect was presented by Mr. Solomon Adams, of Lunenburg, found in Winter street, Boston.

The Curator of Herpetology reported the collection under his charge as in good order, and that some valuable additions had been made to it, principally through the services of Mr. Samuels in California. From him between two and three hundred specimens had been received, many of which were new to our Cabinet. To Mr. Kennicott, one of our Corresponding Members in Illinois, the Society was also indebted for a considerable number of valuable specimens.

The Curator of Oology reported that the collection of eggs had received many additions during the year from Mr. E. Samuels, obtained in California.

No report from the Curator of Ornithology was made. Two specimens of South American birds had been presented to the collection by Mr. N. H. Bishop.

The Curator of Crustacea and Radiata reported that his department was indebted to Mr. Thos. Tallant of Concord, for some corals from California; Capt. Geo. E. Tyler for one large specimen; Capt. J. P. Couthouy for corals from the wreck of a Spanish vessel sunk off the Island of Magdalena; Capt. N. E. Atwood for Corals and a starfish; and to Dr. J. T. Parkinson for a crustacean from St. Simon's Island, Georgia.

The Curator of Ichthyology reported the collection of his department as in fair condition, and that the Society was indebted to Dr. A. G. Hamlin of Bangor, Dr. S. Kneeland, Jr., Mrs. Geo. S. Hillard, Dr. S. Durkee, Rev. J. P. Robinson, Dr. D. H. Storer, and to himself, for specimens received during the year.

The Curator of Conchology reported the following donations: A collection of land and fresh water shells from Dr. James Lewis of Mohawk, N. Y. A box of land and fresh water shells from R. Kennicott, Illinois, some marine shells from Capt. N. E. Atwood, and a small collection of shells from John Jas. Dixwell.

The Curator of Botany reported that but little damage had been done to the herbarium during the year, and that the plants were generally in good condition.

At the election of officers for the year, Capt. N. E. Atwood was chosen Curator of Ichthyology in place of Dr. Samuel Kneeland Jr.; Theodore Lyman, Curator of Crustacea and Radiata in place of Dr. John P. Reynolds, and John Green, Curator of Comparative Anatomy in place of Dr. Jeffries Wyman, elected President the previous June.

The reception of the splendid bequest of Prof. Bailey seemed to inspire some of the members with a desire for microscopic research, and in June a Section for the special purpose was formed, called the Section of Microscopy. This, all members of the Society interested in the object, were invited to join. It was provided that a Curator of the department should be chosen yearly at the annual meeting, whose duty it should be to take charge of all specimens belonging to it, and to preside at its meetings. It was also further provided that at the first regular meeting of the Society each month, the presiding officer shall call for microscopical papers, remarks or exhibitions, and that these shall be in order during the continuance of the meeting, excepting that no business matter properly belonging to the annual meeting of the Society shall be superseded. The proceedings of this department were to be published in the Journal and Proceedings of the Society, subject to the decision of the Publishing Committee.

At the first meeting in June, Dr. Silas Durkee was elected Curator of the new department of Microscopy.

Mr. Charles J. Sprague announced the donation by Dr. Benjamin D. Greene, the first President of the Society, of his large and valuable Herbarium. This was stated to be particularly rich in specimens collected by the various exploring expeditions, both of Europe and this country.

In September of this year, the department of Crustacea and Radiata was divided,

Mr. Theodore Lyman who had been its Curator, becoming Curator of Radiata; and Dr. H. R. Storer, Curator of Crustacea.

1858. April. The President stated that a considerable sum of money had been subscribed for the purchase and stocking of an Aquarium, and that it would be advisable to appoint a Committee to attend to the matter. Accordingly Dr. Samuel Kneeland, Jr., Mr. L. B. Stone, and Mr. Theodore Lyman were chosen for this purpose.

From the record of the annual meeting in May, the following is presented :

The Report of the Auditing Committee upon the finances, exhibited a balance due the Treasurer of $2074.25. To meet this there were available assets consisting of uncollected bills in the hands of the Collector, and a sum in the Treasurer's hands belonging to the Building fund, $1306.00, leaving the Society in debt $768.25, and this providing that all the uncollected debts should be paid in full.

The Librarian reported that since the last annual meeting there had been added to the Library, seventy-four bound volumes, and one hundred and five pamphlets or parts of volumes, exclusive of those deposited by " A Republican Institution," of which there had been forty-three bound volumes. To Dr. Benjamin D. Greene the Society was indebted for some of the most valuable works that had been presented. The Librarian in presenting his report took occasion to remark upon the small sum used for the purchase of books, stating it to be far short of what the reasonable wants of the Curators required. He strongly recommended that one-third of the income of the Courtis fund should be, as formerly, appropriated strictly for the increase of the library.

The Curator of Mineralogy, reported that his department had received donations during the year from Dr. Chas. T. Jackson, Dr. Samuel Kneeland, Jr., Dr. Henry Bryant, Mr. Thos. J. Whittemore, Mr. R. H. Eddy and Mr. S. M. Major. Those from Dr. Kneeland were numerous, comprising an extensive series of minerals from the Lake Superior region. That of Mr. Eddy consisted of a considerable supply of native borate of lime from South America, valuable for exchanges, etc.

The Curator of Geology reported that there had been but few additions to the collection under his charge during the year. The large collection belonging to the State, illustrative of its geology, and which had been for many years under the charge of the Society, had been removed to the State House. This enabled him to place in sight all the specimens in the department of sufficient interest for exhibition, a considerable number having been previously kept in drawers for want of room in the cases.

The Curator of Botany reported that extensive additions had been made to the Herbarium during the year. By the donations of Dr. Benj. D. Greene, and the bequest of the late Prof. Bailey, the number of specimens had been increased ten-fold. Dr. Greene's collection had been incorporated with our own, and the two united form one of the richest, most extensive and most valuable herbariums in the country. The bequest of Prof. Bailey had made our collection of Algae the most complete of any. The Curator expressed his intention to give particular attention to the plants received, to take measures for their preservation by poisoning every specimen, and to arrange them according to their genera and species. When this work was completed, he proposed to make a detailed report on the whole herbarium of the Society.

The Curator of Conchology reported that but few additions had been made to the collection of shells. He complained of want of case-room to arrange species now ready for exhibition.

The Curator of Herpetology reported the condition of the collection good, and stated that the most important additions to it had been some specimens from Lake Superior, presented by Dr. S. Kneeland, Jr.

The Curator of Radiata reported that the collection had been increased during the year by donations from Dr. A. A. Gould, Prof. Agassiz and Capt. N. E. Atwood. He remarked that when he took charge of it the previous year, he found it in a state of confusion and disorder, but that now it was properly arranged, and the specimens mostly labelled. The collection embraced about one hundred species of Polypi, representing thirty-nine genera, and about eighty-nine species of Echinodermata, representing about forty genera. Besides these there were a few Medusae in alcohol.

The Report upon the Entomological department was brief, being limited to a statement of the means used to prevent injury to the specimens, by baking, and the free use of camphor.

The Curator of the Microscopical section dwelt at some length upon the great value of the collection, and stated that from the duplicate material belonging to it, specimens had been furnished to a large number of scientific persons in different parts of the country, who had applied for them.

No reports were made by the Curators of the departments of Ichthyology and Crustacea, by reason of absence from the city.

At the choice of officers, the only changes made were in the election of Amos Binney as Treasurer in the place of Dr. Nathaniel B. Shurtleff, Alexander E. R. Agassiz, Curator of Entomology, in place of Dr. Silas Durkee, who had been made Curator of the department of Microscopy, and Dr. Samuel Kneeland, Jr., Curator of Ichthyology instead of Capt. N. E. Atwood.

In July the death of Dr. James Deane of Greenfield, a Corresponding Member, was announced. He had manifested great interest in the Society, and to him it was indebted for much advice and assistance in procuring the magnificent slabs with impressions of the foot marks of animals, which have since found place in the entrance hall of the Museum. A full sketch of the life and labors of Dr. Deane, read at a meeting of the Society, July 7, 1858, by the writer of these pages, may be found in the sixth volume of the Proceedings.

For the first time the Society took a recess in the summer. The members voted July 7 to have no meeting until the first Wednesday in September.

In September the death of another of the Corresponding Members was announced, that of Dr. Francis W. Cragin, of Surinam. He well merits notice here, as having been for many years one of the Society's generous benefactors, from whom were received large numbers of donations, of great zoölogical and anatomical interest.

It will be borne in mind that as early as 1855, complaint was made that owing to want of sunlight and proper ventilation, the collection of the department of Comparative Anatomy was suffering injury from the dampness of the cases in which the specimens were contained. The trouble was increasing, and subsequently the Curators of several of the departments reported injury from the same cause to the collections under their charge.

The erection in 1853 of the Boston Theatre, a large building adjoining the Museum, which cut off its light and air, had produced a change, rendering the latter far less suitable for the requirements of the Society than when it was first occupied. Moreover, with the ever increasing collections of the several departments it had become too small for the proper exhibition of its cabinet.

As early as 1857, Mr. Jas. M. Barnard had suggested that in view of the necessities of the Society, and of the opportunity of purchasing at a low price a good site for a new building, some action should be taken to secure land for the purpose. The unsatisfactory condition of business affairs at that period, however, precluded any action.

1859. Early this year Mr. Wm. E. Baker of Boston presented a plan for the accommodation of the several institutions of art and science of the city in a large building, which he called the Conservatory of Art and Science, to be erected on the new land then being formed by the State on the Back Bay. There was certainly much in the project to commend it to the serious attention of the institutions referred to, but it did not meet with full approval. The zeal and public spirit manifested by Mr. Baker deserved the gratitude of all interested. The presentation of the plan proposed had the good effect to call attention to the necessity of some action in favor of securing early a grant of land from the State for the Society, and accordingly a committee was appointed, consisting of Dr. Cabot, Prof. Rogers, and Messrs. Barnard, Bouvé and Whittemore, to act in connection with committees of other institutions in petitioning the Legislature for sufficient territory to meet the requirements of all. This was done, but the lateness of the season prevented action during the session.

The annual meeting was held on May 4.

The Report of the Treasurer, Mr. Amos Binney, was very gratifying. An arrangement had been made with the former Treasurer, by which the amount shown by the accounts as due to him was liquidated without full payment in money. The income of the Society had been from all sources $1986, and the expenditures, $949.04, leaving in the Treasurer's hands, $1036.96. Deducting from this amount a small debt, $89.70, and there was shown as available assets, $947.26. Besides this cash balance, the Society held ten shares of stock in the Bank of North America, at the market price, $1035.

The Librarian reported that there had been seventy-five volumes, and one hundred and twenty-six pamphlets and parts of volumes added during the year, of which thirty-seven had been deposited by "A Republican Institution;" six hundred and eighty-nine volumes had been borrowed from the library.

The Curator of Mineralogy reported that only few donations had been made to the collection during the year. These were chiefly from Dr. C. T. Jackson and Dr. Samuel Kneeland, Jr. He stated that valuable accessions might be expected when the Society could provide adequate accommodations for their arrangement and exhibition.

The Curator of Geology reported the condition of the collection good, but that there had been few specimens presented to it. A series of thirty-six vertebræ, twenty-six fragments of ribs and other bones of the Zeuglodon from the eocene deposits of Alabama, had been deposited by Mr. C. S. Hale of Burlington, N. J. These, and many other fossils from the same locality in the possession of that gentleman, would undoubtedly become the property of the Society, it being his expressed intention to provide that this should be the case.

The Curator of Entomology reported upon the great accession to the department in Dr. Thaddeus W. Harris's collection of insects. The native specimens in this, he mentioned, had a peculiar value, for they included many typical species described by himself, Say, and other naturalists, and because of the completeness of the collection. It was stated to contain 4838 specimens of 2241 species of Coleoptera, 181 specimens of 76 species of Orthoptera, 620 specimens of about 300 species of Hemiptera, 267 specimens of 146 species of Neuroptera, 1125 specimens of 602 species of Hymenoptera, 1931 specimens of 900 species of Lepidoptera, 796 specimens of 395 species of Diptera. In all 9758 specimens of 4660 species, besides quite a number not yet classified. The general collection was stated to be in good condition.

The Curator of Comparative Anatomy, Dr. J. C. White, reported that the department contained at this time the following specimens: crania 257, skeletons 88, membra disjecta 172, wet preparations 123, skins 43, dried preparations 10. Total 693. Many of these were packed away and could not be put upon exhibition for want of room. The additions during the year had been few, but were valuable. Donations had been made by Drs. Kneeland, J. Mason Warren, E. S. Holden, J. C. Warren, Mr. C. B. Fessenden and Mr. J. C. Reinhardt. Dr. White stated that upon taking charge of the department he found the specimens almost without exception covered more or less with fungoid growths, the mycelium of which penetrates and destroys the organic parts of the bones. The ligamentous skeletons had also been injured by the ravages of Dermestes. The growth of these fungi, of which three species had been detected by him, was caused by the dampness and want of light and ventilation, unavoidable in the building. Dr. White hoped that he had prevented further injury by carefully brushing the specimens and thoroughly washing them with an acid solution of corrosive sublimate, strychnia and camphor. He had also taken the precaution to place in each compartment dishes of chloride of calcium to absorb the dampness.

The Curator of Microscopy reported that such had been the drafts upon the crude material belonging to the collection received from Dr. Bailey that he thought the time had arrived when the kindness of the Society must be limited so far as related to donations from it. What remained he thought would be wanted by the active members of the Society in coming years for study. He advised, therefore, that there should be no further disposal of it, except when required for special and important microscopic researches.

Of the other departments nothing was stated important to present here.

The changes made in the officers at the election were as follows: Samuel H. Scudder was chosen Curator of Entomology in place of Alexander E. R. Agassiz; F. W. Putnam was chosen Curator of Ichthyology in place of Dr. Samuel Kneeland, Jr.; Albert Ordway was chosen Curator of Crustacea in place of Dr. H. R. Storer.

In November, a plan having been proposed for a large building to accommodate both the Horticultural Society and the Society of Natural History, a petition was presented to the legislature asking the grant of one of the squares of land on the Back Bay for its erection, and another for the use of the contemplated Institute of Technology. Great efforts were made by Prof. Rogers, Messrs. Emerson, Ross, Waterston and Binney in behalf of the project through addresses before the Committees of both branches of the Legislature. Considerable opposition however on the part of many Senators prevented favorable action at that time, though it did not cause defeat. The petition was finally referred to the next General Court.

1860. To awaken interest in the work of the Society, and to justify its claims in the minds of the public, it was thought best to have an address delivered at the time of the annual meeting in May, and Prof. Rogers was invited to prepare one for the occasion. It was read before a very large audience at the new hall of the Mechanic's Charitable Association in Bedford Street. The record states that he "delivered a most eloquent and pertinent address on the progress of natural science for the last thirty years, dating from 1830, the year in which the Society was organized. A large, highly intelligent and enthusiastic audience honored the occasion with their presence, and the Society had great reason to be proud of this successful and brilliant revival of their annual address."

The Reports of the Treasurer, Librarian, and Curators at the annual meeting, furnish information which is presented as follows:

The Treasurer exhibited an account showing receipts for the year, including the balance on hand at its commencement, and also the proceeds of sales of bank stock held by the Society to be $3559.13; and expenditures, including an amount paid to Dr. N. B. Shurtleff, the former Treasurer, in settlement, $3,399.48, showing a balance of $159.65 on hand in cash, and no debt. The Society having disposed of its bank stock, held at this time no other property available for its future requirements.

The Librarian reported the accession to the library of 540 volumes and pamphlets during the year; about 300 volumes of these were very valuable works on entomology, from the library of the late Dr. Thaddeus W. Harris, which were purchased by J. P. Cushing, Esq., of Watertown, and generously presented by him to the Society.

There was nothing in the reports of the Curators of Mineralogy, Geology, Herpetology, Oology or Microscopy, calling for notice here, and none was made upon Ornithology.

The Curator of Entomology mentioned but few additions, but stated that much work had been done by him towards checking the further ravages of destructive insects.

The Curator of Radiata stated that the department had been indebted to Drs. Bryant and Winslow for several additions to it.

The Curator of Ichthyology reported an accession of about 200 specimens. The donors had been Dr. Henry Bryant, who presented a very valuable collection from the Bahamas, Dr. C. F. Winslow, a valuable collection from the Island of Maui, and the Museum of Comparative Zoology.

The Curator of Comparative Anatomy, Dr. James C. White, reported as might have been expected, considering his indefatigable labor upon the collection of his department, that this was now in good condition and systematically arranged. He stated that the means adopted by him mentioned in the report of the previous year, to free the specimens from the ravages of insects, had been completely successful, and that even the growth of the destructive fungi had been prevented by the applications made. Every specimen too, had been numbered, and had had attached to it a label giving its name, locality and donor. A new catalogue had also been prepared for the whole collection.

During the year 275 specimens had been added to the cabinet, many of which were quite valuable. Of these may be mentioned a large collection of mammalian skulls and skeletons presented by Dr. Samuel Kneeland, Jr.; and the lower jaws of an immense sperm whale from F. W. Choate, Esq.

The Curator of Conchology reported that little or no progress had been made in his department for want of room to arrange specimens. The collection was stated to comprise about 4000 species. It had had donations as follows: from Dr. Aug. A. Gould, 37 species from Cumana and Hayti, new to the cabinet; from Dr. J. Lewis, a collection of shells from the Mohawk valley and neighboring lakes; from Dr. Simon Shurtleff, 23 species, many of which were new to the cabinet; and from Dr. C. F. Winslow, specimens from the Hawaiian Islands.

The Curator of Crustacea reported that the cabinet of his department was generally in good condition, but that many of the dried specimens had suffered from the ravages of insects. He had arranged, labelled and catalogued about half the collection, and hoped soon to finish the work upon it. He complained seriously of the lack of room to properly display the specimens, and also that a considerable number were comparatively worthless because their localities were unknown. The donations had been numerous. Dr. Henry Bryant had presented a large collection from the Bahamas; Prof. Agassiz also a large collection from the Hawaiian Islands, and the Essex Institute many specimens from our coast. In all, there had been added during the year 366 specimens, comprising 78 species and 55 genera.

The Curator of Botany reported that the Herbarium was in good condition. A series of valuable Swiss plants collected by Mr. Godet, and another of southern plants collected by Prof. Gibbes in the Carolinas were presented by himself.

At the election of officers the following changes took place: Dr. Augustus A. Gould was elected second Vice-President in room of Dr. D. Humphreys Storer, resigned; Dr. B. Joy Jeffries, Curator of Microscopy, in room of Dr. Silas Durkee, resigned; Mr. A. T. Lyman, Curator of Conchology, in room of Mr. Thomas J. Whittemore, resigned; and Dr. Samuel A. Green, Curator of Herpetology, in room of Dr. J. N. Borland, resigned.

Votes of thanks were passed to the retiring officers for their long and efficient services. Those of one of them call for particular mention.

Dr. D. Humphreys Storer.

Whatever reason there may be generally for hesitating in writing freely of the services of the living and yet active members of the community, there are none that should prevent full expression here of such as were rendered to the Society by Dr. D. Humphreys Storer during the first thirty years of its existence. Those for the Museum were invaluable, and it is due to him to make such mention of them while treating of the period of his labors, as will in some degree serve to do what the visible result of his own work as exhibited in the magnificent collection made by him of the Fishes of Massachusetts would have done much better, had this not been destroyed. This collection, obtained through arduous effort, put up by his own hands and presented by him to the Society, was allowed to go to ruin, through causes, perhaps unavoidable at the time, but not therefore the less to be deplored. It was made by Dr. Storer when preparing his valuable report on the Fishes of Massachusetts, published by order of the Legislature of the State in 1839, and at the same time in the Boston Journal of Natural History. It embraced, as has been before stated, ninety out of the one hundred and twenty then known species of the coast, a large number of which were type specimens, and from which the descriptions of the species were drawn. When engaged in collecting and in seeking information concerning them, he visited the market daily and examined all that were to be seen there. He made the acquaintance of those engaged in selling fish and through them with the fishermen themselves, often going to their boats and interesting them in his work, so that many were led to aid him by bringing for his use every species that came into their possession. His ever genial manner served to make him very popular among them, and he thus became a welcome visitor whom they were ready to serve with alacrity. On obtaining any specimens wanted he conveyed them home, or to the rooms of the Society, where they were studied for description and prepared for preservation. For the greater part of two seasons, that is, during the spring, summer and autumn months, when the temperature of the weather would allow of work in unheated rooms, he, in company with Dr. Augustus A. Gould, might be found busily engaged on specimens of their respective departments, from five o'clock in the early morning until their breakfast time. Mr. Teschemacher, who had the care of the herbarium at this period, generally joined them previous to their departure, having breakfasted before leaving home. He worked until his business engagements called him away, perhaps an hour later. These glimpses of the doings of some of the earlier workers are not unworthy of contemplation by those who occupy their places and who would do justice to their memory. Dr. Storer's labor on fishes and reptiles was often of a very disagreeable character, the specimens received requiring transfer and preparation, being often in a condition far from pleasant to work upon. Alas, that a great part of this labor should have resulted, so far as the Museum is concerned, in scarcely more than the valuable lesson it, with other experience, has taught; that the voluntary work of Curators cannot be relied upon alone, to preserve collections that are subject to ruin without constant supervision and care. In subsequent years nearly all the work of Dr. Storer's hands was allowed to perish. The Society will not have done its duty until it has replaced all the species obtained by him of the fishes of Massachusetts waters, every one being labelled as a substitute for the original presented by him. It is pleasant to know that this is recognized as a duty, and as one likely to be accomplished.

Mention has been made of aid afforded Dr. Storer by fishermen, at the time he was engaged in collecting specimens. To two of these he was very much indebted, not only for many of the species described by him, but for a great deal of information concerning them. He would feel it an injustice not to have their names recorded with his, in any description given of the work done by him. These men were Capt. Blanchard of Lynn and Capt. N. E. Atwood of Provincetown. The latter, particularly, furnished many species that could not otherwise have been procured, and which were of invaluable service.

Indirectly Dr. Storer did much for the Society in introducing to it Capt. Atwood. He became a Corresponding Member and ever after manifested great interest in its proceedings. When in the city, he has attended the meetings, and often addressed them, giving always a vast deal of information concerning fishes, their habits and the methods adopted for their capture, not possessed by any other man.

Dr. Storer's services whilst an active member of the Society were by no means limited to his labors for the Museum; on the contrary, few, if any, were more earnest in devotion to its general welfare. Was there money wanted for any special purpose, what he could spare was freely given. Was an appeal to be made for help from others, he was never backward in taking steps towards rendering it effective.

The part he took in the meetings was a prominent one, and the communications made by him were often of great value. No one can look over the records of the Society without recognizing the importance of the work performed by him in building up the institution he loved so well. There was one trait manifested by him when an active member that will not be forgotten whilst yet members who were associated with him live, and that was a disposition to encourage young and deserving members to take part in the proceedings.

Dr. Storer, though not strictly speaking one of the original members of the Society, may well be considered such, as he became an associate with them immediately after its formation, and in September of the same year was elected Recording Secretary, which office he held until May, 1836. He was a Curator before there were special departments of the Museum from 1836 to 1838, afterwards of the department of Reptiles and Fishes from 1838 to 1843. Elected Vice-President in 1843, he remained in this position until 1860, when he resigned. He thus held office for the long period of thirty years, with honor to himself and with great advantage to the Society.

Of Dr. Storer's life and work otherwise than as connected with the Society the following is presented:

Dr. Storer was born in Portland, Maine, March 26th, 1804. He was educated at Bowdoin College; graduated there in 1822 and had the degree of LL.D. conferred upon him by that institution in 1876. His scientific tastes led him to associate himself, as has been mentioned, with the Boston Society of Natural History soon after its formation, but the particular attention he subsequently gave to ichthyology was entirely the result of fortuitous circumstances. When Dr. Hitchcock was authorized to re-survey the State in 1837, he expressed a strong desire that there should also be made a more full examination of its Natural History. A committee of the Legislature therefore met the one on the part of the Society in conference, the result of which was that George B. Emerson, President of the Boston Society of Natural History, Chester Dewey, Professor of Botany in the Berkshire Medical Institution, Ebenezer Emmons, M. D., Professor of Natural History in Williams College, Rev. William B. O. Peabody of Springfield, T. W. Harris, M. D., Librarian of Harvard University, D. Humphreys Storer, M. D., and A. A. Gould, M. D., of Boston, Curators in the Boston Society of Natural History, were commissioned to take charge of the Botanical and Zoölogical survey. These gentlemen met and agreed among themselves as to the part they should respectively take in the work. Prof. Emmons undertook to report upon the Mammals, Dr. Storer upon the Fishes and Reptiles, Mr. Peabody upon the Birds, Dr. Harris upon the Insects, Dr. Gould upon the Mollusks, etc.

The division was unquestionably a wise one, but it required of Dr. Storer a scientific report within a year on a subject of which neither he nor any one else in the community knew anything beyond what was known to the fish dealer and the cook. Laughingly he has since remarked that he could scarcely at the time have told a flounder from any other flat fish. This was not all. There was not in New England an ichthyologist with whom he could consult, and scarcely a book that would aid him in his investigations. Sufficiently discouraging all this, but Dr. Storer did not despair. If he knew but little of ichthyology, he had a scientific mind, sharply observant, quickly perceptive and nicely discriminating. Moreover he was indefatigable in performing whatever he undertook, never relaxing in his work until it was done and well done.

The Commissioners came to an understanding that they all should endeavor as far as possible to extend the boundaries of knowledge in each department, and not confine themselves to merely presenting catalogues of species. It was soon perceived that the work expected of them could not possibly be done within the allotted time, and leave was asked and obtained to defer the reports until a later period.

Before another year, however, had elapsed, several were ready, and we can only wonder, in looking over the volumes produced, that so much could have been accomplished within so limited a period. The result of Dr. Storer's labor was what Dr. DeKay described as a "masterly report" on the Fishes of Massachusetts. This was published by an order of the Legislature in August, 1839, and also appeared in the Boston Journal of Natural History at the same time. Previous to this, Dr. Storer had presented some papers before the Society on fishes, which had also appeared in the Journal. In April, 1845, he communicated to the meeting of the American naturalists at New Haven, a very valuable paper called "A Synopsis of the Fishes of North America." This was published in the Memoirs of the American Academy. Subsequently there appeared in the same Memoirs what Dr. Storer termed his final report on the fishes of Massachusetts, the species being all illustrated by fine engravings, and this was also published in a separate volume.

The third decade of the existence of the Society having now passed, some mention will be made of what has not been referred to during the period.

The Journal of the Society had been published from time to time, but not quite with the regularity that distinguished its earlier issues. Volume VI and part of Volume VII had appeared with many articles of great value. The Proceedings appeared more frequently. A part of Volume III, and Volumes IV, V, and VI, and a considerable portion of Volume VII had been printed and circulated. The scientific character of both series had been well sustained, and had helped much to extend the reputation of the Society abroad.

The average attendance on the meetings each year may be seen by the following table:

For the year ending				For the year ending		
For the year ending	May	1851	23	For the year ending	May 1856	20
"	"	1852	16	"	" 1857	26
"	"	1853	14	"	" 1858	28
"	"	1854	17	"	" 1859	30
"	"	1855	17	"	" 1860	30

Those who took a prominent part at the meeetings of the Society during the first five years of the ten, by presenting communications, participating in the discussions, or otherwise, were Dr. Charles T. Jackson, Count Desor, Dr. Wyman, Dr. Burnett, Dr. Gould, Dr. Durkee, Mr. W. O. Ayres, Dr. Cabot, Mr. William Stimpson, Dr. J. C. Warren, Dr. Samuel Kneeland, Jr., Dr. A. A. Hayes, Prof. William B. Rogers, Mr. Teschemacher, Dr. Thomas M. Brewer, Dr. D. H. Storer, Dr. H. R. Storer, Mr. Charles J. Sprague, Mr. Wells, Prof. Henry D. Rogers, Dr. J. Mason Warren and Mr. Thomas T. Bouvé.

Those who were prominently active during the last five years of the ten were Dr. C. T. Jackson, Prof. William B. Rogers, Dr. A. A. Hayes, Mr. Charles J. Sprague, Dr. Thomas M. Brewer, Dr. Samuel Kneeland, Jr., Dr. Jeffries Wyman, Professor Agassiz, Dr. Gould, Dr. J. C. White, Dr. Henry Bryant, Dr. Samuel L. Abbot, Dr. J. N. Borland, Mr. J. Whittemore, Dr. Silas Durkee, Dr. John Bacon, Jr., Mr. Charles Stodder, Mr. Theodore Lyman, Dr. B. J. Jeffries, Dr. C. F. Winslow, Mr. Samuel H. Scudder, Dr. Samuel Cabot, Dr. D. H. Storer, Dr. Charles Pickering, Mr. John Green, Dr. D. F. Weinland, Capt. N. E. Atwood, Mr. Nathaniel H. Bishop, Dr. J. B. S. Jackson, Prof. H. D. Rogers, Mr. J. M. Barnard, Prof. Theophilus Parsons and Mr. Thomas T. Bouvé.

The financial condition of the Society at the close of the decade differed but little from that at the commencement. There had been during the ten years, periods of considerable indebtedness, but the economical course of the government had prevented its increase, and at the annual meeting, as stated in the Treasurer's report, there was a small balance in the Treasury.

The Library had increased from about 3500 volumes reported as in the possession of the Society in 1850, to nearly 5000, including 1012 deposited by Mrs. Binney, and 767 deposited by " A Republican Institution". Besides these there were 681 pamphlets, or parts of volumes.

The number of Resident Members of the Society at this time were about 206, exclusive of Life Members, of whom there were 18.

The Standing Committees of the Council, through which much of the important business of the Society was transacted, had faithfully attended to the duties assigned them.

The members of each during the decade were as follows:

On the Library: Drs. A. A. Gould, S. Kneeland, Jr., Henry Bryant, and D. Humphreys Storer, and Messrs. C. K. Dillaway and Charles J. Sprague.

On Finance: Dr. N. B. Shurtleff, Messrs. J. J. Dixwell, Thos. Bulfinch, P. T. Jackson, Amos Binney, C. C. Sheafe, Jas. M. Barnard, Thos. T. Bouvé, and George B. Emerson.

On the Library: Drs. A. A. Gould, D. Humphreys Storer, S. Kneeland, Jr., John Bacon, S. Cabot, Jr., Henry Bryant, and Messrs. C. K. Dillaway and Chas. J. Sprague.

On Publications: Drs. D. Humphreys Storer, Jeffries Wyman, Samuel Kneeland, Jr., Samuel L. Abbot, Samuel Cabot, Jr., Benj. S. Shaw, and Mr. C. K. Dillaway.

DECADE IV. MAY, 1860–MAY, 1870.

Soon after the annual meeting, Mr. Arthur T. Lyman, who had been elected Curator of Conchology, resigned, and in June Mr. Nathan Farrand was elected his successor.

In October of this year the Society was notified that the late Jonathan Phillips had made to it the magnificent bequest of $10,000. It will be remembered that in the latter part of 1849, when the Society was suffering from debt, this gentleman manifested his interest in its welfare by a timely donation of $2,000, which relieved it from all liability.

The exertions of the members of the Society towards accomplishing the objects in view, viz., that of securing land from the State on which to build, and help from the public to enable the Society to erect a structure suitable for its wants, were constant. In December a Committee was appointed by the Council, consisting of Prof. Rogers, Dr. A.

A. Gould and Mr. Amos Binney, to prepare a pamphlet setting forth the claims and wants of the Society. This was published and distributed among the members of both houses of the Legislature.

In December also it was voted by the Council that a course of lectures be given during the winter by members of the Society, free to the public, and Profs. Rogers and Wyman, with Dr. Gould, were appointed to prepare a plan of such a course, with full powers to make all the necessary arrangements.

1861. The most important event of the year to the Society, and one of the most important in its history, was the munificent donation by Dr. William J. Walker of his estate in Bulfinch Street.

As this act was the first of a series of great donations on the part of Dr. Walker to the Society, it may be well to state what is known that led to such manifestation of interest in its welfare. For some time previous to the event mentioned Dr. Walker had boarded in the same house at Cambridge with the President of the Society, Prof. Wyman, and an intimacy had arisen between them which led the former to regard with attention whatever the latter was particularly engaged in. Noticing among the documents brought home and laid upon the table of their common sitting room by Prof. Wyman, some of the publications of the Society, Dr. Walker became interested in their perusal and finally in the work of the Society itself. This led to many conversations between them respecting the aims and objects in view, which resulted in the donation mentioned, and eventually in Dr. Walker becoming the great benefactor of the Society.

In announcing the pleasing event Prof. Wyman made the following remarks, which are worthy of mention here:

"I have great pleasure in stating that since our last meeting, Dr. William J. Walker has presented, and by the necessary legal process has conveyed to this Society, the estate recently occupied by him in this city. The property has been placed in the hands of trustees, to be devoted, under wise and liberal conditions, in such a manner as they may deem most expedient, for the promotion of our best interests and of the study of natural history. This is the largest gift that we have received from a single individual. Under any circumstances it would be munificent. Now it is both munificent and timely. It is all the more gratifying inasmuch as it was wholly unsolicited. It naturally follows, from the emotions which this beneficence calls forth, that we should rejoice at being the recipients of such a gift, and, in accepting it, should express our gratitude and sense of deep obligation. But we must not rest here; there are other considerations to which we must allow a place at this time.

"Standing before a community identified with the study of natural history and the diffusion of a knowledge of it, we have been liberally endowed in this and other ways. I believe that with our very inadequate means, we have done much to justify our benefactors and the public in their encouragement of us. But every benefaction has imposed, and every new one will impose, additional and more exacting obligations. Societies are often charged, and it is to be feared too often justly, as less faithful to their trust than individuals. We must have care that such a charge may not apply to us. In accepting the gift now offered us, we bind ourselves, though tacitly yet firmly, to fulfil all the obligations which belong to it, implied no less than direct.

"We have recently set forth our claims upon the community for patronage. It should be remembered that the public, though it does not formally set forth its claims upon us, has them, and with a deeper interest in the study of nature than has been known before, judges us with a severer scrutiny and by a higher standard than at any previous period. So long as we make our collections useful and our studies conducive to the public good, and thus show ourselves faithful to our trusts, we are justified in the belief that we may confidently expect to receive hereafter, as we have received already, every necessary support and encouragement."

Professors W. B. Rogers and Agassiz congratulated the Society upon the addition to their means at such an opportune moment, and Dr. Augustus A. Gould offered the following resolutions, which were unanimously adopted:

"*Resolved*, That the Society accepts with gratitude the donation of Dr. Wm. J. Walker on the terms stipulated.

"*Resolved*, That the accession of so munificent a sum to our funds at a moment when further expansion with our actual resources must have been very limited, greatly encourages us to new and more efficient exertion.

"*Resolved*, That it shall be our diligent care that the avails from the donation shall be applied prudently and practically towards the cultivation and diffusion of useful knowledge; specially aiming to modify the direction of our endeavors, as the spirit of the age may from time to time indicate."

The conditions upon which this donation was made have always been sacredly regarded by the Society.

During the session of the Legislature in the winter of 1860-61, strenuous efforts were made by several members of the Society, and of the Institute of Technology, to obtain the grant of land wanted for the use of each, particularly by Prof. Wm. B. Rogers and Mr. M. D. Ross, which were finally successful, the grant of one square, so called, having been made on certain conditions which seemed objectionable at first, but which turned out to be of no detriment. Of this "square" one third was to be for the use of the Boston Society of Natural History, the other two-thirds for the Mass. Institute of Technology.

In March, it having been intimated that possibly the city might be willing to buy the building of the Society in Mason Street, for the enlargement of the Normal School House near to it, a committee consisting of Mr. Bouvé, Mr. Binney, the Treasurer, and Dr. Kneeland was appointed to confer with the City Government on the subject.

In April, the Treasurer with such other members as saw fit to join him, were appointed a committee to solicit subscriptions for a building fund, and in the same month a Building Committee was appointed consisting of President Wyman, Mr. Binney, Professor Rogers, Dr. Jeffries and Mr. Bouvé, to consider and propose a course of proceedings in relation to the new hall, accompanied by such general plan of grounds and buildings as they might deem expedient, and to report from time to time to the Society, making no engagements without further authority.

The reports of the Curators at the annual meeting in May present but little of interest. Generally, complaint was made of want of room for the proper display of specimens, and the expectation expressed that when this lack should be supplied there would be a much greater disposition manifested to make donations. The Curator of Geology reported that his department was better circumstanced than the others so far as the collection belonging to the Society was concerned, inasmuch as by the removal of that belonging to the State, ample space was now afforded for the reception of specimens and their display.

The Conchological department had received between four hundred and five hundred specimens, many of them species new to the collection, the donors being the Smithsonian Institution, Mr. E. R. Mayo, Dr. A. A. Gould and Mr. H. Davis.

The Mineralogical department had received but few donations, but two of these were quite valuable, one being a large mass of amethystine quartz from Salto, Uruguay, the other a large geode of the same from Uruguay, both the gift of R. B. Forbes, Esq.

The Curator of Comparative Anatomy reported that by the precautionary measures adopted, the collection had been kept in good order, and that donations of considerable value had been received, principally from Dr. Henry Bryant and Mr. Du Chaillu.

The Treasurer's report was exhilarating. He congratulated the Society upon a state of financial prosperity unprecedented in its history. It had received during the year the legacy of the late Jonathan Phillips of $10,000, a donation of an estate from Dr. Wm. J. Walker valued at $30,000 and the grant of land from the State for the erection of a new structure.

The Librarian reported the number of volumes now in the Library as exceeding 5000.

At the election of officers the only change made was in substituting Dr. Francis H. Brown Curator of Herpetology for Dr. Samuel A. Green, who had tendered his resignation.

A special meeting of the Society was called in July to consider upon accepting the offer of $28,000 which has been made on the part of the city for the building of the Society in Mason street. It was voted to accept that price, and a committee consisting of Professor Rogers and Mr. Bouvé was appointed to complete the sale. This was subsequently done and the Society received the amount mentioned.

In August Mr. Amos Binney resigned the position of Treasurer of the Society through a letter to the President, in order that he might accept a commission in the military service of the United States. Mr. Thomas T. Bouvé was unanimously elected Treasurer in his place.

After the sale of the building in Mason Street had been consummated, it was determined on the part of the Society to temporarily occupy the Bulfinch estate for the storage of its collection and for meetings, until a new museum should be erected for its use. Accordingly the house was prepared for the reception of the collection and for the accommodation of the meetings, the parlors on the lower story being fitted up for the latter purpose, and occupied at the same time as a library. All this being accomplished, the Society in August left the home it had occupied for thirteen years, and where its growth had been such as to render more extensive apartments necessary for its expanding wants.

Not without kindly thoughts of many pleasing and instructive hours passed in the cosy meeting room of the Society, was the old building left for new quarters. Here, with the library arranged in the cases around and a large table serviceable for multifarious purposes, might have been seen almost every afternoon several of the Curators at work upon specimens or investigating their character; here too, for several of the later years might have been heard at the meetings as able scientific discussions, as any hall ever echoed to, for it was here that Agassiz, William B. Rogers and Henry D. Rogers made their power felt in warm though most friendly conflict of opinion, exciting the intense interest of all who had the good fortune to be present.

Dr. Kneeland made a proposal to.the Society to occupy with his family some rooms in the Bulfinch St. house, and thereby ensure the greater safety of the buildings and contents, on certain conditions. These were acceded to and Dr. Kneeland and family subsequently occupied the premises.

The Building Committee promptly and industriously devoted themselves to the work put into their hands. They studied the wants and requirements of the Society, conferred among themselves as they met from time to time, as to the interior arrangements suitable for the accommodation of the several departments, and subsequently consulted with architects respecting the exterior, and the cost of building. In the meantime one of their number, Mr. Amos Binney, having entered the Army, Dr. Jas. C. White was substituted in his place, and the committee subsequently now consisted of the President, Dr. Jeffries Wyman, Prof. Wm. B. Rogers, Dr. Jas. C. White, Dr. B. Joy Jeffries, and Mr. Thomas T. Bouvé. They frequently met for consultation at the house of Professor Rogers, where they examined plans submitted to them and then discussed their merits. After two or three months of close attention to the subject, and after considering fully several plans brought before them, they finally reported to the Society in November, as their choice after mature and long deliberation, one offered by Mr. Jonathan Preston. Dr. White explained the details of the plan and presented estimates of the cost, showing that a handsome building could be erected, and such portions finished as would serve the immediate wants of the Cabinet and Library for about $62,000. The Report was quite satisfactory and the Society voted that the plan be accepted "as at once graceful and ample in its proportions and well adapted for all the purposes which the Society has in view."

The Building Committee was requested to have detailed specifications prepared, in order to obtain positive estimates of the cost of finishing such portion of the building as was referred to in the report, and it was empowered to make arrangements for the construction, if such estimate should show that the cost would not exceed the available fund increased by further contributions.

The Society also voted that the Building Committee be authorized to take such steps as they judged proper to raise an additional amount towards paying for the new structure, and also to add to the committee Geo. B. Emerson, Esq., and Rev. R. C. Waterston.

In November of this year, a fire occurred in Boston, by which a menagerie of wild animals was destroyed, the poor beasts being suffocated in their cages. The skins were greatly damaged by fire and water, but the bodies were generally not much injured. Through the exertions of Dr. White, the Curator of Comparative Anatomy, he obtained for his department the animals, and they were dissected, part of them at the Medical College, and the rest at the private dissecting room of the President at Cambridge. Dr. White in making a report of the matter, stated "that the Society may consider itself fortunate in having secured so valuable an acquisition to its already extensive osteological collection. Such an opportunity will probably never occur again. It raises this department of the Cabinet far above any in the country in importance, and will enable us to grace our new halls with an almost perfect collection of skeletons of the large cats of the old and the new worlds."

The specimens obtained were, one fine male lion from Delagoe Bay, Africa; a very large lioness, mate of above; lioness from Cape of Good Hope, presented to Prof. Wyman; one male jaguar; female of same, presented to Prof. Agassiz; young Bengal tiger, female; hunting leopard, female, from Asia; young leopard, male, from Asia; cougar, male, from South America; ocelot, female, from Central America; civet cat, female, Asia; spotted or laughing hyena, male, Cape of Good Hope; jackal, Cape of Good Hope, presented to Prof. Wyman; young black bear; two raccoons, male and female; llama, female, from South America; American opossum; peccary, female, Brazil; three monkeys, one baboon, domestic goat, skull of gnu; eagle and various other birds.

1862. In January of this year, the Boston Marine Society presented to the Society a valuable collection of objects in natural history, and of specimens of the workmanship of different East India and Pacific nations, such as models of canoes and junks, war clubs and insignia of office, cutting weapons, bows and arrows, quivers and paddles, native cloth and tanned skins, etc., etc.

The presentation of so many objects of art, led the Council to recommend the establishment of a department of Ethnology, and in accordance with this suggestion, the Society formed such a department and elected Dr. Charles Pickering its Curator.

In March of this year, Dr. Kneeland entered the Medical Corps of the Army, and at his request a vote was passed that his family be allowed still to occupy rooms in the building as a residence. Dr. Kneeland was the third officer of the Society that the war had called into active service.

The Building Committee, now having in charge not only the construction of the proposed new edifice, but the raising of additional means to meet the cost, omitted no effort to accomplish the objects in view. They exhibited publicly the plan of the structure, with detailed specifications prepared by Mr. Preston, and invited proposals from mechanics for the execution of the work. No less than sixty-four were presented and considered, but not until subscriptions had been received sufficient to cover the entire estimated cost, was any contract made involving expenditure. To obtain subscribers they took most efficient measures. They met together, they discussed plans, they consulted with others interested, they decided what persons should be appealed to, and finally distributed among themselves the names of such as each one would undertake to solicit, so that there might be no conflicting action. On account of the very great service rendered by Mr. M. D. Ross, for the Society at this time, it is proper to state that though not upon the committee he offered his valuable aid in furtherance of its objects, met with them, gave good advice, and finally took an active part in appealing to such parties for money as he thought he could best influence. To aid the committee in their work they issued a circular prepared by Drs. Jeffries and White giving the reasons for the appeal made to the public, accompanied by lithographic views of the exterior of the proposed building, as well as some representation of the plan for its interior arrangement. While thus engaged in preliminary movements towards personal appeals, what was their joy and how great their encouragement, to have the announcement made to them, as was done by President Wyman, that a gentleman, whose name was to remain for awhile unknown, had offered towards the Building Fund, the munificent sum of $20,000, provided a like sum should be secured by subscription from other parties! This enabled the Committee to head the subscription papers quite effectively, and no doubt had great influence in securing signatures to them. The success which followed soon justified active measures for the construction, and contracts for the execution of the work, and for delivery of material, such as stone, bricks, &c., immediately followed.

In May it was found that $20,000 had been subscribed, and Professor Wyman was requested to communicate the fact to the gentleman who had made the offer alluded to. At a subsequent meeting of the committee Professor Wyman mentioned that he was none other than Dr. Wm. J. Walker, to whom the Society was indebted for the house it occupied, and stated that he was ready to pay over the $20,000 at once.

At the meeting of the Society, June 4, the President announced the reception of the $20,000 from Dr. Walker, and besides other appropriate action the following resolutions were passed:

"*Resolved*: That the Society hereby tender to Dr. Walker their most grateful acknowledgement for the renewed and munificent proof of his interest in their prosperity, and for the occasion and the incentive which it had afforded to other friends of the Society to contribute an equal aggregate amount.

"*Resolved*: That in view of this and the previous benefactions, by which Dr. Walker has marked his appreciation of our scientific labors and aspirations, we feel that to his liberality, chiefly, we are indebted for the enlarged opportunities of usefulness now so brightly opening before us, and that, in offering him the homage of our grateful hearts, we have no need to assure him of the enduring honor which will associate his name with the future successes and the whole history of the Society."

While yet engaged in getting subscriptions, the committee kept busily at work upon matters pertaining to the building, and as soon as it became clear that means enough would be secured to meet the cost, they made contracts for the principal part of the work, including the filling in of the land.

From the estimates made of the probable cost of the building completed, it appeared that not less than $87,000 would be required exclusive of cases, but that by leaving unfinished certain portions not needed for early occupancy, about $80,000 would suffice.

It was therefore voted not to exceed $80,000 upon the building, exclusive of cases and furniture.

It has been thought well to give somewhat in detail the action of the Building Committee in the preliminary steps taken to erect the grand structure since occupied by the Society, and in obtaining the necessary means to accomplish its completion. To do anything like justice to the devoted service of a most faithful and industrious committee would require a much fuller record of their doings than can be given here. The result of their endeavors to erect a building satisfactory to the Society will be stated further on. Notice must now be taken of other matters of interest concerning the Society that transpired during the year.

The Reports of the Treasurer, Librarian and Curators were presented as usual at the annual meeting, and were, considering circumstances, satisfactory. The department of Comparative Anatomy had been enriched by the addition before mentioned of a valuable collection of the skeletons of animals suffocated at the fire in Portland Street, by the osteological collection of the late Dr. Lane, by a series of crania from Dr. Henry Bryant, and by a skull and nearly a perfect skeleton of a gorilla presented by Dr. Otis of the Navy.

The department of Geology had also been enriched by the addition of specimens showing tracks of animals, purchased from Mr. Field of Greenfield.

The Curator of Ethnology, the department of which had been recently formed, acknowledged the reception of the various objects of art and manufacture presented to the Society by the Boston Marine Society, as before mentioned.

At the election of officers, Mr. S. H. Scudder was chosen Recording Secretary in place of Dr. Samuel Kneeland, who had entered the service of the United States as surgeon in the army.

The office of Curator of Crustacea, made vacant by the resignation of Mr. Albert Ordway, who had also entered the army of the United States, was not filled.

This year, so full of events gratifying to the members and cheering to their hopes for the future, did not pass without one that caused sadness in the hearts of all, but more particularly to such as had been associated in the work of the Society in its earlier years. Reference is here made to the death of Dr. Benjamin D. Greene, which took place on the 14th of October, and which was announced to the Society on the 15th.

Dr. Benjamin D. Greene.

When the good and the wise participate in the formation and in the work of an institution, they leave an impress upon its character not to be effaced, whilst the memory of their deeds is yet fresh in the minds of those who succeed them; and as what they were, and what they accomplished is not only a delight to contemplate but an inspiration to endeavor, it becomes a sacred duty to extend and perpetuate a knowledge of their worth and labors. It was the good fortune of the Society to have associated among its members at the period of its origin and in its subsequent history, some of the noblest and purest minded men that the community has produced. This is not expressed without due consideration, and will not be questioned when the names of Dr. B. D. Greene, Rev. F. W. P. Greenwood, Dr. John Ware, Dr. J. B. S. Jackson and Dr. Jeffries Wyman are recalled to mind as active workers, to say nothing of many others whose attainments and deeds justly earned for them the esteem and regard of all who knew them.

Among those mentioned, none enjoyed the respect and love of contemporaries more than the honored First President of the Society, Dr. Benjamin D. Greene, and a knowledge of his virtues is only necessary to cause his memory to be revered by all who come after, as long as the Society shall exist. It is to impart this knowledge that the following account of him is given.

Dr. Greene was born in Demarara, in 1793, during a temporary sojourn of his parents there. In 1812 he graduated at Harvard College in the same class with Charles G. Loring, Peleg Sprague, Henry Ware and others who became well known to public fame in later days. After leaving Cambridge he studied law at Litchfield, Conn., where was then a well-known law school, and was later admitted a member of the Boston bar. His subsequent career cannot be better given than by quoting the words of a near and dear friend and

connection, Mrs. Robert C. Waterston, sister of Mrs. Greene, embodied in a letter respecting him. They were as follows: "Dr. Greene's studies at Litchfield were rather to acquire a general knowledge of law than from an intention to pursue it as a profession, and his tastes for natural history, especially botany, led him to turn his attention to medicine. To pursue this study he went abroad and was a student in London, but more especially in Edinburgh, where he passed several years. Here he formed the acquaintance of men who were afterwards widely known in their different departments. Among them was William J. Hooker, afterwards Sir William Hooker, with whom a friendship arose which continued through life. The intimacy was renewed on Mr. Greene's various visits to England and Scotland; and always maintained by correspondence and the interchange of botanical books and information, as well as by mutual expressions of lasting affection.

"Mr. Greene's botanical studies greatly interested him both in Europe and America. Forgetful of time and even of hunger, he would go out in the country in the morning and not return until night, coming back laden with botanical boxes filled with specimens, and then spend half the night in laying each in its separate papers with the careful and tender touch peculiar to his hand.

"Thus besides acquiring two professions, he gained a reputation as a botanist in the front rank of that department of natural history. Added to these attainments he had command of several modern languages. He knew much and said little. Constitutionally reserved and silent, it was impossible for him to impart what he had acquired.

"Once only I heard him express a regret that fluency of speech or writing had been denied to him. Few knew how richly his mind was stored on almost every subject. His taste for the fine arts made him a just judge of both music and painting. Of pictures he had a great love and knowledge. His ample fortune was the means, not only of adorning his own house with works of the old masters, and those of a more modern school, but also of encouraging and aiding many struggling workers in various departments of 'man's endless toil and endeavor,' who but for him had been 'desolate and oppressed.' His library was well chosen and filled, and there he loved to abide — and when at last he passed on to wider regions of knowledge, the works on natural history as well as his Herbarium were at his request transferred to the Boston Society of Natural History. Mr. Greene's life was one quite aside from the hurry and self-assertion of American careers. He possessed many qualities, which, had he practised the profession of medicine, would have made him an able and certainly a beloved physician. His was the magnetic touch of a born healer, and the strength and tenderness of his presence in the sick room was of itself a restorative power. I knew well that character whose 'still waters ran deep.' His low voice was seldom raised except to rebuke wrong, but the flash of his wrath was all the more startling, because it so seldom fell from the calm and quiet sky of his serene days. After he left us in 1862, I arranged at my sister's request a simple monument to be placed over his resting place at Mount Auburn. An ivy plant climbs over the tablet and half hides a cross on its summit, typifying that sincere faith and reverence which lay in his soul, seldom outwardly revealed. To please a wish of my own heart there was cut on the marble the grass which was named for Mr. Greene, by Thos. Nuttall, when he discovered it on the Western plains, the *Greenia Arkansia*." To this beautiful and just tribute of one who knew more of Dr. Greene in his domestic life, than any other who has written of him, it may seem unnecessary to add anything touching his private character and its influence. Yet the subject is too interesting not to dwell upon, especially as there are words of Dr. Asa Gray, not in print, concerning Dr. Greene, which should not be omitted here. In referring to a brief notice written by himself of Dr. Greene, published in the Proceedings of the American Academy of Arts and Sciences, and in which remarks were made upon his well known generosity in placing the results of his observations and his collections in the hands of those who could make the best use of them for the advancement of science, he says that the notice given "does not make enough of the liberality, the winsomeness and the very quiet generosity of Mr. Greene, which made itself felt in a most spontaneous, unobtrusive way, as if it were something in the atmosphere, a delicate, grateful, subtle aroma, rather than anything consciously put forth." Most fitting words these will be judged by all who had the pleasure of personal intercourse with the subject of them.

Of Dr. Greene as a botanist it may be said that he stood deservedly high in the estimation of those who knew him best in this relation. He collected extensively the plants of our country, and studied them carefully, so that his knowledge of them was thorough. Dr. Gray, in writing of him, states that after he ceased to collect, from failing health, he still showed a real interest in his plants and from time to time "verbally gave me critical remarks such as would only be made by a keen and accurate observer."

Of Dr. Greene's botanical work less can be said than might be expected concerning the knowledge he possessed on the subject, and his desire that others should profit by his acquirements. No doubt this was largely due to that want of fluency in expressing what he knew either in writing or by speech, to which he himself feelingly alluded. Dr. Gray, who knew more discriminately what he accomplished in his favorite pursuit, said that his retiring, contemplative, unambitious disposition rendered him averse to the toils, and wholly indifferent to the fame of authorship; that his services to science were in his helpfulness to others, by making botanical collections, and by forming a library of botanical works; the plants and the books being always at the disposal of those who needed them for scientific research.

The action of the Society upon the death of Dr. Greene is presented as follows:

On the 15th day of October, as before mentioned, the Rev. Mr. Waterston announced to the Society the death of the First President of the Society, Dr. B. D. Greene. He spoke of the high personal character and the attainments of the deceased, and of the great interest he had ever felt in the welfare of the Society. Remarks were also made by the President, Jeffries Wyman, and by Professor Agassiz and Dr. Pickering, expressive of their great respect for his memory. Upon motion made by Mr. Waterston, a committee was appointed to take such action as seemed proper in view of the sad event, consisting of Dr. Gould, Professor Rogers, Professor Agassiz and Mr. Waterston.

At the next meeting of the Society, held Nov. 5th, Dr. Gould made a brief address, giving an account of Dr. Greene's participation in the formation of the Society and in the proceedings of its early days, after which Professor Rogers followed, dwelling more at length upon some points of interest in the life and character of the deceased. "It is not often," he said, "that the possessor of a liberal fortune is found giving his heart and time to the labor of scientific studies which, however ennobling and replete with the finest of enjoyments, have as we know, nothing in sympathy with the luxurious ease and brilliant excitements of what is called society."

"Such tastes and labors as marked the life of our late colleague are the exception, and we are therefore especially called on to honor the memory of him who furnished so beautiful an example. But qualities still more rare characterized the pursuits and conversation of Dr. Greene. No one could fail to remark his singular freedom from the ambitious impulses which, whilst they stimulate the labors of men of science, so often dim their aspirations for what is true and beneficent. With him the love of knowledge was a sufficient incentive and adequate reward. Delighted to store his mind with the beautiful truths gathered from the ample sources around him, and ever ready to help others devoting themselves to kindred branches of inquiry, and indeed to any scientific pursuits, his singular modesty shrank from the least public exhibition of his various knowledge, and in the eyes of those who knew his solid and diversified culture, gave to his social character its most peculiar and winning charm." Professor Rogers closed by offering the following resolutions:

"*Resolved*, That while it is the duty of the Society to hold in grateful recollection all who at any time have participated in the labors or helped to enlarge its means of scientific usefulness, it is under especial obligations to honor the memory of the founders and early patrons of the Society, whose earnest zeal gave the first strong impulse to the pursuit of natural history in the community, and whose liberal contributions and fostering care laid the foundation for those labors which have won for the Society an honorable place in the history of scientific investigation.

"*Resolved*, That the Society, while deeply regretting the loss which it has sustained in the death of its late associate, Dr. Benj. D. Greene, has a sad pleasure in placing on record an expression of its grateful and enduring reverence for his memory as one of the most zealous of its founders and its first acting President, and as one of the most liberal of the patrons and co-workers of the Society.

"*Resolved*, That in expressing our sense of the great value of the services of our late associate in this Society, and of his work as a cultivator and promoter of natural science, we would dwell with affectionate interest on the gentle graces of character for which he was remarkable, and especially on the shrinking modesty and reserve which veiled so beautifully the knowledge and culture they were unable to conceal."

Nov. 19th, 1862, by vote of the Society, the names of all persons who had contributed one hundred dollars or upwards towards the erection of the new building, were entered in the records as Patrons.

1863. In April of this year there arrived from London casts from the bones of the Megatherium in possession of the British Museum, presented by Joshua Bates, Esq. These were subsequently mounted by Mr. George Seeva, under the direction of Dr. James C. White. The huge animal form thus reconstructed has since been one of the most striking features of our main hall.

At the annual meeting in May it was announced that the Society had been the recipient of a bequest of $9,000 from our late associate and first President, Dr. Benjamin D. Greene.

The Treasurer's Report showed receipts of $72,507.76, and expenditures $61,224.31, leaving in his hands $11,283.45. Of the receipts $46,267 had been paid in especially for building purposes, and of the expenditures $58,685.75 had been paid towards the new building.

The Report of the Librarian mentions the munificent bequest of the library of Dr. Greene, comprising 1,500 volumes or parts, many of which were costly illustrated works, mostly upon botany. This was the largest addition ever made to the Library at any one time.

The Curators had but little to report except that the collections were safely housed, awaiting accommodations for exhibition in the new building.

At the election of officers for the ensuing year, Mr. William T. Brigham was chosen Curator of Mineralogy in place of Dr. John Bacon, and Mr. Thomas T. Bouvé was chosen Curator of Geology and Paleontology instead of Curator of Geology alone, which office he had previously held, the two being combined in one department.

The Building Committee had continued to act vigorously in the business of construction and finish. Already the structure was approaching completion, and questions concerning ornamentation, railing for balconies, tiling, heating apparatus, library and other cases, had recently occupied their attention.

In October the announcement was made of the sudden death of Dr. George Hayward, one of the members of the Linnæan Society, and subsequently one of the founders and original members of the Boston Society of Natural History. He was First Vice-President from May, 1830 to May, 1832.

October 21st Mr. Alpheus Hyatt was elected Curator of Conchology.

On the 4th of November, the President of the Society reported on behalf of the Building Committee that the new building was nearly ready for occupancy and that the Library room was quite so. It was therefore voted — That the Library be moved forthwith and that the next meeting of the Society be held at the new building, if gas is previously introduced into it. It was also voted — That the Curators be authorized to remove their collections as soon as convenient. In accordance with the vote, and gas having been in the meantime carried into the library room, the Society on the 18th of November for the first time, met in their new and capacious building, 79 members being present. The library had already, since the previous meeting, been removed to the room, and now occupied the shelves of the cases.

In November of this year, another of the founders of the Society passed away, Mr. Francis Alger.

At the meeting held Dec. 2d, Mr. T. T. Bouvé remarked that before proceeding to business it seemed meet that the members of the Society should express their appreciation of the loss it had sustained in the death of their friend and associate, Mr. Francis Alger.

"Public spirited, he always felt a strong interest in all institutions designed for the welfare of the people, and often gave of his means for their endowment. Especially was he interested in the promulgation of knowledge relating to his favorite branch of science, that of mineralogy. To further this he was always ready to give specimens, inviting those interested in the study to select from his duplicates."

"But a few days since he suggested to me his intention to send some very large specimens of beryl and other minerals to adorn our grounds, and such was his interest in the Society that I cannot but think his large collection would have come into our possession at an early day, if his sudden departure had not prevented the fruition of his wishes."

At the request of the Society, Dr. Chas. T. Jackson prepared a notice of Mr. Alger for the Proceedings, a considerable portion of which will be presented here.

"Our late associate, Francis Alger, son of Cyrus Alger, was born in Bridgewater, in this State, March 8th, 1807. In youth he was not studious, and had only a common school education. His taste for study commenced in 1824, when his attention was first drawn to the science of mineralogy. To his love for that science he attributed his after progress in general learning and scientific attainments. One branch of natural history leads to another, and Mr. Alger soon found himself engaged in the study of shells and plants, first the fossils and then their analogues in the living world. His library shows how extensively he studied in the various branches of natural history; but it was to his first love, mineralogy, that he devoted his chief attention."

Having occasion to accompany his father on an excursion for business purposes to Nova Scotia, Mr. Alger collected minerals from near Digby Neck, and in the trap rocks of Granville, a list of which he published in the Boston Journal of Philosophy and Arts, upon his return home. He also published a brief description of Nova Scotia minerals in the American Journal of Arts and Sciences.

In 1827, Mr. Alger and Dr. Chas. T. Jackson made a full exploration of Nova Scotia, and collected a large number of minerals, the species of which they described by a joint essay in the 14th and 15th volumes of the American Journal of Science, extra copies being freely distributed gratuitously to scientific men.

In 1829, Mr. Alger and Dr. Jackson again visited Nova Scotia, and making many new discoveries, prepared a revised memoir for the American Academy of Arts and Sciences.

Dr. Jackson in his notice went on to say, referring to their work together:

"In the second joint excursion a schooner was chartered for the voyage, and served as a home along the wild coasts of Nova Scotia. Though Mr. Alger was always very sea sick when in the rough waters of the Bay of Fundy, he bore the affliction with great patience, and when on shore worked with the most enthusiastic zeal in exploring for minerals. It was a great pleasure to witness his joy when a new crystal oven in the trap rocks, or brilliantly studded agate ball was broken open, disclosing to view the 'flowers of the mineral kingdom.' He fairly danced with delight, and thought no labor too severe, when such rewards were to be won. His part in the Memoir was fairly borne, the work of writing the descriptions being carefully and equally divided. Soon after its publication, Mr. Alger was elected a Fellow of the American Academy, and took an active interest in the meetings, occasionally communicating some of his scientific observations.

. . "Having become interested in the iron and zinc mines of Sussex Co., New Jersey, he made that locality, before well known to the scientific world, still more famous for its rare and unique minerals, and spread them broadcast over the mineralogical world. He often made excursions into the state of New Hampshire, and purchased some of the interesting mines more for the sake of obtaining specimens of the minerals they produced than from any hope of pecuniary gain. He would never sell any mine without reserving the right to all the fine specimens of crystals that should be got out in mining. Finding that he could not extract and bring home to his cabinet a large beryl of five tons weight which exists in Grafton, N. H., he purchased the hill, had the crystal uncovered of rock, and considered it as in his cabinet and one of his specimens.

"His zeal, instead of cooling off, seemed constantly to be inflamed, and I never knew the time when his eyes would not sparkle at the sight of a new or beautiful mineral. . . . In New York he met a young man who had a guard-chain made up of fine crystals of gold, every one of them far better than could be found in the cabinets of Europe. He at once bought the chain at a high price, and had the crystals carefully removed and added to his cabinet."

In 1849 Mr. Alger received the honorary degree of A. M. from Harvard University.

Of Mr. Alger's personal character we know that he was a kind hearted man, a firm friend and worthy Christian. He was always disposed to apologize for the short-comings and faults of others, and he never spoke a hard word except of those whom he considered irreclaimably vicious, and such men he loathed and did not like even to name. Francis Alger's career in this world is now ended. He died in the field of his public duty. He was engaged in the city of Washington in perfecting shrapnel to be employed in restoring the union of our divided States. Exposure to cold and wet weather, with fatigue and neglect of proper personal care of himself, brought on a sudden attack of congestion of the lungs which terminated in typhoid pneumonia, of which he died on the 27th of November, in the fifty-sixth year of his age.

Mr. Alger's scientific writings were mostly essays upon minerals published in the American Journal of Science and Arts, in the Proceedings of the American Association for the Advancement of Science, and in the Journal and Proceedings of the Boston Society of Natural History. His most important work was what he modestly entitled "Alger's Phillips's Mineralogy." It was an edition of Phillips's Mineralogy increased by Mr. Alger's additions more than one half, the result of his labor for many years.

The Society passed the following resolutions:

"*Resolved*, That the Boston Society of Natural History has learned, with profound sorrow, the death of their late associate and friend, Francis Alger, one of the founders of the Society and for years an efficient Curator in the department of Mineralogy.

"*Resolved*, That this Society recognizes in Mr. Alger a true lover of science, an active and earnest collaborator, animated with a kindly spirit, calculated to win the friendship of all who knew him, and to excite an interest in the branches of science to which he was devoted."

On December 2d, Mr. A. S. Packard, Jr., was elected Curator of Crustacea.

1864. The new year opened auspiciously for the Society, and yet there were sufficient reasons for anxiety concerning the future. Dazzled by the success which had followed their endeavors to secure for themselves a structure adequate to the requirements of a great institution, they but imperfectly realized the enormous expenses that necessarily attend such work as that to which they were now pledged. There was imminent danger that the income derivable from all sources at command would fall far short of the amount required to accomplish what was now expected of them. The following extracts from the records of the first meeting of the Society held January 16th, will show what reasons the members had for new joy and congratulation:

"Mr. T. T. Bouvé arose to speak of the financial condition of the Society and its enlarged needs in the new building, showing that the capital which had hitherto barely supported the Society, would now be manifestly insufficient for its maintenance. He then read a letter recently received from Dr. William J. Walker, to whom the Society was already so largely indebted, wherein he promised to give $20,000 more on condition that others would subscribe a like amount, the whole to be funded and used by the Society as a working capital. In conclusion Mr. Bouvé urged very strongly that every member should give his direct personal effort toward the raising of the sum requisite to secure so generous a donation."

Rev. Mr. Waterston thought "the time auspicious for the endeavor, since the Society, within the means given for the object, has erected a handsome and spacious edifice, an ornament to the city, and most suitable for its wants. We have done all we proposed to do in the outset and have not overburdened ourselves with debt by overstepping the limits of the fund set apart for this special purpose, and now in order to secure a working capital which shall forever place in security our valuable collections, enable us to make a proper exhibition of these to the public, and put us upon a proper basis as an active, progressive Society, we call upon the public to subscribe for this object, $20,000; failing to secure which, we have barely enough to maintain the building in proper repair, leaving out of consideration our necessities for the proper exhibition and ultimate security of our cabinet, and for the publication of our Proceedings and Memoirs."

Others spoke earnestly upon the matter, urging prompt action, and finally a Committee of Subscription was appointed, consisting of Prof. Jeffries Wyman, Dr. A. A. Gould, Dr. C. T. Jackson, Prof. William B. Rogers, Rev. R. C. Waterston, Dr. Samuel Cabot, F. W. Lincoln, Dr. Henry Bryant, Dr. Charles Ware, Dr. D. Humphreys Storer, George B. Emerson, Thomas T. Bouvé, Dr. S. L. Abbot, M. D. Ross, R. C. Greenleaf, J. D. Philbrick, Edward Pickering, N. L. Hooper, Lemuel Shaw, C. J. Sprague, Charles C. Sheafe, J. D. Kidder, Thomas Gaffield, M. S. Scudder, and Dr. J. C. White.

This committee issued a circular setting forth the need of a working fund to carry on efficiently the objects of the Society, and mentioning the munificent offer of Dr. William J. Walker to give $20,000 towards this, if a like sum should be obtained by subscription.

To facilitate obtaining signatures for $100, an alteration was made in the By-laws by which the payment of this sum would be requisite to constitute any one a life member, and it was understood that all parties subscribing that amount towards the working fund should be made life members.

In April, Mr. Bouvé announced the death of Dr. Edward Hitchcock of Amherst, an honorary member, and subsequently made a short address upon his character, ending with a presentation of the following resolution:

"*Resolved*, That the members of the Boston Society of Natural History recognize in the death of their late distinguished associate, Dr. Edward Hitchcock, the loss to themselves, and to the public, of a man of comprehensive ability, of untiring devotion to the cause of science, and of great private worth."

A few days previous to the annual meeting of this year, died one who had been the first of the Second Vice-Presidents of the Society at the time of its foundation, Dr. John Ware.

He was the son of the Rev. Henry Ware, for thirty-five years Professor of Theology at Harvard University, and was born at Hingham, Mass., Dec. 19th, 1795. He graduated at Harvard in 1813, and received the degree of M. D. in 1816. In 1817 he removed to Boston, where by steady devotion to his profession, he gradually built up an extensive practice.

In 1832 he was appointed adjunct Professor of the Theory and Practice of Medicine in Harvard University, and succeeded Dr. James Jackson in 1836, holding the chair until 1858. He was President of the Mass. Medical Society from 1848 to 1852.

Dr. Ware was one of a family distinguished for the talents of its members. His father and several brothers were eminent as preachers and theological writers; one, William, was the author of the widely known classical novels of "Zenobia" and "Aurelian;" and Henry possessed a fine poetical talent. More than one of the brothers achieved great success in the practice of medicine.

Dr. Ware's contributions to the literature of his profession were numerous and very able; and some of them exercised a great influence, especially the essays on delirium tremens and on croup. He was a most careful observer, a mature thinker, and very thorough as a teacher. His great liberality and candor were as marked as his ability; and his gentle and lovable nature rounded off a character which was appreciated as it deserved to be, by all who had the good fortune to be cared for professionally by him, or to enjoy his friendly intercourse. As a physician, he was wholly devoted and faithful, as he was in all other relations of life.

Dr. Ware died in Boston on the 29th of April, 1864, in the seventieth year of his age.

At the annual meeting in May, the Treasurer, before presenting his report, announced the agreeable intelligence that the subscriptions to the working fund had reached the required sum of $20,000, and that consequently the $40,000 was secured.

His report stated that the receipts for the year amounted to $24,955.90, which added to the balance of last year, made $36,239.35; the expenditures had been $32,121.16, leaving a cash balance of $4,118.19.

Of the $24,955.90 received, $7,700 were from subscriptions already paid on the working fund. Of the $32,121.16 paid $27,773.07 had been on the new building.

The Librarian, Mr. Chas. K. Dillaway, after serving the Society for the long period of thirty-one years, having been elected in 1833, in tendering his thirty-first and final report, resigned the position so long and faithfully held, much to the regret of the members, to whom he was endeared by long and intimate association. The record of the meeting states that in presenting the report, Mr. Dillaway gave an interesting account of the progress of the Society in every department during his connection with it. The Library, he said, at the time of his first annual report contained about 200 volumes; now we have over 6000 of great value. In 1833 we had published nothing and had no exchanges; now our Journal and Proceedings go to every kindred Society in America and Europe. Since the last annual meeting there had been received from donations 915 volumes and 559 pamphlets and parts of volumes, including the munificent bequest of the late Dr. Greene; from exchanges 40 volumes and 197 parts of volumes, making with some from other sources an addition of 970 volumes and 778 parts of volumes. Since our removal to this building every book has been numbered, labelled, catalogued and placed upon the shelves, for a great part of which labor the Society was under obligations to Mr. Samuel H. Scudder.

The warm thanks of the Society were voted to Mr. Dillaway for his long and efficient services, and he was requested by unanimous vote to make use of the rooms of the Society for private instruction as heretofore.

The Curators having now placed their collections in the new building were enabled generally to report upon their magnitude and condition. It will be well to present here, now that the Society starts upon a new era of activity, the substance of what was stated respecting the cabinet.

The Curator of Ornithology reported the collection of birds, notwithstanding the time it was stored in Bulfinch Street, to be in as good order as when it was taken from the old building in Mason Street; that several large additions had been made to it since entering the new building, principally by the Smithsonian Institution and by himself; and that the whole number of mounted birds is now more than twenty-five hundred.

The Curator of Comparative Anatomy reported that the collection of his department had all been removed in good condition, and that the skeletons and parts of skeletons had been arranged in the places allotted to them; that the skins not in the hands of the taxidermist, for want of money, were in the cellar exposed to injury from insects. The collection was briefly described as follows:

Mammals: skeletons, mounted 73, unmounted 25; parts of skeletons, 107; skulls, 279; teeth, 93.

Birds: skeletons, 25; parts of skeletons, 56; skulls, 87.

Reptiles: skeletons, 13; parts of skeletons, 8; skulls, 21.

Fish: skeletons, 0; parts of skeletons, 57; skulls, 21.

Alcoholic specimens, 100; horns, 50; miscellaneous, 25; skins not estimated.

During the past year the large collection of mammalian skeletons which came into the possession of the Society at the burning of the Menagerie in 1861, had been mounted in a very correct and beautiful manner by Mr. George Sceva.

Several valuable donations had been received, the principal donors being Dr. Henry Bryant, Mr. George Sceva, Mr. C. J. Sprague, Dr. Borland, Mr. W. H. Dall, Dr. B. Joy Jeffries and Mr. J. M. Barnard.

The Curator of Herpetology reported that there were in the collection representatives of 500 species. During the winter and spring much work was done in arranging them and in placing a certain number of each species in fresh bottles and clean alcohol. Some specimens had become worthless and were thrown away. The reptiles of Massachusetts were tolerably well represented, but many common species were lacking which the Curator hoped to obtain before the next annual meeting.

The Curator of Ichthyology reported that the fishes had not been materially injured by their storage in Bulfinch Street. He stated, however, that when they were carried there from Mason Street the poor specimens thrown away left a deficiency in Massachusetts fishes which he expected might be supplied during the season. This is the first indication given of the fate of the magnificent collection of Massachusetts fishes, largely type specimens, collected by Dr. D. Humphreys Storer, and presented by him to the Society. The want of jars and alcohol was strongly urged to the attention of the Society.

The collection was stated to consist of 280 species, 800 specimens from North America; 80 species, 250 specimens from the West Indies and Bermuda; 45 species, 62 specimens from the fresh waters of South America; 8 species, 9 specimens from Africa; 14 species, 16 specimens from Europe; 115 species, 197 specimens from the Hawaiian Islands; 60 species, 236 specimens of duplicates for exchange; 25 species, 200 specimens dry, from various localities. In all 627 species, and 1770 specimens.

The Curator of Crustacea reported that the collection had been removed without serious injury. The additions during the year were a few native forms, presented by Mr. W. H. Dall of Medford. The collection contains 122 species of alcoholic specimens, 198 species of dry specimens.

The Curator of Oology reported that the original collections of the Society had been increased by the local collections of Mr. Thoreau of Concord and Mr. W. H. Henck of Dedham. The number of specimens belonging to the department was not reported.

The Curator of Conchology reported considerable donations of shells from Dr. Gould, Dr. Gundlach of Cuba, and Mr. J. M. Barnard, together about 500 species, but made no mention of the number in the cabinet.

The Curator of Botany reported an immense amount of work done by him in arranging the plants of the collection in the most scientific manner, and in thoroughly protecting them by means of poison from the attacks of insects. There were many packages still unarranged, but which had been carefully examined. A collection of dried plants had been commenced, and the Curator had incorporated his own private specimens with those of the Society. The number of seed vessels and fruits he reported as 230.

The Curator of Mineralogy reported the safe removal of specimens in his department, and their favorable arrangement for exhibition. He mentions the donation by Dr. Charles T. Jackson of a portion of his private collection which had been for a long time stored in the apartments of the Society.

The Curator of Microscopy reported the safe deposit of the collection of this department, embracing the magnificent gift of Prof. Bailey, in the room allotted to it.

The Curator of Ethnology made a full report upon the collection of this department. It embraced stone implements of the aboriginal inhabitants of New England, collected by the late Mr. Thoreau; hat, bows, models of paddles and canoes of the Chinnook or maritime tribes around Puget Sound; hat, dress, models of canoes, and other articles from Russian America; pottery from Central America or Peru; sharks' teeth swords, war implements of the Kingsmill Coral Islands; articles from the Hawaiian Islands, some of them now unknown on those islands; stone adzes from the Hervey Islands; war club from the Samoan Islands; articles from New Zealand; clubs, female dress and bark cloth from the Feejee Islands; implements from various other localities; Hindoo idol, African krisses, Egyptian relics, Roman lamp, &c.

The office of Cabinet Keeper was abolished at this time and that of Custodian created. The duties of this officer were defined as follows:

The Custodian was to be a person of acknowledged scientific attainments. He was to have general charge of the building and its contents, have free access to the collections at all times, and act in concert with the Curators, to whom he should bear the relation of advisor and assistant. In case of absence or neglect of Curators, he was to act in their stead and perform their duties. He was required to prepare and read at the annual meeting a report of the state of the museum, compiled from the special reports of the Curators. He was to keep a Donation Book and record the names of donors, and perform such other duties as might be prescribed by the Council, and mutually agreed upon.

At the election of officers which followed the reports of the Curators, S. H. Scudder was chosen Recording Secretary, Librarian and Custodian, and A. E. Verrill Curator of Radiata in place of Theodore Lyman who had engaged in the service of the United States.

It was voted by the Council at a meeting held on May 4th that the new building should be known as the "Museum of the Boston Society of Natural History."

On May 27th the Council directed that the Museum be open to the public on Wednesdays and Saturdays, and that it also be open to the members and patrons, or to such as have tickets, on Thursdays.

The Committee of Arrangements for the dedication of the Museum announced that those only would be admitted to the ceremonies who presented tickets, which had been distributed to all the members and patrons.

DEDICATION OF THE MUSEUM.

This notable event in the history of the Society took place on the afternoon of June 3d, the ceremonies being in the main hall of the Museum. At about 4 o'clock the President invited the Rev. Dr. Hill of Harvard University, to offer prayer.

After this service the President made some remarks appropriate to the occasion, expressive of gratitude felt for the liberality of the Commonwealth and the munificence of individuals, which had resulted in placing the Society in the high position it now occupied. He then introduced Prof. Wm. B. Rogers, who gave a brief history of the movements made by the Society, which had resulted in its possession of the beautiful edifice to which the audience were now welcomed. He alluded to the fact that even whilst the flames of civil war were lighting up the country, the legislature of the State made the grant of land the Society asked for, adding that for this gift it was as much indebted to Governor Andrew as to any other man.

Prof. Rogers then spoke of the progress of the Society and of the means it would now afford the student in scientific pursuits. He regarded the interest shown in the Society during these years of war as evidence of the desire of the community for truth, ending by gratefully referring to those who were struggling through conflict for peace, without which many of the blessings we enjoy would vanish like smoke.

His Honor the Mayor, F. W. Lincoln, Jr., next addressed the assembly, and in the name of the citizens of Boston bade the members God speed in all their honorable efforts.

Rev. Dr. Waterston followed, giving a very interesting address upon the importance of such an institution as that of the Boston Society of Natural History. Its objects, like those of the Public Library and the Institute of Technology, were important for the higher education of the community. All citizens might take an interest in it with great advantage to themselves, for it furnishes the means of enlarging their sphere of knowledge. He thought its success should be viewed with reverent gratitude, since all who participated in its benefits would find an increased enjoyment.

Lieutenant Lutke of the Russian Navy, aide-de-camp of the Grand Duke Constantine, who had been invited to be present, made a few remarks expressive of his high gratification in being able to participate in the ceremonies of the dedication.

After further remarks by Professor Rogers upon the taste displayed by the architect in the construction of the building, and the conscientious devotion constantly manifested by him while erecting it, the audience was invited by the President to remain and examine the collections.

The account thus given of an exceedingly interesting occasion is largely derived from the newspapers of the day, the records of the Society being meagre.

In June of this year the Society lost one of the most promising of its younger members, Carleton Atwood Shurtleff. He was particularly interested in entomology, and had recently prepared a paper upon the general plan of venation in the orders of insects, which was presented and read by Mr. S. H. Scudder at a meeting in September, accompanied by some remarks upon the scientific character and attainments of the deceased. The collection of insects and plants made by Mr. Shurtleff, and his scientific papers, were sent to the Society by the bereaved family, with the expressed wish that they should be regarded as a bequest from him who had manifested such an interest in its welfare.

The collection consisted of a considerable number of native plants, over a hundred bottles of alcoholic specimens, mostly insects, quite a large number of dried chrysalids of insects, and a cabinet of dried insects containing about six thousand specimens beautifully prepared, mostly from the vicinity, but including several hundred from China and Japan.

At a special meeting on the 12th of August, it was announced that the twenty thousand dollars offered by Dr. Walker, towards a working fund for the Society, on condition that other individuals should subscribe a like amount, was secured, as one hundred and thirty-five persons had subscribed twenty thousand, seven hundred and five dollars.

The income receivable from the amount given by Dr. Walker was subjected by him to certain conditions which are shown by the following extract from the agreement with him.

"The said aggregate sum of money (forty thousand seven hundred and five dollars), shall be invested and kept invested in some productive real estate, or if such cannot be conveniently obtained, in mortgages, bonds, stocks, or other personal property, and shall form a permanent fund, the principal of which shall not be infringed upon under any circumstances, but if through unavoidable casualties, or otherwise, any portion of said aggregate fund should be lost, the whole income of the remainder of said aggregate fund shall be retained and added to said fund until said loss is fully made up; all investments and changes of investments of said funds, are to be subject to the approval of the supervisors hereinafter named ; all deeds, certificates and evidences relating to said aggregate fund, are to be kept distinct from those of all other investments of said Society ; and the accounts of the principal thereof shall be kept separate from all other accounts of the Society.

"John A. Andrew and Samuel K. Williams of said Boston, County of Suffolk, Jeffries Wyman of Cambridge, of the County of Middlesex, Thomas T. Bouvé of the said Boston, and George A. Kettell of Charlestown, of said County of Middlesex, shall be the supervisors of the funds of the trust hereby erected; and during their lives, the approval in writing of the major part of them, or of the major part of the survivors of them, or of their successors in the trust, shall be requisite to the validity of any sale or investment of the trust property.

"From one half of the income of the said aggregate fund representing the gift of the said William J. Walker, there shall be annually offered two prizes for the best memoirs, and in the English language, on subjects proposed by a committee appointed by the Council of said Society, as follows :

"*First*, for the best memoir presented, a prize of sixty dollars may be awarded. If, however, the memoir be one of marked merit, the amount awarded may be increased to one hundred dollars, at the discretion of the committee.

"*Second*, for the next best memoir, a prize not exceeding fifty dollars may be awarded at the discretion of the committee; but neither of the above prizes shall be awarded unless the memoirs presented shall be deemed of adequate merit.

"*Third, Grand Honorary Prize.* The sum of two hundred dollars shall be set aside each year from the income of the trust fund representing the donation of the said William J. Walker, and shall with the accumulations therefrom, form a prize fund; when said prize fund amounts to the sum of two thousand dollars, the Council of the Society may award and pay therefrom the sum of five hundred dollars for such scientific investigation, or discovery in natural history, as they may think deserving thereof; provided such investigation or discovery shall have first been made known and published in the United States of America, and shall have been at the time of said award, made known and published at least one year; if in consequence of the extraordinary merit of any such investigation or discovery, the Council of the Society shall see fit, they may award therefor the sum of one thousand dollars.

"After the said prizes shall have been thus awarded, the residue of said fund shall be retained, and a certain portion of the income of the trust fund, not exceeding two hundred dollars, shall be annually appropriated by a vote of the Council of the Society, to the formation of a new prize fund of one thousand dollars, and when, and as often as said prize fund amounts to said sum, the Council of said Society may again award a prize therefrom in the manner above stated; provided, however, that the said prize shall not be awarded oftener than once in five years; and also, as said prize is to be awarded for merit solely, if no sufficiently meritorious investigation or discovery is brought to the notice of the Council, they may withhold said prize at their discretion, until an investigation or discovery of sufficient merit shall be published and made known.

"After the above appropriations have been set aside from the annual increase of said trust fund, given by the said William J. Walker, the residue of said income is to be applied as follows:

"*First*, to pay for procuring the necessary means for the preservation and exhibition of the specimens belonging to the cabinet of said Society, such as the purchase of alcohol and other antiseptics, jars, bottles, barrels, and the materials for the proper mounting, labelling and displaying of the specimens, but not to expenses in the nature of salaries or wages, or for labor, or instruction, or for cases or other furniture, nor for the purchase of specimens, but may be economically applied to the necessary repairs of the building in which the collections of the Society are preserved, and for gaslights and fuel.

"*Second*, should the whole income of the fund not be required for the above named purposes, the balance thereof may be reserved and used for such purposes in future years, or added to the principal of the fund at the discretion of the Society."

In November, the Curator of Entomology reported the collection of insects of the Society in a dangerous condition, requiring prompt and close attention which he could not give; another evidence that without parties paid to constantly look after the collections, and adequate means to provide all possible protection for the specimens, it was worse than useless to make them.

In this case a paper was circulated for subscriptions among the officers of the Society that enough money might be realized to hire an assistant.

It will be remembered that a Section of Microscopy was founded in 1857, and that for sometime afterwards it showed signs of activity, which were manifested less and less until all mention of its existence ceased to be made in the records. In December of this year, in response to an invitation from the Curator of Microscopy, sixteen gentlemen interested in the revival of the Section, met and appointed a committee of reorganization. This committee reported a series of rules for the government of the Section a fortnight later, which were adopted. Among them there was one providing that the meetings should take place on the second Wednesday of every month in the room of the department.

1865. At a meeting held on the 15th of February the Rev. Mr. Waterston addressed the meeting upon some of the educational instrumentalities which he thought within reach of the Society, ending with a motion:

"That a committee of three be appointed to consider the subject of courses of lectures to the public school teachers of this vicinity with full powers to act."

This motion was strongly seconded by Mr. John Cummings, and upon his suggestion a vote was passed that the committee be nominated by the chair.

The Rev. Mr. Waterston, Dr. Augustus A. Gould and Dr. James C. White were made this committee.

The action thus taken by the Society is well worthy especial notice for several reasons. ne is that it clearly shows to whom is due the first conception of a plan to impart instruction to the teachers of the public schools. To the Rev. Mr. Waterston unquestionably belongs that honor. Another is that it indicates the early interest felt in such teaching by the gentleman who seconded with much earnestness the original motion. Many years afterwards several courses of lectures to the teachers of the public schools were given under the auspices of the Society, the whole expenses of which were generously borne by the gentleman alluded to, Mr. John Cummings.

Still another reason why this action merits attention is the surprising fact that there is not to be found in the subsequent records of the Society, or of the Council, one word implying that anything grew out of the proposition and motion of Mr. Waterston. It is hard to believe that this can be said relative to one of the most commendable acts the Society ever engaged in, and yet it is strictly true. Fortunately for the presentation of what followed, the Report of the Superintendent of Public Schools enables the writer to do that justice to the Society which its own records fail to do.

John D. Philbrick was then the Superintendent, and his report of September, 1865, to the Board of School Committee, embraces the following paragraphs:

"During the past year, an event worthy of record, and highly gratifying to the friends of education, may be found in the fact that one of the most important and well endowed scientific institutions in this community, made arrangements for a series of lectures on different branches of natural history, which were prepared expressly for the teachers of the public schools of Boston.

"The large hall belonging to the Society of Natural History was thronged with earnest listeners. The lectures were amply illustrated by specimens and diagrams, and at the close of each lecture the rich and extensive cabinets of the Society were generously thrown open for the inspection of all present. At the introductory meeting, the teachers were addressed by His Excellency Governor Andrew, His Honor the Mayor, President Hill of Harvard University, George B. Emerson, LL.D., and other eminent friends of education.

"The lectures which followed in successive weeks were by Professor Wyman, President of the Society of Natural History, Professor Rogers, of the Institute of Technology, Dr. Augustus A. Gould, Rev. R. C. Waterston, D.D., and Professor Gray of Harvard University. They embraced branches of natural history of the deepest interest, and when it is remembered that here were assembled some six hundred teachers, having daily under their care more than twenty-seven thousand children, it may readily be believed that a fresh impulse must have been given, which could not fail to be beneficial and widely felt. Wholly aside from the valuable knowledge thus imparted and acquired, the memorable fact not to be overlooked or forgotten, is this, that one of the ablest bodies of scientific men in our community thus publicly extended the most courteous hospitalities to the teachers of the public schools, inviting them to meet, through successive weeks, at the spacious hall, arranging gratuitous lectures upon various branches of natural history, by men especially qualified to give valuable information, and to awaken interest among the teachers for whose particular advantage they were given."

At the close of the last lecture, the teachers unanimously passed resolutions expressive of their recognition of the generous action of the Society, thanking the lecturers warmly, and especially the Rev. R. C. Waterston, for the interest he had manifested in the success of the intellectual entertainments to which they had been invited.

On the 5th day of April, 1865, the President announced the death of Dr. William J. Walker, which event took place at Newport, R. I., on the 2d inst. He remarked upon the great interest Dr. Walker had shown in our welfare, and offered the following resolution, which was passed unanimously:

"*Resolved*, That the Boston Society of Natural History recognize in the death of Dr. William Johnson Walker the loss of their greatest benefactor, and in view of his munificent gifts to this Society and his beneficent aid to the cause of education and science, we would ever hold his name in honorable and grateful remembrance."

A motion was made at this meeting significant of the anxious feelings that pervaded the public mind at this important crisis in our country's experience. The rebel army under Lee had just been forced from Richmond and was being pursued by General Grant with all the forces at his disposal. Everybody was in hourly expectation of decisive news, and too much excited to calmly consider ordinary matters.

Dr. Augustus A. Gould therefore moved: "That in view of the absorbing interests of the hour in national affairs, the Society adjourn, and hold an informal meeting for the expression of sentiment."

This motion was passed, and the Society as such adjourned. An informal meeting then followed, and brief addresses were made on the subject that agitated all minds, by Drs. Wyman, Gould and Jeffries, Prof. Chadbourne, and Messrs. Ross and Bouvé.

Of the great benefactor of the Society, concerning whom action was taken by it as mentioned above, the following notice is presented:

Dr. William Johnson Walker.

Dr. William Johnson Walker was born March 15th, 1789, at Charlestown, Mass. His father, Major Timothy Walker, was a prominent citizen of the town, and came originally from Burlington, Mass., where he, as well as his wife, was born.

Dr. Walker was the second son in a large family of children. He was educated in the public schools of Charlestown, prepared for college at Phillips Academy, and graduated at Harvard in the class of 1810. He studied medicine with Dr. (afterward Governor) John Brooks at Medford, giving particular attention to the branches of physiology and anatomy. While yet a student, he won the prize of the Boylston Medical Committee at Harvard College for an essay on Hydrocephalus, in 1813.

Graduating the same year at the Massachusetts Medical College, he sailed for France and entered the Paris hospitals, where he found unusual opportunities for study and practice on account of the scarcity of French students, caused by the rigid conscriptions of Napoleon. He had the advantage of being under the instruction of many of the ablest French surgeons of the time, and subsequently was a pupil of Sir Astley Cooper in London, where he spent six months in the hospitals. Then, returning home, he entered upon the practice of his profession in Charlestown, and soon established his reputation as a very able practitioner. He was appointed physician to the Massachusetts State Prison and consulting surgeon to the Massachusetts General Hospital. He practised in Charlestown about thirty years, but finally withdrew from his profession, and moved to Boston. This course was looked upon by his numerous patients with the greatest disappointment and sorrow, as he had devoted himself to them with the utmost faithfulness and kindness, and was universally beloved by all whom he had occasion to care for professionally, more especially by those who were poor and helpless.

Although probably while he practised, he had no superior in surgery, yet he was among his contemporaries quite unpopular as a man, owing to his marked peculiarities. But with all this, he was very kind toward young physicians, and was much consulted by them. He had an extensive experience as a medical instructor, and was very successful. His well known accurate knowledge of anatomy and careful investigation into the natural history of disease, caused him to be widely looked up to, and his pupils were numerous.

Upon removing to Boston, he interested himself in financial and business matters, especially in manufactures and railroads, and from his great shrewdness in investments, rather than in speculations, rapidly amassed a large fortune, which he no sooner obtained than he set himself to expend in the most enlightened and generous manner. He gave away during his lifetime very great sums to various of the educational institutions of his native State and at his death left still larger amounts for such noble purposes. He was a most munificent friend to the Society of Natural History. The amounts of money which he gave outright and willed to the Society are elsewhere summed up in detail, and it is only necessary here to say that without his magnificent generosity, the Society would have been to-day in far different circumstances from those in which it finds itself; owing as it does in great measure to him the building in which is its home. It can never forget its great obligations to him, and will hold his memory in grateful remembrance.

Dr. Walker died in Newport, R. I., whither he had removed the latter part of his life, on the 2d of April, 1865. He had married in 1817, Eliza Hurd, daughter of Joseph Hurd of Charlestown. By her he had eight children, five of whom, with the widow, survived him.

On the 15th day of April a special meeting of the Council was held for the purpose of hearing a statement from the executors of the will of the late Dr. William J. Walker rela-

ative to the provisions of that instrument, and to take such action as might be necessary to see that the purposes of Dr. Walker were carried into effect.

The Treasurer, Mr. Bouvé, who was also one of the executors, read a statement of some of the provisions of the will, and gave some account of the property, by which it appeared that the whole amount probably exceeded $1,250,000. Of this, $10,000 was bequeathed to the Redwood Library, $26,500 in various sums to friends, and there were annuities to be paid out of the estate amounting to $1,280 during the lives of certain individuals mentioned. To his family was left $200,000, and to the Boston Society of Natural History, the Massachusetts Institute of Technology, Amherst College and Tufts College, the remainder of his estate in equal proportions.

It was also provided that if his children, to whom the $200,000 was left, die childless, then this amount also should be divided between the residuary legatees.

It was also stated by Mr. Bouvé that Mr. Wheeler, one of the executors, and a friend of the heirs, had asked in their behalf that the four residuary legatees would consent to the further payment to them of $300,000 from the estate without conditions. He gave reasons why he thought this request had better be promptly complied with, and wished action taken upon the proposition whether the Society, as one of the four residuary legatees, would consent to such payment. If this were done, and the others concurred in it, each would soon receive from $175,000 to $180,000, with a fair prospect that this would at some time be increased to $200,000, whereas if it were not done, the whole sum might be lost in litigation, or much lessened after years of strife, of which there was imminent danger.

Following this statement by Mr. Bouvé, a motion was made that he be authorized to act for the Society with full powers. Upon his suggestion, however, that it would be better to have parties selected for the purpose who were not also executors of the will, Dr. Gould and Prof. Rogers were appointed, and authorized by an unanimous vote to make such settlement on behalf of the Society with the executors and the heirs-at-law of the late Dr. William J. Walker, as they should see proper.

The annual meeting of the Society was held on May 3d. The report of the retiring Treasurer, Mr. Bouvé, who declined re-election, was in substance as follows:

That as Treasurer of the general account of the Society, he had on hand at the beginning of the year, ... $4,118.19
And that he had received since, including amount borrowed of the Courtis fund and return of amounts loaned, ... 115,432.32

$119,550.51

And that he had paid on account of new building and furniture . . $12,527.12
Journal and Proceedings, ... 129.04
General expenses, ... 3,014.38
Cabinet, ... 838.32
Library, ... 71.89
Temporary loans, ... 62,010.00
Investments of Walker fund, ... 41,105.00
Interest, ... 251.81
——————— $119,947.56
Showing a balance due him of $397.05

As Treasurer of the Courtis Fund he reported that it consisted of an amount due from
the Society itself, borrowed $8,339.71
and a mortgage note of 3,000.00

As Treasurer of the Bulfinch Street Estate he reported receipts amounting to . . $1,073.00
And expenditures of 341.39

Showing a balance on hand of $731.61

As Treasurer of the Walker fund, he reported receipts amounting to . : $1,226.97
And expenditures of 1,080.02

Showing a balance of $146.95

The balances in his hands belonging to the Bulfinch Estate and Walker fund amounted to $878.56
Balance due him on general appropriations, ... 397.05

Actual balance in his hands of all the accounts rendered, ... $481.51

He presented estimates of the value of the property belonging to the Society at different times for purposes of comparison; in May, 1862, the value was $85,001.49; in May, 1863, $133,497.80; in May, 1864, $142,512.47; at the present time, $167,881.51.

These estimates included the buildings and furniture, but not the library or the cabinet.

In retiring, the Treasurer said he would not undertake to estimate the value of our property, in the estate of our late benefactor, Dr. Wm. J. Walker. It was sufficient for him to know that in resigning the office of Treasurer, he left to his successor the pleasing task of showing on the next anniversary, means of usefulness beyond what the most sanguine expectations could have looked for.

On behalf of the Building Committee, Mr. Bouvé announced that the full cost of the new building, including commissions for architectural services, but not including the cases, had been $94,393.80, and that the cases had cost $10,003.36, making the total amount expended $104,397.16, a result with which the Society had reason to be gratified, considering that such a structure with the cases would have cost much more if the construction had been delayed, by reason of the greatly enhanced prices of material and labor. With this report presented as a final one, the committee asked the Society to accept the building and discharge them from further duty, which was done with warm thanks.

By the Custodian's report it appeared that much work had been done in the several departments towards perfecting the arrangement of the specimens and adopting means for the safety of such as were perishable. Not without great regret, however, did the members learn of the extent of the injury done to the collections by the ravages of insects, and of the absolute unfitness of the cases throughout the building for the preservation of the specimens from dust and destructive vermin. Already had it become apparent that there yet would have to be a large outlay in substituting other cases before the treasures of the cabinet could be regarded as secure. It had not been recognized when those now in use were constructed, that they should be made practically air tight in order to render them suitable for what they were designed.

The Library now contained 11,191 volumes and pamphlets. The additions through the year had been 1319, or between 11 and 12 per cent. The greater part of the increase was stated to have come from exchange with kindred institutions.

The Botanical department had had during the year an accession of about 1800 New England plants, the bequest of Mr. C. A. Shurtleff, and over 1200 German plants from Col. Joseph Howland.

The Geological and Palaeontological department had received in exchange a series of casts of large animals from Prof. Ward, a collection of fossils from the Andes presented by Dr. Winslow, and a natural cast in Red Sandstone of the bones of one of the animals that probably made impressions upon the rocks of the Connecticut river.

The most important and interesting addition to the collection during the year, was the cast of the Megatherium presented by the late Joshua Bates of London, and which had been mounted on a platform in the eastern part of the main hall. This was done by Mr. Sceva with artistic skill, under the superintendence of Dr. James C. White, and it is believed in a posture consonant with what the character and habits of the animal required. The whole collection of the department was stated to consist of about 3250 specimens.

The Mineralogical collection was reported to have undergone a thorough revision during the year. The specimens suitable for exhibition and arranged upon the shelves, numbered about fifteen hundred.

The department of Comparative Anatomy and Mammals had received an accession of eighty-four specimens in all, including seventeen skins of mammals. Skeletons of the white whale, porpoise and dromedary had been set up, and much work done by the Curator, in making sections of skulls representing the various orders of mammalia. The Curator again called attention to the unsafe condition of the skins in his department.

The Ethnological department had received from many donors, principally Commodore Charles Stewart, Dr. C. F. Winslow, Mr. E. A. Brigham, Mrs. James Phillips, and the Smithsonian Institution, articles from Japan, Siam, California, Mexico, and from localities in Massachusetts, all of which had been placed in the collection.

The Ornithological department was represented to be in good condition, but the Curator complained sadly of the unsuitableness and imperfect construction of the cases.

The Oölogical collection had been increased by donations from Dr. Henry Bryant, Dr. A. S. Packard, Jr., John R. Willis, Esq., of Halifax, and Dr. Chas. T. Jackson, in all numbering forty-five specimens.

The Conchological department had received a donation from Dr. Henry Bryant, of a collection of shells from Cape St. Lucas, and from Dr. Gundlach of a series of Cuban shells identified by him.

The Herpetological department was reported as containing about five hundred species, half of which had been identified and arranged for exhibition, the others remained unarranged for want of bottles, alcohol, &c.

The Ichthyological department had received many additions, the donors being Prof. F. Poey of Havana, the Lyceum of Natural History of Williams College, Dr. H. Bryant, the late C. A. Shurtleff, Mr. S. M. Buck, Mr. W. A. Nason, Mr. W. H. Dall, Mr. E. T. Snow, Mr. H. C. Whitten, Dr. C. F. Winslow, Dr. B. S. Shaw, Mr. David Pulsifer, and the Curator, F. W. Putnam.

The department of the Radiata had received donations from Dr. H. I. Bowditch, Dr. Samuel Kneeland, John B. Willis, Esq., Dr. A. S. Packard, Jr., and the Essex Institute of Salem. The Echinoderms had been fully catalogued and arranged, with the exception of the alcoholic specimens, which required bottles and fresh spirit before they could be put on exhibition.

To the collection of Crustacea a large number of specimens had been added during the year.

The collection of the Microscopical department remained about as before reported, but few additions having been made to it.

It was sad to learn what indeed had been partially known before, that a large part of the Entomological collection was well nigh ruined by the Anthreni, which, from want of secure cases and continuous care, had been able to attack the specimens and accomplish their destruction. The magnificent collection of Professor Hentz, purchased at considerable cost many years since through private subscription, and being then altogether the finest in country, might be said to be entirely destroyed, inasmuch as not one-fiftieth part of the whole remained fit to serve the student for purposes of comparison and identification, much less to place on exhibition. The same could be said of all the old collections presented to the Society by Dr. Gould, Dr. Harris and others.

How forcibly in this statement is brought to mind the truth often alluded to in these pages, that it is worse than useless to form large collections of perishable objects unless the means are at hand to command the accommodation and the unremitting care and watchfulness necessary for their preservation.

The late collection of Dr. Harris, purchased and presented to the Society by several gentlemen after his death, and that of the late C. A. Shurtleff, which came to the Society by bequest, were reported to be in fair condition. These were receiving proper attention, and a large number had been put upon exhibition.

The whole number of specimens of every kind added to the cabinet during the year, the Curator stated to be 21,155, of which half were insects, the bequest of Mr. C. A. Shurtleff.

The very efficient Curator of Botany, Mr. Charles J. Sprague, much to the regret of every member of the Society, resigned his office at the annual meeting, after a long service of twelve years, during which time, he had brought order out of disorder, so far as the herbarium of the department was concerned, and accomplished an amount of work in identifying, arranging and poisoning the plants, of incalculable value to the Society, and such as few persons in active business could have found time to do.

The thanks of the Society were unanimously voted to him, and also to the retiring Treasurer for their services in its behalf.

At the election of officers, Edward Pickering was chosen Treasurer, in place of Thomas T. Bouvé; Thomas T. Bouvé Curator of Mineralogy in place of William T. Brigham; and Horace Mann Curator of Botany in place of Charles J. Sprague. The office of Custodian was left vacant, Mr. Scudder declining to act longer as such. In the August following, Dr. A. S. Packard, Jr., was appointed by the Council Acting Custodian.

In October of this year, Dr. Henry Bryant announced his intention of presenting to the Society a large collection of birds recently purchased by him when in Europe, and asked that an appropriation of $4,000 be made, for the purpose of fitting up two of the rooms in the second story for their reception. This was voted, and a committee consisting of Dr.

Bryant and Dr. J. C. White, was appointed to attend to the proper construction of the cases.

The collection, which was purchased by Dr. Bryant of Count Lafresnaye de Falaise for the purpose of presentation to the Society, was the largest and most valuable private one in Europe. It contained nearly 9,000 specimens, all finely mounted, and from 4,500 to 5,000 species. Of these, 700 to 800 were from North and South America, many being type specimens described by the Count himself, an able ornithologist..

October 18th, Dr. Burt G. Wilder was elected Curator of Reptiles in place of Dr. Francis H. Brown, who had resigned at the previous meeting.

A special meeting of the Society was called to consider the subject of creating the office of Director of the Society, whose duty it should be to administer the affairs of the Museum and Library, with the intention of inviting Dr. Jeffries Wyman to take such office.

With great unanimity of feeling and action it was voted to invite Dr. Wyman to fill such office, with a salary of $2,500 per annum, clerical assistance in the administration of the Library and such scientific assistance as might be necessary. To the great regret of all the members, Dr. Wyman, after much consideration, declined to accept the position tendered him. The office designed for him was not therefore created.

In December, the Treasurer announced the reception by him of the first instalment of the Walker bequest, amounting to $100,000 in various stocks, and that it had now become the duty of the Trustees to assume the management of this property.

1866. From the report of the Acting Custodian, Dr. Packard, made at the annual meeting in May, we learn that there were twenty stated meetings of the Society, and eight of the Microscopical section. These had been well attended, and the communications presented were of an interesting and instructive character. Forty-four Resident and eleven Corresponding Members had been elected.

The Society had again resumed publication, after having omitted to issue any of its Proceedings for a year, and not having continued its Journal beyond Volume VII, printed in 1863. In resuming publication it was thought best to change the form of the Journal from octavo to quarto, and also to change the title to "Memoirs." It was also decided not to furnish the Proceedings to members free of cost, as hitherto, the state of the Treasury not warranting it. The first part of Volume I of the Memoirs, and nearly one half of Volume X of the Proceedings, including the records of the meetings held in 1864 and 1865, were mentioned as having been issued.

The Treasurer's report for the year showed that there had been an excess of expenditure over receipts, not including borrowed money, of $2,890.19. The amount expended, however, included $5,030.61, the cost of fitting up rooms with cases for the Ornithological collection.

The Librarian reported an accession of 981 volumes, parts of volumes and pamphlets, of which 767 had been received in exchange for our publications. He stated that the Library now contained 7622 volumes, 2097 parts of volumes, and 2462 pamphlets.

The Curator of Microscopy stated that the collection was in good preservation, though not in such order as it should be. Donations had been received from Dr. S. A. Bemis, Dr. C. F. Winslow, and Messrs. C. G. Bush and J. S. Melvin.

The meetings of the Section had been well attended, with advantage to its members and to the Society.

The Curator of Comparative Anatomy reported the addition to his department of 2 skeletons, 10 parts of skeletons, 20 skulls, 4 skins of mammals, 5 mammals in spirit, and miscellaneous 3; total 44 specimens. The donors were Drs. C. T. Jackson, A. A. Gould, A. S. Packard, Jr., H. Bryant, B. J. Jeffries, S. Kneeland, and Messrs. H. Mann, C. A. Kirkpatrick, J. K. Warren, and the Boston Milling and Manufacturing Company.

The specimens belonging to the department were represented to be in good order with the exception of the skins.

The Curator of Ornithology reported the collection in good order. He stated that the Lafresnaye collection, before mentioned as purchased by him for the Society, arrived safely in the autumn of the previous year, and upon being unpacked had been found in perfect condition. He himself had personally superintended the packing while in France. The whole number of specimens received had been found to be 8,656.

The Curator of Ichthyology reported valuable donations to the department from the Smithsonian Institution, of 54 specimens of North American fishes; from Dr. A. S. Packard, Jr., of 10 species comprising about 100 specimens Labrador fishes, and from the Curator of about 40 species comprising 1000 specimens from Lake Erie, and about 20 specimens from Dr. B. S. Shaw, Messrs. C. J. Sprague, W. H. Dall, J. S. Lewis, Samuel Hubbard, R. C. Greenleaf and Caleb Cooke. The latter presented a fine specimen of the rare *Leptocephalus gracilis* Storer, one of six collected by him on Nahant beach.

To the Entomological Cabinet about 600 specimens had been added, the principal donors being Drs. H. Bryant, S. A. Bemis, C. F. Hildreth, A. A. Gould, C. T. Jackson, S. Kneeland, Jr., C. F. Winslow, Messrs. A. R. Grote, Samuel Hubbard, S. H. Scudder and Prof. J. L. Smith.

To the collection of Crustacea 440 specimens had been added. Of these, 50 species, comprising about 340 specimens, represented the Crustacean fauna of Labrador, and 25 species, comprising 80 specimens, that of Maine. The Worms, now united with the Crustacea in the department, included 55 species, of which 30, comprising 115 specimens, were from the coast of Labrador; and 14, comprising 65 specimens, from Maine, had been obtained by the Curator.

The donors to the department of Crustacea and Worms, were Drs. A. S. Packard Jr., B. S. Shaw, A. A. Gould; Messrs. E. R. Mayo, Samuel Hubbard, C. Stodder, F. G. Sanborn, C. C. Sheafe; and Captain E. Smith.

The Conchological department had received about 1,500 specimens, many of them of great value, the donors being Dr. A. S. Packard, Jr., Dr. Gundlach, Dr. Henry Bryant, Dr. A. Chapin, Dr. C. T. Jackson and Mr. A. Coolidge.

The department of the Radiata had received from the Essex Institute 10 species, from Dr. A. S. Packard, Jr., 250 specimens, from N. Appleton 3 species, and from Yale College in exchange 59 specimens, comprising 34 species.

The Curator of Mineralogy reported the whole number of specimens on exhibition to be about 2,000. The department had received donations from Drs. C. T. Jackson, Henry Bryant, A. S. Packard, Jr., the Agassiz Natural History Society, Prof. Jeffries Wyman, and Messrs. G. P. Huntington and W. H. Dall.

The department of Botany had received very valuable donations of mosses and lichens from the former Curator, C. J. Sprague, Esq., comprising about 500 species. Specimens had also been presented by Drs. C. Pickering, C. F. Winslow, A. S. Packard, Jr., S. Kneeland, Jr., and Messrs. Gunning, E. R. Mayo, H. M. McIntire, William Nelson and S. Wells, Jr.

The Curator of Herpetology reported 69 additions to the department during the year, the donors being Drs. A. S. Packard, Jr., S. Kneeland, Jr., C. F. Winslow, and Messrs. S. Hinckley, F. Andernach, D. White, and Captain Barber.

The Ethnological department had received a few donations from Dr. H. Bryant, A. E. L. Dillaway and Horace McMurtrie.

To the Oölogical department there had been no additions.

In June, the sad intelligence of the death of Prof. Henry D. Rogers of Glasgow was received.

Henry Darwin Rogers was born at Philadelphia, in 1809. He early became interested in scientific pursuits, and while still quite young engaged as State Geologist of Pennsylvania in an extended and very thorough survey of that State. His great work on the geology of Pennsylvania, subsequently published, placed him at once in the front rank of American geologists, and his later Report on the Geology of New Jersey was a valuable contribution to science.

His eminent attainments led to his being invited, in 1857, to take the chair of Regius Professor of Geology and Natural History in the University of Glasgow, Scotland. He accepted this position, which he filled to the time of his death, which took place on his return from a visit to his native land, at his residence, Shawlands, near Glasgow, May 29th, 1866, in the fifty-eighth year of his age. He was a brother of Professor William B. Rogers, and for several years was a resident member of the Society; while so, manifesting much interest in its welfare. Valuable communications were frequently made by him, reports of which may be found in the Proceedings.

In September a special meeting of the Society was called upon the occasion of the death of one of its founders and most eminent members, Dr. Augustus A. Gould. This event was announced by the President, and a committee, consisting of the President, Thomas T. Bouvé and S. H. Scudder, was appointed to report a suitable address upon the occasion. A vote was unanimously passed that the Society attend the funeral, and four members were appointed to act as pall-bearers in connection with those appointed by the Suffolk District Medical Society. The four were the President, Dr. C. T. Jackson, Mr. George B. Emerson, and Mr. C. K. Dillaway. The services were at the Rowe Street Baptist Church, of which he was a member, and were attended by a large concourse of friends.

At the regular meeting on Sept. 19th, on behalf of the committee appointed at the special meeting the President read the following notice:

"Dr. Augustus Addison Gould, for many years one of the Vice-Presidents of this Society, died at his home on the morning of the 15th day of September. By this sad and sudden event, the Society loses one of its most honored and respected associates, and science a disinterested and truthful worker. From the beginning of our existence to the day on which he died, his hand was never weary in our service. Through many years we have leaned on him for his wise counsel; his thought and labor more than any other have helped us in our progress, and it is to his name and fame at home and abroad, that we are very largely indebted for what we most prize in our own. It is not we alone that suffer from his death. His interests were broad and catholic and embraced whatever was good and excellent, and his helping hand was not withdrawn whenever sought, whether in behalf of the interests of science, education or humanity. The loss to these will be truly great. For all his disinterestedness he was not without his reward. The profession of which he was so distinguished an ornament gladly bestowed upon him its highest gifts, and the community of which he was so worthy a member gave love and honor for his many graces of character and for his work in life so full of christian excellence. With head and hand still busy and with a heart still earnest in his chosen work and still warm in all his relations to friends and kindred, it was God's will that he should pass away. The Society would express its gratitude for the example of his life, and offers its deepest sympathy to those to whose hearts his death brings so much sorrow."

Dr. Wyman then stated that a more full notice of the scientific labors of Dr. Gould would be presented by the committee at a later meeting.

Dr. C. T. Jackson followed with remarks upon Dr. Gould's character and work, passing in review the various stages of his scientific career; and Mr. C. K. Dillaway read an interesting autobiography of him which had been written in 1850, and which he had in his possession as secretary of his college class.

It was then voted that a copy of the notice of the committee be furnished to the press, and that out of respect to the memory of our lamented friend and associate the Society adjourn without the transaction of business or the hearing of scientific papers.

A considerable portion of the obituary notice of Dr. Gould, prepared by Dr. Wyman in behalf of the committee and published in the Proceedings of the Society, Volume IX, page 188, is here given:

Augustus Addison Gould was born in New Ipswich, New Hampshire, on the 23d of April, 1805. His early life was passed there, and as soon as he was old and strong enough to labor, the larger part of the year was given to his father's farm, and the rest to the common school. At the age of fifteen he took the whole charge of the farm; nevertheless a part of the year was devoted to study, and some progress was made in the classics. By the careful husbanding of the odds and ends of time and a year's teaching at an academy, he was prepared to enter college, and entered at Cambridge in 1821. With his college life came a struggle, the forerunner of many such by which his strength was to be tried. He had already come to know something of the barrier which limited means had put between himself and the things he aspired to, and now this assumed larger proportions, such as to most persons would have been disheartening. College duties and exercises demanded his time, nevertheless his education must be paid for, and he must do largely towards earning the means; and so by strict economy, by performing various duties for which indigent students received compensation, and also by hard work in vacations and on those days which others gave to relaxation, he says he at length fought his way through, and attained to respectable rank.

In college he was noted among his classmates for industry, and it was there, too, that his taste for natural history began to show itself. He became familiar with the most of our native plants and to the end of life never lost his love for them. After leaving college, he

held the office of private tutor in Maryland, and at the same time began the study of medicine. The rest of his pupilage was passed in Boston, and the last year of it at the Massachusetts General Hospital as house student. He was graduated in medicine in 1830, and at once began the practice of his profession, having given good grounds to his friends for expecting future eminence. But his struggles with poverty were not yet ended. Until his profession could yield him a support, he was obliged to go out of it, to earn the necessaries of life. To this end he undertook burdensome tasks; one of them, the cataloguing and classification of the fifty thousand pamphlets in the library of the Boston Athenæum, was Herculean, as any one may see who will take the trouble to look over the four large folio volumes he wrote out, monuments of his patient industry and handiwork, and for which he got only a pitiful return.

The study of natural history was nearer to his heart than all other pursuits, and to that he could always turn, and did, whenever he could command a few spare hours or moments to do so. As a matter of course, he became a member of this Society. This was soon after its organization, and to the time he died he labored for us without stint. When his studies began to assume a methodical shape, his first investigations were in the class of insects, of which, at one time, he had a large collection. Among his first published works was a monograph on the Cicindelae of Massachusetts, printed in 1834, and in 1840 he published an account of the American species of shells belonging to the genus Pupa, in regard to which he found much confusion. These shells are very small, and Mr. Say, who named all the species previously described, gave no figures, and consequently naturalists fell into error. " I have received from our best conchologists," Dr. Gould says, " a single species under four of the names that Mr. Say applied to as many different species." Dr. Gould then points out how, by the use of the microscope, and a careful study of their minuter details, the classification of them might be improved. The paper was illustrated by about thirty figures carefully drawn by himself, with the aid of the microscope.

In 1841, he read before this Society a paper entitled " Results of an examination of the species of shells of Massachusetts, and of their geographical distribution." This is the more noteworthy since the geographical distribution of animals had at that time attracted but little attention, and none amongst us. Now it involves one of the most important zoölogical problems.

Dr. Gould also points out in this paper the influence of shore outlines, and shows from a comparison of species, that Cape Cod, which stretches out into the sea in a curved direction some forty or fifty miles, forms to some species an impassable barrier. Of two hundred and three species, eighty do not pass to the south, and thirty have not been found to the north. In the same paper he calls attention to the importance of the fact that certain species appear and disappear suddenly, and of the necessity, in order to construct a correct catalogue of the shells of any region, to extend observations through a series of years, a consideration by which many naturalists, even of the present day, might profit.

One of the first results of the joint action of the members of this Society, and of which it has more reason to be proud than any other, was the part taken by some of them in the series of admirable reports on the natural history of the State, presented to the General Court in compliance with a legislative enactment. The report on the Invertebrate Animals, excepting insects, was by Dr. Gould.

The Molluscs were Dr. Gould's favorite subject for study, and his attention was chiefly given to them. Up to this time, few if any attempts had been made to give as complete a zoölogical survey as practicable of any particular region of the United States. As regards the Molluscs, the descriptions of Say, Conrad and others, pioneers in conchology, pertained more to the Middle and Western States, than to New England. Their writings were fragmentary and scattered through the narratives of travels, journals of science, and even newspapers. It was no small labor, therefore, to become acquainted, merely as a preparation for his task, with the writings of his predecessors. To make his report as complete as possible, and to ascertain what changes in the classification of Molluscs recent important progress growing out of the study of them would indicate, he opened correspondence for information and exchanges with European naturalists interested in the same branch of study, who obligingly and courteously lent their aid, and out of this correspondence grew up long continued friendships.

The report fills a volume of nearly four hundred pages, illustrated by more than two hundred figures skillfully drawn from nature by himself. "Every species described," he says, "indeed almost every species mentioned, has passed under my own eye. The descriptions of species previously known, have been written anew, partly that they be more minute in particulars, and partly with the hope of using language somewhat less technical than is ordinarily employed by scientific men." The number of species described was about two hundred and seventy-five of Molluscs and nearly one hundred of Crustaceans and Radiates.

As a contribution to zoölogical science, this report gave him an honorable name and an eminent position among the naturalists of Europe and America.

Dr. Gould edited the admirable work entitled "The Terrestrial Air-breathing Molluscs of the United States," prepared, but left unfinished at the time of his death, by his intimate friend, Dr. Amos Binney, formerly the respected president of this Society, and whose name we hold in grateful remembrance, not only for his contributions to science, but for the munificent bequest which fills so large a space on the shelves of our library.

In 1848 he was associated with Prof. Agassiz in the preparation of the Principles of Zoölogy.

His largest and most important contribution to natural history was the description of the shells of the United States Exploring Expedition. This was prepared under circumstances somewhat embarrassing. The collection was not made by himself, but by the late Capt. Joseph P. Couthouy, well remembered as one of the most zealous and active members of this Society. Capt. Couthouy had drawn up full notes on the external characters of the soft parts, habits, geographical description, and other important points. Before the voyage was completed he left the expedition, but the notes and collections were sent to Washington. The former were unaccountably lost, and no trace of them was found. The collections, when they came into the hands of the Navy Department, were repacked by incompetent hands, the arrangement of them disturbed, labels in many cases lost, and the whole thrown more or less into confusion. Dr. Gould was called upon to save this wreck, but in accepting the task was obliged to submit to various arbitrary restrictions, and to leave undone many things he deemed of much importance.

The Otia Conchologica was the last of his printed volumes, but this was merely a reprint in a condensed form of the descriptions of species of shells previously published separately in different works. Besides the works already mentioned, there is a long catalogue of communications made to the Boston Society of Natural History, which may be referred to as showing that he did not allow himself to become a mere specialist, but kept his mind awake to the relation of individual forms to higher and more general truths.

We must not forget that Dr. Gould was a member of the medical profession, and that his time was of necessity chiefly devoted to this, while the scientific labors we have been considering were the yield of spare moments made useful. He was an active member of the medical societies of this city and of the State, and held offices of trust in them. The Massachusetts Medical Society conferred on him the honors which it has to bestow upon its fellows. In 1855 he delivered the annual address, which was marked for the soundness of its views and the characteristic clearness and elegance with which they were presented He took for his text the advice of Harvey to the Royal College of Physicians of London when he founded the annual oration which bears his name, and in which, among other things, he enjoins upon the orator "an exhortation to the members to study and search out the secrets of nature by the way· of experiment." Dr. Gould was elected president of the Medical Society, and his term of office ended within a few months of his death. He was for several years one of the physicians of the Massachusetts General Hospital, was an efficient member of the Boston Society for Medical Improvement, where he often communicated valuable observations, and took an active part in its discussions. He labored much and long in preparing the vital statistics of the State from the official returns.

At one of the meetings of the National Academy of Sciences, of which he was a member, he presented an important paper on the distribution of certain diseases, especially consumption, in reference to the hygienic choice of a location for the cure of invalid soldiers.

As a citizen, Dr. Gould made a principle of going out of the ordinary routine of life to lend a helping hand wherever it was desired, and he could. He served the public in many capacities; in the religious society of which he was from early life a member, and in the public schools, where he took an active interest in all attempts to improve the ways and means of instruction. He from time to time gave public lectures, and although in this capacity he could not be said to be brilliant or highly accomplished, yet his unostentatious manner and simplicity, his knowledge of his subject and hearty interest in it, always gained him attentive listeners, who went away instructed.

In his temperament he was genial, and drew friends around him, retaining the old and attracting the new. He came to the social gathering with joyous face and kindly feelings. His love for natural scenery was genuine and hearty, and whatever personal enjoyment came from this source, it was always enhanced if others partook of it with him. There are too many naturalists who stand in the presence of nature all their days, but see her not. To them the world offers nothing but the forms they would technically describe and arrange in their cabinets. Take away this object and all becomes a waste, for they are neither warmed nor enlivened by the world around them. Not so with our associate; no one toiled more industriously than he over individual forms and specific descriptions; but all this aside, every aspect of nature touched him to the innermost. Those who have been intimate with him know how his face would light up while in the presence of the least as well as of the greatest natural objects! the flower of a day, or the sturdy tree that had known its centuries of life, the quiet or the grander scenes of the world. His emotions were not those of an enthusiast, but rather came of a clear perception and calm contemplation of the things around him, and of his own responsive nature.

His life, all too poorly and inadequately represented in this sketch, was throughout a consistent one, and to the end each day was full to the round. He was still endeavoring to improve what had been done before, and looking forward to the accomplishment of new and better ends, when suddenly it was closed. He had been less well than usual; on the afternoon of September 14th, 1866, he manifested the usual symptoms of an attack of Asiatic cholera, soon after fell into a state of collapse, and on the following morning just before the dawn, he died.

The office of Custodian, it will be remembered, was created in May 1864, and Mr. Samuel H. Scudder was elected to fill it. He held it one year only, when it became vacant and remained so until October 3d of this year, Dr. Packard performing its duties temporarily by appointment of the Council. The great importance of having the constant services of some able person who would at the same time perform the special duties appertaining to this office and also act as Librarian and Recording Secretary, led the Committee on nominations to propose Mr. Scudder again to the Society for Custodian, and he was elected. An arrangement was then made by the Council with him, by which it was agreed that he should give his undivided attention to the wants of the Society throughout the year, excepting such time as might be allowed him for a vacation of from one to two months, and that he should perform all duties of Custodian, Librarian and Recording Secretary. The Society to provide permanent assistance in the Library department as heretofore, and also in the special manipulation of specimens which require immediate care for their preservation.

Before the death of our lamented associate, Dr. Gould, there had been some negotiation with him for the purchase of his cabinet of shells, as he had expressed a willingness to part with it to the Society at a price much less than he would be willing to accept from any other party, as he desired it should finally have a place in the Museum. The only reason why the purchase had not been consummated was that Dr. Gould first wished to put it in good order, and to properly label all the specimens. This work he did not find leisure to do, and consequently much time of an able conchologist would be required to perform it. It was deemed therefore inexpedient to compete with others who offered more than the Society could afford to pay. This was more to be regretted because of its having been the collection of one so much revered by the members, and because it contained many type specimens of species described by him. A large number of the species were, however, already in our cabinet.

In November, the Society, upon motion of Dr. J. C. White, passed resolutions expressing appreciation of the value of the gift of Mr. Peabody to Harvard University for the foundation of a Museum and Professorship of American Archaeology and Ethnology, and great pleasure in the recognition on his part of the relation of this Society to that important department of Science in the selection of its President for one of the Trustees of the munificent endowment made by him.

By the terms of this donation, the President of the Society is, *ex-officio*, one of the Trustees.

At the meeting of Nov. 2d, Mr. Thos. T. Bouvé was elected Vice-President of the Society, to fill the vacancy made by the death of Dr. Gould.

A Section of Entomology was formed at the meeting of Nov. 28th. Members of the Society only to be members of the section, the President of the Society to be ex-officio President of the section, and the Recording Secretary of the Society Recording Secretary of the section. The meetings to be held on the evening of the 4th Wednesday of each month.

1867. In January of this year, Palaentology, which had been combined with Geology, was raised to a separate department, and Thomas T. Bouvé was made its Curator. Wm. T. Brigham was chosen Curator of Geology.

Early in this year the Society was the recipient of a munificent bequest from Miss Sarah P. Pratt. This lady had long been interested in the study of conchology, and had made a large collection of shells obtained from every quarter of the globe, many of them being of rare species. The whole cabinet, consisting of more than 4000 specimens, was bequeathed to the Society, together with her library and works on conchology, and the sum of $10,000 to be held as a fund for the increase and maintenance of the department devoted to that science.

As with individuals, so with institutions, events often succeed each other of the most diverse character, those of a joyful following such as are painful, and the reverse. Not a week had elapsed after the announcement of the bequest above-mentioned, when news was received of the death of one of the great benefactors of the Society, Dr. Henry Bryant. At a meeting held on the 20th of February, after some remarks by Mr. Bouvé expressive of the feeling that pervaded and saddened all hearts, a committee consisting of Drs. S. L. Abbot and J. C. White, and J. E. Cabot, Esq., was appointed to prepare a notice of the professional and scientific life of the deceased.

In behalf of this committee, Dr. S. L. Abbot subsequently read before the Society a very full and discriminating notice of Dr. Bryant, which appeared in Vol. XI of the published Proceedings, and from which the following brief abstract is given.

Dr. Henry Bryant was born in Boston, May 12, 1820. He entered Harvard University in 1836, graduated in 1840, then studied medicine in the Tremont Medical School, from which he received the degree of Doctor of Medicine in 1843. He afterwards studied in Paris and subsequently joined the French army in Africa as a volunteer surgeon, in which capacity he served during the winter campagn of 1846. He returned home in 1847, and commenced the practice of his profession. His health failing him he was obliged to give up practice, and he ever after devoted himself to the study of Ornithology, which had always been a favorite pursuit with him. The precarious state of his health compelled him to take a great deal of outdoor exercise, and his active, energetic temperament led him often to the most distant parts of the country for the purpose of collecting specimens of Ornithology. He had a singular power of endurance, and invalid as he was, a most stoical indifference to considerations of personal comfort on these expeditions, which sometimes lasted for months, many of them being out of the country among the West India Islands.

On the outbreak of the civil war, he offered himself as a candidate for the position of assistant surgeon in the regular army, and after a very severe examination was accepted, but subsequently was appointed surgeon of the 20th regiment Massachusetts Volunteers, being promoted to be brigade surgeon, in September, 1861. He was afterwards Medical Director in the army of General Shields, in the Shenandoah Valley. While engaged in this service he was severely hurt by his horse falling upon him, and confined to his bed for a portion of the many months during which he suffered from his injuries. Yet, although it was even thought for a while that he might have to undergo amputation of his foot, he continued on duty all the time, and in the midst of his sufferings organized the military hospitals at Winchester. In August, 1862, he took charge of the Cliffburn hospital near Washington, and in December, 1862, was ordered to assume the care and operation of the Lincoln hospital, in Washington, which under his thorough and most excellent administration, was regarded as a model hospital. But close confinement and excessive mental labor broke down his health and strength, and he was eventually compelled in May, 1863, to resign his commission. His faithful service in his country's cause very nearly cost him his life, so utterly exhausted had he become by unremitting work.

After the close of the war he went to Europe twice, and in December, 1866, visited Porto Rico. For some weeks he travelled about the island, suffering extremely from ill health all the time, but working at his favorite pursuits uninterniittingly, until the 1st of February, when he was taken with what proved to be his last violent attack of illness, while on an expedition in the country, and died the next day.

Dr. Bryant was no common man. He was peculiar in certain ways, but much of this peculiarity arose undoubtedly from his ill health and bodily suffering. His thoroughness, intellectual honesty, and faithfulness to duty were marked characteristics through his whole career. He was as true as steel, through and through genuine, and with far more kindliness and wider sympathy than he ever liked to show. Dr. Bryant was elected a member of this Society in November, 1841. He served as Cabinet-keeper for a part of 1843, and took charge in 1855 of the Entomological collection for a time. From 1854 to the time of his death, he was Curator of Ornithology.

He was a most munificent friend to the Museum of the Society, his donations embracing reptiles, fishes, crustaceous insects, minerals and birds. His most valuable gift was the magnificent Lafresnaye collection of birds, which amounted to nearly nine thousand fine specimens. Extensive pecuniary aid was also received from him whenever the purchase of collections was desirable for the museum.

Dr. Bryant married in 1848, Miss Elizabeth B. Sohier, daughter of W. D. Sohier, Esq., of Boston.

In March of this year Professor Baird, of the Smithsonian Institution, expressed a strong desire that the Society should coöperate with that institution in extending the system of explorations undertaken by it, in return for which the Society should receive the first choice among the duplicates of objects of natural history. He desired a yearly appropriation of $500.

There was a unanimous wish on the part of the Council to act favorably upon the proposition which resulted in a vote: "That the sum of $500 be placed at the disposal of the Assistant Secretary of the Smithsonian Institution for the purpose mentioned, and that the Secretary intimate the desire of the Council to assist further at a future time."

April. The necessity of refraining from any account of the scientific papers brought before the Society or of the discussions that took place at the meetings, in order to confine this sketch within reasonable limits, has often prevented even a reference to much of public interest. There was one subject, however, brought before the meeting of April 17th of this year, which is here mentioned, because there is yet quite as much diversity of opinion upon it as at that time, and some readers may be interested to learn where to look for the views of two distinguished members of the Society whose investigations led them to diametrically opposite conclusions. This subject was practically what was likely to be the result of the introduction here of the common house-sparrow of Europe. Dr. Charles Pickering ably presented his ideas on the question, maintaining that nothing but evil would follow their increase; that its habits were of the most destructive character and that it had been the enemy of mankind for five thousand years. Dr. Thomas M. Brewer, on the other hand, at a subsequent meeting, defended the bird from the charges preferred against it, claimed that it had already accomplished much good in the destruction of insects, and cited the authority of many authors in proof of its great usefulness. The papers presented were meagrely reported, but may be found in the eleventh volume of the Proceedings.

The establishment of the Museum of American Archaeology and Ethnology at Cambridge through the munificence of George Peabody, Esq., gave rise to the question whether it was worth while for the Society to continue its department of Ethnology. After much consideration it was judged best to abolish it, and this was accordingly done by a vote of the Council. The collection was afterwards presented to the Peabody Museum of American Archaeology and Ethnology at Cambridge.

Some of the rooms of the Museum which had remained unfinished were at this time prepared for use by laying the floors and building cases. The lecture room was also finished.

Just before the annual meeting the Society was the recipient of a bequest from a former patron, Mr. Paschal P. Pope, of $20,000. This large sum was most gratefully received. Mr. Pope had been a successful merchant and had accumulated a large fortune, the greater portion of which he bequeathed to various public institutions. He had the reputation of being a highly honorable man, and died at an advanced age, much respected by all who knew him.

At the annual meeting, May 1st, the Custodian reported that there were now held every week meetings of the general Society, or of the sections of Entomology and Microscopy. There had been thirty-five meetings of the Society; forty-four communications on various branches of natural history had been read; forty-one Resident, seven Corresponding, and four Honorary Members elected. The first number of the Memoirs in quarto had been issued, and the first quarter of Volume XI of the Proceedings completed. The museum had been open one hundred and one days, with an average of three hundred and twelve visitors per diem.

The Library had increased in size, mainly through the efforts made to effect exchanges for our publications by the Librarian when in Europe. It will perhaps surprise readers to learn that an amount equivalent to 400,000 octavo pages of the publications of the Society had been sent away during the year..

The donations to the cabinet had been less numerous than usual. Including the bequest of Miss Pratt, there had been added 20,202 specimens. Among these and worthy of mention, was a valuable collection of volcanic specimens from the Hawaiian Islands, presented by Mr. Wm. T. Brigham.

The Treasurer's report showed receipts from all sources, of $13,281.23, and expenditures of $11,022.93.

There had been no essays offered in competition for the annual Walker prize.

The changes in the officers at the election were in Alpheus Hyatt being chosen Curator of Palaeontology in place of Thomas T. Bouvé; J. Eliot Cabot, Curator of Ornithology, in place of Dr. Henry Bryant, deceased; and Edward S. Morse, Curator of Conchology, in place of Alpheus Hyatt.

At a meeting in June of this year, the death of Thomas Bulfinch, long a member of the Society, and for six years its Recording Secretary, was announced by the Rev. R. C. Waterston, with appropriate remarks upon his life and character.

Mr. Bulfinch was deservedly held in great esteem by all the members of the Society. His faithful devotion to his duty, his genial manner, his loving and sympathetic nature, all conspired to endear him to them and to make his loss deeply felt, particularly to those with whom he was associated in the work of the Society in earlier years.

On motion of Dr. C. T. Jackson, Mr. Waterston was requested to prepare a fitting tribute to the memory of the departed for the Proceedings, which he did by an exceedingly interesting sketch of his life and character, and which may be found in Volume XI. The following is a brief abstract from this paper.

Thomas Bulfinch was born July 14th, 1796, at Newton, Mass. He was the second son of Charles Bulfinch, whose reputation as an architect at that day stood among the highest in the profession. Graduating from Harvard University in 1814, he numbered among his classmates Prescott the historian, the Rev. Dr. Greenwood and the Rev. Dr. Lamson. After leaving college, Mr. Bulfinch was chosen usher in the Latin School. Here he remained fourteen months, when feeling no very strong inclination for either of the professions, he entered upon the active duties of a business life. Two years were thus spent in Boston, when he was led to remove to Washington, where his father was engaged as architect in the erection of the Capitol. Here he resided seven years, when in 1825 he returned to Boston, entering into a copartnership with his relative, Mr. Joseph Coolidge. This connection continued until 1832, when he was chosen to a responsible position in the Merchant's Bank, which he held until his death, a period of thirty years.

Devoted as he was to the duties devolving upon him as a man of business, he had tastes aside from this, yet more congenial to his nature, which he followed with quiet but persistent enthusiasm. Thus it was that he became an active member of the Society and its Recording Secretary.

His mind balanced for a time between science and literature. There was that in both which awakened his admiration and exerted an attractive power. At length, literature gained the ascendancy, though science always continued to possess a peculiar charm.

In 1855 he published the Age of Fable, in which he relates the stories of Mythology, Greek and Roman, in a way to render them attractive to the lovers of general literature. This was followed in 1858, by a volume on the Age of Chivalry, or the Legends of King Arthur, presenting in the same spirit pictures of a later age. In 1863 he published the Legends of Charlemagne, or the Romance of the Middle Ages.

There were other works of less importance, all of which were the fruit of care, written in hours rescued from the pressure of active business.

Mr. Bulfinch devoted much time to social intercourse among a circle of friends who highly appreciated his worth. Modest he was, but not morose, for a more genial and generous nature could not be found. Keenly sensitive to the gentle sympathies of life, he truly lived in his affections, and never was he weary of extending kindness, not only to companions and friends who valued his friendship, but to the needy and tried, young or old, whoever they might be.

Much more might be said of Mr. Bulfinch, but it is not needed. His excellences were familiar to all. His quiet and respectful manner, his gentlemanly consideration, his conscientious fidelity, his love of learning, his Christian trust and faith; these were an indispensable part of himself.

Members of the Society and other visitors to the Library will recall with pleasure, not unmixed with sadness, a very agreeable young lady of great excellence who at this period and for several years was an assistant in the Library. Her beauty of person, her vivacity, her pleasing address and manners, combined with her intelligence and readiness to meet all the requirements of her position, made her a general favorite. She was the daughter of the Rev. Mr. Blaikie, a Presbyterian clergyman of the city. She left the service of the Society because of her marriage, and soon after died, to the great grief of all who had been associated with her.

It was quite apparent before the close of this year that further assistance than what had hitherto been employed was required in the Museum, if the collections were to be preserved from ruin. It was therefore voted in Council to employ Mr. F. G. Sanborn as assistant in the Museum from the 1st of January, to act under the direction of the Custodian.

Two courses of lectures were authorized by the Society for the winter of 1867-8. One given by Edward S. Morse, consisting of six on the natural history of the mollusca, or shell fish, on Saturday afternoons, commenced Dec. 7th, and continued weekly. The other by Horace Mann, consisting of eight, on structural botany, commenced March 7th. The lecturers were paid $25 for each lecture, and an admission fee of $1 for the course was charged those who attended. The cost of giving these lectures exceeded the amount received from the sale of tickets, $114.37.

1868. From the Report of the Custodian, made at the annual meeting in May, we learn how much had been done during the year towards preparing unfinished portions of the building for use. Besides the lecture room, in which for the first time the annual meeting was held, the rear library room had been furnished for use and was now occupied, two exhibition rooms fitted up, and new cases built for several of the departments. A printing office had been prepared in the basement, and the Janitor's apartments remodelled.

There had been twenty general meetings of the Society, seven of the Section of Microscopy, and nine of that of Entomology. The average attendance at the general meetings was about forty, and at each of the sections about nine.

There had been eighty-six communications made, of which fifty-six were at the general meetings of the Society, the others being at meetings of the Sections. One Honorary, two Corresponding, and forty Resident Members had been elected.

There had been issued of the publications of the Society, the second and third parts of the Memoirs, and the fourth and concluding part of the first volume was in press. The eleventh volume of the Proceedings had been completed, and a new edition of six signatures of the eighth volume printed.

Great additions to the Museum had been made during the year, the most important being a very fine series of humming birds, embracing over 700 specimens, comprising about 300 species, from Mrs. Henry Bryant; a large collection of eggs, numbering 1500 specimens, comprising more than 350 species, from the same lady; a collection of more than 2000 Guatemalan birds purchased; a large donation of several thousand rock and fossil specimens from Dr. C. T. Jackson; and a collection of skulls from Arizona, given by Dr. J. W. Merriam.

The collections of the several departments were reported generally to be in good condition, though that of Entomology had suffered some injury from the ravages of Anthreni. These pests, had however, been entirely eradicated, and it was hoped that by constant vigilance they would be prevented from doing further harm. Some remarks made by the Custodian before closing his report, are worthy of notice. He said, in referring to the growth of the Society: "The small collections received at first had a certain charm of novelty which attracted the lovers of nature, and were undoubtedly a principal means of sustaining the interest of its members; but the times have greatly changed; for while the number of members who give their personal attention to the care of the collections is scarcely greater than in former years, the collections have increased an hundred fold, and the ratio of increase does not seem to lessen. Now it is manifestly impossible for such a state of things to continue, if the Museum is to maintain an appearance creditable to the name and honor of the Society. On this account several years ago a regular Custodian was appointed; for the same reason the Council found it necessary, within a few months, to engage the services of a regular assistant, whose labors have been already felt in every department. On similar grounds, I believe that in a short time, the services of many assistants will be indispensable; indeed I am convinced that at least one or two more are needed at the present moment, and that from this time forward the greater part of the work of the Museum should be done by regular salaried assistants, under the direction of the officers."

The report of the Treasurer showed, including all sources of income available for general purposes, an excess of expenditures over receipts of $208.05.

Dr. J. C. White, notwithstanding urgent solicitation that he would continue to hold the position in which he had faithfully served the Society, positively declined reëlection. He had been Curator of the department of Mammals and Comparative Anatomy for nearly ten years, devoting a considerable portion of his time to laborious work upon the collection, not a small part of which his wise and skilful management saved from destruction. He was, moreover, very efficient in obtaining specimens for the department, thus contributing to its large increase.

At the election, all the officers were re-chosen excepting Dr. White. No one was substituted in his place.

It may be remembered by the reader that in 1837 permission had been given to members to bring with them to the meetings ladies of their families and such others as they might choose to invite, and that the temporary effect of this at least had been beneficial, leading to a better attendance on the part of the members themselves. As stated subsequently, there is no record of the permission having been withdrawn, but as ladies ceased to attend, it is fair to presume they did so from lack of interest in the proceedings. Twenty years had elapsed, and again an effort was made to have their attendance. The Council at a meeting in June of this year voted: "That members have permission to invite ladies to attend the second meeting of each month."

Previous to the summer recess the Lecture Committee of the Council, reported in favor of having three courses of lectures during the next succeeding winter, one course of four by Dr. Jeffries on the anatomy of the eye, one by Mr. W. H. Niles, of ten or twelve on the Geological History of North America, and one by Mr. Wm. T. Brigham on some botanical subject. The report was accepted and adopted.

In October Dr. Burt G. Wilder resigned his position as Curator of Herpetology, being about to remove from the State.

November 18th, Dr. Chas. F. Folsom was elected Curator of Comparative Anatomy, and J. A. Allen Curator of Herpetology.

In November the death of Mr. Octavius Pickering, long a member of the Society and one of the founders of the Linnaean, was announced with appropriate remarks by the President.

At the next meeting, the Society was called upon to deplore the loss of another member by the death of Mr. Horace Mann, the youngest officer in its service, Curator of Botany. The remarks upon the occasion by Mr. Wm. T. Brigham, his intimate friend, were very appropriate and the following particulars are abstracted from them.

In his earliest youth Mr. Mann imbibed a love of nature from the teachings of his father, and in opposition to the advice of many of his friends who wished him to have a collegiate education, entered the school of Prof. Agassiz as a student of zoölogy and geology. He was at the same time deeply interested in botany, and it was from this taste that his friendship with the speaker commenced. In company they visited the Hawaiian Islands and studied the peculiar flora of that group. Soon after his return to Cambridge, Mr. Mann was appointed assistant to Dr. Gray, and subsequently instructor in botany in Harvard College. Besides the work of arranging the Thayer Herbarium, and of aiding Dr. Gray both in preparing material for his classes, and in revising proof for his two botanical manuals, he worked steadily in spare hours, often late into the night, upon his Hawaiian collections, many thousand specimens of which were determined, labelled and distributed. His enumeration of Hawaiian plants, which has given him a good botanical reputation, was published by the American Academy of Arts and Sciences, of which body he was elected a fellow on the very evening of his death. As the result of these Hawaiian explorations, five new genera and sixty-seven new species were added to the flora.

Early in October, Mr. Mann yielded to the solicitations of his friends, and resigned his college classes; but the worst forms of pulmonary complaint had gone too far to be checked; and although at times his recovery was hoped for, he continued to fail rapidly, and passed away on the evening of November 11th.

1869. Mr. Edward S. Morse, then residing in Salem, was engaged to work on the shells of the Pratt collection, for three alternate days of each week through the year, the other three days being devoted to work on the collections of the Peabody Academy.

A new arrangement was also made with the Custodian, by which he was to give his undivided attention to the duties of the position through the year, with the exception of five weeks between the first of May and the first of November, and three weeks between the first of November and the first of May, he to have permanent assistance in the Library and Museum.

Upon application to the City Government, two police officers were detailed for duty at the Museum on public days of exhibition.

An idol obtained in purchasing other objects from Guatemala was, by vote of the Council, presented to the Peabody Museum. Authority was also obtained from the Marine Society by which the antiquities formerly given by that institution were transferred to the same Museum.

The Trustees of the Society, after calling attention to the greatly increased expenses of the year, and mentioning the necessity arising therefrom to sell stocks to the amount of $4,000 to meet indebtedness, made a protest against such large expenditures.

The Council voted that authors should be allowed twenty-five copies of their productions from the publications of the Society, free of expense.

From the Report of the Custodian at the annual meeting in May, and doings of the Society for the year ending May, 1869, may be learned as usual much of interest. There had been twenty general meetings of the Society, ten of the Section of Entomology, and six of Microscopy. At the general meetings, the average attendance of members had been thirty-three, of the Section of Entomology twelve, and of that of Microscopy eight. The number of ladies who attended in response to the invitation of the Society, of course is not included. Very few, however, availed themselves of the opportunity offered. One hundred and five scientific communications had been presented by forty-nine persons, of which the titles are given in the report. Five Corresponding and twenty-nine Resident Members had been elected during the year.

There had been three courses of lectures given during the winter and spring; the first by Dr. B. Joy Jeffries, consisted of four upon Optical Phenomena, the second by Mr. W. H. Niles, of twelve upon the Geological History of North America, and the third by Mr. Wm. T. Brigham, of twelve upon Plant Life. The first, not having been advertised and the subject being of limited interest, failed to draw many hearers, the second was attended by an average of sixty-six persons, the third by an audience averaging about ninety-nine persons. The last course was in the evening, which may in part account for the greater attendance.

The Custodian dwelt with satisfaction upon the large amount of the Society's publications, as well he might if only their extent and value were considered, and the consequent cost ignored. When, however, it is learned that what was done in this way led to an excess of expenditures over receipts to the amount of thousands of dollars, and obliged the Trustees of the property of the Society to encroach largely upon its capital to meet this excess, one is inclined to judge there was little cause for exultation. A few years of such lavish expenditure could have had but one result.

The issue from the press of the publications of the Society had been double that of any previous year, being not less than an equivalent of one thousand two hundred and twenty-nine octavo pages. The twelfth volume of Proceedings begun a year previous, had reached the four hundredth page. The annual report, the first issue of the publication called the "Annual," a physical map of North America, the fourth part of the Memoirs, and the first volume of the Occasional papers had all appeared, the latter containing the Entomological correspondence of the late Dr. T. W. Harris, embellished with steel plates and wood cuts.

It will be remembered that in 1867, an appropriation of $500 was made by the Council towards the expenses of some explorations to be made under the auspices of the Smithsonian Institution, with the understanding that the Society should receive the first choice among the duplicates of objects of Natural History collected by the explorers. Under this arrangement the Society received within the first year a series of birds from the Island of Socorro, the natural history of which had been explored by Col. Grayson. The specimens received were of peculiar interest, being nearly all new to science, and distinct from the species of the neighboring continent, or of islands nearer the coast. Only a portion of the sum appropriated having been called for, the Council again voted in 1868, that $200 should be at the disposal of the Smithsonian Institution for further explorations by Col. Grayson in Central America, and $100 towards an expedition to be made by Prof. Sumichrast in Tehuantepec, the $300 being what remained unexpended of the original appropriation.

During the past year, after leaving the Island of Socorro, Col. Grayson had been studying the natural history of the Sierra Madre, from which, however, returns had not been made of objects obtained by him. A fine collection of birds had, nevertheless, been presented to the Society, by Prof. Henry of the Smithsonian Institution, collected at Costa Rica.

From the Isthmus of Tehuantepec, for the exploration of which by Prof. Sumichrast the Society contributed $100, news had been received of a very promising character. The Smithsonian Institution had already received specimens which had been distributed for identification.

One of our own members, Mr. W. H. Dall, had been employed by the Society for several months selecting specimens from the Smithsonian duplicates, partly in return for the contributions made by the Society towards the explorations referred to, and partly as a donation from the Institution.

Already many fossils and mollusks had been received by the Society, and a collection of the nests and eggs of birds was expected to arrive.

The visitors to the Museum had exceeded thirty-six thousand. It had been open to the public one hundred and four days.

In the department of Mammals and Comparative Anatomy, a movement had been made towards obtaining specimens of all our New England mammals, and to make room for them, the Ethnological collection was to be removed. A black bear and an antelope, one the donation of Mr. W. T. Adams, the other of the City, had already been received.

The collection of birds had been increased by a donation of twenty-five specimens of the land species of Massachusetts, from Mr. L. L. Thaxter of Newton. Mrs. Bryant had again shown her interest in the Society by the gift of a large and valuable collection of unmounted birds from the West Indies and Central and North America, and from Professor Henry of the Smithsonian Institution, eighty specimens from Costa Rica had been received, all labelled by Mr. Lawrence.

The collection of Nests and Eggs of birds had been entirely rearranged. A statement was made showing the collection at this time to consist of the eggs of seven hundred birds, of which four hundred were American. A large number of duplicates, valuable for exchange, had been presented by Mrs. Bryant, and about two hundred and fifty nests and eggs by the Smithsonian Institution.

The Curators of the departments of Reptiles and Fishes mentioned great deficiencies in the representation of Massachusetts species, and in the latter the need of help in order to identify and label the specimens.

The Entomological collection was stated to be in better condition than it had been a year previous, much attention having been given to its improvement and preservation.

In referring to the condition of the department of Mollusks, the Custodian made some remarks of more than temporary value. With the exception, he stated, of work done by the last Curator, there is no evidence of any attention having been bestowed upon the specimens for fifteen years. It was now in a worse condition than it had been years before, showing that gratuitous aid had proved a failure. The Curator's entire attention had been given to the Pratt collection, the arrangement of which would be completed before other work was done in the department.

Of the other collections nothing was said of sufficient importance to repeat here.

The report of the Treasurer was startling. It showed an excess of expenditures over receipts of more than $6,000, and a diminution in the value of the Society's property of over $13,000. Much of this latter was accounted for by the reduction in the estimated value of the stocks which had been received under the Walker bequest, but it was only too evident that there had not been a due economy exercised in the administration of the business of the Society. Well might the Trustees protest as they did, and well it was, too, that the Council heeded their warning. The lesson taught was not lost upon the members, and finally led to measures tending to prevent, under any ordinary circumstances, more expense of means than income warranted. Among these was that of requiring from the Trustees at the commencement of each year an estimate of the probable receipts from the various sources tabulated, and also one showing what expenditures might be incurred in the different departments based upon such receipts; there being a clear understanding that under no avoidable circumstances should there be expended more than the income. This met the hearty approval of all, and the policy adopted has been faithfully adhered to ever since. It was not, however, intended that the expenditure yet necessary in finishing the rooms of the Museum and in supplying cases should be paid for from the ordinary income. Whatever was done in this way it was expected would necessarily be paid for in part, at least, from the principal of the Society's property. At the meetings of the Council following the general meeting, there was much discussion concerning retrenchment, a strong disposition being manifested to reduce expenses within the probable income.

At a regular meeting in June the Rev. Robert C. Waterston reminded the members of the approaching centennial anniversary of the birthday of Humboldt, and suggested the public celebration of it by the Society. He remarked that it was wholly unnecessary in such a presence to speak of Alexander Von Humboldt in order to impart information concerning one whose illustrious reputation in so many departments of knowledge had made his name familiar over the civilized world. Yet in view of what he had done for science by his explorations on this continent, it seemed particularly appropriate that a Society like this should do honor to his memory. He further remarked that there was one among the members, preëminent in science, who had been his pupil and his personal friend, Louis Agassiz, who was specially qualified to speak upon such an occasion. That to hear him menof science and letters from every part of the country would gladly assemble to listen and to respond.

Although the matter had not been apparently thought of by any of the members, all present heartily concurred in the sentiments expressed by Mr. Waterston, recognizing that in the Society thus paying a tribute of respectful homage to one of the noblest of men, it could not but do itself great honor. The proposal therefore met with a hearty response, and the following resolution, offered by Mr. Waterston, was unanimously adopted:

"*Resolved*, That it is highly desirable that the Boston Society of Natural History should hold a public celebration of the centennial anniversary of the birth of Alexander Von Humboldt, and that a committee of five be appointed to consider the whole subject and empowered to make all arrangements." The President appointed on this committee the Rev. Robert C. Waterston, Dr. Samuel Kneeland and Mr. Samuel H. Scudder. To these were subsequently added the President, Jeffries Wyman, His Honor the Mayor, N. B. Shurtleff, and Col. T. W. Higginson.

It is due to Mr. Waterston to state that a large part of the work attendant upon the celebration was done by him. That it might be a thorough success and redound to the credit of the Society and the community, he gave up his whole time to it, remaining in the city during the hot summer months, and exerting himself to the utmost that nothing might be left undone that would add to the interest of the occasion. He not only arranged for the meeting at which the address was to be delivered, but for a reception in the evening, at which distinguished men should be invited to speak, and he induced the City Government to take part in it and to provide an entertainment at the expense of the City.

The celebration which followed on the 14th of September was in every respect a success, far exceeding the anticipations of all who had favored it. Probably nowhere throughout the civilized world was the day more appropriately observed. The address by Agassiz was worthy of the man and the occasion. It was delivered at the Music Hall before an audience which filled every available place in it. Delegates from the leading literary and scientific societies of New England and representatives from the colleges of Yale, Bowdoin, Brown, Dartmouth and Harvard were present, as were likewise His Excellency the Governor of the Commonwealth, His Honor the Mayor of the City and members of both branches of the City Government. President Wyman presided at the meeting.

The evening reception was at Horticultural Hall. A large and distinguished audience attended it, including invited guests from literary and scientific societies, members of the City Government, and many gentlemen interested in the cause of education from every part of the country. Interesting mementos of Humboldt, including several portraits of him, were placed upon the platform and about the hall. The Rev. Mr. Waterston presided, and after welcoming the delegates from the different societies present and making some appropriate remarks, introduced successively the Rev. Frederick H. Hedge, Mr. Ralph Waldo Emerson and Prof. E. J. Young, all of whom made interesting addresses. Among the portraits exhibited, was one by Mr. Wight, painted at Berlin in 1852 from life, when Humboldt was eighty-three years of age. It had been loaned to the committee for the occasion by the artist. The chairman, calling attention to it, stated that an order had been given to the artist to execute an exact copy. This would be unveiled, and if it was found in every respect satisfactory, he, the chairman, would take great pleasure in presenting it on this centennial anniversary to the Boston Society of Natural History. The covering was removed and the resemblance was found to be so perfect as to call forth spontaneous applause. A letter from the artist was read giving an account of his personal observation of Humboldt when he was engaged upon his portrait. Accompanying it was an autograph note of Humboldt, which was also presented to the Boston Society of Natural History by the chairman. In behalf of the Society, Dr. Charles T. Jackson, Vice-President, accepted the portrait and autograph with expression of thanks. He stated that Humboldt himself had declared that the original by Wight was the best ever painted of him.

Dr. Jackson then gave some pleasant reminiscences of Humboldt, whom he had often met in Paris at Cuvier's lectures in 1833. He also made some interesting remarks upon his works and character.

The chairman then called upon his Honor the Mayor, who, in responding briefly, said that the City Government, being desirous of expressing its respect for the memory of Alexander Von Humboldt, had passed resolutions and had made a generous appropriation. In behalf of both branches, he invited all present to partake of a collation prepared for them in the hall below. The company accepted the invitation and proceeded to the place assigned, where they enjoyed an excellent supper, during which at intervals the Germania band added their enlivening music to the entertainment.

After refreshment at the tables, a poem upon Humboldt, prepared for the occasion by Oliver Wendell Holmes, and another by Mrs. Julia Ward Howe, were read. During the evening, several communications from distinguished persons unable to be present, were presented, one from the Hon. Theo. S. Fay, one from Prof. William B. Rogers, one from the Rev. Noah Porter and one from John G. Whittier. The address by Agassiz, with a full account of the proceedings at the evening meeting, may be found in pamphlet form published by the Society.

In October, Dr. C. F. Folsom resigned his position as Curator of Comparative Anatomy and Mammals.

At a meeting of the Council, held Nov. 17th, it was voted that the net proceeds of the celebration of the Centennial Anniversary of the birth of Humboldt, together with the money received from the sale of Prof. Agassiz's address previous to Jan. 1, 1870, and the money subscribed at the solicitation of the Society's Committee, be given to the Trustees of the Museum of Comparative Zoölogy at Harvard College, in trust, for the establishment of an endowment under the title of the "Humboldt Scholarship," the income of which should be solely applied, under the direction of the Faculty, toward the maintenance of one or more young and needy persons engaged in study at said Museum. The reception of the money, amounting to $7,040.66, was gratefully acknowledged by the Trustees of the Museum of Comparative Zoölogy, under the conditions expressed in the vote of the Council.

Mention was made in giving an account of the proceedings at the evening reception on the day of the Humboldt celebration, of a fine portrait presented by the Rev. Mr. Waterston to the Society. This may now be seen in the Library of the Museum.

The hearty thanks of the Society were passed to Mr. Waterston not only for the valuable portrait and autograph, but for the unflagging energy with which he had labored for the success of the Humboldt celebration. Testimony was borne to the untiring zeal manifested by him in obtaining subscriptions for the fund, and in performing a large part of the work consequent upon the celebration. The Society also expressed its obligations to Prof. Agassiz for his able address, a copy of which was asked for publication. Thanks were also voted to the Orpheus Musical Association, and to Mr. Carl Zerrahn, for their welcome aid in the performances of the occasion; also to Mr. J. H. Paine, who presided at the organ.

1870. On January 19th, Dr. Thomas Waterman was elected Curator of Comparative Anatomy and Mammals.

At the meeting of April 20th, in view of contemplated changes in the administration of the Society, certain alterations were made in the Constitution and By-laws to go into effect on and after the annual meeting. The most important of these arose from the substitution of Committees for Curators in the care of the Museum.

The Constitution was made to express that the officers of the Society shall consist of a President, two Vice-Presidents, a Corresponding Secretary, a Recording Secretary, a Librarian, a Custodian and a Committee of three on each department of the Museum, etc., etc.

The By-laws were so altered as to define that the Committees should be entrusted with the care of the Museum; that they should be designated for particular departments at the time of their election, and consist of not more than three members, one of whom should be named by the nominating committee to act as chairman. The duties mentioned were such as the By-laws previously active expressed for those of the Curators.

Annual meeting. The Custodian's report gave the following summary of the doings of the Society during the year:

There had been eighteen general meetings, the average attendance at which had been thirty-two: eight of the section of Entomology, with an average attendance of eleven: and seven of the section of Microscopy, with an average attendance of nine. Forty-seven scientific communications had been made by twenty-five persons, all of which had been printed in full or by title in the Proceedings.

One Honorary, three Corresponding and thirty-nine Resident Members had been elected.

Three courses of evening lectures had been arranged for by the Council. One of twelve, entitled Sketches of Animal Life, by Mr. Edward S. Morse, delivered in the early part of the season, had an average audience of seventy-six persons; the second, consisting also of twelve, given by Mr. William T. Brigham, entitled The Earth we live on, had an audience averaging ninety-eight persons; the third, not concluded at the time of the annual meeting, consisted of four, entitled Familiar Talks about Insects, given by Mr. F. G. Sanborn. The average attendance at these was about sixty.

Of the Publications it was stated that from economical considerations the issue of a large number of the Memoirs had been postponed. Of the Proceedings the twelfth volume had been printed, and a part of the thirteenth. The address of Prof. Agassiz at the recent celebration of the Humboldt Centenary, with an account of the evening's festivities, forming an octavo pamphlet of one hundred and seven pages, had been also published and distributed.

The Custodian expressed strongly the feeling that a further postponement of activity in this direction could not fail to be disastrous. Yet there had been sent abroad of parts of Memoirs and of the Journal, of copies of Harris' Correspondence, of the Proceedings, what was equivalent to about two hundred and sixty-five volumes of the Proceedings, and over 200,000 octavo pages. Besides all this the Society had distributed in behalf of the Commonwealth, three hundred copies on the Report of the Invertebrates of Massachusetts, recently published by the State.

The judicious action of the Legislature, the Custodian remarked, in placing its scientific publications where they will be of the greatest permanent benefit, merits the commendation of all who, like ourselves, are aiming at the widest diffusion of knowledge.

An enumeration of the books in the Library had been recently made. They were counted as bound, whether containing more than one volume, as frequently the case, or not; and the parts had been estimated at their proper proportions of the volumes to which they belong, and the pamphlets counted separately. The enumeration therefore gave the number as proportionably smaller than previous estimates. There were found to be 9396 volumes, and 2677 pamphlets. Of these volumes ten hundred and ten were of a general literary character, mostly deposited by "A Republican Institution"; eight hundred and six were botanical; four hundred and fifty-three entomological; four hundred and two geological and mineralogical; five hundred and ten encyclopaedic; six hundred and thirteen upon vertebrates; five hundred and thirty-six upon travels and local fauna, and forty-one hundred and seventy-three journals and publications of Societies.

The Custodian announced the death of our esteemed coadjutor, Col. A. J. Grayson, to whose explorations it will be recollected the Society contributed in connection with the Smithsonian Institution. It had been the strong wish of both parties interested, that he should visit the Sierra Madre of North Western Mexico, that he might make there a careful investigation of its fauna. He arranged to be there in June, that being considered the most favorable month for his purposes. Prior to that period he visited the Island of Isabella off the coast to study the habits of sea fowl during their breeding season, and there he contracted a malarious disease that led to his death in August.

The amount contributed by the Society being unexpended, was returned by his wife to the Smithsonian Institution. By advice of Prof. Henry, this was transferred by vote of the Council to Prof. Sumichrast, to be used in the explorations undertaken by him on the Isthmus of Tehuantepec.

An arrangement had been made by the Custodian with the Secretary of the Smithsonian Institution, by which a large number of unassorted specimens of various character were sent to the Society with the understanding that they should be returned in orderly condition, compensation for the labor being made by a selection from the duplicates for the Cabinet.

The number of visitors to the Museum during the year exceeded forty thousand. It was open to the public one hundred and four days. The largest number present on any one day was seven hundred and eighty-one.

The Custodian reported the collections of the different departments of the Society to be in good condition. That of Mammals and Comparative Anatomy had received a stuffed specimen of the great Antarctic seal collected in the exploring expedition of Commodore Wilkes. A living opossum and its young had also been received from Dr. C. Kollock of South Carolina, and had been mounted in characteristic attitudes. Other interesting specimens had been received from the Union Street menagerie.

In the Ornithological department, the mounted birds had had special attention, every specimen having been taken down, thoroughly examined, and where necessary treated with benzine and other materials. The cases had all been made as nearly air tight as possible and in fact every possible measure adopted to prevent the further ravages of insects. To accomplish this, four or five persons had worked continuously for two months. Donations had been received from the Smithsonian Institution, F. E. Everett, S. Mixter, H. A. Purdie and others.

Quite extensive additions had been made to the collection of nests and eggs, mostly in exchange. To Mr. B. P. Mann and Mr. S. Mixter, the department had been indebted for the presentation of many specimens.

The Entomological collections were reported in better condition than at any time within ten years. Mrs. Stratton, Mr. H. Edwards and others, had presented many specimens, and there had been a valuable accession from Tehuantepec collected by Professor Sumichrast.

There had been considerable work done upon the Reptiles, and one hundred and fifteen specimens had been added to the collection. A marked deficiency of native species was mentioned, particularly of turtles.

The Fishes, numbering three thousand eight hundred and ninety-six specimens, were reported in good order and mostly identified.

Some work had been done by Mr. S. I. Smith upon the Crustacea, and the whole collection placed in satisfactory condition.

The Curator of Mollusks reported much progress in mounting the gasteropods of the Pratt collection, and mentioned that a valuable series of British shells had been received from the Smithsonian Institution, and many specimens from Mr. H. Edwards and others.

The collection of Radiates had been greatly improved, and a large portion of the corals and sponges mounted in an erect position upon black tablets.

The Botanical department had received an important addition in the herbarium of Hon. John Amory Lowell, containing many thousand species carefully labelled, mounted and catalogued.

By the subscription of some gentlemen, a ring of the bark of a Redwood tree of California had been purchased, measuring forty feet in circumference. This had been mounted under the direction of Mr. Brigham, the acting Curator, and now forms a conspicuous object in the entrance hall of the Museum.

The arduous task of rearranging and labelling the entire Mineralogical collection had been completed by the Curator, and the whole was now in perfect order. The number of specimens was about 2800.

Mr. S. H. Scudder, the Custodian, in presenting the annual report, took occasion, as this was to be the final one by him, to review somewhat at length the experience of the Society in the past, and to suggest considerations in relation to its future policy. He said that " while some collections need a good deal of revision and many are not yet entirely supplied with the uniform system of labelling lately adopted, the Museum is in much better order and in a much safer condition than it has been at any time since our removal to this building. The Library has increased, and the lectures have proved a success, but in our publications and in the interest of our meetings, we have sadly fallen off."

The Custodian further remarked upon the great importance of the publications of the Society as a means through which the researches of the members might be promptly made known, and the fame which it has fairly won at home and abroad be sustained.

In relation to the Museum, after mentioning its large collections, he expressed the view that, with some exceptions, they embraced sufficient for all the purposes of the Society. That its principal aim should not be to sustain a great museum or an industrial one, but rather seek to maintain first, a popular educational one, in which all and none but the characteristic forms of life and inorganic nature should be displayed, and second, a complete local collection, restricted at widest to our New England flora and fauna. To effect this, it was important that more skilled labor should be regularly employed, and a man of broad scientific culture placed at the head of the Museum, with its interests alone in charge.

The Custodian then spoke of his endeavors to faithfully perform the duties of his office, and expressed warmly his appreciation of the devotedness of those who had been engaged to assist him in the various departments of the Society's operations.

Upon motion of Mr. F. W. Putnam, who thought something more was due the retiring Custodian than a simple vote of thanks for his services, it was unanimously voted that the rules be suspended and Mr. Scudder be made a Life Member of the Society.

The Treasurer's report showed, including all sources of income available for general purposes, a balance of receipts over expenditures, of $160.49.

The Prize Committee reported through Dr. J. B. S. Jackson, that only one essay had been offered in competition for this year's prize, and this was not deemed worthy of it. They announced for the subject of the prize for 1872, "The Darwinian question; its bearings on the development of animal life."

Letters from the President, Dr. Jeffries Wyman, at this time in Europe, positively declining to be a candidate for the office so long held by him, had been received. The Nominating Committee however, thinking that he might be induced again to accept the position, asked further time for consideration before any action was taken in electing a President. They also asked further time before presenting names for the Committees on the departments of Mammals and Comparative Anatomy, as the Council had, but a few hours before the meeting, divided the department of Comparative Anatomy, which before embraced Mammals, into two departments. They likewise asked further time before nominating the Committee for the department of Microscopy.

The list of officers proposed by them was then presented, the Rev. Joshua A. Swan being named as the successor to Mr. S. H. Scudder, for the positions of Custodian, Librarian and Recording Secretary. A strong objection was made to the nominee for the former office, many present favoring the election of Mr. Alpheus Hyatt. A prolonged and very earnest discussion followed, the whole policy of the Society and the comparative merits of the two persons mentioned for the position being ably presented. Those who participated in the discussion were N. S. Shaler, J. B. S. Jackson, J. C. White, E. S. Morse, R. C.

Greenleaf, F. W. Putnam, W. H. Niles, T. M. Brewer, W. T. Brigham, J. D. Runkle and Thomas T. Bouvé. Upon balloting, it was found that Mr. Alpheus Hyatt was elected Custodian and Mr. Swan, Librarian and Recording Secretary, the majority of the members thus electing two officers to fill the three positions, instead of one as hitherto. One objection to this was the largely increased expense thereby incurred, but the result was generally satisfactory.

The Committees chosen for the several departments were as follows:

On Birds.
Thomas M. Brewer, M. D.,
Samuel Cabot, M. D.,
J. A. Allen.

On Fishes and Reptiles.
D. Humphreys Storer, M. D.,
F. W. Putnam,
N. E. Atwood.

On Insects.
F. G. Sanborn,
A. S. Packard, Jr., M. D.,
Edward Burgess.

On Crustacea and Radiates.
A. S. Packard, Jr., M. D.,
A. E. Verrill,
Alexander Agassiz.

On Mollusks.
Edward S. Morse,
John Cummings,
Levi L. Thaxter.

On Palaeontology.
W. H. Niles,
N. S. Shaler,
Thomas T. Bouvé.

On Botany.
William T. Brigham,
Charles J. Sprague,
J. Amory Lowell.

On Minerals and Geology.
Thomas T. Bouvé,
Charles T. Jackson, M. D.,
William T. Brigham.

The election of Committees for the departments of Comparative Anatomy, Mammals and Microscopy was postponed to allow time for further consideration.

The fourth decade of the existence of the Society was now completed. It had been a period of great events in its history. Its commencement found the country involved in a war which, by rapidly wasting its resources, threatened alike its material prosperity and its progress in art, science and literature. There was sadness in the hearts of men and an undefined dread of evil pervading their minds, tending to concentrate all thought upon the movements of armies and the tidings of conflict. Thank God, too, there was an unfaltering faith in the final success of the struggle for the nation's integrity, which kept alive hope and encouraged exertion for the advancement of all movements promising future good to the community. Thus was it that in the midst of a dreadful civil war the Society was enabled, through the untiring devotion of its own members and by the exertions, the contributions and bequests of many friends, to erect the fine structure that now adorns the city, and to place therein the great collections of natural history that now minister to the delight and the instruction of multitudes.

In referring to the period of the civil war, it may not be amiss to state that besides the members of the Society mentioned as having resigned their official positions in it to enter the service of their country, there were several others who took an active part in the conflict. Among them was one whose great interest in the welfare of our institution for many years as shown by his exertions in its behalf when in distant regions, entitles him to respectful notice in these pages. That he died by the hands of the enemy makes it all the more a duty to render a tribute to his memory.

Joseph P. Couthouy was born in Boston, January 6, 1808. He was educated at one of the schools in the town, and when yet a lad, made a voyage in his father's ship. His tastes leading him to prefer a sea life, he applied himself to the calling he had chosen, and became, when old enough, the captain of a vessel.

He early developed a love for science, and had progressed in his studies to such an extent that when the American Exploring Expedition was organized under command of Lieutenant Wilkes, he was appointed one of the scientific corps to accompany it, his specialty being that of Conchology. The expedition sailed from Hampton Roads, Aug. 18th, 1838, and, although the state of his health obliged him eventually to abandon his share of the enterprise at the Samoan Islands, yet he had already made very valuable collections of shells and illustrated his numerous notes and descriptions concerning the many species obtained, with drawings and colorings which would have been of invaluable assistance to Dr. A. A. Gould, who subsequently published the elaborate report on the shells secured by the expedition, had not these papers been in some unexplained way lost or destroyed when the cases containing the specimens were unpacked after arrival.

Captain Couthouy afterwards went to South America and the islands of the Pacific Ocean, making numberless valuable observations on the natural history of the countries which he visited.

In the year 1854, he was engaged to take command of an expedition to the Bay of Cumana, for the purpose of exploring for the wreck of the Spanish man-of-war San Pedro, lost there nearly half a century previously, which was supposed to have had a great amount of treasure on board. After three years spent in an unsuccessful search for this, the vessel returned to the United States, and was lost in a violent snow storm on Cape Cod, the crew being saved with the greatest difficulty.

When the war of the rebellion broke out, Captain Couthouy offered his services to the government. They were at once accepted, and he was placed in command of the U. S. barque "Kingfisher," in which he was actively engaged against the enemy. Being transferred to the command of the U. S. steamer "Columbia," he joined the blockading squadron of the South Atlantic, and upon his vessel being wrecked in a storm at Masonboro Inlet, he was captured and sent as a prisoner of war to Salisbury, where he remained three months. After being exchanged he was placed in command of the monitor "Osage" of the Mississippi river squadron under Admiral Porter, and subsequently, being transferred to the "Chillicothe" of the same squadron, was ordered up the Red River. In this expedition he met his death. On the 3d of April his ship was engaged with a large body of rebel troops on the shore. Captain Couthouy was on deck directing the fire of his guns, when a rebel sharp-shooter on the bank fired at and mortally wounded him. He died the next day, universally regretted by officers and men, and by no one more than the Admiral, who, in a letter to the Secretary of the Navy, bore witness to his zealous, patriotic and estimable character.

Captain Couthouy was a man of rare and varied ability. He was a fine linguist, and spoke with great elegance the Spanish, French, Italian and Portuguese languages. An interesting example of the beauty of his pronunciation of the Spanish was given the writer by one of his intimate friends. Being in Spain at the time of the Carlist wars, he was repeatedly under suspicion on the part of the officers of the government, who could not believe him to be a foreigner, the purity of his accent and thorough knowledge of the language leading them to think that he must necessarily be a native Spaniard. He had also in the course of his travels mastered more than one of the unwritten languages of the South Pacific Islands.

He was described by intimate friends and associates as being a man of the utmost fascination of manner, and one whose wide and varied information made him one of the most interesting of companions.

Elected a member of the Society on the 6th of April, 1836, he was often before it while at home, at the meetings, with communications or remarks relating to facts of scientific interest which had come to his knowledge during his wide-spread investigations abroad. He also, from time to time, presented many specimens to the Society.

His memory should be held in tender regard by the Society, for while, in former years, an active and valued associate, his death in battle in the service of his country added another to the list of those who have passed away, leaving, through faithful work in the cause of science, a lasting lustre on its roll of membership.

Captain Couthouy married Miss Mary G. Wild of Boston. His wife died in 1857, and at the time of his death, in 1864, he had three daughters living. His only son had died previously.

It having been necessary in quite a number of instances during the first half of this decade to record the fact of several of the officers having resigned or temporarily vacated their positions in order to engage in the military or naval service during the war for the suppression of the rebellion, it is fitting that the part which was taken in the great conflict by members of the Society should be recognized; and the following roll gives the names and branch of the service to which they belonged, of such as are, or have been, borne upon its list of membership.

Dr. Samuel Kneeland, Surgeon 45th Mass. Infantry, Brevet Lieut. Colonel.
Dr. Henry Bryant, Surgeon 20th Mass. Infantry, Brigade Surgeon U. S. Vols.
Dr. Samuel A. Green, Asst. Surgeon 1st Mass. Infantry, Surgeon 24th Mass. Infantry.
Dr. Burt G. Wilder, Asst. Surgeon 55th Mass. Infantry.
Dr. B. Joy Jeffries, Sergeant 1st Corps Cadets M.V.M., Acting Assistant Surgeon U.S.A.
Dr. Francis H. Brown, Acting Assistant Surgeon U. S. Army, Private 12th unattached company Mass. Infantry.
Theodore Lyman, Colonel U. S. Vols., aide-de-camp to Major General Meade.
Albert Ordway, Lieut. Colonel 24th Mass. Infantry. Brevet Brigadier General.
Amos Binney, Major and Paymaster U. S. Vols.
Dr. John Stearns, Surgeon 4th Mass. Heavy Artillery.
Dr. Lucius M. Sargent, Jr., Surgeon 2d Mass. Infantry, afterwards Major 1st Mass. Cavalry. Killed in battle.
Dr. Hall Curtis, Asst. Surgeon 24th Mass. Infantry, Surgeon 2d Mass. Heavy Artillery.
Dr. Robert T. Edes, Passed Assistant Surgeon U. S. Navy.
Dr. Z. Boylston Adams, Asst. Surgeon 7th Mass. Infantry, Surgeon 32d Mass. Infantry, afterwards Major 56th Mass. Infantry.
Dr. A. S. Packard, Jr., Asst. Surgeon 1st Maine Veteran Volunteer Infantry.

Dr. Calvin G. Page, Surgeon 39th Mass. Infantry.
Dr. Franklin Nickerson, Acting Assistant Surgeon U. S. Navy.
Dr. F. P. Sprague, Acting Assistant Surgeon U. S. Army.
Dr. Algernon Coolidge, Acting Assistant Surgeon U. S. Army.
Dr. Edward Wigglesworth, Jr., Hospital Steward 45th Mass. Infantry, Volunteer Surgeon.
Dr. J. Collins Warren, Volunteer Surgeon U. S. Army.
Dr. Francis C. Ropes, Assistant Surgeon U. S. Army.
Dr. H. M. Saville, Surgeon 4th Mass. Infantry.
Dr. George Derby, Surgeon 23d Mass. Infantry, Brevet Lieut. Colonel.
Dr. H. P. Bowditch, Major 54th Mass. Infantry, Captain 1st Mass. Cavalry, Major 5th Mass. Cavalry.
Dr. John McLean Hayward, Surgeon 12th Mass. Infantry.
Dr. C. F. Crehore, Asst. Surgeon 15th Mass. Infantry, Surgeon 37th Mass. Infantry, Medical Inspector on staff of Major General Sedgwick.
Dr. Oliver F. Wadsworth, Asst. Surgeon 5th Mass. Cavalry, Brevet Captain U. S. Vols.
Dr. Allston G. Bouvé, Private 6th Mass. Infantry.
Dr. John Homans, Assistant Surgeon U. S. Navy, Asst. Surgeon U. S. Army.
Dr. William Ingalls, Surgeon 5th and 59th regiments Mass. Infantry.
Dr. William Henry Thayer, Surgeon 14th New Hampshire Infantry.
Dr. John C. Dalton, Asst. Surgeon 7th New York V. M., Surgeon U. S. Vols.
Dr. S. W. Langmaid, Acting Asst. Surgeon U. S. Army.
Dr. Charles W. Swan, Acting Asst. Surgeon U. S. Army.
Dr. Samuel G. Webber, Asst. Surgeon U. S. Navy.
Dr. Charles B. Porter, Acting Asst. Surgeon U. S. Army.
Dr. Frederick S. Ainsworth, Surgeon 22d Mass. Infantry.
Dr. Thomas B. Hitchcock, Asst. Surgeon 42d Mass. Infantry.
Dr. George J. Arnold, Acting Asst. Surgeon U. S. Army.
Dr. Charles E. Hosmer, Private, Steward U. S. Navy, Acting Asst. Surgeon U. S. Navy.
Dr. John G. Park, Acting Asst. Surgeon U. S. Navy.
Dr. Charles Thacher Hubbard, Asst. Surgeon U. S. Navy.
Dr. James E. Walker, Acting Asst. Surgeon U. S. Army.
Dr. Henry G. Clark, Inspector-in-chief of the Sanitary Commission.
Dr. J. Nelson Borland, Inspector of Hospitals for the Sanitary Commission.
Dr. Samuel L. Abbot, " "
Dr. Henry I. Bowditch, " " Surgeon to the Board of Enrolment in Boston during the war, and Volunteer Surgeon in the Army.
Dr. Samuel Cabot, Jr., Inspector of Hospitals for the Sanitary Commission and Volunteer Surgeon.
Dr. William Edward Coale, " "
Dr. Calvin Ellis, " " and Volunteer Surgeon.
Dr. Augustus A. Gould, " "
Dr. J. B. S. Jackson, " "
Dr. Francis Minot, " "
Dr. Benjamin S. Shaw, " "
Dr. Charles E. Ware, " "
Dr. Henry W. Williams, " "
Dr. W. W. Morland, " "
Dr. Winslow Lewis, " "
Dr. Henry K. Oliver, " "
Dr. D. D. Slade, " "
Rev. Warren H. Cudworth, Chaplain 1st Mass. Infantry.
T. Wentworth Higginson, Captain 51st Mass. Infantry, Colonel 33d U. S. Colored Troops (1st South Carolina Infantry).
Francis A. Osborn, Colonel 24th Mass. Infantry, Brevet Brigadier General U. S. Vols.
Joseph P. Couthouy, Acting Volunteer Lieutenant U. S. Navy. Killed in battle.
Alpheus Hyatt, Jr., Captain 47th Mass. Infantry.

BOSTON SOCIETY OF NATURAL HISTORY. 137

T. W. Clark, Colonel 29th Mass. Infantry.
Edward C. Cabot, Lieut. Colonel 44th Mass. Infantry.
Hiram S. Shurtleff, Captain 56th Mass. Infantry.
Nathaniel S. Shaler, Captain 5th Kentucky Artillery.
Nathaniel Bowditch, 1st Lieut. 1st Mass. Cavalry, A.A.G. U. S. Vols.   Killed in battle.
Charles W. Folsom, 1st Lieut. and Q.M. 20th Mass. Infantry.
Huntington F. Wolcott, 2d Lieut. 2d Mass. Cavalry.   Died in the service.
Edward T. Bouvé, 1st Lieut. 32d Mass. Infantry, Captain 4th Mass. Cavalry, Major 26th N. Y. Cavalry.
Joseph H. Lathrop, Sergeant 43d Mass. Infantry, 1st Lieut. and Adjutant 4th Mass. Cavalry.
John E. Alden, 2d Lieut. 1st unattached company Mass. Infantry.
Nathan Appleton, 1st Lieut. 5th Battery Mass. Light Artillery, Capt. and A.D.C. U. S. Vols.
Louis Cabot, 2d Lieut. 1st Mass. Cavalry, Capt. 2d Mass. Cavalry, Major 4th Mass. Cavalry.
Fletcher M. Abbott, 1st Lieut. 2d Mass. Infantry.
John Ritchie, 1st Lieut. and Q.M. 54th Mass. Infantry.
William E. Endicott, 2d Lieut. 30th unattached company Mass. Heavy Artillery.
Lorin L. Dame, 1st Lieut. 15th Battery Mass. Light Artillery.
Albert S. Bickmore, Private 44th Mass. Infantry.
A. P. Cragin, Private in a Mass. Cavalry regiment.   Killed in battle.
John Jeffries, Jr., Major 1st Corps Cadets Mass. Volunteer Militia.
George Brooks, Private 45th Mass. Volunteers.   Died in the service at Newbern, N. C.
Robert M. Copeland, 1st Lieut. and Q.M. 2d Mass. Infantry, Major and A.A.G. U. S. Vols.
Alfred P. Rockwell, Captain 1st Battery Conn. Light Artillery, Colonel 6th Conn. Infantry, Brevet Brigadier General U. S. Vols.
Stephen M. Weld, Captain 18th Mass. Infantry, Colonel 56th Mass. Infantry, Brevet Brigadier General.
E. R. Cogswell, Corporal 44th Mass. Infantry.
Jonathan Dorr, Private 44th Mass. Infantry.
Nathaniel Willis Bumstead, Captain 45th Mass. Infantry.
Carleton A. Shurtleff, Medical Cadet U. S. Army.
Joseph T. Rothrock, Private 12th unattached company Mass. Infantry, Captain Pennsylvania Cavalry.
Copley Amory, 1st Lieutenant 4th U. S. Cavalry.
Rev. George H. Hepworth, Chaplain 47th Mass. Infantry.
William Ellery Copeland, Private 44th Mass. Infantry.
Lewis W. Tappan, Jr., Captain 45th Mass. Infantry.

The writer can scarcely hope, notwithstanding great care taken, that no errors will be found in this roll of honor. He would especially regret the omission of the name of a single member of the Society, who manfully went forward to serve the nation in its hour of peril.

Early in the decade now passed was received the bequest of Mr. Jonathan Phillips of $10,000. This was followed by the grant of land from the State on which the Museum was afterwards erected. Then came the first of the series of donations from our great benefactor, Dr. William J. Walker, of his house in Bulfinch Street, followed by the second and third of $20,000 each, and finally by the great bequest from him which established the institution on such a firm foundation as to secure its perpetuity so long as wisdom shall prevail in its councils.

The Society had also been the recipient during the decade of the bequests before mentioned, from Paschal P. Pope, $20,000; Miss Sarah P. Pratt, $10,000, with a large collection of shells; Dr. Benjamin D. Greene, $9,000, with a large library of valuable books; and Mr. Henry Harris, $5,000. It had likewise received for the establishment of a fund for the Library, $5,000 in the name of Huntington Frothingham Wolcott, who died in the military service of the country in the war of the rebellion.

Of the donations made towards building and other purposes in the early part of the decade, Mr. Nathaniel Thayer contributed $2,500, Mr. Thomas Lee $1,000. Mr. John L. Gardner $1,000, Dr. Benjamin D. Greene $1,000, Mr. Henry B. Rogers $1,000, and an anonymous friend $1,000. A considerable amount of the money subscribed towards the building and working funds was from donors of sums varying from $500 to $100 and less. Besides money, the Society received during the decade the magnificent donation of the Lafresnaye collection of birds from Dr. Henry Bryant.

There was a very valuable donation made to the Society by Mr. James M. Barnard in 1864, notice of which has not been given. This consisted of a large collection of fossil echinoderms made by Dr. A. Krantz of Bonn, and was second in the country only to that in the Museum of Comparative Zoölogy in Cambridge, presenting as it did good types of nearly every group of the class.

Mr. H. F. Wolcott mentioned above was a young member of the Society whose great interest in it led to the endowment after his death of the fund referred to in his name by his father, Mr. J. Huntington Wolcott, as a memento of that interest, and as a recognition of what would have been pleasing to him if living. The fund is known as the *Huntington Frothingham Wolcott Fund*, and now amounts to over $6,000, the interest at first having been allowed to accumulate and having been added to the capital. It is held is trust, the income alone being available for the purchase of books for the Library. The service of this fund to the Society has been very great, as without it, there would not have been means to supply works actually indispensable for the use of the members. Mr. Wolcott was born in Boston, February 4th, 1846, and died June 9th, 1865.

In mentioning the bequests of Mr. Jonathan Phillips made during the decade, no such notice was given of this benefactor of the Society as seems fitting should appear concerning him. A few brief remarks are therefore added here.

Hon. Jonathan Phillips was born in Boston, April 24th, 1778. He was the son of Lieutenant Governor William Phillips and was educated for mercantile life, but never engaged in much active business. Upon the death of his father in 1827 he became the possessor of a very large fortune, and the remainder of his life was mostly passed in literary culture, travel, and in. taking an active share in many of the benevolent and educational movements of his day, all of which he generously aided. He was at one period a member of the Senate of Massachusetts, but his tastes and inclinations were such as to lead him to shrink from public life. For a number of years he held the office of President of the Massachusetts Bank. He was an associate with Dr. William Ellery Channing, Rev. George Ripley, Dr. Charles Follen and many other prominent men, in the well-known Progress Club, and was a very intimate friend of Dr. Channing. Among many other bequests and donations he contributed $30,000 in aid of the Boston Public Library, first making a donation of $10,000 and afterwards bequeathing by will $20,000, the interest of which sums alone is available for use. He bequeathed likewise the sum of $20,000 to the City in trust, the income of which is to be expended in adorning and embellishing the streets and public places. To this last-mentioned bequest, the City owes the statue of

Josiah Quincy in front of City Hall, that of John Winthrop in Scollay Square, and that of Samuel Adams on Washington Street.

Mr. Phillips died in Boston on the 29th of July, 1860, at the age of eighty-two years.

Of the publications during the ten years, the seventh volume of the Journal and the last of the series, was completed in 1863. The Memoirs in quarto form which succeeded the Journal had been delivered to members in parts from 1863; the whole of the first volume being completed in 1869. Of the Proceedings the twelfth volume and part of the thirteenth had been issued.

The members of the several standing committees of the Council during the decade were as follows:

On Publication. Drs. Jeffries Wyman, Augustus A. Gould, S. L. Abbot, Samuel Kneeland, Charles Pickering; and Messrs. S. H. Scudder, William T. Brigham and Charles J. Sprague.

On the Library. Messrs. Charles K. Dillaway, Charles J. Sprague, S. H. Scudder, Horace Mann, J. Elliot Cabot; and Drs. John Bacon and A. S. Packard, Jr.

On Finance. Messrs. Thomas T. Bouvé, James M. Barnard, Edward Pickering and Amos Binney.

The average attendance at the general meetings during the ten years was as follows:

For the year	1860–61	37	For the year	1865–66	34
" "	1861–62	37	" "	1866–67	39
" "	1862–63	33	" "	1867–68	40
" "	1863–64	44	" "	1868–69	33
" "	1864–65	33	" "	1869–70	32

The average attendance at the meetings of the Section of Microscopy after its formation was for the months December 1864 to May 1865, 9; for the year 1865–66, 9; 1866–67, 12; 1867–68, 12; 1868–69, 8; 1869–70, 9.

The average attendance at the meetings of the Section of Entomology after its formation was for the months November 1866 to May 1, 1867, 12; for the year 1867–68, 9; 1868–69, 12; 1869–70, 10.

The members who took the most active part in the proceedings of the Society during the first five years of the decade were Drs. Jeffries Wyman, C. T. Jackson, B. Joy Jeffries, James C. White, Charles Pickering, Augustus A. Gould, Henry Bryant, Burt G. Wilder, C. F. Winslow, William Stimpson and Thomas M. Brewer; Profs. Louis Agassiz, William B. Rogers and H. J. Clarke; Messrs. S. H. Scudder, F. W. Putnam, Alexander Agassiz, A. E. Verrill, Horace Mann, C. J. Sprague, Charles Stodder and Thomas T. Bouvé. Those who were most active during the last five years were Drs. Jeffries Wyman, C. T. Jackson, B. Joy Jeffries, James C. White, Charles Pickering, Hermann A. Hagen, J. B. S. Jackson, Thomas M. Brewer; Messrs. S. H. Scudder, Charles Stodder, William T. Brigham, R. C. Greenleaf, N. S. Shaler, Horace Mann, B. P. Mann, F. G. Sanborn, E. Bicknell, C. S. Minot and Thomas T. Bouvé.

Walker Prizes. In accordance with the provisions in an agreement made with Dr. William J. Walker by which the Walker Prize Fund was established, offers were made for the best and second best memoirs presented on subjects proposed by a Committee of the Council, as follows:

Subject for 1865: "Adduce and discuss the evidence of the coëxistence of man and extinct animals, with the view of determining the limits of his antiquity."

Subject for 1866: "The fertilization of plants by the agency of insects, in reference both to cases where this agency is absolutely necessary, and where it is only accessory."

No essays having been presented, or none deemed by the Council worthy of a prize, the same subjects were proposed again for the years 1867 and 1868, but still without bringing forth any response from writers. Other subjects were therefore proposed for the two subsequent years, viz:

For 1869: "On the range of arctic and alpine plants in Northern America, with an enumeration of species."

For 1870: "The reproduction and migration of Trichina spiralis."

As with the case of previous subjects, neither of these last elicited any response, or any of sufficient merit in the estimation of the Council to call for an award. It will be seen later that those proposed for the immediately succeeding years were more successful in calling forth essays upon them.

The property of the Society at the end of this decade, besides the building, and the collections and library which were of inestimable value, consisted of investments belonging to the various funds amounting in the aggregate to $186,898.20; this included, however, several bequests left under restrictions, a part of the income of which must be expended only for special purposes, and can never be available for general uses or expenses.

The library at this time had nearly doubled in size during the ten years, and consisted of 9396 volumes, and 2677 pamphlets, as before stated. But if the members had cause to rejoice at the material prosperity of the institution, they too had often cause to lament the loss of faithful workers for its interests, many of whom had been companions in their labors. Among those taken by death during the ten years were Dr. B. D. Greene, Dr. Geo. Hayward, Mr. Francis Alger and Dr. Augustus A. Gould, all original members of the Society; Dr. Wm. J. Walker, its great benefactor; Dr. Henry Bryant, Mr. Octavius Pickering, Mr. Thomas Bulfinch, Mr. Horace Mann, Mr. Huntington Frothingham Wolcott, Mr. Carleton Atwood Shurtleff and Capt. Joseph P. Couthouy.

DECADE V. MAY, 1870 — MAY, 1880.

1870. The fifth decade commences with the office of President vacant, by the resignation of Dr. Jeffries Wyman; with Mr. Alpheus Hyatt, Custodian; Rev. Joshua A. Swan, Recording Secretary and Librarian; Dr. Samuel L. Abbot, Corresponding Secretary; Mr. Edward Pickering, Treasurer; Mr. F. G. Sanborn, Assistant in the Museum; Miss Lillias Blaikie, Assistant in the Library, and Mr. George Coles, Janitor.

It will be recollected that at the annual meeting the Committees for the several departments of Comparative Anatomy, Mammals and Microscopy were not elected. At the first meeting succeeding, the following persons were chosen to these respectively:

Mammals. J. A. Allen, Thomas Waterman, Jr., M.D., J. B. S. Jackson, M.D.

Comparative Anatomy. Thomas Dwight, M.D., Jeffries Wyman, M.D., J. C. White, M.D.

Microscopy. Edwin Bicknell, R. C. Greenleaf, B. Joy Jeffries, M.D.

The following changes were made in the members of the Committees as elected at the annual meeting: J. A. Allen was transferred from the Committee on Ornithology to that of Fishes and Reptiles, taking N. E. Atwood's place on the latter; and J. Elliot Cabot was chosen one of the Committee on Ornithology.

It was decided to change the Janitor's room from the north-west corner of the basement to the south-west corner, at an expense of $1500, it having been found that from lack of sunshine in the apartments, the health of members of his family had been seriously impaired.

Under the new condition of affairs inaugurated by the election of Mr. Hyatt as Custodian, certain changes were desirable in the Regulations and By-Laws. The Librarian, besides such duties as defined hitherto, was given the sole direction of the Janitor so far as related to work expected of him in the delivery of publications, care of office, lecture room, &c. He was also to have sole charge of the assistants in the Library. The office hours were fixed at from 9 A. M., until the closing of the Library in the afternoon, except an intermission not exceeding two hours at noon. A vacation of two months was allowed him during the year.

The Custodian, in addition to duties defined in By-laws, was to have the immediate charge of the Museum, and the sole direction of the assistants employed there. Also the sole direction of the Janitor, excepting in such duties as are mentioned in the authority given the Librarian over him. He was empowered to decide in all cases relative to the arrangement, care or use of the collections not otherwise specially provided for, and his decision was to be binding, unless overruled by the Council. When any department suffered by neglect or other cause, he was authorized to take charge of it and report to the Council. He was required to prepare a report as early as possible on the state of the Museum, and a plan for the definite arrangement of the collection, so as to best illustrate what the Society had in view by the formation of its Museum. He was required to give twenty-four hours each week at least, of undivided attention to the Museum; six hours each for four days, or eight hours each for three days. A vacation of two months was granted him.

The Assistant in the Museum was authorized to act for the Custodian in his absence. A vacation of six weeks was allowed him, the time to be fixed by the Custodian.

The Assistant in the Library was required to act for the Librarian in his absence. Her attendance was fixed at seven hours per day. She was to be allowed six weeks vacation during the year, the time to be appointed by the Librarian.

It was understood that an appeal might be made to the Council on the part of any one employed who felt aggrieved.

At a meeting of the Society on the 1st of June, a Committee was appointed, consisting of five members, to present a candidate for the office of President at the next meeting. Mr. Edward Pickering, Dr. C. F. Winslow, Mr. Chas. J. Sprague, Mr. R. C. Greenleaf and Mr. William H. Niles composed this Committee.

At the next meeting, held on the 25th of June, Mr. Edward Pickering, the chairman, reported that the name that first suggested itself to the Committee was that of the First Vice-President, Dr. Charles T. Jackson, one of the earliest, most constant and devoted of the friends of the Society. Upon his unwearying interest in its welfare, his liberal contributions to its treasures, his courtesy as a presiding officer, his well known scientific attainments, it was not necessary to enlarge. But the reception of the following letter prevented the Committee from offering his name as a candidate.

EDWARD PICKERING, Esq., *Chairman of Committee of Nomination.*

Dear Sir: Having been informed that the Committee on the Nomination of President for the Boston Society of Natural History are disposed to offer my name as a candidate for that office, I beg leave to say to the Committee, through you, that however highly I consider the honor, I cannot consent to become a candidate, since my health, which is often impaired, especially in the winter, might be inadequate to the very important duties and constant attention required of the first officer of the Society. So far as my health and ability will permit, I shall always be happy to labor for the interests of the Society, and whatever influence I can exert will be in its favor.

A younger man than myself I believe would be able to serve the Society much better than I can, and my personal preference would be in favor of the promotion of the Second Vice-President, Mr. Thomas T. Bouvé, to the Presidency of the Society.

Most cordially thanking the Committee for their favorable consideration, I have the honor to be Your obedient servant,

CHARLES T. JACKSON.

Under these circumstances the Committee proposed for the office of President of the Society the name of the Second Vice-President, Thomas T. Bouvé.

The report was accepted.

Dr. C. F. Winslow moved that the Society proceed to ballot for the candidate nominated.

This led to considerable discussion, there being the feeling on the part of some present, that the proposed action was hasty, and that no harm could result from postponing the election to a future period. A ballot, however, was ordered by a large majority of the members, which resulted in the election of Mr. Thomas T. Bouvé to the Presidency of the Society, there being but two dissenting votes.

Early in this official year a letter was received from Prof. Runkle of the Institute of Technology, expressing a desire for the coöperation of the Boston Society of Natural History with the Institute. This was warmly responded to by the Council, and the President, Mr. Bouvé, was requested to write an answer to Professor Runkle expressive of the readiness of the Society to meet his wishes, it being thought that an arrangement might be made which would be of service to both institutions in the furtherance of the purpose each had in view, to extend a knowledge of science in the community.

A plan was subsequently adopted by which the Institute had permission to use the halls of the Museum and the collections for the instruction of its students, subject to such restrictions as the Council might impose for the preservation of the specimens, it being understood that the Society should be paid a certain sum therefor, and that the Institute should deposit the collections and charts of the late Prof. H. D. Rogers with the Society, grant the use of the Huntington Hall for lectures, if required, and contribute specimens of natural history towards an educational series. Under this arrangement, Dr. Samuel Kneeland delivered several lectures on Zoölogy in the lecture room of the Society the first year, and the Custodian delivered a course on Palaeontology.

It is well, perhaps, before proceeding to detail further the doings of the Society, to dwell at some length upon the necessity of a change in the management of its interests, which had led primarily to the election of Mr. Hyatt as Custodian, and subsequently to the adoption of a more defined policy in its administration. It is manifestly unjust to the memory of the many distinguished and devoted members of the Society who, from its earliest period to that now under consideration, were active in its affairs, to imply that no plan of organization, or policy of administration had been acted upon. A common sentiment influenced all of them, that of affording means by which a better knowledge of natural history might be attained by themselves and disseminated in the community, and to act upon this they deliberately planned for the accomplishment of their purposes and organized means for the object. They established a Museum, they founded a Library, they held meetings, gave lectures, and published scientific papers. Simply, they did not define their course of action or their arrangement of the Museum, as more advanced knowledge and experience suggested in 1870. What they did was in accordance with the best thought prevailing anywhere in relation to such institutions as that of the Society.

If the several departments of the Museum they formed were not placed in such sequence as to form together as now, the best means for the education of visitors, the collections of each were arranged in thorough scientific order. The time had however come for a more definite statement of what was proposed on the part of the Society, especially as views were held by some members tending to prevent such change in its policy and in the arrangement of the collections as seemed desirable for its best good. The Custodian, Mr. Hyatt, was therefore required, as has been before mentioned, to prepare a report as early as possible, on the state of the Museum and a plan for its definite arrangement, so as to best illustrate what the Society had in view in its foundation. This he did soon after, and a vote was passed by the Council, adopting the proposed plan as a basis for action until the annual meeting in 1871.

This plan was not limited in its application to the Museum. The paper presented by the Custodian and adopted by the Council, was termed "Proposed Plan of Organization," and embraced views and suggestions concerning the meetings, the publications, and the library, as well as the Museum. The essential details of this plan may be found in the annual report for the year ending May, 1871, published in the fourteenth volume of the Proceedings. Here only such portions of it will be referred to as tended to excite opposition and to lead to a conflict of opinion and action upon measures deemed essential to the interests of the Society.

After stating that the Museum of the Society was intended especially for the instruction of teachers, general students and the public, and that therefore its collections should be arranged according to some easily understood and comprehensive plan, illustrating the general laws of natural science, the Custodian added, "All the different departments should be connected as closely as possible, and form together a series of lessons in the structure of the earth and its constituent parts, and in the organization of the plants and animals living upon its surface."

A clear understanding of the defective general character of the arrangement of the Museum, as judged in the light of present experience, is necessary in order that the reason for a radical change in the location of the several departments in the building, involving large expenditure of time and money, may be manifest.

As recently as when the new building of the Society was constructed, it is doubtful if in any of the great museums of the world, the importance was recognized of arranging the several departments in such relation to each other as would best serve educational interests; certain it is, that not a member of the Society gave a thought to it. The only idea that moved the minds of the Curators in selecting rooms for the collections was that of obtaining such as would meet the requirements of each department without reference to the rest. Thus it happened that those brought in contact had no relation to each other, and others closely allied by nature, were far remote in location. On the lower floor, where are two exhibition rooms, one was appropriated to Botany, the other to Geology, whilst the department of Minerals, which should have had a place with that of Geology, and immediately preceding it, was far away in another part of the building.

To act upon the advanced views expressed by the Custodian upon the arrangement of the departments in consecutive series, a radical change was necessary, involving great expense, particularly in the reconstruction of cases, so that there might be a proper adaptation of them to new uses. Perhaps it was fortunate that as constructed originally, none of them were fit for the purposes designed. They were, undoubtedly, as suitable as those generally then found in Museums, but experience had taught the Curators that there was a necessity for much better, if the collections were to be saved from ruin. This fact made it easier to accomplish the radical change in arrangement desired on scientific considerations, as it was seen that the necessary expenditure would accomplish a double object. There was no intention to do all or much at once, towards effecting the change, but only to establish the policy of placing the collections in such consecutive order as suggested, and act upon it as time and means would allow. The President heartily approved of the change. He was strongly averse to encroaching on the principal of the property of the Society for any but the most weighty reasons, but he regarded the end to be attained as fully justifying the means, and he gave the policy of re-arrangement of the Museum all the individual and official influence he could bring to bear in its support.

Besides the re-arrangement of the several departments, the proposed plan contemplated the formation of separate New England collections in each, and an epitome collection of the organic sections of the Museum, containing the types of the vegetable and animal kingdoms, classified to show the approximations of the lower, and the great differences of the higher orders of each, with the zoölogical succession of the types of each. It will be seen in the remaining pages of this volume how steadily the policy was adhered to of effecting the object mentioned, and how gradually but surely the great work was accomplished; although not without opposition, and not without the manifestation of unpleasant feeling on the part of some who failed to recognize the wisdom of what was proposed. This was to be expected, even on the part of members devoted to the interest of the Society. The Custodian indicated his appreciation of this in the following remarks upon the plan submitted.

"The difficulties to be encountered in carrying out the details of any scheme, will be great or small, precisely in proportion to the feeling which governs the officers entrusted with its execution. If a broad, catholic spirit of consideration for the interests of the Museum obtains, there need be no doubt of its ultimate success. On the other hand, if regard for the interests of any special departments is allowed to interfere with the uniform arrangements and proper scientific use of the whole Museum, no very beneficial results can be anticipated." The course pursued has, it is believed, received the commendation of all naturalists who have made themselves acquainted with it, and witnessed the results.

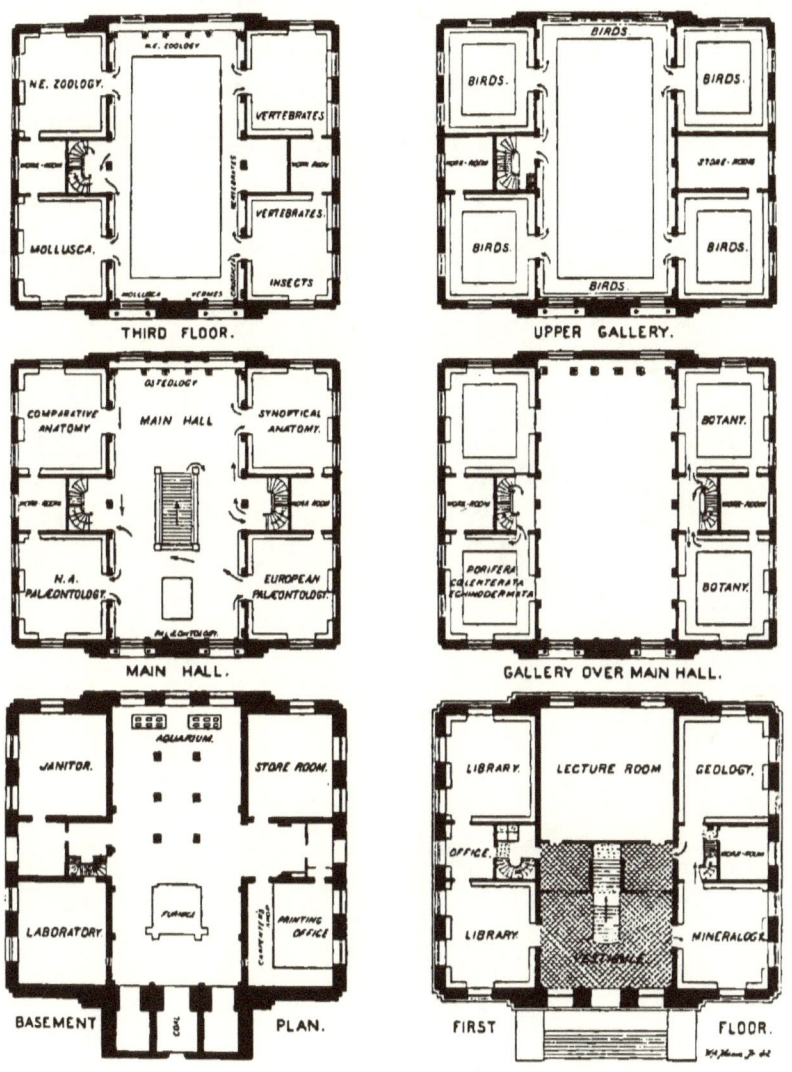

MUSEUM OF THE BOSTON SOCIETY OF NATURAL HISTORY.

FLOOR PLANS.

In October of this year, a large fin-back whale was exhibited in one of the docks of the harbor, exciting much interest in the community, and attracting a large concourse of visitors. The matter was brought before the Council by a motion being made that Dr. Thos. Dwight, Jr. and the Custodian be a committee to procure if possible the skeleton of this huge animal for the Museum. At the next meeting Dr. Dwight reported that the carcass had been presented to the Society by Mr. Harvey T. Litchfield, had been accepted by the committee, and had been towed to and stranded upon Spectacle Island. Upon the suggestion of Dr. Dwight, three hundred dollars were voted to cover expenses of transportation, cleaning, and delivering the skeleton at the Museum.

This fine specimen now adorns the main hall of the Museum, being suspended from the roof of the building. Dr. Dwight gave a large part of a year of scientific labor in the preparation and final arrangement of the skeleton in the position it now occupies, and to him the Society is mainly indebted for such an important acquisition to its collection. The skeleton is undoubtedly the finest in the country, and its perfection is largely due to his personal care and watchfulness over the carcass until all the bones were safely removed.

The lack of means at this time necessary to accomplish all the objects the Society had in view for the instruction of the public in science, weighed upon the minds of the active members, as indeed it has ever since. They were, therefore, much gratified to learn from the President that he had had an interview with Mr. John Amory Lowell, the Trustee of the Lowell Institute, who had kindly expressed a willingness to provide for several courses of lectures from the Lowell fund, to be given in our building under the auspices of the Society ; the lectures to be selected by the Council, and the subjects to be such as pertained to natural history.

In accordance with this favorable provision for continued instruction by lectures, seven courses were given during the season of 1870–71. The first six lectures were by the Rev. J. L. Russell, on Cryptogamic Botany, the second course of two lectures by Prof. J. S. Newberry, on the Cañons of the Colorado and Ancient Civilization of America, the third course of six lectures by Dr. Thos. Dwight, Jr., on the Comparative Anatomy of the Mammalia, the fourth course of four lectures by Dr. P. P. Carpenter, on a General Sketch of Mollusca, the fifth course of two lectures was by the Rev. R. C. Waterston, on some of the remarkable natural features of California ; the sixth course of twelve lectures by Prof. W. H. Niles on the Principles of Geology, and the seventh course of six lectures by the Rev. E. C. Bolles, on the Revelations of the Microscope. These lectures were generally attended by large numbers and were of a very interesting and instructive character.

In December, 1870, Miss Blaikie, whose services as assistant in the Library had been very valuable, and whose presence had always diffused cheerfulness, resigned on account of her approaching marriage. The thanks of the Council were presented to her for the very efficient manner in which she had discharged the duties of her office.

1871. By vote of the Council in January of this year, as one of the precautions against fire, smoking in every part of the building was prohibited. On Feb. 7th, Mr. John Cummings presented to the Society five hundred dollars to be applied for educational lectures to teachers during the next winter, that of 1871–72. Mr. John Cummings, the President, Mr. Bouvé, the Custodian, Mr. Hyatt, and Mr. Wm. H. Niles, were appointed a Committee to employ the gift in accordance with the wishes of the donor. This was the first open manifestation made by Mr. Cummings of his intention to afford an opportunity to the teachers of Boston to become acquainted with natural history. His mind had for some time dwelt upon a plan by which the public might possess a better scientific culture than hitherto, and thus share in its refining influences. The general lectures delivered each winter, though undoubtedly of great service to many, seemed to him to accomplish but inadequately the object he had in view. He finally came to the conclusion that by interesting the teachers in the several branches of science, and by affording them an opportunity of receiving practical instruction, better and more lasting results might follow than from any other course. Possessing themselves a knowledge of botany, of mineralogy, or of any other branch, they could not fail to exert a great influence upon the many thousand minds that came under their instruction, in favor of its study, and thus another generation be led to show greater interest in pursuits of an elevating tendency. The members of the committee other than Mr. Cummings himself, feeling a great interest in the proposed plan, early issued a circular to the teachers, calling attention to the generous proposal made by him, and invited their co-operation. A committee on the part of the masters of the Grammar Schools was appointed to learn the feelings of the teachers generally on the matter, and to report results. The circular referred to, after mentioning the proposal of the donor, stated that teachers of every grade were invited; that the lectures would be given on Wednesday or Saturday afternoons, as the teachers might decide, commencing in October and continuing through the winter at the Museum of Natural History; that the earlier courses would be on Physical Geography, Botany and Geology, and that they would be given by Professors familiar with the object method of teaching and skillful in the use of chalk; that it was designed that the lectures should be practical and familiar, questions and answers to be allowed, and the whole subject slowly developed; that the Professors were anxious to know how large classes they could rely upon before leaving the Museum for summer work, and therefore asked all teachers who desired to avail themselves of the offer to sign the circular.

It was gratifying to find that the movement excited great interest on the part of those to whom it was addressed, manifested by the prompt signing of the circular by upwards of seven hundred teachers. The great success which followed this preliminary action will be given in the account of proceedings hereafter.

In March of this year, a bequest of one thousand dollars was received from the late Mr. Sidney Homer for the general purposes of the Society. The Council subsequently voted to appropriate the amount for New England mammals.

The assistant in the Museum, Mr. Sanborn, was authorized to devote two mornings each week to giving instruction at the Bussey School of Agriculture, upon his consenting to have his salary reduced, and Mr. P. S. Sprague was employed to work in the collection of Insects.

At the annual meeting in May, the Custodian read his report for the year. Much of it was devoted to general considerations concerning the objects of the policy of the Society which, having been referred to earlier, will not be dwelt upon here. Of the meetings, it was stated that there had been eighteen of the Society, with an average attendance of forty-one persons, eight of the section of Microscopy with an average attendance of eleven, and seven of the section of Entomology with an average of ten. Thirty-seven written communications had been made by thirty-six persons. Of these, thirteen were presented in the section of Entomology and thirteen in the section of Microscopy.

Of the publications, eleven signatures of the Proceed'ngs, completing the thirteenth volume, had been issued, and of the Memoirs, one paper, Historical Notes on the Earthquakes of New England, by William T. Brigham, had appeared.

The Library had received during the year by gift, purchase or exchange, 215 volumes, 765 parts of volumes, 183 pamphlets and 22 maps and charts. The use of the Library had been extended to members of the Institute of Technology and to others pursuing some branch of natural science, who made application.

Of the departments of the Museum, the Custodian reported as follows:

That of Mineralogy had received a large accession by the purchase of a fine series of specimens, and by the presentation of several, and the reception of others by exchange. The whole collection was in perfect order, and every specimen labelled.

The Geological collection was in good order, and fully arranged and labelled. There had been no important additions.

The Palaeontological collection had had much work done upon it in identifying and labelling the specimens.

The condition of the Botanical collection was stated to be good, being entirely free from insects. It contained about 25,000 specimens labelled and glued to papers, and many hundred duplicates for exchange. A considerable number of plants from various expeditions yet required much study and work for their identification and arrangement.

The department of Comparative Anatomy had been enriched by the important addition made to it of the skeleton of the whale before mentioned, of the reception and mounting of which the particulars have been given.

The corals and the sponges of the Radiata had been rearranged by Mr. Sanborn, and placed on black tablets. The labelling was reported, however, as incorrect in many cases, and it was recommended that measures should be taken to secure the services of Prof. A. E. Verrill for the naming of the species.

Much work had been done on the Insects by Mr. P. S. Sprague, and it was stated that the cases recently procured would obviate all danger of future damage from moths and Anthreni. Valuable additions to the collection had been made by Messrs. Sanborn, Swan, Trouvelot, Sprague, Dickenson, Minot, and Scudder.

The department of the Mollusca required much attention from able conchologists. The services of Dr. P. P. Carpenter were obtained for a short period on the general collection, and Mr. L. Lincoln Thaxter continued work on the New England collection.

The collection of Fishes was in good order and Mr. Putnam had been engaged in labelling the specimens, which work was reported as nearly completed.

The Reptiles were stated to be in the same condition as the previous year. The collection was reported as small, and needing many additions.

The department of Ornithology had received many valuable additions of fresh eggs of Arctic birds from the Smithsonian Institution, and some rare specimens of birds from Mr. Thure Kumlein.

The Custodian had adopted many expedients to stop the ravages of the Anthreni, but with only partial success. Constant work alone, he said was the most effectual. Every bird had been soaked in benzine or naptha. The great want was such cases as are the best adapted to keep out the pests that do the injury. Those in use were not fit by their construction to contain specimens liable to attack.

The department of the Mammalia was reported as rapidly improving. The New England collection had received many accessions obtained by expenditure of a portion of the bequest of Mr. Sidney Homer, the Council, as before stated, having appropriated the sum thus received for the purpose of adding to this collection.

At the election of officers, Mr. R. C. Greenleaf was chosen Second Vice-President, and Mr. J. A. Allen one of the Committee on birds in place of Mr. J. Elliot Cabot, resigned.

Walker Prizes. At a meeting of the Society in June, the President, Mr. Bouvé, presented the report of the committee on the Walker prizes.

To Prof. Albert N. Prentiss of Ithaca, New York, the first prize of one hundred dollars was awarded, and to Mr. Daniel Milliken of Hamilton, Ohio, the second, of fifty dollars, for their competitive essays "On the mode of the Natural Distribution of Plants over the Surface of the Earth."

In October, Mr. F. W. Putnam called the attention of the Society to the great loss the Chicago Academy of Science had suffered in the destruction by fire of their valuable collections in the various departments of natural history and of archaeology, and offered a resolution of sympathy on the part of the Boston Society of Natural History, and the offer of such of our publications and duplicate specimens as might be acceptable. This was ably seconded by Professor Agassiz, who mentioned that the Museum of Comparative Zoölogy had suffered greatly by the fire, as all of Count Pourtalés' collections on the Deep Sea dredging expedition were deposited there. The resolve was unanimously passed.

At a meeting of the Council it was voted that Miss Lucinda Foster be employed to succeed Miss Blaikie as assistant in the Library.

The death of the Reverend Joshua Augustus Swan, the Recording Secretary and Librarian of the Society, occurred on the 31st of October. At the meeting on November 1st, the President, Mr. Bouvé, paid the following tribute to his memory:

"I know not how to utter the deep grief I feel and which I know is shared by you all in the death of our dear companion, Mr. Swan, the Secretary of the Society. No one, I am sure, who has had the pleasure of personal intercourse with him, but will feel that he has lost a near and dear friend. To me his presence even has always seemed a benediction. I do not think I ever was so much impressed by the personal character of any man with whom I have come in contact as with that of Mr. Swan. He seemed always overflowing with love for, and a desire to aid, all about him. What might excite in other men feelings of bitterness or anger, moved him only to sorrow, and no one was more charitable in his judgments of the acts of others. Truly we have lost from our circle a man devoid of guile, upright in conduct, lovable beyond expression, pure in heart and faithful in every duty. God grant that his family, so dear to him, may have strength to bear the loss that falls so much more heavily upon them than upon all others."

The following resolution, with others offered by Prof. J. D. Runkle, was then unanimously passed:

"*Resolved*, That in the death of Mr. Swan the Society recognizes the loss of not only a highly efficient officer and member, but of an associate greatly respected for his attainments as a scholar, admired for his noble qualities as a gentleman, and loved for his many virtues as a man and a Christian."

Before the close of the year it had become so evidently necessary to have cases of better construction for the birds than those in use, and in furtherance of the plan of reorganization adopted, the Council voted that the entire income from the Bulfinch Street fund for one year, be expended in fitting up cases in the upper gallery for that purpose.

1872. In February, Mr. Edward Burgess was elected Recording Secretary and Librarian of the Society in place of Rev. J. A. Swan, deceased.

The necessity for the presence of police officers on public exhibition days to preserve order and to see that the specimens of the Society suffered no harm, was now so apparent that at the meeting on March 6th, the President was authorized to petition the City Government to appoint such officers.

At a meeting of the Section of Entomology, on the 27th of March, the death of an active member of that section, Mr. William Hales Dale, was feelingly referred to, and the following resolution unanimously passed:

"*Resolved*, That in the death of our late associate, William Hales Dale, we mourn the loss of one whose many graces had endeared him to us, and whose researches in natural science, now abruptly arrested by this inscrutable dispensation, commanded our highest respect."

This gentleman bequeathed to the Section of Entomology his cabinet of insects, and five hundred dollars.

The annual meeting of the Society was held on May 1st. From the report of the Treasurer it appeared that the receipts, including donations amounting to $1249.26, and a bequest of $500, exceeded the expenditures $3649.89.

The Custodian's report for the year embraced much matter of importance, but nothing more gratifying that what he expressed relative to the Teachers' School of Science, by which name he designated the school formed through the liberality of Mr. John Cummings. It will be recollected that this gentleman in the early part of the previous year presented to the Society $500 to be applied for educational lectures to teachers, to be given during the succeeding winter. This sum he afterwards increased to cover all expenses occurred in carrying out his design, so that instead of $500 he really paid $950 to the Society. The remarks upon the result are here given.

"The Teachers' School of Science was conceived and has been carried into successful operation during the past winter, under the patronage of Mr. John Cummings, a well known member of the Society. Under the direction of the Committee in charge, courses of lessons have been given in Physical Geography, by Prof. W. H. Niles; on Mineralogy, by W. C. Greenough; on Zoology, by the Custodian; and one is now in progress by Dr. W. G. Farlow, of Cambridge, on Botany.

"Prof. Niles delivered the first six. He undertook to give the more general features of the earth's surface, and then to apply these general principles to the explanation of the physical characteristics of Massachusetts. The success of this course may be judged by the average attendance, which was about six hundred teachers of all grades, and by the fact that the methods of teaching geography in some of our public schools are now undergoing a change in favor of the more natural method introduced by him.

"The necessity of actually handling and dissecting specimens obliged the Committee, after consultation with the masters of the Public Schools, to confine the issue of tickets to about two for each school. This limited the average attendance at the succeeding lessons, six on mineralogy, eleven on zoology, and ten on botany, to about fifty-five. Specimens were distributed and studied at every lesson, and we know that in many instances the instruction was repeated at the schools. We have without doubt excited an interest in natural history, which must speedily effect a marked improvement in the system of public instruction.

"The lectures of the first course by Professor Niles were given in the commodious hall of the Institute of Technology, the others in the lecture room of the Society. The materials for the course of zoölogy were largely furnished by Prof. S. F. Baird, United States Commissioner of Fisheries, and those of the botanical course by Prof. Asa Gray, from the Botanic Garden at Cambridge.

"The expenses of the Society in connection with these lectures were but trifling, and it received donations incidental to their delivery of considerable value. Among these were a full suite of the marine animals of Wood's Holl, a full and complete collection of the fauna of the southern coast of Massachusetts, and also a complete collection of the marine animals of the coast of Maine. These collections were purchased for the Teachers' School of Science by Mr. Cummings, but as the duplicates were sufficient for the distribution at the schools, a series from all of them was first selected for the Museum to be the property of the Society. Many of the species thus obtained were not before in the cabinet. The visit of the Custodian to Wood's Holl to procure the specimens required for the school, enabled him fortunately to procure a complete set of the skins of sharks, rays, skates and other large fishes, which were collected by the vessels and the men in the employ of the U. S. Commissioner of Fisheries."

The Custodian, in addition to what has been given above, stated that at his solicitation Mr. Charles J. Sprague had generously given two hundred dollars towards preparing the skins mentioned above for the New England collection.

The rearrangement of the Museum in accordance with the plan adopted by the Society, had been commenced by removing the birds to the upper gallery, where suitable cases had been prepared for their reception. As the experience of the Society may be of service to some who read these pages, the statement of the Custodian concerning these cases is given entire. "Extraordinary precautions were taken to render them absolutely insect tight. The lumber was very carefully selected and kept heated while the work was going on. All joints were tongued, grooved and glued. The tops, bottoms and sides were built into the plastering, the sashes grooved and tongued and locked by wedge-shaped bolts. The latter were arranged so as to draw the sashes up tightly and firmly against the tongues at the top and bottom and completely close the fronts of each case. Morse's patent brackets were used to suspend the shelving, which hangs upon the wall and has no connection with the fronts. The success of these precautions is shown by the air tight condition of the cases. By suddenly opening or closing a sash, one can readily crush in or burst out the neighboring glass panes. The resistance of the air is so great that it has to be overcome by a steady slow pressure. The plan was similar to one adopted in the Smithsonian Institution and was recommended by Professor Baird."

The Custodian reported that the effort to free the Ornithological collection from the further ravages of Anthreni had been successful. Some of the birds had been so badly affected as to require their being operated upon over twenty-five times before they were entirely freed from the pests.

In the Conchological department much work had been done by Dr. P. P. Carpenter, and by exchange with him a valuable collection of British shells had been procured for the Society.

In the department of Entomology also much work had been done by Mr. Sprague in completing the general collection of Coleoptera placed in the rail cases of the upper gallery. The specimens of Coleoptera were mentioned as numbering about 10,000, and are in the improved boxes adopted by the Council.

The Mineralogical department had received by donation from Mr. F. Alger, the large specimens of beryl which have since occupied the window recesses in the hall of entrance to the Museum, exciting the interest of beholders.

The Geological department had been enriched by the presentation on the part of the Technological Institute of the magnificent mass of hematite iron ore and jasper which may be seen with the beryls above mentioned in the hall of the Museum. From Mr. L. S. Burbank a series of specimens had been received illustrative of a paper by him upon the Eozoon canadense, from Dr. S. Kneeland some lavas, and from Mr. Thomas T. Bouvé a set of polished marbles.

The other collections were mentioned as in fair condition. Much work was constantly required upon many of them in consequence of defective cases.

Of the publications two quarterly parts of the fourteenth volume of the Proceedings had been issued, and four articles of the Memoirs.

The Library had received 424 volumes, 943 parts of volumes, 268 pamphlets and 32 maps and charts.

There had been eighteen general meetings with an average attendance of thirty-two persons, nine of the section of Microscopy with an average of ten, and eight of the section of Entomology with an average of eleven. Six Corresponding and thirty-four Resident Members had been elected. There had been eighty-two communications, of which seventeen were before the Entomological section and twelve before the Microscopical section.

Previous to the election of officers, the department of Geology and Minerals was divided, and at the election the following members were chosen on the respective committees: Geology; William H. Niles, William T. Brigham and Thomas T. Bouvé;—Minerals; Thomas T. Bouvé, Charles T. Jackson, M. D., and L. S. Burbank. The only other change made at the election was in substituting Dr. Samuel Kneeland in place of Mr. J. A. Allen on the Committee for Fishes and Reptiles.

Leave of absence was granted in June to the Custodian for one year, his salary to be relinquished until his return to the duties of his office. He wished to visit Europe and make himself acquainted with its museums and men of science.

Walker Prizes. In June the Council awarded the first prize of one hundred dollars to E. D. Cope, and the second of fifty dollars to Benjamin G. Ferris, for their competitive essays on "The Darwinian Question; its bearing on the Development of Animal Life."

In August of this year, the Council passed votes implying some action on the part of members not entirely satisfactory, and at the same time defining limits for the future, viz.:

All donations shall be submitted to the Committees of departments, before final deposition.

All work rooms in use by Committees are to be regarded as private and shall not be exposed to intrusion except by members of the Council.

In September, Prof. Shaler proposed that notices of each meeting be mailed to members designating the subjects that would be brought before it, hoping this might lead to better attendance. Before this time simple notice of other meetings had been published in two daily papers. The suggestion of Prof. Shaler was approved and adopted.

In October, the Council, in view of the fact that the City Government did not furnish regularly such police officers as were necessary on public days, passed the following vote:

"That in consequence of injuries done the Society's building and collection by visitors, the Museum will be closed to the public after October 19th, until measures can be taken to properly protect the property; and the Secretary is instructed to advertise the same in six daily papers for one week." This determined action led to officers being furnished for a while satisfactory to the Society.

During the summer of the year, there had been three field excursions of the members of the Entomological section, resulting in their obtaining a large collection of specimens. The places visited were first Mattapan and vicinity, second Peabody, and third, Waltham and Waverly.

1873. The Museum of the Society was closed to the public on the first day of March, because the police officers had ceased to attend. This led to an interview on the part of the President, with the Mayor and Chief of Police, resulting in a promise on their part that officers should be present on public days.

At the annual meeting in May, in the absence of the Custodian abroad, the Secretary, Mr. Burgess, presented the yearly Report upon the condition and operations of the Society. From this is given the following abstract.

During the year, two Honorary, one Corresponding, and twenty Resident Members had been elected.

There had been eighteen general meetings of the Society, six of the section of Entomology, and six of the section of Microscopy. The average attendance at the general meetings had been twenty-five, showing perhaps a diminished interest in them.

There had been four courses of Lowell Lectures given under the direction of the Society, and a fifth was in progress. The first was upon "The Principles of Zoölogy," by Prof. Edward S. Morse, and had an average audience of sixty persons; the second upon "Mineralogy," by Mr. L. S. Burbank, and had an average audience of forty persons; the third upon "Evenings with the Microscope," by the Rev. E. C. Bolles, and had an average audience of two hundred and fifty, and the fourth on " Chemical and Physical Geology," by Prof. T. Sterry Hunt, and had an average attendance of one hundred and fifty. The fifth course by Mr. B. Waterhouse Hawkins, upon "Comparative Anatomy," so far as they had progressed, had had an average attendance of fifty.

The Teachers' School of Science was necessarily suspended, much to the regret of a great number who desired to avail themselves of its privileges. The publications had been satisfactory. Two numbers of the Memoirs and two parts of the Proceedings had been issued.

The additions to the Library during the year had been 277 volumes, 852 parts of volumes, 189 pamphlets and 20 maps and charts.

In the Museum the necessary alterations in the cases had progressed as fast as regard to financial considerations warranted. New and admirable ones for the reception of the valuable Herbarium presented by John Amory Lowell, Esq., had been made and were in use.

The change in the location of the collections of the various departments so as to bring them in the designed relation to each other had proceeded steadily, and at this time the work was so far accomplished as to enable visitors to the galleries, by entering the first and passing round to the right, to study the zoölogical collection in order, beginning with the sponges and passing to the higher groups.

A beginning had been made on a comprehensive system of labelling, a great step towards publishing a visitors' catalogue, so important as a means of instruction.

Much work had been done on the collections during the year by Messrs. Emerton and Sprague, the former having labelled over 2,000 bottles of Crustacea and many of New England worms and radiates, and the latter being engaged nearly all the year on insects. Dr. Carpenter had likewise done much in studying our Mollusca and in labelling them. They were sent to him at Montreal for identification.

Valuable donations had been received from many parties, among them birds from the Smithsonian Institution, insects from Mr. Sanborn and Mr. Ernest Papendiek, a fine fossil tree from the Joggins Mine, Nova Scotia, presented by the Institute of Technology and a beautiful Japanese crystal globe by Mr. Thomas Gaffield.

The collection of Minerals had been much enriched by a large and valuable addition made to it by purchase from Dr. Beadle of Philadelphia. The expense was but trifling to the Society, as two members paid a large sum towards the purchase, and considerable money was received from the sale of duplicates.

The number of visitors to the Museum seemed steadily to increase, schools often coming with their teachers. It was open to the public daily during the Peace Jubilee, so called, when the City provided special police for its protection.

The Treasurer's account for the year exhibited an excess of receipts over expenditures of $1,342.98. The Society suffered a loss of $6,280 from the great fire of November, 1872, it having held stocks in insurance companies that became worthless. It was obliged to pay also assessments to the amount of $2,346, levied by the companies.

The changes made in the officers at the election were as follows: John Cummings was chosen on the Committee of the department of Geology, from which William T. Brigham and Thomas T. Bouvé resigned. J. Henry Blake was chosen on the Committee of Mollusks in place of John Cummings, transferred to Committee on Geology. Richard Bliss, Jr., was chosen on the Committee for Fishes and Reptiles in place of Dr. D. Humphreys Storer resigned. J. H. Emerton was chosen on the Committee for Mammals in place of Thomas Waterman, Jr., M. D., resigned. Samuel H. Scudder was chosen on the Committee for Insects in place of F. G. Sanborn.

In June of this year the gallery was added, with the cases, to the rear library apartment. The want of more room for books had been long felt but was now indispensable. A case was also built for the reception of the moose which had been procured for the Society.

At a meeting of the Council it was voted to present the specimens belonging to the Society which were formerly in the Ethnological department to the Peabody Museum.

Walker Prizes. The first prize of sixty dollars was awarded in June to Dr. A. S. Packard, Jr., for an essay by him on the subject proposed for this year " On the development and transformations of the common house-fly."

The Grand Honorary Prize was awarded this year by the Council to Alexander Agassiz for his investigations in the Embryology, Geographical Distribution, and Natural History of the Echinoderms, and the sum of one thousand dollars, the highest amount the Council was authorized to grant, appropriated for the purpose.

In November, Mr. William T. Brigham offered to present to the Society the casts of the busts of several naturalists, if it would pay the cost of transportation from Europe. The offer was accepted with thanks; these busts, being those of Cuvier, A. L. de Jussieu, Adrian de Jussieu, Buffon, Linnæus, and Charles Girard, were subsequently received and now adorn the main hall of the Museum.

A meeting of the Council was called by the President on December 15th. Upon assembling, he addressed the members, stating that in view of the great calamity that had befallen the community and particularly upon all interested in scientific culture and progress, by the death of our distinguished member Louis Agassiz, he had thought it well that they should come together and take such immediate action in relation thereto, as might seem fitting upon the occasion. He then recommended as a manifestation of respect to the memory of our honored associate, that the usual second monthly meeting be omitted on the next Wednesday evening and that we communicate to the family of Professor Agassiz our wish to be present at his obsequies if this should be agreeable to them. The proposed action was taken.

Louis Agassiz.

1874. The meeting of the Society on January 7th partook largely of a memorial character, the proceedings generally relating to the death of our distinguished member, Prof. Louis Agassiz. After calling the members to order, President Bouvé addressed them as follows: .

Since we last met an event has occurred that has brought deep sorrow to our hearts, and indeed moved with grief those of the whole community; for whilst in the death of the great naturalist we have lost a distinguished Honorary Member, a pioneer in the paths we love to tread, one whose name deservedly ranks high among the most illustrious of those who have explored the world of matter and of life, the great body of the community has lost one whom it has long and justly regarded as pre-eminently the great teacher in science, the man of all men, who inspired the love of knowledge, and who was never weary in his efforts to impart the best he knew to every seeking soul.

Truly all alike, learned or unlearned, high in attainments and position, or only humble seekers of truth, may well weep the loss of him, whose presence alone was to everybody an inspiration.

To those of us who have been in any degree sharers in his labors, or companions in literary or scientific circles, his loss is irreparable.

The fine physical form, the countenance ever beaming with feeling and intelligence, the expressive utterances, and above all, that subtle influence which came from the whole being of the man, alas! that these are now only matters of memory.

But it is not for me to dwell upon the event I have alluded to. For a fit expression of the loss sustained by the Society, we have the privilege of looking to one whose valuable services to it in its earlier days we have not forgotten, and who was one of the first among scientific men to welcome to our shores and our companionship the great naturalist. I need not say I refer to our former President, Mr. George B. Emerson, whom I now have the pleasure to introduce to you.

Upon the close of the President's remarks, Mr. George B. Emerson gave an interesting address, a large part of which is here presented.

I thank you, Mr. President, for the great honor you do me by inviting me to say something before, and in behalf of, your Society, in commemoration of the most distinguished naturalist that has appeared among us. You know how reluctantly I consented to speak, and I feel how inadequately I shall be able to represent the Society. Yet I cannot but admit that there is some apparent propriety in your request. I was one of those who formed this Society. All the others who first met, except one, are gone; Dr. B. D. Greene, Dr. J. Ware, F. C. Gray and the rest. My old friend, Dr. Walter Channing, alone, in whose office most of the first meetings were held, is still living. Moreover, while I was in the seat you now occupy, it was agreed by my associates that it was very proper and desirable that a survey of the State, botanical and zoölogical, should be made, to complete that begun by Prof. Hitchcock in Geology. At their request I presented to Gov. Everett a memorial suggesting this.

Our suggestion was graciously received. Gov. Everett brought the subject before the Legislature, in which some friends of natural history in the House of Representatives had already been acting toward the same end; an appropriation was made, and he was authorized to appoint a commission for that purpose. On that commission four members of this Society were placed; the reports of three of whom, Dr. Harris, Dr. Gould and Dr. Storer, have been, and still continue to be, considered of signal and permanent value, and Mr. Agassiz himself regarded them as among the best reports ever made. It has given and still gives me the greatest satisfaction to know that the Society has been continually going forward, and that it is now more prosperous than ever.

A little more than twenty-seven years ago, as I was sitting in my study, a message came to me that two gentleman desired to see me. They were immediately admitted, and Dr. Gould introduced me to Louis Agassiz. His noble presence, the genial expression of his face, his beaming eye and earnest, natural voice, at once gained me, and I responded cordially to his introduction. He said, "I have come to see you, because Dr. Gould tells me that you know the trees of Massachusetts; I wish to be made acquainted with the Carya. I have found the leaves and fruit of several species in the Jura Mountains, where they were deposited when those mountains were formed; but, since that time, none have been found living in Europe. I want to know them as they are now growing."

I told him that I knew all the species found in New England, and should be glad to show them to him. "But I have," I said, "presently to begin my morning's work. If you will let me call on you immediately after dinner, I shall be glad to take you to them."

At the time fixed, I called on him at his lodgings and took him, in my chaise, first to Parker's Hill, where one species of hickory grew, then through Brookline, Brighton and Cambridge, where two others were found, and to Chelsea, where a fourth, and one that might be a variety, were growing. I pointed out the characteristics of each species in growth, branching, bark, fruit and leaves, and especially in the buds. He listened with the most captivating attention, and expressed surprise at my dwelling upon the peculiarities of the buds. "I have never known the buds to be spoken of as characteristic," said he; "that is new to me."

We drove on to Chelsea Beach, which stretches off several miles, — apparently without end, — and, as the tide was very low, was then at least a quarter of a mile wide. He was charmed with everything, expressing his pleasure with all the earnestness of a happy child, hardly able to restrain himself in his admiration and delight. He told me that he had never before been on a sea-beach, but that he was familiar with the undulations and wave marks on the old beaches laid open in the Jura Mountains.

I need not say what a pleasant drive this was. I had long felt great interest in various departments of Natural History, but had been so fully occupied with my own duties, as a teacher, that I had been able to indulge myself fully, and that for a small part of the year, in one only. Here was a companion who was intimately acquainted with all, and with the most distinguished men who had been advancing them, and who was ready and happy to communicate wealth of information upon every point I could ask about.

The news of the death of Agassiz caused a throb of anguish in millions of hearts. Such a death is a loss to mankind. What death among kings or princes in the Old World, or among the aspirants for power, or the possessors of wealth, in the New, could produce such deep-felt regret?

He is gone. We shall see his benignant face and hear his winning voice no more; but we have before us his example and his works. Let us dwell, for a few moments, on some features in his life and character, as an inspiration and a guide, especially to those who mean to devote their leisure, or their life, to natural history, or to the great work of teaching! What a change has taken place, in the whole civilized world, and especially in this country, in men's estimation of the value and interest of these pursuits, since he began his studies. To whom is that change more due than to Agassiz?

He was endowed by nature with extraordinary gifts. His fascinating eye, his genial smile, his kindliness and ready sympathy, his generous earnestness, his simplicity and absence of pretension, his transparent sincerity;—these account for his natural eloquence and persuasiveness of speech, his influence as a man, and his attraction and power as a teacher. For the development and perfecting of many of his highest and most estimable qualities of mind and character, Mr. Agassiz was doubtless indebted to his noble mother, who, judging from every thing we can learn, was a very rare and remarkable woman. To the quiet, homely, household duties, for which the Swiss women are distinguished, she added unconsciously, very uncommon mental endowments, which she wisely cultivated by extensive reading of the best authors, and by conversation with the most intelligent persons.

Trained by such a mother, Agassiz grew up in the belief of a Creator, an infinite and all-wise Intelligence, Author and Governor of all things. He was sincerely and humbly religious. During his whole life, while exploring every secret of animal structure, he saw such wonderful consistency in every part, that he never for a moment doubted that all were parts of one vast plan, the work of one infinite, all-comprehending Thinker. He saw no place for accident, none for blind, unthinking, brute or vegetable selection. Though he was a man of the rarest intellect, he was never ashamed to look upwards and recognize an infinitely higher and more comprehensive Intellect above him.

Agassiz's mother-tongue was French, but both this and German were in common use in the Pays de Vaud. He lived, for years afterwards, in several parts of Germany, and thus attained, without special study, the rich language which we Americans have to give so much time to acquire; and he lived, long, a studious and laborious life in Paris, where he became intimately acquainted with Cuvier and other distinguished naturalists, and perfectly familiar with the French language in its best form. More than once, when he was putting his note-book into his pocket, he told me he knew not whether he had made his notes in German or in French.

Agassiz's universality of study and thought suggest a precious lesson. It is never safe to give one's self entirely to one study or to one course of thought. The full powers of the mind cannot so be developed. Nature is infinite; and a small part of one kingdom cannot be understood, however carefully studied, without some knowledge of the rest.

Agassiz took a large, comprehensive view of the whole field of natural history; his thorough education and intimate acquaintance with the works of the highest men in several walks, Von Martius, Cuvier, Humboldt, and others, made it possible for him to do it, and he then fixed on certain departments, and, for the time, he gave himself entirely to one.

Whenever Mr. Agassiz undertook a special work, he prepared himself for it by a careful study of whatever had been done in that particular line by all others. He had seen, everywhere, indications of the action of ice. He determined to investigate. He began by reading all he could find upon the subject, and then set himself to observe, patiently and carefully, what was taking place in the glaciers themselves. He gave the leisure of several years to this examination, and then felt himself ready to observe the effects of similar action in former ages and distant regions. The opinions of such an observer, after such a preparation, cannot be without authority and value; and it is not surprising that he should not himself have been willing to yield them to those of others who had never given the same study to the subject.

His example as a teacher has been of inestimable value, as showing the importance of the best and largest possible preparation, teaching by things really existing and not by books, opening the eye to the richness and beauty of nature, showing that there is no spot, from the barren sea-beach to the top of the mountain, which does not present objects attractive to the youngest beginner, and worthy of, and rewarding, the careful consideration of the highest intellect.

In 1855, with the aid of Mrs. Agassiz, who, from the beginning, did a great deal of the work, Mr. Agassiz opened a school for young ladies. For this he was, in all respects, admirably well qualified. The charm of his manner, his perfect simplicity, sincerity and warm-heartedness, attracted every pupil, and won her respect, love and admiration. He knew, almost instinctively, what we teachers have to learn by degrees, that we cannot really attract, control and lead a child, and help to form his habits and character, without first loving him; that nothing in the world is so powerful as real disinterested affection. He gave, himself, by lectures most carefully prepared, an hour's instruction, real instruction, every day. All his pupils retain their respect and love for him, and some keep the notes they made of his talks, and read them with delight. The school was continued for seven years, with great success, attracting pupils from distant parts of the country.

One of the secrets of his success as a teacher was, that he brought in nature to teach for him. The young ladies of a large school were amused at his simplicity in putting a grasshopper into the hand of each, as he came into the hall; but they were filled with surprise and delight, as he explained the structure of the insect before them, and a sigh of disappointment escaped from most of them when the lesson, of more than an hour, closed. He had opened their eyes to see the beauty of the wonderful make of one of the least of God's creatures. What a lesson was this to young women preparing to be teachers in the public schools of our Commonwealth, showing that in every field might be found objects to excite, and, well explained, to answer the questions, what? and how? and why? which children will always be asking.

He had all the elements necessary to an eloquent teacher: voice, look and manner, that instantly attracted attention; an inexhaustible flow of language, always expressive of rich thoughts, strong common sense, a thorough knowledge of all the subjects on which he desired to speak, a sympathy with others so strong that it became magnetic, and a feeling of the value of what he had to say, which became and created enthusiasm. He thus held the attention of his audience, not only instructing and persuading them, but converting them into interested and admiring fellow students.

The advent of Agassiz is to be considered a most important event in the Natural History of the country. The example of his character, his disinterestedness, his consecration to science, his readiness to oblige even the humblest and most modest, his superiority to self-interest, his sincerity and absence of all pretension, his enthusiasm in all that is noble — all these recommended not only him, but the science he professed. Never was a life more richly filled with study, work, thought; and all was consecrated, not to the benefit of himself, but to the promotion of science for the good of his fellow creatures.

For many years Mr. Agassiz has seemed to live only for the advancement of natural history, by the building up of his Museum, for which he had collected material, of the greatest possible diversity, which would, properly cared for and arranged, form a Museum superior in numbers and variety to any similar collection in the world. Shall this great work be allowed to fail?

Let every person who honors the name of Agassiz, say No! Let every one who regrets that the great main support of the noble structure is taken away, resolve that it shall not fail, but that, so far as depends on him and what he can do, *it shall go on and be built and filled, and stand firm, a glorious temple of science forever.*

At the conclusion of Mr. Emerson's address Rev. Dr. R. C. Waterston in response to an invitation from the chair, spoke as follows of Prof. Agassiz's connection with the Centennial Anniversary of the birth of Humboldt:

At a meeting of the Boston Society of Natural History, June, 1869, it was moved and voted that a celebration of the Centennial Anniversary of the birth of Alexander von

Humboldt, by this Society, was highly desirable. It was also suggested that Professor Agassiz be invited to deliver an address upon the occasion. The invitation was extended to Professor Agassiz and accepted. Various circumstances connected with that memorable occasion, at a time like the present, come to the mind with peculiar power.

In Professor Agassiz's public address, his introductory remarks were, "I am invited to an unwonted task. Thus far I have appeared before the public only as a teacher of natural history. To-day, for the first time in my life, I leave a field in which I am at home, to take upon myself the duties of a biographer."

Thus this Society had the privilege of inviting Professor Agassiz to a duty (most nobly fulfilled), which without this invitation in all probability he would never have entered upon. That being as he himself expressed it, the first time in his life he had undertaken such a task; it was also, as we now know, destined to be the last. This event which, on every account, had great interest, for these reasons possesses a solemn and sacred import. That anniversary we would keep in grateful remembrance, forming as it does, in connection with many reminiscences, an added and, may we not say, an indissoluble tie between us and him.

At the time when the invitation was extended to Prof. Agassiz, he was overwhelmed with work; while by previous labor, both body and mind had already been overtaxed. Under such circumstances, it would have appeared next to impossible for him to comply with the request of the Society, yet so desirous was he to meet their wishes that he undertook the task.

On the 3d of July Prof. Agassiz wrote as follows:—

"For weeks past I have intended every day to write to you, but the fact is that just now I have scarcely time to breathe, and with the sincere desire of accepting the invitation tendered to me through you, I have been trying to free myself in some degree of the tasks before me. It is not so easy to do this as it seems.

"However, I write now to say that I will do my best so far as it depends upon me, to make the Anniversary of Humboldt worthy of his memory, and serviceable to science in the country. The task will be a difficult, and in some respects a painful, one to me, none the less because of my personal relations with him. But I will do my best, and I beg you to believe that the confidence placed in me by those who wish to make this occasion a marked day, has gratified and touched me deeply.

"I wish you would express this sentiment in my behalf, and add that my great cause of hesitation has been the fear that I might not satisfy the expectations of those who have thus honored me. Believe me,

"Ever truly yours,
"Louis Agassiz."

In a note dated July 21st, he says, "I have been completely prostrated this week." Yet notwithstanding this exhaustion (doubtless far beyond what was imagined by his most intimate friends, and, added to this, serious illness among the members of his own family, his son leaving for Europe, on account of his health, the very day upon which the address was delivered), Professor Agassiz most conscientiously devoted himself through the sultriness of an intensely hot mid-summer, to the work of preparation. Few are probably aware what a mind like his would, under such circumstances, consider requisite. Nothing was to be taken for granted; not even the memory of former investigations would be accepted without passing through the process of examination. Every step was to be measured, with critical exactness, through the long progress of Humboldt's scientific career.

Is there not exemplified in this fact, one of the marked characteristics of Prof. Agassiz's mind? Absolute thoroughness; sifting every question and principle down to its first elements; tracing every thought, from its earliest germ through each successive development, until the final result is reached.

In order to secure freedom from all interruption during these researches, he asked for a room at the City Library, which was readily granted. Here he could gather about him papers and books, which during his absence would remain undisturbed. Mr. Winsor, the efficient and obliging Superintendent, tells me that for more than a month Prof. Agassiz passed at least three or four days of each week, from nine o'clock in the morning until generally three o'clock in the afternoon, and that during this time he called for more than two hundred volumes in different languages, always desiring to read each work as it originally came from the mind of the author. Thus every work which Alexander von Humboldt ever wrote passed under careful review; not only every volume, but every pamphlet, with the exception of one, which could not be found in this country.

On the 4th of September he wrote me,

"I have only yesterday finished gathering my materials, and have not yet begun preparing my address."

He adds — "My friends will never know what anxieties I have to go through on this occasion."

Six days after this I received the following:—

"*Nahant, Sept.* 10*th*, 1869.

"MY DEAR SIR:

"I have succeeded this evening in bringing to a close my draft of an address; not exactly as I would like to deliver it, but such as I may be compelled to read should the occurrences of the day unfit me for an extemporized discourse, which I believe might be more effective."

It would thus appear that even after the address was written, he hoped to give, not what he had embodied in manuscript, but the result of which that would be the basis, in the form of an extemporized discourse, for which, as all know from his constant habit of speaking without notes, he possessed the very highest qualifications.

However, to meet every contingency, he adds:—

"As I go to-morrow to Cambridge, I will try to have my illegible manuscript set in type, that I may myself be able to read it. At the same time I shall see how my diagrams are progressing, and if satisfactory, forward them at once to the Music Hall.

"Very truly yours,

"L. AGASSIZ."

On the 13th of September he wrote:—

"DEAR SIR:—

"I hope I may have a proof of my address for your reporters by the time I reach Boston to-morrow, which I shall hand to you. My diagrams went to the Music Hall Saturday afternoon, with the palm-branch worn on Humboldt's funeral.

"The pen taken from his desk the day he died, and sent to me, I shall bring myself, fearing it might be lost if left with bulkier objects. Very truly yours,
"L. AGASSIZ."

Such were some of the preparatory labors connected with the address which was to be heard on that Centennial Anniversary by literary and scientific men from every part of the country. Seldom has there been an occasion in the history of New England, which has brought together so brilliant an assemblage of able scholars and prominent men in every department of thought.

At the evening reception, Mr. Ralph Waldo Emerson, in speaking of what he termed the "delightful address in praise of Humboldt," concentrated his estimate in this characteristic declaration, "our eminent professor never delivered a discourse more wise, more happy, or of more varied power."

These words expressed the universal feeling. And the address, so cordially welcomed by those who heard it, was received when published with equal favor on both sides of the Atlantic.

This very day, I was reading a letter by Sir John Herschel expressing his commendation; and in the Life of Alexander von Humbolt, edited by Professor Karl Bruhns, director of the observatory at Leipzig, the address by Agassiz is referred to, both in the preface, and in the body of the book. In the latter, a lengthy extract is introduced. [See Vol. II, pp. 179, 180 and 181.]

There were several occasions upon which Alexander von Humboldt extended such attention and kindness to Agassiz, at a time when encouragement was most needed, that it seems but an act of justice and gratitude to recall them here. The first was related by Agassiz some fifteen years ago, at a meeting of the American Academy of Arts and Sciences, soon after Humboldt's death.

"May I be permitted," he said, "to tell a circumstance personal to me? I was only twenty-four years of age when in Paris, whither I had gone with means given me by a friend, but I was at last about to resign my studies from want of ability to meet my expenses. Professor Mitscherlich was then on a visit in Paris, and I had seen him in the morning, when he had asked me what was the cause of my depressed feelings, and I told him I had to go, for I had nothing left. The next morning as I was seated at breakfast, in front of the yard of the Hotel, where I lived, I saw the servant of Humboldt approach. He handed me a note, saying there was no answer and disappeared. I opened the note, and I see it now as distinctly as if I held the paper in my hand. It said:

'MY FRIEND:—

'I hear that you intend leaving Paris in consequence of some embarrassments. This shall not be. I wish you to remain here as long as the object for which you came is not accomplished. I enclose you a check of £50. It is a loan which you may repay when you can.'"

That one act of Humboldt, at the turning point in the life of Agassiz, may have affected the whole course of his active career. If Sir Humphrey Davy could say "My best discovery was Michael Faraday,"— what shall we say of this discriminating instance of generous encouragement, which perhaps gave to us Agassiz as a man of science.

In the address upon Humboldt, Agassiz speaks of his studies at Munich, whose University had opened under the most brilliant auspices, and where nearly every professor was prominent in some department of science or literature. "These men," he says, "were not only our teachers but our friends. We were the companions of their walks and often present at their discussions." "My room," he adds, "was our meeting-place, bed-room, study, museum, library, lecture-room, fencing-room, all in one. Students and professors used to call it the little Academy."

It was at this time that Humboldt was preparing for his Asiatic journey. Agassiz was anxious to accompany him, and asked that he might join the expedition as an assistant. This was the beginning of his personal acquaintanceship with Humboldt.

A graphic picture is presented of the student's life in Paris, in the days of Louis Philippe, when Cuvier, just the age of Humboldt himself, was active and ardent in research, his salon frequented by statesmen, scholars and artists.

Cuvier was then giving a course of lectures, in the College of France, on the History of Science. "Humboldt," says Agassiz, "attended these lectures regularly; I had frequently the pleasure of sitting by his side, and being the recipient of his passing criticism." At this period, Humboldt had his working-room at the Rue de la Harpe. "There," continues Agassiz, "it was my privilege to visit him frequently. There he gave me leave to come, to talk with him about my work, and consult him in my difficulties."

At this time Agassiz was twenty-four years of age, and Humboldt sixty-two.

"I had recently," says Agassiz, "taken my degree as Doctor of Medicine, and was struggling, not only for a scientific position, but for the means of existence also. I have said that he gave me permission to come as often as I pleased to his room, opening to me freely the inestimable advantages which intercourse with such a man gave to a young investigator like myself. But he did far more than this, occupied and surrounded as he was, he sought me out in my lodging."

Here he gives a most interesting account of a visit from Humboldt, at Agassiz's narrow quarters, in the Hotel du Jardin des Plantes. After which is an invitation from Humboldt to meet him at the Palais Royal,— where they dine,— "a rare indulgence," says Agassiz, "for a young man, who could allow himself few luxuries." "Here," he adds, "for three hours, which passed like a dream, I had him all to myself. How he examined me, and how much I learned in that short time! How to work, what to do, and what to avoid; how to live, how to distribute my time; what methods of study to pursue; these were the things of which he talked to me, on that delightful evening."

When we reflect upon the extended reputation acquired by Agassiz before he left Europe; of that visit to this country which led him gladly to adopt it as his home, and of the untiring zeal with which he devoted to it the best years of his life; shall we not hold in grateful remembrance the man who gave to him, at the most critical moment, the cordial hand of friendship, and who by his cheering words, inspired fresh ardor, and a hope which no after trial could extinguish?

It is more than a pleasant picture, it is a lesson for all time, and should awaken, through generations, the desire generously to encourage and wisely to aid.

It was in this spirit that a " Humboldt Scholarship " became associated with the Humboldt Anniversary. Through personal solicitation on the part of the committee the sum of seven thousand dollars was subscribed to form a permanent fund, the income of which, under the direction of the Faculty, was to be solely applied to the aid of young and needy students, while pursuing their preparatory studies at the Museum of Comparative Zoölogy, in Cambridge. The founding of this scholarship was the voluntary proposition of this Society as a token of sympathy and hearty good-will.

The gratification of Professor Agassiz was at once expressed. In a note written July 3d, he says:

"Your proposition to connect a scholarship with the Museum of Comparative Zoölogy, in commemoration of this occasion, has had great weight with me. I believe that such an arrangement will not only be an ever-returning memento of the solemnities of this 14th of September, but, if properly conducted, will contribute to the real advancement of Natural History among us."

The origin of this scholarship was by some misapprehended. It was supposed to have been suggested, directly or indirectly, by Professor Agassiz. This is an entire mistake. No one could feel more sensitive than he himself did upon this subject. His feelings are frankly expressed in a note which I received from him, after he had read a paragraph in the daily papers, referring this movement to him.

" MY DEAR SIR: —

" In a paper to-day, giving an account of the proposed celebration, ' a plan ' is alluded to ' of Mr. Agassiz for founding a Humboldt Scholarship in the institution of which he is the head.'

" This is no doubt a simple error of the press, but I should be very sorry to have it stand. It would have been very ungracious in me, and would have shown, to say the least, a great want of delicacy, had I suggested an endowment for the Museum in which I am personally interested. It was, as you know, a proposition made spontaneously, without any reference to me. And though I rejoice in it and feel doubly unwilling, on account of this offer, to shrink from the responsibility connected with the invitation of your committee, yet the suggestion coming from me, under the circumstances, instead of being appropriate, would be wholly unbecoming. You will excuse me for troubling you about this, but I am sure you will see that it places me in an awkward position."

If in any mind there should exist even the shadow of a misapprehension upon this subject, these words will serve to explain fully both the feelings of Prof. Agassiz and the exact facts of the case.

At the close of his public address of the 14th of September, he says:

" I have appeared before you as the representative of the Boston Natural History Society. It was their proposition to celebrate this memorable anniversary. I feel grateful for their invitation, for the honor they have done me. I feel still more grateful for the generous impulse which has prompted them to connect a Humboldt Scholarship, as a memorial of this occasion, with the Museum of Comparative Zoölogy at Cambridge."

Thus, Mr. President and gentlemen, while we cannot but deeply mourn the vast loss which this community and the whole country has sustained by this bereavement, we rejoice in that friendly relationship which so long existed between us, and are thankful that one of the last great public utterances of his life was given under the auspices of this Society.

And now that his life, so beneficently crowded with activity and usefulness, has closed to us in this sphere of being, we are grateful that our mutual efforts established what will not only be a perpetual bond of union between this Society and the institution of which he was the honored head, but which, we trust, through successive years, may prove a source of practical help and encouragement to numberless students, who, by their future efforts, may extend the boundaries of knowledge, thus aiding in the work of human progress, while they carry forward to yet further completion, those investigations and discoveries which, in our own day, have given immortality to the names of Humboldt and of Agassiz.

There was much feeling manifested at this time concerning the safety of the Museum and collections, now of inestimable value. At a meeting of the Council, the Custodian brought up the question of prohibiting the use of workrooms after dark. This led to the appointment of a committee to take the whole subject of securing the building and contents against fire. At a subsequent meeting, the President, in behalf of this committee of which he was chairman, reported, recommending several changes in regard to unsafe gas fixtures, and the erection of stand pipes for water. By vote, the committee was authorized to do all they deemed wise and necessary in the matter.

In January, the President, Mr. Bouvé, again brought before the Council the necessity of continued action in order to place the collections of the Museum in proper sequence, in accordance with the plan of arrangement which had been adopted. He thought that extensive changes were desirable at once. These would involve the fitting up of two galleries in the side rooms of the main hall for the reception of the Botanical collection, as well as the fitting up of the north rooms on the first floor for the Mineralogical and Geological collections. To carry out these changes would require an expenditure of about five thousand dollars. After discussion, a committee was appointed, consisting of Messrs. Bouvé, Hyatt, Brigham, Cummings and Scudder, to consider the matter and report at the next meeting to be held a week later. When the Council again met, the President in behalf of the committee, presented plans and estimates relative to the proposed alterations. He stated, however, that the majority of the committee recommended that the Botanical collections be placed in the gallery on the north side of the main hall, rather than on the south side. To this, Mr. Brigham, in behalf of a minority of the committee, strongly remonstrated. A prolonged discussion followed. The Council, after mature deliberation, finally voted, with but one dissenting voice, to make the alterations as proposed by the majority of the committee, and full authority was given the President, Custodian and Treasurer to carry them out. The Council also voted that the southeast room in the basement be fitted up as a work room under the direction of the same parties.

As indicative of thought given by members of the Society to matters affecting the public interest not pertaining especially to its work, it may be stated that in February of this year, the Council passed a vote for presentation to the city authorities remonstrating against licensing "Jourdain's Museum of Anatomy" so called, on the ground of its tendency to offend decency and public morality, whilst subserving no good purpose.

It being understood that persons were in the habit of entering the building during the evening hours for other purposes than that of working upon the collections, the Council voted in March: That after the closing of the building, no person shall be allowed to pass into it, except through the apartments of the Janitor.

Some alterations were proposed and adopted in the Constitution and By-laws at this time, the most important of which was the addition to the latter of a section, providing that whenever any existing or anticipated vacancy in the list of officers was to be filled by election, a nominating committee should be appointed by the Society at a stated meeting to bring in at a subsequent meeting one or more nominations of persons to fill such vacancy. And providing also that no person should be elected to any office until his nomination had been under consideration by the Society at least two weeks.

In April of this year, Mr. S. H. Scudder spoke of the great importance of a re-survey of the State of Massachusetts, topographical, geological and biological. It was the first in the Union to provide for a survey, but while almost all the principal States had now finished or begun a second one, no steps had been taken by Massachusetts in this direction. The original survey was wonderfully well done, yet incomplete, and the advance of scientific knowledge since rendered a re-survey very desirable. The American Academy of Arts and Sciences had taken the matter into consideration and had appointed a committee to memorialize the Legislature on the subject.

Prof. Niles, Mr. John Cummings and the President all addressed the meeting in favor of the project, and finally it was voted on motion of Mr. Putnam: That the President appoint a committee including himself to petition the Legislature for a re-survey of the State. Messrs. Niles, Cummings, Putnam, Jeffries, Hyatt, and Morse with the President, were accordingly made this committee.

In the following May Mr. S. H. Scudder reported that the subject of a re-survey of the State had duly come before the Legislature and had been referred to the Committee on Education with every prospect of a favorable report. He also referred to the question of a public park now agitated, thinking that the idea of the establishment of a zoölogical garden should be considered by the Society in connection with it.

The annual meeting was held on May 6th, Vice-President R. C. Greenleaf in the Chair.

The report of the Treasurer showed that the expenditures of the Society had exceeded its receipts $1874.12. Among the former, however, was included the sum of $1754.22 paid for insurance of property for five years. The alterations and improvements in the building indispensable for the safety of the collections, and to bring them into proper relation to each other, had cost $3423.81.

The report of the Custodian, Mr. Hyatt, who had returned home and resumed the duties of his office, after appropriately referring to the decease of Prof. Agassiz, gives a summary of the work of the year, from which the following is presented.

Mr. Hyatt's visit to Europe afforded an opportunity to fill out the Palaeontological collection. A fair collection of species from Western Europe was needed in order that we should be able to compare them in a general way with their synchronous representatives in North America. To meet this want Mr. John Cummings generously furnished the necessary means for their purchase. By good fortune Mr. Hyatt was able to buy the very valuable collection of Oberfinanzrath Eser of Stuttgart. This was very rich in the fossils of the Tertiary, Secondary and Triassic periods, and also contained a fair representation of the Carboniferous, and some of the Devonian and Silurian types. All these had been selected with great care, and Herr Eser had expended the leisure hours of nearly forty years in accumulating them.

Speaking of this collection, the Custodian remarked that the "unique specimens which it contains are both remarkable and numerous. Many of these were found during the building of the extensive fortifications at Ulm, and were selections from all the fossils obtained, which were sent by the chief architect to Herr Eser. The most valuable single series consists of the two head pieces and detached bones of Belodon Campbelli, the only remains of this remarkable animal ever found. There are specimens of tertiary plants, which are of such delicacy that they are mounted like botanical specimens on paper."

Besides the collection mentioned, Mr. Hyatt purchased also while abroad, through the generosity of Mr. Cummings, several large specimens for the Palaeontological department quite essential to it, among the species several Ichthyosauri and Teleosauri, and a magnificent plate of the expanded species of the Pentacrinus Briarius.

A splendid collection of Devonian fossils collected near Ithaca, New York, had also been added to the Palaeontological series, partly by donations of Mr. John Cummings and Mr. Thos. T. Bouvé, and partly by purchase.

The illness of Mr. Sprague had interrupted work in the Entomological department. It was reported by Mr. Emerton, free from destructive insects. Dr. Carpenter had continued work on the Mollusca. To the Comparative Anatomy department a prepared skeleton of a horse mackerel had been added. Work on the Fishes had been begun by Mr. Putnam, Chairman of the Ichthyological Committee.

The Ornithological collection had been frequently inspected through the year. It was reported as free from insects. Considerable work had been done in the Botanical department by Miss Carter, employed at the expense of Mr. John Cummings, to inspect and arrange the duplicates.

During the year five Corresponding and thirty-one Resident Members had been elected. There had been seventeen general meetings of the Society, eight of the section of Entomology, and seven of the section of Microscopy.

The plan of notifying each member by postal card of the general meetings and of the papers to be read at each, adopted in the autumn, had been attended with great success. The numbers present since Oct. 15th, have averaged sixty-four, whereas the average number the previous year was but twenty-five. The greatest number of persons present at one meeting was one hundred and twenty-four, the largest Society meeting ever held in this building.

Only one course of the Lowell Institute Lectures was given. This was by Dr. Thos. Dwight, Jr., upon living animal tissues.

The disastrous effects of the great fire of November, 1872, had prevented the continuance of the lectures to teachers, so generously provided for hitherto by Mr. John Cummings.

Of publications, four articles in the Memoirs had appeared, and four parts of the Proceedings. The library had received during the year three hundred and twenty-three volumes, eight hundred and thirty-three parts of volumes, one hundred and twenty-four pamphlets, and forty-nine maps and charts.

Respecting the alterations that had been going on, the Custodian remarked that a considerable part of the year had been taken up in making them. There would undoubtedly be experienced some difficulty in the arrangement of details in the separate collections but the natural sequence of forms, whether mineralogical, geological, or zoölogical would be as fully and better illustrated than it ever has been in any printed work embracing similar grounds, an achievement heretofore considered unattainable in Museums of the size of this. He deprecated having ascribed to himself the whole credit of the extraordinary success thus far obtained, mentioning that the President had urged the adoption of the plan of organization presented in the annual report of 1870–71, and had ever since given it his energetic support.

At the election of officers for the year ensuing, Mr. Samuel H. Scudder was chosen First Vice-President, and Mr. John Cummings Second Vice-President of the Society, taking the positions hitherto held by Dr. Chas. T. Jackson, and Mr. Richard C. Greenleaf. T. Sterry Hunt and L. S. Burbank were chosen upon the Committee on Geology, from which John Cummings resigned; R. H. Richards was chosen upon the Committee on Minerals, in place of Dr. Charles T. Jackson; John Cummings was chosen one of the Committee on Botany in place of William T. Brigham.

On motion of Dr. Kneeland the thanks of the Society were unanimously voted to the retiring Vice-President, Mr. Greenleaf, for his valuable services. The following resolution presented by Mr. George Washington Warren was also unanimously passed:

"*Resolved*, That this Society desires to place upon its records, its high appreciation of the eminent services rendered by Dr. Chas. T. Jackson, one of its Vice-Presidents, and of the high honor conferred upon the Society by his long association with it; and it would respectfully tender to his afflicted family its sincere condolence for the malady which has overtaken him, and has so abruptly terminated, for a season only, it is greatly to be hoped, his scientific researches, which have been of inestimable value to the public."

It was voted that a copy of the resolution be sent to the family of Dr. Jackson.

Six years have now passed since the above mentioned action was taken by the Society, and as the hope expressed of the renewal of scientific work on the part of Dr. Jackson, has not been and is not likely to be realized,[1] there can be no more fitting occasion to dwell upon his connection with, and his services to the Society. He was not, strictly speaking, one of its original members, but he, soon after its foundation, was acting among them, and in 1833 was elected to the office of Curator.

To no man was the Society more indebted for constant and active zeal in its welfare than to Dr. Charles T. Jackson during the first forty years of its existence. Others surpassed him in laborious work on its collections when nearly all done upon them was by voluntary effort; others in exerting greater influence in the community for its advantage; but none in a constant manifestation of interest in its proceedings as shown by so long and uninterrupted a participation in them, and by the generous donation of a large por-

[1] Dr. Jackson died, after a long illness, on the 29th of August, 1880.

tion of his mineral collection. No man among the members perhaps manifested more genius for scientific work. Had the truly brilliant suggestions of his mind been always followed up by prompt endeavor to obtain practical results, he would have been recognized everywhere as a great discoverer and benefactor. This is not the place to discuss questions relative to his instrumentality in the introduction of ether as an anæsthetic agent. Suffice it here to express what is clearly true that the friends who knew him the most intimately and who were his constant companions, ever felt that much more was due to him than the world awarded. Whatever may be said, however, upon mooted points, all who were members of the Society in his days of activity will agree that he served it well and faithfully and that he richly earned its gratitude. Possessed of a good memory, and having a great fund of information upon almost all subjects that came up for discussion at the meetings, Dr. Jackson became much relied upon to take part when there was any lack of speakers, and thus often largely contributed to the interest of proceedings that might otherwise have been dull. Moreover, he frequently read papers of great value which appeared in the publications of the Society.

In the Council meeting first held after the annual one of the Society, the usual committees for the year were formed, and a new arrangement was made with the Custodian, by which it was understood that he should give all his time to the Society, excepting such as was required by him for his regular lectures, and be held responsible for the building and all the employees under his charge; these to be considered his assistants and not those of the other officers or of members of the Council. The Custodian or the Museum assistant to be present during office hours. The Secretary to be present only when necessary, and the second assistant to be a general assistant under his charge.

In furtherance of the plan still in progress to arrange the collections in consecutive order, the Council voted, upon representation of Mr. Bouvé in behalf of the committee on alterations, that it was necessary to fit up the gallery on the south side of the building for the reception of Protozoans and Radiates.

Walker Prizes. The subject proposed for the Walker annual prize for 1874 was "The comparative structure of the limbs of birds and reptiles." No essay of sufficient merit for an award was presented.

In June of this year, the subject of a Zoölogical Garden came before the Society and the Council. At a meeting of the former, it was voted, upon motion of Mr. G. Washington Warren, that a committee be appointed by the Chair to urge, in the name of the Society, before the Park Commissioners and the City Council, the importance of providing for the establishment of a Zoölogical Garden and Aquarium in connection with one of the proposed public parks, and that said committee have power to call a special meeting of the Society whenever it may be thought expedient to consider such recommendation as the committee may suggest in relation to the subject.

Whether this committee was appointed and if so what they did, is not reported in the records. The matter is quoted as indicating the readiness of the Society to coöperate with the City government in any movement that may be made towards the establishment of a Zoölogical Garden.

Jeffries Wyman

JEFFRIES WYMAN.

Died 4th Sept., 1874.

The wisest man could ask no more of Fate
Than to be simple, modest, manly, true,
Safe from the Many, honored by the Few;
Nothing to court in World, or Church, or State,
But inwardly in secret to be great;
To feel mysterious Nature ever new,
To touch, if not to grasp, her endless clew,
And learn by each discovery how to wait;
To widen knowledge and escape the praise;
Wisely to teach, because more wise to learn;
To toil for Science, not to draw men's gaze,
But for her lore of self-denial stern;
That such a man could spring from our decays
Fans the soul's nobler faith until it burn.

JAMES RUSSELL LOWELL.

The first meeting of the Society in the autumn was held on October 7th. There were one hundred and fourteen persons present, many of whom had come expressly to testify their great respect and regard for the memory of Dr. Jeffries Wyman, whose death had occurred on the fourth day of the previous month. The President addressed the members as follows:

After our usual summer vacation we meet together with more than accustomed emotion; for mixed with the joy of greeting one another after separation, there is a consciousness of irreparable loss that weighs heavily upon our spirits, a recognition that there have gone away from us a force and a virtue which have so long been a help and inspiration, that we cannot but feel a sense of bereavement such as no words of mine can adequately express. Sad indeed is it for us and for all, that such nobleness of nature, such wealth of acquired knowledge, such purity and simplicity of life, as were manifested in JEFFRIES WYMAN, should pass from the world; for rare, too rare, are to be found examples of such exalted character and attainments.

To our Society Professor Wyman was a great benefactor; not in the sense of a donor especially, but in the higher sense of one imparting to it such honorable fame as enhanced greatly respect for it, both at home and abroad. To him also was the Society mainly indebted for the interest shown in our work by the late Dr. Walker, and which led directly to its large endowment with means of success.

But pleasant as it would be for me, as a personal friend, to dwell upon the transcendent virtues of one whom I have always regarded with the highest respect and most affectionate esteem, I feel it would be unbecoming to further occupy your time in view of those present, who have come here with their tributes of love to the memory of our dear departed friend. I therefore close by inviting others to address you, first calling upon Dr. Asa Gray, who, from his great regard for Professor Wyman has kindly prepared a notice of his life and work to read on this occasion.

Dr. Gray said: —

When we think of the associate and friend whose death this Society now deplores, and remember how modest and retiring he was, how averse to laudation and reticent of words, we feel it becoming to speak of him, now that he has gone, with much of the reserve which would be imposed upon us if he were living. Yet his own perfect truthfulness and nice sense of justice, and the benefit to be derived from the contemplation of such a character by way of example, may be our warrant for reasonable freedom in the expression of our judgments and our sentiments, taking care to avoid all exaggeration.

Appropriate and sincere eulogies and expressions of loss, both official and personal, have, however, already been pronounced or published; and among them one from the governors of that institution to which, together with our own Society, most of Professor Wyman's official life and services were devoted,—which appears to me to delineate in the fewest words the truest outlines of his character. In it the President and Fellows of Harvard University "recall with affectionate respect and admiration the sagacity, patience and rectitude which characterized all his scientific work, his clearness, accuracy and conciseness as a writer and teacher, and the industry and zeal with which he labored upon the two admirable collections which remain as monuments of his rare knowledge, method and skill. They commend to the young men of the University this signal example of a character modest, tranquil, dignified and independent, and of a life simple, contented and honored."

What more can be or need be said? It is left for me, in compliance with your invitation, Mr. President, to say something of what he was to us, and has done for us, and to put upon record, for the use of those who come after us, some account of his uneventful life, some notice, however imperfect, of his work and his writings. I could not do this without the help of friends who knew him well in early life, and of some of you who are much more conversant than I am with most of his researches. Such aid, promptly rendered, has been thankfully accepted and freely used.

Our associate's father, Dr. Rufus Wyman,—born in Woburn, graduated at Harvard College in 1799, and in the latter part of his life Physician to the McLean Asylum for the Insane,—was a man of marked ability and ingenuity. Called to the charge of this earliest institution of the kind in New England at its beginning, he organized the plan of treatment and devised the excellent mechanical arrangements which have since been developed, and introduced into other establishments of the kind. His mother was Ann Morrill, daughter of James Morrill, a Boston merchant. This name is continued, and is familiar to us, in that of our associate's elder brother.

Jeffries Wyman, the third son, derived his baptismal name from the distinguished Dr. John Jeffries, of Boston, under whom his father studied medicine. He was born on the 11th of August, 1814, at Chelmsford, a township of a few hundred inhabitants in Middlesex Co., Mass., not far from the present city of Lowell. As his father took up his residence at the McLean Asylum in 1818, when Jeffries was only four years old, he received the rudiments of his education at Charlestown, in a private school; but afterwards went to the Academy at Chelmsford, and, in 1826, to Phillips Exeter Academy, where, under the instruction of Dr. Abbot, he was prepared for college. He entered

Harvard College in 1829, the year in which Josiah Quincy took the presidency, and was graduated in 1833, in a class of fifty-six, six of whom became professors in the University. He was not remarkable for general scholarship, but was fond of chemistry, and his preference for anatomical studies was already developed. Some of his class-mates remember the interest which was excited among them by a skeleton which he made of a mammoth bull-frog from Fresh Pond, probably one which is still preserved in his museum of comparative anatomy. His skill and taste in drawing, which he turned to such excellent account in his investigations and in the lecture room, as well as his habit of close observation of natural objects met with in his strolls, were manifested even in boyhood.

An attack of pneumonia during his senior year in college caused much anxiety, and perhaps laid the foundation of the pulmonary affection which burdened and finally shortened his life. To recover from the effects of the attack, and to guard against its return, he made in the winter of 1833–34, the first of those pilgrimages to the coast of the Southern States, which in later years were so often repeated. Returning with strength renewed in the course of the following spring, he began the study of medicine under Dr. John C. Dalton, who had succeeded to his father's practice at Chelmsford, but who soon removed to the adjacent and thriving town of Lowell. Here, and with his father at the McLean Asylum, and at the Medical College in Boston, he passed two years of profitable study. At the commencement of the third year he was elected house-student in the Medical Department, at the Massachusetts General Hospital,—then under the charge of Doctors James Jackson, John Ware and Walter Channing—a responsible position, not only most advantageous for the study of disease, but well adapted to sharpen a young man's power of observation.

In 1837, after receiving the degree of Doctor of Medicine, he cast about among the larger country towns for a field in which to practice his profession. Fortunately for science he found no opening to his mind; so he took an office in Boston, on Washington Street, and accepted the honorable, but far from lucrative post of Demonstrator of Anatomy under Dr. John C. Warren, the Hersey Professor. His means were very slender, and his life abstemious to the verge of privation; for he was unwilling to burden his father, who, indeed, had done all he could in providing for the education of two sons. It may be interesting to know that, to eke out his subsistence, he became at this time a member of the Boston Fire Department, under an appointment of Samuel A. Eliot, Mayor, dated Sept. 1st, 1838. He was assigned to Engine No. 18. The rule was that the first-comer to the engine house should bear the lantern, and be absolved from other work. Wyman lived near by, and his promptitude generally saved him from all severer labor than that of enlightening his company.

The turning point in his life, i. e., an opportunity which he could seize of devoting it to science, came when Mr. John A. Lowell offered him the curatorship of the Lowell Institute, just brought into operation, and a course of lectures in it. He delivered his course of twelve lectures upon Comparative Anatomy and Physiology in the winter of 1840–41; and with the money earned by this first essay in instructing others, he went to Europe to seek further instruction for himself. He reached Paris in May, 1841, and gave his time at once to Human Anatomy at the School of Medicine, and Comparative Anatomy and Natural History at the Garden of Plants, attending the lectures of Flourens, Majendie, and

Longet on Physiology, and of de Blainville, Isidore St. Hilaire, Valenciennes, Duméril, and Milne-Edwards on Zoölogy and Comparative Anatomy. In the summer, when the lectures were over, he made a pedestrian journey along the banks of the Loire, and another along the Rhine, returning through Belgium, and by steamer to London. There, while engaged in the study of the Hunterian collections at the Royal College of Surgeons, he received information of the alarming illness of his father; he immediately turned his face homeward, but on reaching Halifax he learned that his father was no more.

He resumed his residence in Boston, and devoted himself mainly to scientific work, under circumstances of no small discouragement. But in 1843 the means of a modest professional livelihood came to him in the offer of the chair of Anatomy and Physiology in the medical department of Hampden-Sydney College, established at Richmond, Virginia. One advantage of this position was that it did not interrupt his residence in Boston except for the winter and spring; and during these months the milder climate of Richmond was even then desirable. He discharged the duties of the chair most acceptably for five sessions, until, in 1847, he was appointed to succeed Dr. Warren as Hersey Professor of Anatomy in Harvard College, the Parkman professorship in the Medical School in Boston being filled by the present incumbent, Dr. Holmes. Thus commenced Prof. Wyman's most useful and honorable connection as a teacher with the University, of which the President and Fellows speak in the terms I have already recited. He began his work in Holden Chapel, the upper floor being the lecture-room, the lower containing the dissecting room and the anatomical museum of the College, with which he combined his own collections and preparations, which from that time forward increased rapidly in number and value under his industrious and skillful hands. At length Boylston Hall was built for the anatomical and the chemical departments, and the museum, lecture and working-rooms were established commodiously in their present quarters; and Prof. Wyman's department assumed the rank and the importance which it deserved. Both human and comparative anatomy were taught to special pupils, some of whom have proved themselves worthy of their honored master, while the annual courses of lectures and lessons on Anatomy, Physiology, and for a time the principles of Zoölogy, imparted highly valued instruction to undergraduates and others.

In the formation and perfecting of his museum — the first of the kind in the country, arranged upon a plan both physiological and morphological — no pains and labors were spared, and long and arduous journeys and voyages were made to contribute to its riches. In the summer of 1849,— having replenished his frugal means with the proceeds of a second course of lectures before the Lowell Institute (viz:, upon Comparative Physiology, a good condensed short-hand report of which was published at the time),— he accompanied Captain Atwood of Provincetown, in a small sloop, upon a fishing voyage high up the coast of Labrador; in the winter of 1852, going to Florida for his health, he began his fruitful series of explorations and collections in that interesting district. In 1854, accompanied by his wife, he travelled extensively in Europe, and visited all the museums within his reach. In the spring of 1856, with his pupils, Green and Bancroft, as companions and assistants, he sailed to Surinam, penetrated far into the interior in canoes, made important researches upon the ground, and enriched his museum with some of its most interesting collections. These came near being too dearly bought, as he and his companions took the fever of the country, from which he suffered severely, and recovered slowly. Again, in 1858–9, accepting the thoughtful and generous invitation of Capt. J. M. Forbes, he made a voyage to the La Plata, ascended the Uraguay and the Parana in a small iron steamer which Captain Forbes brought upon the deck of his vessel; then, with his friend George Augustus Peabody as a companion, he crossed the pampas to Mendosa, and the Cordilleras to Santiago and Valparaiso, whence he came home by way of the Peruvian coast and the Isthmus.

By such expeditions many of the choice materials of his museum and of his researches were gathered, at his own expense, to be carefully prepared and elaborated by his own unaided hands. A vast neighboring museum is a splendid example of what munificence, called forth by personal enthusiasm, may accomplish. In Dr. Wyman's we have an example of what one man may do unaided, with feeble health and feebler means, by persistent and well-directed industry, without eclât, and almost without observation. While we duly honor those who of their abundance cast their gifts into the treasury of science, let us not — now that he cannot be pained by our praise — forget to honor one who in silence and penury cast in more than they all.

Of penury in a literal sense we may not speak; for although Prof. Wyman's salary, derived from the Hersey endowment, was slender indeed, he adapted his wants to his means, foregoing neither his independence nor his scientific work; and I suppose no one ever heard him complain. In 1856 came unexpected and honorable aid from two old friends of his father who appreciated the son, and wished him to go on with his scientific work without distraction. One of them, the late Dr. William J. Walker, sent him ten thousand dollars outright; the other, the late Thomas Lee, who had helped in his early education, supplemented the endowment of the Hersey professorship with an equal sum, stipulating that the income thereof should be paid to Prof. Wyman during life, whether he held the chair or not. Seldom, if ever, has a moderate sum produced a greater benefit.

Throughout the later years of Prof. Wyman's life, a new museum has claimed his interest and care, and is indebted to him for much of its value and promise. In 1866, when failing strength demanded a respite from oral teaching, and required him to pass most of the season for it in a milder climate, he was named by the late George Peabody one of the seven trustees of the Museum and Professorship of American Archaeology and Ethnology, which this philanthropist proceeded to found in Harvard University; and his associates called upon him to take charge of the establishment. For this he was peculiarly fitted by all his previous studies, and by his predilection for ethnological inquiries. These had already engaged his attention, and to this class of subjects he was thereafter mainly devoted,— with what sagacity, consummate skill, untiring diligence and success, his seven annual Reports — the last published just before he died,— his elaborate memoir on shell-heaps, now printing, and especially the Archaeological Museum in Boylston Hall, abundantly testify. If this museum be a worthy memorial of the founders liberality and foresight, it is no less a monument of Wyman's rare ability and devotion. Whenever the enduring building which is to receive it shall be erected, surely the name of its first curator and organizer should be inscribed, along with that of the founder, over its portal.

Of Prof. Wyman's domestic life, let it here suffice to record, that in Dec., 1850, he married Adeline Wheelwright, who died in June 1855, leaving two daughters; that in

August, 1861, he married Anna Williams Whitney, who died in February, 1864, shortly after the birth of an only and a surviving son.

Of his later days, of the slow, yet all too rapid progress of fatal pulmonary disease, it is needless to protract the story. Winter after winter, as he exchanged our bleak climate for that of Florida, we could only hope that he might return. Spring after spring he came back to us invigorated, thanks to the bland air and the open life in boat and tent, which acted like a charm;—thanks, too, to the watchful care of his attached friend, Mr. Peabody, his constant companion in Florida life. One winter was passed in Europe, partly in reference to the Archæological Museum, partly in hope of better health; but no benefit was received. The past winter in Florida produced the usual amelioration, and the amount of work which Dr. Wyman undertook and accomplished last summer might have tasked a robust man. There were important accessions to the archæological collections, upon which much labor, very trying to ordinary patience, had to be expended. And in the last interview I had with him, he told me that he had gone through his own museum of comparative anatomy, which had somewhat suffered in consequence of the alterations in Boylston Hall, and had put the whole into perfect order. It was late in August when he left Cambridge for his usual visit to the White Mountain region, by which he avoided the autumnal catarrh; and there, at Bethlehem, New Hampshire, on the 4th of September, a severe hemorrhage from the lungs suddenly closed his valuable life.

Let us turn to his relations with this Society. He entered it in October, 1837, just thirty-seven years ago, and shortly after he had taken his degree of Doctor in Medicine. He was Recording Secretary from 1839 to 1841; Curator of Ichthyology and Herpetology from 1841 to 1847, of Herpetology from 1847 to 1855, of Comparative Anatomy from 1855 to 1874. While in these latter years his duties may have been almost nominal, it should be remembered that in the earlier days a curator not only took charge of his portion of the Museum, but in a great degree created it. Then for fourteen years, from 1856 to 1870, he was the President of this Society, as assiduous in all its duties as he was wise in council; and he resigned the chair which he so long adorned and dignified only when the increasing delicacy of his health, to which night-exposure was prejudicial, made it unsafe for him any longer to undertake its duties. The record shows that he has made here one hundred and five scientific communications, several of them very important papers, every one of some positive value; for you all know that Prof. Wyman never spoke or wrote except to a direct purpose, and because there was something which it was worth while to communicate. He bore his part also in the American Academy of Arts and Sciences, of which he was a Fellow from the year 1843, and for many years a Councillor. To it he made a good number of communications; among them one of the longest and ablest of his memoirs.

Dr. Gray then went on to give a brief account of Prof. Wyman's scientific work, as recorded in his published papers which have appeared in the Journal and Proceedings of this Society, in the Proceedings of the American Academy, in the Boston Medical Journal, in Silliman's Journal and in the Smithsonian Contributions. Of several of them he presented interesting analyses which may be found in the published records of the meeting. After notice of what he had done Dr. Gray continued his remarks as follows:

The thought that fills our minds upon a survey even so incomplete as this is: How much he did, how well he did it all, and how simply and quietly! We know that our associate, though never hurried, was never idle, and that his great repose of manner covered a sustained energy; but I suspect that none of us, without searching out and collecting his published papers, had adequately estimated their number and their value. There is nothing forth-putting about them, nothing adventitious, never even a phrase to herald a matter which he deemed important.

His work as a teacher was of the same quality. He was one of the best lecturers I ever heard, although, and partly because, he was the most unpretending. You never thought of the speaker, nor of the gifts and acquisitions which such clear exposition were calling forth,—only of what he was simply telling and showing you. Then to those who, like his pupils and friends, were in personal contact with him, there was the added charm of a most serene and sweet temper. He was truthful and conscientious to the very core. His perfect freedom, in lectures as well as in writing, and no less so in daily conversation, from all exaggeration, false perspective, and factitious adornment, was the natural expression of his innate modesty and refined taste, and also of his reverence for the exact truth.

Respecting the views of Jeffries Wyman upon the subject that has most deeply moved the minds of profound thinkers in our day, Dr. Gray remarked:

In these days it is sure to be asked how an anatomist, physiologist, and morphologist like Prof. Wyman regarded the most remarkable scientific movement of his time, the revival and apparent prevalence of doctrines of evolution. As might be expected, he was neither an advocate nor an opponent. He was not one of those persons who quickly make up their minds, and announce their opinions with a confidence inversely proportionate to their knowledge. He could consider long, and hold his judgment in suspense.

And further on he adds:

Upon one point Wyman was clear from the beginning. He did not wait until evolutionary doctrines were about to prevail, before he judged them to be essentially philosophical and healthful, "in accordance with the order of Nature, as commonly manifested in her works," and that they need not disturb the foundations of natural theology.

Perhaps none of us can be trusted to judge of such a question impartially, upon the bare merits of the case; but Wyman's judgment was as free from bias as that of any one I ever knew. Not at all, however, in this case from indifference or unconcern. He was not only, philosophically, a convinced theist, in all hours and under all "variations of mood and tense," but personally a devout man, an habitual and reverent attendant upon Christian worship and ministrations.

Those of us who attended his funeral must have felt the appropriateness for the occasion of the words which were there read from the Psalmist:—

"The Heavens declare the glory of God, and the firmament showeth his handy-work. . . . . . O Lord, how manifold are thy works! In wisdom hast thou made them all; the earth is full of thy riches; so is this great and wide sea, wherein are things creeping innumerable, both great and small beasts. Thou sendest forth thy spirit, they are created, and thou renewest the face of the earth."

These are the works which our associate loved to investigate, and this the spirit in which he contemplated them. Not less apposite were the Beatitudes that followed :—
Blessed are the meek; blessed are the peace-makers; blessed are the merciful; blessed are the pure in heart.
Those who knew him best, best know how well he exemplified them.

Upon the conclusion of the address of Dr. Gray, Mr. F. W. Putnam offered the following Resolutions :—

"*Resolved*, That in the death of Jeffries Wyman the Boston Society of Natural History mourns the loss of a most honored member and efficient officer; one who was untiring in his labors for the Society during his long and active connection with it as Curator, Secretary and President; and that, in his death, Science has lost a most thorough and careful investigator, and the cause of education and truth a most devoted and conscientious disciple.

"*Resolved*, That as members of a Society who gave to Professor Wyman the highest honor and position we could bestow, we acknowledge our indebtedness to him for the thoughtfulness and care with which he guided our labors for so many years, and, while filled with sorrow at our own loss, we ask the privilege, by transmission of these resolutions, of extending our sympathy to his bereaved family in their great trial."

These resolutions were seconded by Dr. D. H. Storer, who said :—

Mr. President, I most cordially second the adoption of the resolutions which have been presented. The scientific reputation of our departed friend was universally acknowledged, but the beauty of his life was equally worthy of admiration. I never knew a gentler purer, nobler spirit. As a brother I loved him, and I mourn him.

The Resolutions were unanimously adopted.

The following letter from Prof. Rogers was then read :

Newport, Oct. 6, 1874.

To President Bouvé,

My dear friend:—I regret that it will not be in my power to attend the meeting of the Natural History Society to-morrow evening, as I should greatly desire to unite with you in an affectionate tribute to the memory of Prof. Wyman, whose long services as President of the Society, and whose peculiar excellences as a student of nature must ever claim our regard and admiration.

From my first acquaintance with him, while engaged in the delicate microscopic dissections with which he illustrated the work of the late Dr. Amos Binney on Land-shells, until within a few years past, I have had frequent opportunities of marking his scientific progress; and although but little acquainted with the inquiries to which he chiefly devoted himself, I have understood enough of his labors to appreciate his singular patience and accuracy as an observer, his ingenuity in devising experiments, and the caution and conscientiousness with which he was accustomed to report the results of his investigations.

These qualities, early recognized by his scientific co-workers abroad as well as at home, placed him in the front rank of the promoters of the biological sciences. To these intel-

lectual gifts were added a modesty and self-forgetfulness which, while they were unfavorable to the more popular recognition of his merits, have rendered his example preëminently worthy of imitation by all honest seekers after truth. Yours faithfully,
                                                                WILLIAM B. ROGERS.

In October the President received a letter from Miss Susan Wyman, Administratrix, stating that the will of her father, Dr. Jeffries Wyman, had an item reading: "I offer to the Boston Society of Natural History my collection of Comparative Anatomy, they paying therefor the sum of three thousand dollars." After considerable discussion it was voted to refer the matter to a committee appointed by the Chair. Dr. B. Joy Jeffries, Dr. T. M. Brewer, and Mr. Chas. J. Sprague, composed this committee. In November, the committee on the bequest reported recommending the Council to accept the offer made in the will, and also, in consequence of the increased value of the collection, to pay $5000 instead of $3000.

Much discussion followed, it being suggested that possibly there might be facts not yet before the Council concerning the later wishes of Dr. Wyman in regard to the disposal of the collection which might influence action. A decision upon the matter was therefore further postponed, and the President was requested to confer with Dr. Morrill Wyman, and to report the result to the Council two days later. This he did at a large meeting of that body, there being twenty-one members present. Much more discussion followed, some members thinking the expense too great for the Society to incur, others that the wish of the late President as expressed in the will should be respected even at some sacrifice. None objected to increasing the amount to $5000 provided the collection was received.

It was finally voted to accept the offer made in the will, and also in consequence of the increased value of the collection since the execution of that instrument, that $2000 additional be paid. Drs. Dwight and White were appointed a committee to take all necessary action to remove the collection and have cases prepared for its reception.

1875. The Report of the Custodian at the annual meeting in May, was as usual full of interest to the members. Respecting the work in the building for the protection of the collections yet in progress, he stated "that such as had been proposed to be done within the year has been completed. More than half the cases are now secured against the entrance of dust and insects, and the most valuable preparations can be safely trusted to their protection. If any member of the Society will take the trouble to walk through our rooms, he will easily satisfy himself of the necessity of these changes. The condition of the collections which still remain in the old cases, whose loose doors cannot be secured either against dust or insects, show this very plainly. The tables in the Palaeontological and Conchological collections, though but recently completed, are more or less disfigured by dust, and where more perishable specimens exist, as among birds and mammals, the amount of damage done will in a few years be irretrievable."

Much work had been done upon the collections during the year. Mr. Emerton had been occupied in removing those of the Geological department, and also the sponges, corals and echinoderms.

The minerals had been rearranged by the President, so as to make a most attractive display in the newly furnished room at the right of the main entrance. In the gallery of this room he had placed a special collection of New England species.

The Eser Palaeontological collection, presented by Mr. John Cummings, had been thoroughly revised by Mr. Crosby, and was being mounted for exhibition by Miss Carter, whose efficient services to the Society were due to the generosity of Mr. Cummings. Mr. Crosby had been also engaged upon the American fossils, and they were being mounted by Miss Washburn, for whose desirable assistance the Society had been likewise indebted to Mr. Cummings.

During the summer of the past year, the Custodian, assisted by Mr. Rathbun, worked for the U. S. Fish Commissioners under the charge of Prof. S. F. Baird, to whom the Society was indebted for the ample opportunities given the Custodian and his assistant for collecting. The valuable additions thus made to our New England collection had been revised and placed in complete order.

The Custodian, in mentioning some work done in preparing models illustrating some of the living forms of the Mollusca, remarked that the experiment had shown the practicability of rendering our collections useful as a means of conveying accurate knowledge to general students, teachers and the public, and he strongly deplored the insufficiency of funds in every department of the Museum, necessary to this being done, except in that of Conchology, which the bequest of Miss Pratt provides for.

The Teachers' School of Science had been resumed with good results, Mr. Cummings liberally furnishing the means. A course of about thirty lessons on Minerals had been given by Mr. L. S. Burbank of Lowell, and the usual plan of presenting specimens used at the lectures had been followed. In order to test the practical results of these gifts, enquiries were made which resulted in showing that in as many as fifty instances the specimens were being intelligently employed in the instruction of students of the teachers.

The Society may therefore congratulate itself upon being the birthplace of the first practicable movement for introducing the study of the natural sciences into the public schools of Boston.

The Botanical collection had received daily attention from Mr. Cummings, and had been much improved by his own work and that of Miss Carter. A beautiful as well as valuable addition to this department had been made by Mr. Edward T. Bouvé, consisting of the preparations of the leaves and stems of New England trees and shrubs pressed under panes of glass so that they can be readily studied without injury to the specimens. These were accompanied by other specimens of the wood and bark of each species. When completed, as it will be as rapidly as possible, this collection will occupy a prominent place among the New England plants.

Among the donations worthy of mention was one of birds, shells and insects, received as a bequest from the family of a deceased fellow-member, Mr. F. P. Atkinson. Although very young, Mr. Atkinson had already shown much interest in the study of natural history, and had attracted the friendly attention of many of the members of the Society, who deeply regretted his early death.

The evening lectures given from the Lowell fund by the Trustee, Mr. John Amory Lowell, consisted of four courses, and in all twenty lectures. Six were upon the "Chemistry of the Waters," by Dr. T. Sterry Hunt; six upon "Injurious Fungi," by Dr. W. G. Farlow; six upon "American Archæology," by Mr. F. W. Putnam; and two upon the "Village Indians of New Mexico," by Mr. Ernest Ingersoll.

There had been eighteen general meetings with an average attendance of fifty-four persons, five of the section of Microscopy with an average attendance of eight persons and six of the section of Entomology, with an average of seven persons. On two occasions one hundred and fourteen persons had been present at the general meetings. One Honorary, four Corresponding and thirty-seven Resident Members, had been elected; seventy-five communications had been presented.

Of the Publications, two quarterly parts each of volumes sixteen and seventeen of the Proceedings, and four articles of the Memoirs had been published.

The additions to the Library had been 297 volumes, 820 parts of volumes, 261 pamphlets, and 19 maps and charts.

The Treasurer's Report showed an excess of receipts over ordinary expenditures of $248.81. There had been besides extraordinary expenses, viz.: for alterations in Museum and cases, $10,689.01, and for the Wyman Collection, $5,000, making a total of $15,689.01.

The changes made in the officers, consisted in the resignations of William H. Niles from the Committee of Palaeontology, J. H. Emerton from the Committee on Mammals, A. S. Packard, Jr., and A. E. Verrill from the Committee on Radiates, Crustacea and Worms, and the election of Dr. H. A. Hagen on the last mentioned Committee.

Walker Prizes. The subject proposed for competitive essays for this year was "Protective coloration in any class or classes of animals." No article was presented in response, or none deemed worthy of a prize.

In May, the Council of the Society, recognizing the importance of the zoölogical and botanical observations made by the U. S. Signal Service Bureau, passed resolutions expressing its interest in the continuance of such observations and their extension, as being of great value, affording as they do, data for important generalizations respecting not only the migrations of birds and the relation of their movements to atmospheric changes; but also respecting the influence of great extremes of temperature, the lateness or forwardness of the season, etc., upon the development and maturation of useful and other plants and the increase or decrease of insect pests; thus possessing not only scientific importance but as likely to lead to valuable practical results, especially in relation to agriculture.

In view of these considerations and of the fact that such observations are beyond the power of private individuals to make, the Council deemed a special appropriation a wise expenditure of the public money.

Resolutions expressing the above were transmitted to General Albert J. Meyer, Chief of the Signal Service Bureau.

A little incident in May was too expressive of the feelings existing on the part of the members towards one of their number to be passed over without mention. Prof. William B. Rogers, who had not for a long period, by reason of illness, been able to attend the meetings of the Society, was present, prepared to offer a communication. Upon the President's introducing him with a few appropriate words of welcome, there immediately followed such hearty plaudits from all the members as could not fail to testify how great the respect and warm the love felt by them for their distinguished associate.

In October of this year, through the bequests of Mr. and Mrs. C. S. Hale of Burlington, New Jersey, the Society came into the possession of a considerable collection of

Cretaceous and Tertiary fossils, including series of the Vertebrae of the Zeuglodon and of the Mosasaurus.

Mr. Hale upon a visit to Boston, many years ago, visited the rooms of the Society, then in Mason street, and was so much gratified with what he saw of the arrangement of the cabinet, and of the care taken to exhibit the specimens to the best advantage, that he proffered to send bones of the Zeuglodon which he had obtained himself in Alabama, and place them in the Society's collection, intimating that they might afterwards be presented. They being received were properly placed for examination, duly labelled, and designated as deposited by him. These were the vertebrae mentioned as included in the bequest. The specimens received numbered about two thousand, of which over one thousand were catalogued and placed in the Cabinet. The others were put aside for exchange. Besides the fossils there were several books upon natural history received, also bequeathed to the Society.

The painting of Prof. Agassiz by Mrs. C. V. Hamilton, which has since been conspicuous among the portraits possessed by the Society, was purchased by the subscription of several of the members.

1876. The writer of these pages has not found it consistent with his feelings to often make personal reference to his own part in the proceedings of the Society. To avoid doing so altogether would be manifestly unjust to those who have been his supporters during his long service as chief executive officer, and to the reader who asks for truth and not its obscuration. An event occurred at the meeting prior to that of the annual election which can not be passed over in silence with due regard to others than himself, and it may be added with justice to his own feelings of gratitude for some of the happiest moments of his official life. He had determined to resign the position he held, really desiring relief from responsibility, and fully satisfied that the Society would suffer no detriment from a change. To his surprise he was called upon at his house prior to the meeting by one of the most honored members, the President of another institution, who, speaking for himself and others, urged that the resignation should not be tendered. The writer had, however, too long considered the matter to readily yield, and went to the meeting firm in purpose to do as he had proposed. To his greater surprise he found there not only a very unusual number of members, but many who had not been in the habit of attending. What was read as a valedictory was listened to with great attention, after which a call to proceed to the business of the meeting was made. Instead of responding to this call, one after another of those whom the writer most respected, addressed him in such terms of affectionate remonstrance against his resignation, as to induce him not only to withdraw it, but to feel that henceforth what had been regarded as a burden would be a joy, that the performance of the duties of his office would be sweetened as never before by the recognition that the respect and regard which he felt towards all the members were fully reciprocated by them.

The very laudatory remarks made by the Custodian upon this matter the writer cannot present here. He does not feel at liberty to refrain from giving one paragraph from his Report.

"An event, which in its results was very satisfactory to the officers of this Society, occurred at the meeting when the President offered his resignation. I allude to the approbation of the policy which had governed the Society during his presidency, expressed by many of our most influential members. The officers of the Society felt themselves to be identified with the President in this matter; and consequently, the ovation which he received, and the absolutely unanimous vote of a large and select meeting of the Society, requesting him to withdraw his resignation, were peculiarly grateful to them."

At the annual meeting in May, very important alterations were made in the Constitution and By-laws, which were primarily suggested by the desire on the part of many that women should be eligible as members of the Society. Others objected to this, partly because of the necessity that sometimes arose to speak upon matters not appropriate to discuss in the presence of ladies. Independently of considerations affecting the admission of women, a large number favored the creation of a new grade of members, to be known as Associate Members, who should be admitted to its meetings and take part in scientific discussions, but who should not be entitled to vote for the officers of the Society, or participate in its business management. All those hitherto known as Resident Members to constitute a higher grade to be known as Corporate Members. New admissions to this grade only to be by election from Associate Members of at least a year's standing and who either were professionally engaged in science, or had aided in its advancement.

The views of those favoring an additional grade of members finally prevailed. They had been embodied in the proposed alterations to the Constitution, and the amendments had received the requisite three fourths vote of the members present at two consecutive meetings. They were finally adopted by a nearly unanimous vote. In the proposed alteration of the By-laws made, the article relating to the election of Corporate Members had been made to express, by a vote of the Society at the previous meeting, that only male Associate Members should be chosen. When final action was called for, Mr. Cummings moved that the word male be omitted. After much discussion the motion prevailed by a vote of forty-eight to twenty. The amendments to the By-laws were then adopted.

Thus after much deliberation and warm discussion, the Society finally by decisive action ceased to make any sexual discrimination in the admission of members.

At the election of officers no changes were made, all serving the previous year having been reëlected.

The report of the Custodian was as usual full of interest to the members. Of the Mineralogical collection, it was said that accessions had been made by the purchase of some desirable specimens from the Jackson collection and that there were in all belonging to the department 3230 trays and single specimens on exhibition, 347 of which were in the New England collection.

In referring to the Botanical collection, it was stated that the New England collection of specimens had been completed, poisoned and catalogued by Miss Carter, and that it contained nearly every species found within the New England States, there being 1984, comprising 3227 specimens. Much work had also been done upon the general collection.

The preparation of the leaves and stems of New England trees and shrubs had been placed on exhibition by the donor, Mr. Edward T. Bouvé, filling, with the accompanying wood sections and specimens of fruit, one entire gallery. With these had been placed a series of plates from the last edition of The Trees and Shrubs of Massachusetts, presented by Mr. George B. Emerson, showing the natural colors of the leaves, flowers and fruit.

Altogether, the Custodian remarked, this collection must be considered one of the most attractive and instructive in the Museum.

The Bailey Microscopical collection had had much labor devoted to it by Miss Washburn, who had spent the greater part of the winter in cataloguing it. Dr. Henry Codman had continued his work upon the Burnett collection of mounted parasites. In the Comparative Anatomy department, Dr. Thomas Dwight had finished the incorporation of the Wyman Anatomical collection with that of the Society, and had prepared many sections showing the structure of bones for the cabinet. There had been an accession of the skeletons of a large sea-lion and of two fur seals, through the liberality of Captain Charles Bryant, the superintendent in charge of the Fur Seal Islands.

A collection of sponges had been acquired by purchase and would form the beginning of a collection of Protozoa. Very valuable though small collections of Australian sponges had been received from Dr. W. G. Farlow and others, making the dried collection of these animals the finest in this country.

The collection of New England Fishes had been considerably enlarged through the facilities afforded the Custodian by the kindness of Prof. S. F. Baird of the U. S. Fish Commission.

In the department of Mollusca, considerable work had been done upon models by the assistants in the Museum, and Dr. Brooks had begun the preparation of an accompanying suite of anatomical preparations for each model. An important addition had been made in the shape of suites of models showing the principal stages in the development of the characteristic types of the Mollusca. Dr. P. P. Carpenter had continued the work of classifying and labelling the shells.

All the Annelids had been reviewed, sorted, and the Entozoa named by the Custodian.

The Insects had received much attention from Mr. Henshaw, who reported that the entire collection was free from Anthreni. To the collection of the Mammalia, a fine Polar bear had been presented by Bishop Williams, the skin of a fine grayhound by Mr. Addison Child and a specimen of the celebrated breed of Ancon sheep by Mr. George William Bond.

The Custodian mentioned that considerable assistance had been received during the year from the voluntary labors of Mr. Edward G. Gardner.

During the year another room had been fitted up with improved cases for the reception of New England fishes, reptiles, birds and mammals, and much had been done in providing for the protection of the Museum against fire. A large service pipe had been introduced, which would give an ample supply of water, and every workroom was provided with screw faucets. One large faucet with hose attached would be always ready in the cellar, and three sets of hose had been distributed about the building for use in any emergency in the work-rooms. On the roof two faucets, one on each wing, had been placed, to which hose could be attached. Buckets of water, with a Johnson pump had also been placed in each workroom, and three patent gas machines in different parts of the building.

The Custodian spoke of continued improvement in the condition and work of the Laboratory under the management of Mr. Crosby. There had been four female students, besides the usual number of students from the Technological Institute.

The Teachers' School of Science had been carried on through the liberality of Mr. Cummings. The statement of the results is given almost verbatim from the Report of the Custodian as follows: Fourteen lectures or practical lessons in Lithology had been given by Mr. L. S. Burbank, during the winter, at which the average attendance had been about 90 out of 100 members. This was a remarkable fact, considering that the class included a large number of the busiest teachers, the masters of the public schools of Boston and the vicinity. Each member of the class was provided with tools, consisting of a small hammer, magnet, file, streak stone of Arkansas quartzite, a bottle of dilute acid with rubber stopper and glass rod, and the scale of hardness previously used in the Mineralogical class of the preceding winter. All these were purchased by the members of the class except the scale of hardness, reserved for future use. One hundred sets of rock specimens were distributed gratis, affording each of the teachers a series. Most of these were large enough for cabinet specimens, and many of the sets had been placed in the collections of the city schools, and used in the instruction of the pupils. The specimens were largely collected in Massachusetts. The course was supplemented by a series of excursions for field work in the vicinity of Boston.

Of the Lowell free lectures given under the direction of the Society by the generosity of John Amory Lowell, Trustee, four courses were given during the winter. These courses consisted of six lectures, by Prof. E. S. Morse, on six New England animals and their nearest allies; six by Prof. G. L. Goodale on Botany; six by Prof. T. Sterry Hunt on Ancient Rocks of North America; and two by Mr. L. S. Burbank on Mineral Veins and Ores. The course on Botany was the best attended, the numbers present averaging 192.

The additions to the Library during the year had been 327 volumes, 1108 parts of volumes, 217 pamphlets and 67 maps and charts.

Of the Publications there had been issued two parts of each of the seventeenth and eighteenth volumes of the Proceedings, and three numbers of the Memoirs. A second volume of the Occasional papers had also been published, of 171 pages and 21 plates.

The Report of the Treasurer exhibited an excess of expenditures over receipts of $522.39.

At the election of officers, L. F. de Pourtalès was chosen on the Committee of Radiates, Crustacea and Worms, and Jules Marcou on the Committee of Palaeontology.

Walker Prizes. The subject for which the annual prizes were offered for this year was "An original investigation of the structure, development, and mode of life of one or more of the fungi which injuriously attack useful plants, such as the potato, the onion, the cranberry, etc., to be prefaced by an exposition of our present knowledge of the structure and development of the lower fungi." No essays were offered on this subject.

At a meeting of the Council in May, a vote was passed, upon the motion of Prof. Shaler, that no existing Council shall formally or informally pledge any part of the Society's income for a future year.

During the summer recess this year, there passed away by death one of the original founders of the Society, Dr. Walter Channing.

Dr. Channing was not only one of the original members of this Society, but he was also one of the founders of the Linnean Society which preceded it. He took an active part in the early formation of both. Upon the organization of the Boston Society of

Natural History, he was elected one of its Curators, and subsequently became one of its second Vice-Presidents. He was born in Newport, R. I., on the 15th of April, 1786. The celebrated Dr. William Ellery Channing was his eldest brother, and Edward T. Channing, who long and ably filled the chair of Rhetoric in Harvard College, was a younger brother. Walter entered Harvard College in 1804, but did not graduate from there, a great rebellion among the students having led to his leaving the institution and devoting himself to the study of medicine in Boston. He afterwards pursued this study with great zeal in the schools of Philadelphia, Edinburgh, and London. In 1812 he established himself in the practice of his profession in Boston, and in the same year was appointed Lecturer in Obstetrics at the Medical College. Three years later he became Professor there of that branch of medical practice, the duties of which position he performed for nearly forty years.

In the practice of his profession Dr. Channing exhibited marked ability, especially in the department to which he gave particular attention. In the reform movements of his day he took great interest, and his pen and voice were very active in advocating them. In social life he was genial, and had the rare gift of being able at all times to interest listeners by the brilliancy of his conversation, enlivened as it ever was by ready wit.

A characteristic anecdote is, that when asked by a stranger who wished to see his more eminent brother, if he was the Dr. Channing who preached, he replied, "No! it is my brother who preaches; I practice."

Dr. Channing died in Brookline, Mass., on the 27th of July, 1876, at the age of 90 years.

In October the attention of the Council being called to the fact that at the meetings of the section of Microscopy the attendance had become very small, a vote was passed to discontinue the notification of them.

Edward Pickering.

At the meeting, December 6th, President Bouvé addressing the members, remarked; "The Society is called to deplore the loss of a valuable member and officer in the death of our late Treasurer, Edward Pickering. Previously to our last meeting, Mr. Pickering had been ill for a day or two from a trouble in his throat affecting the vocal organs, and making it painful for him to converse freely, but he kept about his usual occupations until a few hours before we met, when feeling unable to be with us, he sent to me his regular financial statement for presentation to the Council in the evening. The trouble with him seemed similar to that he had before experienced, and there appeared no reason to anticipate its sad result.

"All, I am sure, were surprised and shocked to learn on the following Tuesday that he had passed away early that morning. Mr. Pickering, though not strictly speaking, a scientific man, was much interested in whatever conduced to the education of the community, and he consequently felt great interest in the well being of the Society. He became a member in 1860, since which, he has always been a regular attendant on our meetings, and I think, from his highly appreciative mind, enjoyed much the proceedings. In 1865, he was elected Treasurer of the Society and he became also ex-officio one of the Trustees, meeting the requirements of these positions with great devotion and efficiency. Our departed friend acquired the high respect of all who knew him, by his general intelligence, his marked integrity, and his faithfulness to all the duties of the various offices he was called upon to fill, and he won the love of all who knew him intimately by his kindly sympathy and his Christian gentleness."

On motion of Messrs. Scudder and Hyatt, it was voted that the Secretary send a copy of Mr. Bouvé's remarks to the family of Mr. Pickering, as an expression of the Society's respect and regard for him.

In December a very fine cast from the bust of Prof. Louis Agassiz, by Preston Powers, was presented to the Society by the Rev. R. C. Waterston.

In Council a vote was passed allowing the use of the Laboratory of the Society to the Boston University for instruction in Zoölogy; the lessons to be given by Mr. Hyatt, as Professor of the Technological Institute, or his assistant Mr. Crosby, and a suitable rent to be paid the Society.

1877. In January of this year, the death of Mr. F. B. Meek of Washington, a Corresponding Member, and one of the most eminent of American palaeontologists, was announced by the Secretary. At the next meeting the following resolutions were passed by the Society.

"*Resolved*, That the members of the Society have heard with the deepest regret of the decease of one of the most highly esteemed of their Corresponding Members, Mr. F. B. Meek of Washington. Their admiration can add but little to his reputation, which is secured by the numerous works of which he has been the author. They feel, however, that a testimonial is due from them to the memory of a man whose knowledge of the whole field of American palaeontology was unsurpassed, and whose life was a model of laborious special investigation and therefore unrewarded by public commendation. As students of natural history, they desire also to record their respect for a life of such modest simplicity and devotion to science for its own sake, that it merits, and will, it is hoped, receive the highest praise from the hands of Mr. Meek's fellow laborers.

"*Resolved*, That this resolution be recorded in the Proceedings of this Society and that copies be forwarded to the friends of the deceased."

At a meeting of the Society February 2d, Charles W. Scudder was elected Treasurer.

In Council a vote was passed to procure a crayon of the late President, Dr. Jeffries Wyman, of life size, with a suitable frame. This was subsequently done, and the fine portrait obtained may now be seen in the Library room of the Museum.

This body also upon hearing that another attempt was to be made to obtain a license for the exhibition of Jourdain's anatomical collection, again successfully remonstrated against one being granted, on the ground that it would be subversive of public morals.

In March, the President announced the death of Mr. Edward Bicknell, the well-known Microscopist, and for several years a member of the Council of the Society.

A petition having been presented to the Council that the Museum of the Society should be opened to the public on Sundays, a committee was appointed to take the matter into consideration and to report upon the subject. This committee consisted of three, the President being of the number. At the next meeting, the committee reported adversely, on the ground mainly that the Society could not afford the additional expense that would be incurred by compliance. The report was approved unanimously.

In March also of this year, Dr. B. Joy Jeffries called the attention of the Society to the necessity of action on the part of the United States Government to prevent accidents by reason of color blindness in the army, navy and merchant service, and the need of the State governments also taking measures to prevent casualties on the railroads from the same cause. Whilst the possible danger arising from color blindness had been mentioned before, this was the first time in this country that the necessity of control on the part of the authorities was brought forward and urged. The action of the government, State and National, and of the railroad corporations since, has proved Dr. Jeffries' position correct.

In April, the Legislature of the State having authorized the licensing of such persons to shoot birds for scientific purposes as the Society might designate, a committee was appointed, consisting of the Custodian, Mr. Hyatt, Dr. Thomas M. Brewer and Mr. J. A. Allen, to issue certificates to such persons as they deemed, upon due enquiry, proper to receive such license.

Many persons desiring admission to the Museum on other days than public days, the Council voted to admit such as the Custodian judged proper, upon the payment of a small entrance fee, to cover such additional expense as might be incurred thereby.

At the annual meeting in May, the reports of the Custodian, and of the Secretary, made in accordance with a new provision in the By-laws, were presented. An abstract from these follows.

During the year one additional room had been fitted up with new cases and brackets, for the reception especially of the birds and mammals of the systematic collection. For further protection against loss by fire, telegraphic communication had been established with the fire engine house on Dartmouth Street by which, in case of necessity, engines could be had for service at the building within a few minutes after giving an alarm.

The Teacers' School of Science was continued, as in previous years, by the liberality of Mr. Cummings. The only course of lessons given, was by Prof. Goodale of Harvard College, but this was a very comprehensive one, comprising twenty-one lectures on Morphological, Physiological and Systematic Botany. The lessons were, as usual, illustrated by specimens which were distributed to the pupils. By the use of blank forms, which were given with the flowers, each teacher was enabled to analyse the specimens independently and record his observations, thus preventing confusion and allowing the instructor to cover more ground than would otherwise have been possible. The analysis of the flowers for the determination of the peculiarities of the floral structure by each teacher, was regarded by Prof. Goodale as an important element in the instruction given. The attendance was large, averaging one hundred.

In the Laboratory much work had been done of a satisfactory character. The collections for the use of students had been largely increased, and it was hoped they might be made complete before another year. The room and the collections had been profitably used by students of the Institute of Technology and of the Boston University.

The condition of the collections was reported to be good, and the progress made in arrangement, labelling, etc., quite satisfactory.

In the Mineral department the only change made was by the addition of new specimens, the greater portion of which had been presented by the President.

In the Palaeontological department under the charge of Mr. Crosby, much had been done by Miss Carter and Miss Washburn, for whose very valuable services the Society was indebted to the generosity of Mr. John Cummings. The former had mounted, catalogued, labelled and placed on exhibition, all the fossils of the Triassic and the Cretaceous periods, together with the larger part of the European Jurassic; whilst the latter had re-arranged, catalogued, and re-labelled all the fossils from the Devonian to the Cretaceous periods inclusive. A great amount of work too had been done in identifying the new specimens; the additions to the collection having been very numerous. The Jurassic, Triassic, and Carboniferous plants of North America had been tripled in number and value by accessions from the Rogers collection, and the Devonian and Cretaceous fossils much increased by additions from the Hale and Cleveland collections.

The Botanical department, under the charge of Mr. Cummings, had received much attention, and great progress had been made in the revision of the general collection by Miss Carter.

The collection of the department of Comparative Anatomy had had much labor bestowed upon it by Mr. Van Vleck. More work was necessary upon this collection than anticipated, and there yet remained much to do before its arrangement would be completed.

The cataloguing of the Microscopical collection had been finished by Miss Washburn early in the year. The whole was reported as consisting of 2606 slides and preparations; of these, 567 were preparations of parasitic insects acquired by purchase from the Burnett estate; 1838 were received in the bequest of Professor Bailey, and consisted largely of foraminiferae and diatoms; 135 were miscellaneous preparations of worms, crustacea and embryos of various kinds, prepared by Mr. J. H. Emerton when assistant in the Museum, and 113 were preparations of the anatomy and skeletons of sponges, prepared by Mr. Crosby and the Custodian. Besides these, there was reported a great quantity of unmounted material. Subsequently to the close of Miss Washburn's work, the collection was enriched by the presentation to it of 477 slides prepared by Mr. William Glen, formerly of the Museum of Comparative Zoölogy of Cambridge. These were purchased and given to the Society by Mr. R. C. Greenleaf and Dr. A. D. Sinclair. This collection was especially rich in sections of the spines of Echini and the tongues of Mollusks. Including this accession and some specimens of miscellaneous character presented by Messrs. E. Samuels, C. S. Busch and others, the Society collection was reported as containing, exclusive of duplicate material, 3356 slides and preparations.

The collection of Corals and Echinoderms was reported as undergoing revision by Mr. Van Vleck, who was likewise preparing the specimens for labelling. The Poriferae were receiving the same attention from the Custodian.

In the Molluscan department valuable work had been continued by Dr. W. K. Brooks upon the models of the animals, anatomical preparations of them, and in explanatory outline drawings. He had also completed the re-arrangement of the shells. Much to the regret of the Society, Dr. Brooks removed to Baltimore, having been appointed assistant professor in the Johns Hopkins University. After his departure the work upon the collection of the Mollusca was continued under the direction of Mr. Van Vleck, who reported that about one third of the specimens on exhibition had been re-labelled by Miss Washburn. Dr. P. P. Carpenter of Montreal had continued the work of identification and had completed a large part of the terrestrial shells.

In the Entomological department Mr. Henshaw had continued his valuable labors. The New England collection of the Coleoptera had been completed, and the Neuroptera, Orthoptera, Hymenoptera and Lepidoptera re-arranged. Very important additions to the collection of Coleoptera had been made from the collection of Mr. Sprague, the late assistant of the Museum. The Society was permitted, in accordance with the verbal request of Mr. Sprague, to select from the specimens left by him all that might be valuable to its collection, and thus additions were made to it of 600 species and 2000 specimens.

A revision of all the New England collections at this time showed them to consist of Hymenoptera, 157 species; Lepidoptera, 711 species; Coleoptera, 1810 species; Orthoptera, 59 species; Neuroptera, 65 species.

To Dr. Hagen the Society was indebted for a revision and identification of all the Neuroptera, and to Mr. Burgess for the revision and identification of the Diptera of the Harris collection. The entire Harris collection had been transferred to the new style of boxes, and was considered safe from the ravages of Anthreni. It is due to Mr. Henshaw to state that he voluntarily gave professional labor in the department of Entomology, equal to about seven hours daily during the year, the means of the Society not enabling it to adequately compensate him for his services.

The alcoholic collection of Reptiles had been sent to the Museum of Comparative Zoölogy for identification by Mr. Garman, who had kindly consented to examine and name them. It was understood too, that under the instruction of Mr. Alexander Agassiz, the director, he would add such species from the duplicates of the Museum as were needed in the collection of the Society. Mr. Garman had already been instrumental in increasing our collection of fishes in the same manner, and the Society had to some extent reciprocated the favor by sparing specimens from its duplicates.

The Custodian closed his remarks upon the collections of the Museum by stating that there was now a New England collection in every department, and that there was a great need of a new gallery around the main hall, which should be devoted exclusively to the New England department, so that a visitor could see arranged in one continuous series all the natural products of New England. It is certainly a matter to be deeply regretted that the Society has not since been able to put up such a gallery as suggested by the Custodian.

From the Secretary's Report, the following is given: to the Library there had been added of volumes, 357; parts of volumes, 977; pamphlets, 188; maps, charts and photographs, 98; making 1620 accessions in all. Nothing had been done in binding for want of the necessary means. The use of the Library seemed to be regularly increasing. During the year 1019 books had been borrowed by 119 persons.

The publications of the Society had been considerably less than during previous years. Two parts, concluding Vol. XVIII, of the Proceedings, had been issued, and the first part of Vol. XIX was in press. Of the Memoirs, the second part of Prof. Hyatt's Revision of North American Poriferae was in press.

The meetings of the Society had been well attended, and the interest in the communications presented well sustained. In consequence of the formation of the Boston Microscopical Society, the section of Microscopy had been given up. The section of Entomology had held monthly meetings, with a small but regular attendance.

The Section of Botany formed within the year had held bi-monthly meetings, and these had been fairly attended.

During the year four Corresponding Members, six Resident, under the old Constitution, and twenty-five Associate Members under the new Constitution, had been elected.

Of the Lowell free courses of lectures, there had been given under the direction of the Society; six on Comparative Embryology, by Dr. Chas. S. Minot; four on North American Archaeology and Ethnology, by F. W. Putnam; three by Maj. J. W. Powell on the Cañons of the Colorado, Indian Life in the Rocky Mountains, and Indian Mythology; six by Prof. N. S. Shaler, on the Geological problems of Boston and its vicinity; and five by S. H. Scudder on the Organization and Metamorphoses of Butterflies. The courses were very interesting and well attended.

From the report of the Treasurer there was an excess of receipts over expenditures of $1081.12, the most of which, however, it was necessary to reserve for Prize purposes in accordance with the conditions of the Walker bequest.

At the election of officers for the ensuing year the only changes made were as follows:

In the department of Microscopy, Samuel Wells was chosen on the Committee, in place of Edwin Bicknell deceased, and in the department of Fishes and Reptiles, S. W. Garman was chosen in place of Richard Bliss, Jr.

It is pleasant to observe the persistent efforts made to prevent the expenditures of the Society from exceeding its income. At the first meeting of the Council, after the annual meeting of the Society, the Trustees reported that after a careful examination of the invested funds, they estimated the income for the year then commencing, applicable to the general purposes of the Society, as not likely to exceed $8500. "To all who are conversant with the state of affairs in the business world," they said, " the estimated reduction from the income of the past year will not be surprising, though most unwelcome. Let us be thankful it is no larger, and by a wise and careful economy endeavor to discharge the manifest duty of keeping our expenditures within the limits of our income." The following appropriations were recommended:

For salaries and wages, $6000; gas and fuel, $400; general expenses, $900; cabinet, $300; publications, $900.

These appropriations allowed of no contingences, but it seemed impossible to lessen any of them.

Walker Prizes. In October of this year the first prize of sixty dollars was awarded to Mr. C. Riley, for his essay upon the subject proposed for this year, viz.: A complete life history of the army worm, Leucania unipunctata, and its parasites.

In November the Laboratory of the Museum was rented to the Technological Institute for a course of thirty lectures, upon the payment of ninety dollars.

1878. In March of this year occurred the death of Dr. Charles Pickering, a greatly respected member of the Society, whose interest in its proceedings had been for many years manifested by constant attendance at the meetings and often by taking part in them. A man of very remarkable scientific acquirements, and of personal character corresponding to his intellectual attainments, he merits more than a passing notice.

Dr. Charles Pickering.

Dr. Charles Pickering was born at Starucca, Susquehanna County, Pennsylvania, November 10th, 1805. His father, Timothy Pickering, Jr., was born in Philadelphia, October 1st, 1779, graduated at Harvard College, entered the navy, served creditably as midshipman under Decatur, and resigned in 1801. His grandfather was Colonel Timothy

Pickering of the Revolutionary Army, a friend of Washington, and a member of his Cabinet. The Colonel had acquired large tracts of "wild land" in western Pennsylvania, and after retiring from the Cabinet, removed thither with his son, whose wife, Mrs. Lurena Pickering, subsequently became the mother of the subject of this notice and his brother Edward.

In the year 1809, Timothy Pickering, Jr. died, and his father afterwards returned to Massachusetts, settling in Wenham, near Salem. He brought with him his son's wife and her two boys, and it was under his supervision and that of their mother, an admirable woman, that they were brought up.

Charles early showed a taste for natural history, roaming about the country in search of birds, eggs, insects, plants and quadrupeds, with specimens of which he would return from his excursions loaded. He entered Harvard College in 1823, but did not graduate with his class, subsequently taking the degree of M. D. at the Medical School in 1826. His love for natural science increased with his years, and while living at Salem, he was associated with William Oakes in botanical investigation, and it is thought that the two first explored the White Mountains together.

He was elected a correspondent of the Academy of Natural Sciences of Philadelphia, November 28th, 1826, in the twenty-second year of his age; and the next year he removed to Philadelphia, and became a member of that Society. The scope of his various scientific attainments, even at that early period of his life, may be estimated from the fact that he served on the Zoölogical Committee for ten years (from December 25th, 1829); on the Botanical Committee for eight years, half this time as chairman; on the Publication Committee four years; on the Library Committee a year; as Librarian five years, and as Curator for four years, discharging all the duties of these several positions with the utmost faithfulness and efficiency.

He prepared a Catalogue of American Plants in the Academy's collection, in 1834, and was intrusted with the transfer of the great collection of plants bequeathed to the Society by Von Schweinitz. His great services in collecting and arranging the extensive herbarium of the Society, merited and received its thanks, presented through a resolution unanimously passed on motion of Prof. Henry D. Rogers. He also was made the recipient of the grateful thanks of the Society on motion of Dr. Samuel George Morton, for his services in selecting from Mr. Maclure's library the 2300 volumes designed for the Academy.

He was elected a member of the American Philosophical Society, January 15th, 1828, having previously (Oct. 19th, 1827), read before this Society his paper "On the Geographical Distribution of Plants." He was a member of the Yale Natural History Society, and read, conjointly with James H. Dana, before that Society the "Description of a Crustaceous Animal, belonging to the genus Caligus, C. Americanus," published in Silliman's Journal, Vol. XXXVIII. He served as Recording Secretary of the Pennsylvania Horticultural Society, from February 1830, till September 1837.

On the organization of the U. S. Exploring Expedition under Lieutenant Charles Wilkes, Dr. Pickering's reputation was such that he was at once selected as chief zoölogist, and placed on board the flagship Vincennes. The expedition sailed from Hampton Roads, Aug. 19th, 1838, and on its return reached Sandy Hook, June 10th, 1842. During the four years' voyage, Dr. Pickering turned his attention to anthropology and to the study of the geological distribution of animals and plants; especially to the latter, as affected by, or as evidence of, the operations, movements and diffusion of the races of man. To the collections and investigations of Dr. Pickering and Professor Dana, the scientific fame of the expedition is principally due.

In October, 1843, Dr. Pickering again went abroad, visiting during his tour Egypt, Arabia, India, and eastern Africa, more particularly for the purpose of verifying observations made while with the Exploring Expedition. On his return he settled in Boston, and occupied himself in preparing his "Races of Man and their Geographical Distribution," published in 1848, being Volume XI, of the Exploring Expedition. In 1850, appeared in the "Edinburgh New Philosophical Journal," his "Enumeration of the Races of Man."

In 1854, his work "The Geographical Distribution of Animals and Plants," was published. This work constituted Volume XV of the Exploring Expedition.

The proceedings of the American Academy of Arts and Sciences, contain the following articles by Dr. Pickering: Observations on the Egyptian Computation of Time, appearing in October, 1849; on the Egyptian Astronomical Cycle, in May, 1850; on Sulphur Vapor, in December, 1856; on the Coptic Alphabet, in March, 1859; on the Geographical Distribution of Species, in March 1859, and December 1860; and on the Jewish Calendar, in October, 1864.

In June, 1867, he prepared a paper "On the Gliddon Mummy case in the Museum of the Smithsonian Institution," published in Volume XVI of the Smithsonian Contributions to Knowledge.

In 1876, was published at Salem the "Geographical Distribution of Animals and Plants; Part II; Plants in their Wild State."

The great work of his life was "The Chronological History of Plants." This truly remarkable production, to which he had devoted sixteen years of indomitable industry and laborious research, was going through the press at his own expense at the time of his death. While the form in which it is cast will prevent its use as a book for popular study, to the thorough student and teacher it must ever be unequalled as an exhaustive authority on the subjects of which it treats.

Dr. Pickering was elected a member of the Boston Society of Natural History, March 3d, 1858. As a member, his attendance upon meetings was constant, and his communications, whether elaborately written out, or merely remarks upon the subject at the time before the Society, were always indicative of thorough knowledge and acquaintance with the matter. The range of his general information was very extensive, and whether he was speaking of Feejean pottery, or rare botanical forms found in the mountains of New England; of the character of the alluvial deposits of South American rivers, or the origin of the Esquimaux; whatever he might have to say was interesting and instructive in a high degree. Most of the present members of the Society will recall his controversy with the late Dr. Thomas M. Brewer, relative to the introduction of the European sparrow, in which Dr. Pickering took very strong ground adversely to the naturalization of the bird, quoting a formidable array of authorities in support of his position, and predicting very undesirable results in case the proposed experiment should be attempted—and prove successful—as to the ability of the sparrow to exist in this climate.

Dr. Pickering, while it could be truly said of him by one of his biographers, that there was probably not a more learned naturalist in the world, was yet one of the most modest of men. His simplicity of character, inflexible integrity, loyalty to truth, tranquillity of temper, and kindly though somewhat reserved disposition, were thoroughly consistent with his great and extremely accurate acquirements, and that love of knowledge which was his grand passion. The following extract from a biographical notice published with his " Chronological History of Plants," speaks thus of him:

" We doubt if any one naturalist ever united in himself so far as he did, the qualities of an exact original observer on the most enlarged scale, and of an inquirer into all that had been learned before. His minute, laborious and extended explorations into all possible records of past ages, seemed of themselves more than enough for the work of a lifetime. * * * He not only visited every quarter of the earth, but went through the whole range of history, wherever it could bear upon his subject, in quest of anything that might help him better to understand " The Races of Man and their Geographical Distribution," " The Geographical Distribution of Animals and Plants," and " The Chronological History of Plants."

Dr. Pickering married in 1851, Sarah S., daughter of the late Daniel Hammond, Esq. He died of pneumonia, in Boston, March 17th, 1878, leaving a widow but no children.

In April the death of Prof. C. F. Hartt, a highly valued Corresponding Member of the Society, was announced. As he was for some time an active member of the Society, it is due to the eminence attained by him as a scientific explorer and investigator, to give some account of the great work achieved by him in the short time of his active life. The sketch here presented is drawn entirely from an elaborate and excellent paper prepared by Mr. Richard Rathbun and published in the nineteenth volume of the Society's Proceedings.

Professor Hartt was born in Fredericton, New Brunswick, August 23d, 1840. He graduated from Acadia College in 1860. At an early age he manifested much interest in the study of natural history, and whilst in college labored zealously in exploring geologically the Province of Nova Scotia, in doing which he made large collections. Subsequently he gave much attention to the study of the rocks in the vicinity of St. John, New Brunswick, and it was by his researches there that he first became extensively known to the scientific world. The discovery there of fossil insects in the Devonian shales, led to Professor Agassiz' knowledge of him, and to his being invited to become a student in the Museum of Comparative Zoölogy, where he passed much time during the succeeding four years, making great progress in science and preparing himself for future usefulness. During this period he made excursions to his native province and to Nova Scotia, making investigations of important character. To him, the scientific world is indebted for very much of the knowledge possessed by it of the ancient strata of New Brunswick. Mr. Hartt was appointed by Professor Agassiz one of the two geologists who accompanied the Thayer expedition to Brazil in 1865, and it was whilst engaged in this service, that he became so much interested in the geology of that empire as to lead to his extensive work there in after years. He made a second trip there in 1867.

In 1868 he was appointed Professor of Natural History in Vassar College, which position he soon resigned to take the head of the department of Geology in Cornell University, which he held until the time of his death.

Whilst at Cornell, when not engaged in the duties of his position, he prepared his report as geologist of the Thayer expedition. This embraced so much of value upon the subject treated, as to lead to its being published in a volume by itself under the title of "The Geology and the Physical Geography of Brazil." It formed a large octavo volume of over six hundred pages.

In 1870, Prof. Hartt organized another expedition to Brazil, taking with him Prof. Prentice and eleven of the students of Cornell University. This party, after exploring in the vicinity of Para, proceeded to the Amazonas where were found the first Devonian fossils east of the Andes in South America. Prof. Hartt soon after made another trip to the Amazonas in company with Mr. O. A. Derby, with important results. He returned to Ithaca in 1872, where he remained from two to three years, giving such time as he could spare to studying up the material obtained in his Amazonian trips, aided by two assistants, Mr. O. A. Derby and Mr. Richard Rathbun, and in preparing papers for publication. These appeared in various scientific journals.

In 1875, the government of Brazil, appreciating the labors of Prof. Hartt, invited him to submit a proposition for the systematic geological exploration of the Empire. He accordingly proceeded to Rio Janeiro, where he was received with great enthusiasm. The suggestions made in his proposition were not fully complied with from economical considerations, which is much to be regretted, considering his early death. In May, 1875, Prof. Hartt was made chief of a commission for the geological survey of Brazil with six assistants, among whom was Mr. Rathbun, also a member of the Boston Society of Natural History. The party was soon in the field, and its active work continued almost uninterruptedly until the close of 1877. The amount of work done during this period was immense, and the investigations made of the most important character. No wonder that the Emperor upon his return from a visit to the Museums of North America and the old world, should have expressed his astonishment when he found that the small party which he had left eighteen months before working hard among the rocks of a portion of the Empire, had created a large Museum containing the collections made, and having connected with it biological, chemical and photographic laboratories.

This brief notice of Professor Hartt will be closed by a few words given in abstract from the paper alluded to, prepared by Mr. Rathbun.

"In order to judge of the real character and value of his investigations, we must refer to his publications. These, however, give us but a glimpse of the vast store of knowledge he had accumulated. He has left a number of volumes in manuscript, which when published, will add greatly to his scientific standing, by making known to the world the variety and excellence of the work he had accomplished. Judging from his brilliant beginning, we are confident in asserting that had he lived, he would have won for himself a place by the side of such investigators as De la Beche, Murchison, Logan and others, like whom, he was a pioneer in the special field of research he had entered."

The reports of the Custodian, Secretary and Treasurer were looked forward to with much interest, the members generally realizing the difficulty of accomplishing the necessary work of the Society within the means at its disposal, without incurring debt or lessening its funded property. When listened to at the annual meeting, they gave great satisfaction, showing as they did much progress in several departments of the Museum, continued growth of the Library, a fair amount of publication, and good attendance at the meetings. It will be borne in mind that the period was one of prolonged business depression, rendering the income from the Society's funds quite uncertain, and that the Council at the beginning of the year had decided to limit the expenditures to the least possible sum consistent with the Society's future welfare. The Custodian commenced his report by deploring that this decision, though necessary, had prevented continued improvement in the cases, and thus arrested work, the accomplishment of which alone could render the collections secure from damage by dust and insects.

From the remarks of the Custodian upon the state of the collections, the following is presented.

The Minerals remained in the good condition of the previous years and had received valuable accessions from the President.

The Palæontological collections had had much labor bestowed upon them by Mr. Crosby, the assistant in the Museum, and by Miss Washburn and Miss Carter, who had aided him in mounting and labelling the specimens. The whole department was stated to be divided into sections according to locality, and collections of it arranged entirely to illustrate the stratigraphical relations of fossils. There were of the North American collection on exhibition, 1040 genera embracing 2034 species, and 7834 specimens. These had been derived from the following sources: Mass. Institute of Technology, 2223; C. S. Hale collection, 1013; Cleveland collection, 627; various, 3971; making a total of 7834.

The most valuable parts of this collection are specimens of Paradoxides from Braintree, embracing the original from the Jackson Cabinet; a fine suite of Crinoids from Mr. J. M. Barnard; the coal plants of the Rogers Cabinet; the fine animal impressions on stone from Turner's Falls; the reptilian bones from the red sandstone of the Connecticut valley, presented by Prof. W. B. Rogers, and the fossils from Attleboro, Mass.

Of the Eser collection of European species, there were on exhibition 1306 genera, embracing 2563 species, and 8809 specimens.

The Botanical department under the charge of Mr. John Cummings had been steadily progressing. Three-fifths of the flowering plants had been revised, and work had only been suspended awaiting the reception of a further number of the "Genera Plantarum." Miss Carter had been engaged much of the time in assorting, condensing and properly arranging duplicates. She had also sorted, mounted and labelled a large and valuable collection of lichens under the direction of Mr. C. J. Sprague, who reported that "this formed the Lichen-herbarium of Dr. Thomas Taylor, an Irish botanist, to whom Sir W. J. and Sir Joseph Hooker communicated the whole of their extensive collections of lichens gathered during many exploring expeditions. Dr. Taylor published descriptions of these plants in the London Journal of Botany, 1844-46, and many of the specimens are the originals of the descriptions. Mr. John Amory Lowell purchased the collection of

Dr. Taylor's heirs, and afterwards presented it to the Society, with the rest of his herbarium.

The knowledge of the structure of lichens has advanced much since Dr. Taylor's day, and the nomenclature has undergone extensive changes, so this herbarium, though containing over a thousand species, might have remained comparatively useless to the American student had it not been for the voluntary services of Prof. Edward T. Tuckerman. He examined and named very nearly the entire series, a work which no one else in this country could have done, and has given it au authentic value, otherwise unattainable.

The decease of Dr. P. P. Carpenter of Montreal, to whom had been intrusted the work of naming the collections of shells, had prevented its final completion. Fortunately for the Society, not much remained undone. At the time of Dr. Carpenter's death, he had in his possession at Montreal a very large portion of the collection belonging to the Museum. The specimens were subsequently received in admirable condition, not one having been lost, and all had been unpacked and arranged in the cabinet by Mr. Van Vleck. Miss Washburn had been engaged in re-mounting, labelling and cataloguing them.

The Systematic collection of Mollusca, consisting of 630 genera, represented by 2600 species and 9000 specimens, had been completed by Mr. Van Vleck, and placed on exhibition.

The alcoholic collections of Reptiles and Batrachians had been in large part revised and named by Mr. Garman of the Museum of Comparative Zoölogy. Considerable additions had been made to them by the kindness of Mr. Garman, who selected from the duplicates of the Museum by permission of Mr. Agassiz, the director, such specimens as were needed for the collection of the Society.

The New England collection of birds had been much increased by donations from various parties, and by exchange. Eighty species had been added, some of which were of great rarity. The donors were Messrs. Weeks, E. A. & O. Bangs, C. B. Corey, F. B Loring, W. B. Greene, H. D. Morse, Wm. Brewster, Arthur Smith, Geo. A. Boardman, and H. O. Ryder.

The Entomological collection had been enriched by valuable donations received from Messrs. Smith, Bryant, Thaxter and Mrs. Möring. Mr. Henshaw's labors in this department had been continued.

To the Anatomical collection a number of preparations had been added by the assistant, Mr. Van Vleck, and by Dr. Thomas, a student in the Museum.

To the collection of Echinoderms had been added a suite of Ophiurans received from the Museum of Comparative Zoölogy. These having been identified and named by Mr. Theodore Lyman, the labelling may be relied upon as correct.

Of the Laboratory, the remarks of the Custodian are presented in full, as they give briefly a good idea of the practical means taken to advance the knowledge of natural history in the community.

"The work in this department has greatly increased. The educational collections, if they continue to be improved at the same rate, will, within a year or two, be entirely completed, with of course, the exception of those rarer preparations and specimens which never seem to be within the reach of moderate means. They embrace typical zoölogical, palaeontological and geological collections, already sufficiently perfect for the ordinary purposes of general instruction.

"The room and the collections have been used by the Institute of Technology for a class in Palaeontology; by the Boston University for a class in Zoölogy and another in Botany; and by the Teachers of Boston, for a class in Zoölogy. This last was composed of the teachers of natural history in the High Schools of Boston, and other teachers, numbering about thirty in all.

"The lessons are necessarily given on Saturday, and are limited to two hours, though the laboratory is open throughout the day for those who wish to remain.

"This course was instituted in order to support the movement made by the School Committee to introduce the teaching of Zoölogy into the High Schools. Miss Crocker, the supervisor having this branch under her charge, applied to the Custodian for assistance, and the Council of the Society assenting, the laboratory and its facilities were placed at her disposal. The course will not be finished until the spring of 1879, and will comprise nearly one hundred lessons, illustrated in the usual way by the study and dissection of specimens. The instruction so far, has consisted of a series of practical lessons, given by Messrs. Crosby and Van Vleck, interspersed with lectures of a more general character, by the Custodian."

The Teachers' School of Science was continued, as in previous years, through the liberality of Mr. John Cummings. One course of twenty lectures was given by Professor Goodale of Harvard University. The teachers were provided with printed synopses of the lectures as aids in taking notes, and with dried and named specimens of native plants. About one hundred and fifty sets of these were distributed during the course. The average attendance was about one hundred and twenty.

From the report of the Secretary, Mr. Edward Burgess, it was shown that the condition of the departments under his charge was satisfactory.

Of the Library, he stated that the increase was very constant. The additions during the year had been in slight excess of the previous year, and were as follows: volumes 255, parts of volumes 966, pamphlets 236, maps and charts 1999. From lack of the necessary means, no binding had been done.

Of the Publications, two parts of the Proceedings of the Society had been issued and a third was nearly ready. The second volume of the Memoirs had also been concluded.

Of the meetings, there had been sixteen general ones of the Society, at which the average attendance had been forty persons; nine of the section of Entomology and eleven of the section of Botany, at each of which the average attendance had been about ten. Nearly forty papers read at these several meetings had been published.

From lack of means, the Society was not enabled to give any public lectures during the winter.

Of members, four Honorary, seven Corresponding, and twenty-two Associate, had been elected during the year.

The Report of the Treasurer showed an excess of receipts over expenditures of $1336.73, a considerable portion of which could only be used for specific purposes. The receipts available for general purposes had been $9098.75, and the expenditures for general purposes, $8903.82; leaving a balance of $194.93, showing that the Society through great economy had succeeded in accomplishing its purpose of limiting expenditure within its income.

At the election of officers for the ensuing year, Theodore Lyman was chosen on the Committee for Fishes and Reptiles in place of Dr. Samuel Kneeland, resigned, and Jules Marcou was left off the Committee on Palaeontology, by reason of prolonged absence abroad.

Previous to the adjournment of the annual meeting, Mr. Charles J. Sprague, in view of the great aid given him by Prof. Tuckerman, in enabling him to put on exhibition a very considerable portion of the Cryptogamous plants of the Society, offered the following resolution, which was passed unanimously:

"That the thanks of the Society be conveyed to Prof. Edward Tuckerman, for the voluntary, generous and invaluable service he has rendered it by elaborating and naming the Lichen herbarium of Dr. Thomas Taylor, now forming a part of its collection; a service which no one in this country but he could have performed, and which gives to the herbarium an authentic value it could not otherwise have possessed."

At the Council meeting subsequent to that of the annual meeting of the Society, the Trustees reported that they had made an estimate of the probable income of the Society for the year entered upon, showing that not much over $9000 could be relied upon as available for general purposes. Considering, however, that there would be a call for the payment of insurance on property for five years, amounting perhaps to one thousand dollars, they advised that appropriations be made to the extent of $9500 in order to cover this item.

The Society being at considerable expense of time and money in carrying out the intention of the legislature of the State in giving it authority to designate persons who should have the right to kill birds for scientific purposes, voted to charge for the certificates so issued, the sum of two dollars each.

Walker Prizes. The subject proposed for the Walker prizes was the same practically as that of 1876, two years before, and upon which no essay had been presented, viz:
" An original investigation of the structure, development and mode of life of one or more of the fungi which injuriously affect useful plants."

This second attempt to interest writers in treating upon this subject was not successful in eliciting essays, as none were presented.

In August of this year, the Society lost a young member by death, to whom it seems fitting to pay a tribute of affectionate remembrance by a brief mention of his life, and of the interest manifested by him in natural history.

Gurdon Saltonstall, the son of Henry and Georgiana C. Saltonstall, was born in Salem, on the 15th day of August, 1856, soon after which the family made Boston their winter residence. Being obliged, by trouble in his eyes, to leave school, and having at a very early age exhibited a strong inclination to acquaint himself with objects of natural history, he was led, in January 1871, when but fifteen years of age, to become a member of the Society, in the work of which he was exceedingly interested, proffering his services in aid of the Custodian and the working members, and identifying himself with their labors in almost every department. In turn, he was aided by them in the acquisition of the knowledge he sought, and thus the association was of advantage to both himself and the Society.

The summer of 1872 he passed at Eastport with the United States Fish Commission, studying and preparing specimens for the Society, and in a subsequent year he worked with this Commission at Noank, with Professor Hyatt.

In 1873 he was able to return to school, where he rapidly and thoroughly mastered the necessary studies and entered Harvard College with honor in the Freshman class of 1874, in which he passed one year with great credit, taking high rank as a scholar and gaining the respect and affection of his associates and instructors. But early in his second year his health suddenly gave way and he was obliged to leave home. Passing part of one winter at Nassau, he sent valuable specimens and information to the Society, his association with which was always one of his greatest pleasures. In this association he exhibited such kindly and lovable traits of character as served to endear him to all the working members, and they sadly deplored the necessity of his leaving home for his health, and still more sadly learned of his early decease.

He died at Pau in France on the 21st of May, 1878, beloved by all who knew him, and happy in the assurance of immortal life.

At a meeting of the Society held Oct. 2d, Mr. Scudder, being in the Chair, alluded feelingly to the death of Prof. Henry, a distinguished Honorary Member, which had recently occurred, and at the close of his remarks introduced Dr. Asa Gray, who addressed the Society upon the life and character of "that eminent man whose death, full of years and honors, had been so sensibly felt throughout the country and the scientific world."

Leaving to others the duty of portraying his great scientific services and researches, Dr. Gray gave a brief sketch of Prof. Henry's life, mentioning his birth at Albany, N. Y., near the close of the last century, his restricted opportunities for early education, his becoming a pupil at the Albany Academy, and afterwards receiving an appointment as Professor of Natural Philosophy at that institution. He then spoke of his brilliant discoveries in electricity and magnetism, which made his name prominent throughout the scientific world, and his acceptance in 1846, of the office of Secretary of the Smithsonian Institution. Referring to this, Dr. Gray remarked, that to the simple sense of duty which impelled Prof. Henry to interrupt a career of research of almost unequalled brilliancy, by an undertaking which was sure to absorb his best years in administrative and perplexing cares, was to be attributed the result that the noble bequest of Smithson "for the increase and diffusion of knowledge among men" was rescued from waste and misappropriation. Dr. Gray insisted that the great benefits which the scientific world at large, and science in America especially, are receiving from the Institution, were mainly owing to the practical wisdom, the catholic spirit, and the just conception of the founder's intent, and the indomitable perseverance of its first Secretary and Manager. In concluding his remarks, of which this notice gives but a brief abstract, Dr. Gray spoke of "the serene simplicity and loftiness, as well as kindliness of spirit, shown by Prof. Henry, of his devotion to what he deemed his duty, often exhibited in the extreme patience with which he attended to the applications of projectors and crotchety discoverers who sought his advice." Much of the prominent influence which he wielded at Washington, was attributed "to his transparent and spotless character, the complete subjection of all considerations of personal advantage, or even of personal ambition, and the atmosphere of purity in which his official as well as private life ever moved, and upon which never fell even the shadow of a shade."

The fall and winter of this official year were characterized by a degree of work done in direct instruction by the Custodian, and other officers of the Society and assistants, so unexampled in character as to call for special and full notice.

The study of natural history had been recently introduced into the public schools, and it was thought by those who had been instrumental in effecting this, particularly by Miss Lucretia Crocker, the supervisor of that department, that the teachers generally of the schools should have such instruction in the several branches, as could be well given under the auspices of the Society. An appeal to its officers was therefore made by Miss Crocker for assistance, and as this was urged as essential to success, the call was cheerfully responded to. The opportunity of interesting the children of the public schools in natural history through lessons given to the great body of their teachers, seemed too much in the line of the Society work to be lost, and strenuous efforts were at once made to do all that was possible in furtherance of the object.

The Council appointed the President, Mr. Bouvé, Vice President, Mr. Cummings, and the Custodian, Mr. Hyatt, to take charge of the matter, giving them full authority to arrange for the lectures, obtain specimens for illustration and distribution, and to approve bills for such expenses as might necessarily be incurred, it being understood that, excepting the time and labor devoted to the object, the cost should be defrayed by subscription.

The wonderful success that attended the movement will be presented in the annual report of the Custodian at the yearly meeting in May.

Dr. J. B. S. Jackson.

1879, January 15th. After calling the meeting of this date to order the President said: Since we last met, Death has once again entered our circle and borne from us one of the oldest and most highly respected of the active members of the Society, Dr. J. B. S. Jackson.

To those of you who have not been members for more than the last decade or two, there can be but little appreciation of the feeling experienced by those of us who were contemporary, or nearly so, with the founders and early members of the Society, when one of their number passes the limit that divides the seen from the unseen. Among these were men of noble characters and impulses, with whom to be associated was to be impressed with such sense of their great excellence and purity of purpose as no subsequent experience through life could obliterate. Claiming but little knowledge of natural history, but strongly appreciating the importance of its study both for themselves and the community, they came together for mutual help in the acquisition of knowledge, and to combine their efforts for its dissemination, modestly expressing in the preface to the first number of the Journal "that having but small claims to the character of naturalists, they nevertheless are desirous of contributing something to the common stock of information."

In the greater light of the present day, and reflecting upon the little aid attainable by them through books or collections, we may well exclaim, Noble men! Simple seekers of truth, not only for your own good but for that of all others; you grandly did your work! And so they did. The many volumes of their papers and proceedings attest this: the State reports upon the geology; the invertebrate animals; the fishes; the insects injurious to vegetation; the trees and shrubs of Massachusetts; all by early members resident or corresponding, speak unceasingly of the value of their labors. And the magnificent development of the Society until it has become what it now is, with its great collections and its wide felt influence, — how much of this is due to their early strivings who shall say ? Certainly all is but the fruition of their hopes and desires.

Among these early members were Dr. Benjamin D. Greene, an accomplished botanist and the first President of the Society; Dr. Augustus A. Gould, the author of the Report upon the Invertebrates of the State, and who became one of the most able naturalists of New England; Dr. D. Humphreys Storer, the author of the very valuable Report upon the Fishes of New England; Dr. Amos Binney, an accomplished conchologist, afterwards President; George B. Emerson., author of the great work upon the Trees and Shrubs of the State, and who also subsequently became President of the Society; Dr. Martin Gay, an able chemist; Dr. Charles T. Jackson, well-known as an accomplished chemist, mineralogist and geologist; Francis Alger, the author of a valuable work on mineralogy ; the Rev. Dr. F. W. P. Greenwood, who seemed more divine than human in the loveliness of his character; Dr. T. W. Harris, author of the Report on Insects injurious to Vegetation, and last o mention, though by no means the least in his influence upon the affairs of the Society and its character, Dr. J. B. S. Jackson, whose loss we now deplore.

The particular investigations of Dr. Jackson were generally not of a nature to bring him prominently before the Society as an instructor in any branch of natural history, his labors being largely confined to a class of subjects more generally interesting to students in pathology. Yet the Journal of the Society presents to us several papers of great value to naturalists, and the Proceedings contain remarks made by him at various times embodying much useful information.

Dr. Jackson was elected a member in the fall of 1831, the Society having been incorporated the previous February.

In 1837 he read before the Society a paper which was published in the Journal, giving an anatomical description of the Gallapagos Tortoise, which was a valuable contribution.

In 1842 the Journal gives an account read by him of the dissection of two adult dromedaries, male and female.

In 1845 there is in the Journal a paper upon the dissection of a spermaceti whale and three other Cetaceans.

Of his remarks made from time to time upon scientific subjects and published in the Proceedings of the Society, may be found some of interesting character upon the teeth of *Delphinus globiceps*, upon fossil bones of the *Mastodon giganteus* from Schooley's Mountain, N. J., and upon bones from Indian tumuli.

As said before, Dr. Jackson's most important work was in pathology rather than natural history. He became Professor of Pathological Anatomy in the Medical School of Harvard University in 1847, and was ever after a most diligent laborer in its interests, investigating with great patience and with keenness of observation arising from constant experience, the morbid effects of disease upon the organs, and writing out fully and carefully the results of his examinations, which have been of invaluable service in the cause of medical science. Much of his work for many years was in the building of the Cabinet of the Society of Medical Improvement and its arrangement for study, and in the care and arrangement of the Warren Museum. Of these two fine collections Dr. Jackson published descriptive catalogues, containing much matter of great interest to students in medicine and surgery. Others can write and speak more wisely and instructively of these great services than can the writer, who has only been associated with him in the Society of Natural History and as a personal friend. His work for the Society has been spoken of, but what he did for it in labor and through publications was but a small part of the aid he was able to render. No member ever felt more interest in its welfare, and if this was not manifested to the same degree in actual devotion to work upon its collections and to investigations in natural history subjects, it was only because his valuable time was preoccupied by the duties owed to his official position. He was always in the habit of attending the meetings of the Society, and always exhibited a strong desire that they should be made as instructive as possible to younger members, to such particularly as were entering the paths of science. He was ever urgent, too, that all the specimens of the collections of the Society should be so distinctively and fully arranged and labelled that all visitors might clearly understand their character and relations. He indeed sometimes felt impatient that this was not already accomplished, so important did he regard it as a means of education; though he did not fail to recognize that with the means at the Society's disposal this work must necessarily be slow. He lived to see great progress towards the realization of his wishes in this respect, and if his life had been spared a year or two longer his fullest desire might have been satisfied.

One marked peculiarity of Dr. Jackson was his great interest in the advancement of worthy members to positions of honor and usefulness in the Society. Entirely free from any ambitious desire for office himself, he wished to gratify the feelings of those whom he thought deserving and to whom position might be an inducement to exertion. It is pleasant to dwell upon the special characteristics that made our departed friend a useful member of the Society, but with what additional pleasure can we recall the traits that made him the delightful companion, the beloved friend, the dear husband and father; that led all with whom he came closely in contact to regard him with affection and respect. Simple, unostentatious, true in all the relations of life, honest in the expression of his convictions, and pure in heart, he lived amongst us a blessing to his friends and the community, and has passed away leaving only the most tender memories. May we be helped by his example to live and do our life's work so that it may be said of each of us when we likewise depart, what may be truly said of him : Those who knew him the best loved him the most.

At the close of the President's address, Dr. D. H. Storer said :

Mr. President : — I rise merely to express my thanks for your faithful and most appropriate remarks respecting our departed friend. I should have regretted not to have heard them. I rejoice that nothing ever occurred to alienate him from the Society — that he continued to feel the same interest, and to evince the same zeal in its prosperity as long as he was with us.

Jackson and Wyman I always associated together — in my heart they were one — ever faithful and true.

Again I thank you, Mr. President, for your heartfelt tribute.

At the annual meeting the reports of the Custodian and Secretary were as usual interesting and gratifying.

The Mineralogical cabinet was stated to be in good condition and order.

The Geological collection had been undergoing re-arrangement, this being necessary by recent advances in science, especially in Lithology. The principal accession to this department consisted of a suite of 250 specimens of the rocks of New Hampshire, collected in the recent geological survey of that State, by Prof. C. H. Hitchcock.

The revision of the Palaeontological collections had been finished. To the North American had been added forty specimens of Cambrian, Silurian and Devonian fossils, collected by Prof. F. H. Bradley and given by Mr. John Cummings; nearly 500 sub-carboniferous crinoids, obtained by exchange from Prof. A. H. Worthen, State geologist of Illinois; 125 specimens of Cretaceous fossils from Texas, obtained by purchase; and 100 specimens of Cretaceous vertebrate remains from Kansas, purchased from the State geologist, Prof. B. F. Mudge.

The New England collection had received twenty specimens of fossiliferous rock from the drift of Truro, Cape Cod, probably Eocene.

The North American collection, with the accessions reported, consisted of:

	Genera.	Species.	Specimens.
Cambrian	112	214	645
Silurian	136	241	656
Devonian	208	376	1127
Subcarboniferous	99	215	650
Carboniferous	79	288	1089
Triassic	35	29	51
Jurassic	5	5	40
Cretaceous	90	177	883
Tertiary and Post-tertiary	306	548	3086
	1070	2093	8227

The Triassic fishes and plants, and most of the foot-tracks, a good collection of Devonian bivalves, and several other small lots of fossils wanting identification, were not included.

The South American collection, including the West Indian, was mentioned as insignificantly small, numbering but twenty-four genera, twenty-eight species, and one hundred and seventy specimens, all Tertiary, or Post-tertiary, excepting one Cretaceous. The African was said to be still more lacking, comprising only five genera, six species, and fourteen specimens, all Tertiary.

The Asiatic collection, including specimens from the Malay Archipelago, Australia and Oceanica, had been mounted during the year. This was stated to contain many large specimens, chiefly casts of the Miocene Mammalia from the Sivalik Hills, also Cretaceous fishes from Mt. Lebanon, casts of Carboniferous shells from Australia, and casts of the bones of the Dinornis and Palaeopteryx from New Zealand. The whole embraced 46 genera, 84 species, and 170 specimens.

The principal work done on the European collection during the year had been to mount the Palaeozoic fossils. There had been an accession to these of 380 specimens, received from Mr. John Cummings in exchange. The European specimens at this time numbered 13,655.

The aggregate of the several collections of the Department was as shown by the following table:

	Genera.	Species.	Specimens.
From North America	1070	2093	8227
" South America	24	28	170
" Africa	5	6	14
" Asia and Australia	46	84	170
" Europe	1631	3623	13655
	2776	5834	22236

The Custodian in referring to the fact that the laborious work of the arrangement and cataloguing of the Palaeontological collections was finished, justly ascribed, not only the magnitude of these to the great liberality of Mr. John Cummings, but also their condition, which was attributable entirely to the valuable services of the two assistants employed by him.

In the Botanical department, the work of sorting the duplicates and supplying the deficiencies in the general collection had steadily progressed under the direction of Mr. Cummings. The specimens of wood, fruit, etc., on exhibition had been catalogued, mounted on tablets, and labelled by Miss Carter. They numbered 2583 specimens, representing 304 genera, and 492 species. To Mr. Chas. J. Sprague this department was indebted for 250 specimens of dried plants from Florida, collected by Mr. A. H. Curtiss, and for 50 rare New England species, collected by Mr. C. J. Pringle, of Vermont. Mr. E. T. Bouvé had continued his work on the trees and shrubs of New England, and added a number of species to the collection.

In the Anatomical department, a new section had been established. In this section had been brought together preparations made by Mr. Van Vleck, exhibiting the general anatomy of the invertebrates and the typical forms of the different sub-divisions of the animal kingdom.

The New England collection of Birds had been considerably increased through the exertions of Dr. Brewer, thirty to forty species having been added.

The Entomological department had received several important donations, one from Mr. F. C. Bowditch, of useful insects of all orders; another from Dr. C. S. Minot of his entire collection of insects, containing very desirable additions to the New England collection. A part also of a collection made by the late Mr. Gurdon Saltonstall had been received from his family, and several valuable specimens of which the Society stood in need from Mr. Roland Thaxter.

The remarks of the Custodian upon the other collections do not call for repetition.

In the Laboratory there had been much activity. The room and the collections had been used for the past year by a class in Zoölogy and Palaeontology from the Mass. Institute of Technology; one in Zoölogy, from Boston University; and one in Zoölogy composed of the teachers of the Boston High Schools. This last class was particularly mentioned in the report of the previous year. The course of instruction had been prolonged and was not yet quite finished.

Reference was made on a preceding page to the great work accomplished, through the instrumentality of the Society, in direct instruction during the last autumn and winter months. The importance of what was done justifies the presentation of nearly the full statement of the Custodian, though it involves some repetition.

"*Teachers' School of Science.* The Teachers' School of Science has this year attained extraordinary size and importance. So sudden and unexpected was this development that for the last six months it has almost completely arrested all efficient work in other directions. The study of nature having been introduced in a definite form into the public schools, and the supervisor of this department, Miss Lucretia Crocker, having assured us that our assistance would be of great benefit, and was in fact essential, it was determined to institute appropriate courses upon elementary Botany, Zoölogy, and Mineralogy, if the means of paying the expenses could be raised. Mrs. S. T. Hooper and Miss Crocker undertook and successfully completed this part of the work, and also a considerable amount of harassing clerical labor, which subsequently arose out of the success of their own exertions. Fortunately for their schemes these ladies met with substantial appreciation from Mrs. Augustus Hemenway, who both subscribed most liberally, and also encouraged them to accept the very considerable pecuniary responsibilities, which began to block their way at the very beginning of operations. In fact, without these assurances of further support and interest, we should not have dared to begin.

"These obstacles arose from two causes, the number of applicants, and the necessity of providing identical specimens for all. The specimens and materials for two hundred, which was the maximum number anticipated at first, could have been readily furnished, but when the applicants reached six hundred, it became exceedingly questionable whether such a number could be provided for, and properly instructed by one person, all at the same time. Feeling, however, that the cause of science demanded that these difficulties should be met and supported, and relying on the hearty coöperation of Professor Goodale and the ladies mentioned above, the course was begun.

"The association and sympathy of Mrs. Elizabeth Agassiz with the undertaking has been particularly gratifying, since Prof. Louis Agassiz was the first naturalist who ever taught a popular audience in this country with the specimens in hand.

" The enterprise was in large part the work of women and affords pleasing evidence of the activity and usefulness of this new class of members in our Society.

" The following is a list of the donors:

Mrs. Augustus Hemenway . . . $1000.00	Mrs. Sarah S. Russell . .	$50.00
Mrs. Quincy A. Shaw 500.00	Mrs. John E. Lodge . .	50.00
Mrs. John M. Forbes 100.00	Mrs. Richard C. Greenleaf .	50.00
Miss A. S. Hooper 100.00	Miss Anna C. Lowell . .	50.00
Mrs. H. P. Kidder 100.00	Mrs. E. W. Gurney . .	50.00
Miss M. A. Wales 50.00		

"Smaller sums were contributed by Mrs. Elizabeth C. Agassiz, Mrs. Samuel Hooper, Miss S. Minns, Miss E. Mason, Miss M. C. Jackson, Miss Stone, Miss Abby W. May, Mrs. James Freeman Clarke, Miss Cora H. Clarke, Miss Lucretia Crocker, Mrs. Thomas Mack, Mrs. A. S. Farwell and others.

"Many of these ladies were very active in securing the success of the course and the Society thanks them and others; especially Mrs. E. D. Cheney, Miss J. M. Arms, Miss C. J.

Ireland and Mrs. Samuel Wells for their personal efforts in behalf of the Teachers' School of Science.

"The teachers themselves, at our solicitation, joined in making up the fund. The contributions from this source amounted to $789.

"Notwithstanding this generous assistance, it would hardly have been possible to carry on the several courses without the friendly aid and direct assistance in various ways of the following institutions and persons.

"The Institute of Technology, which most generously gave us the use of Huntington Hall, upon the payment of a merely nominal sum for cleaning and heating.

"The Museum of Comparative Zoölogy, under the direction of Mr. Alexander Agassiz, which, through Count Pourtalés, Dr. Hermann Hagen, and Mr. E. C. Hamlin, at various times assisted us by donations of specimens from the respective departments superintended by these gentlemen.

"Mr. Henshaw, my right hand assistant in all the work of preparation and distribution, whose untiring energy contributed largely to secure the success of every lesson; Miss Hintz, of the Normal School, who drew with remarkable skill the diagrams used in the Zoölogical course, and enabled the Custodian to illustrate fully all subjects; Mr. Van Vleck for aid in the preparation of models; Mr. L. S. Burbank; Miss Nunn, Professor of Biology at Wellesley College; Mr. Robert McCarthy, of New York; Captain Horsfall, of Steamer Canopus; Mr. Eugene G. Blackford, of New York; and the proprietors of the Parker House and Young's Hotel, for donations of specimens and assistance in various ways.

"Mr. E. G. Gardiner, Mr. E. A. W. Hammatt and Mr. G. H. Barton of the Institute of Technology, have also kindly assisted at the lectures in various capacities. To many of my own students, teachers and others I am also indebted for assistance.

"Since the lectures were begun in 1871, they have been continued without interruption, except during the winter of 1872–73, under the patronage of Mr. John Cummings; and previous to this winter about 75,000 specimens of minerals, plants, and animals had been studied and distributed to teachers of the public schools. The applications for tickets rose during those years from an average of 55 to 166.

"The number of recorded applications for the course now approaching completion is 616, or nearly four times as many as in previous years, and the number of specimens which will have been distributed during this winter alone cannot fall short of 100,000.

"After an introductory lecture in which the Superintendent of the Public Schools, the President of the Society, and the Custodian delivered addresses appropriate to the occasion, Professor Goodale completed a course of six lessons on Botany in which he instructed the whole audience of five hundred with apparently as much readiness as if it had been but fifty. Mr. Jackson Dawson, Mr. Watson and Mr. Greenleaf were of great assistance to Professor Goodale in the procuring of the vast number of live plants and the great amount of other material required for his lessons. Mr. Charles W. Spurr, 522 Harrison Avenue, Boston, prepared, for the purpose of illustrating the subject of wood sections, 500 packages of excellent specimens of the following woods: tulip-tree or whitewood, rose-wood, ash, oak, pine, mahogany, walnut, butternut, maple, cedar, birch, cherry, elm and holly. Many of these were in duplicate, exhibiting both plain and figured texture. The specimens, more than ten thousand in all, were gratuitously presented to the class by Mr. Spurr.

"The Custodian followed with twelve lessons on Zoölogy, which will be completed on the 10th of this month, and Mr. Burbank is to continue with five on Mineralogy. The average attendance on fair days, so far, has been about five hundred.

"The course was supplemented by the publication of a series of small pamphlets, under the general title of Science Guides, which were intended to assist the teachers in the application of the knowledge imparted by the lectures. These are described in the Report of the Secretary.

"Perhaps the most gratifying and encouraging facts are derived from an examination of the statistics of the past seven years. Thus out of the 616 applicants of this winter, there are 155 who had attended at least one previous course,[1] 119 who had attended two or more previous courses, and 44 who had attended all of the courses. Some of these last, I may add, are masters of public schools."

The Secretary's report was interesting, as he compared the condition and the work of the departments under his charge during the ten years then closing. As in this volume it will be better to present such comparisons at the close of another year, they are here omitted.

Of members, twenty-four Associate, five Corporate, and fourteen Corresponding had been elected. Of the meetings there had been sixteen of the general Society, seven of the section of Botany, and eight of the section of Entomology. The average attendance had been twenty-two at the general meetings, eight at the Botanical, and eleven at the Entomological. The meetings of the last had been unusually interesting.

The history of the Botanical section begun, as stated by the Secretary, "under hopeful auspices three years ago, is far from satisfactory." "With so much popular interest in the study of Botany, the result was unexpected, and is to be regretted."

The condition of the Library was stated to be good and its usefulness never to have been so great—1169 books having been taken out by 123 persons.

The Society was indebted to the Museo Civico of Genoa for a valuable and complete series of its publications; to Prof. Joachim Barrande of Prague, for a set of his extensive works; and to Prof. J. O. Westwood of Oxford, for a number of his papers. The additions to the Library are as follows: volumes, 252; parts of volumes, 1005; pamphlets, 214; maps and charts, 221; total, 1692.

Of Publications, two numbers of the Memoirs, and three quarterly parts of the Proceedings had been issued.

A new volume of Occasional Papers, the third, had been put in press, and would soon be printed. Besides these, a series of Guides for Science Teaching had been prepared for use in the courses of lectures to the teachers, three of which had been published and distributed, the cost being defrayed by sales. The three already issued were, About Pebbles, by Prof. Hyatt; A few Common Plants, by Dr. Goodale; and Commercial and other Sponges, by Prof. Hyatt. These were to be followed by other numbers. The Secretary stated the exchange list as numbering 352 Societies or Journals, of which 50 were United States and Canadian.

---

[1] It must be remembered that the highest number of attendants at lessons reached in previous years was 166.

The Treasurer's account for the year showed that the income applicable for the general purposes of the Society had not come up to the estimate made at its commencement, and that the expenditures had been about three hundred dollars in excess of such income. As, however, insurance on the property had been paid for five years in advance, the spirit of the policy not to expend beyond the income had been adhered to. There had been an excess of all receipts over expenditures of $835.90, all of which and probably more it would be necessary to reserve for prize and other special expenses in accordance with the conditions attached to the use of the Walker Fund.

At the election of officers but few changes were made, and these only in the Committees on the departments of the Museum. M. E. Wadsworth was chosen on the Mineral Committee instead of L. S. Burbank, Rev. G. Frederick Wright on the Geological Committee instead of T. Sterry Hunt, W. F. Whitney, M. D., was added to the Committee on Comparative Anatomy, C. O. Whitman was chosen on the Committee of Mollusks, in place of L. Lincoln Thaxter, and E. L. Mark in place of Dr. J. B. S. Jackson, deceased.

At the meeting of the Council following the general annual meeting of the Society, the trustees presented their estimate of the probable income of the Society, applicable for general purposes for the ensuing year, as $8538.16. As a portion of the income for special uses, amounting to several hundred dollars, might be expended for general purposes, they recommended that $8800 be appropriated for expenditure, not well perceiving how less could be used without detriment to the interests of the Society.

Walker Prizes. The subject proposed for this year was "The structure, history, and development of some cryptogamous plant." One essay was presented, but it was not deemed worthy of a prize, and no award was therefore made.

In October the Woman's Educational Association having requested the use of the lecture room of the Society for botanical lectures on Mondays and Fridays, the Council granted the request upon the condition that the expense of heating the room, and of the janitor's services, should be paid by the Association. The Council appointed at this time committees to act upon special matters as follows: On the grand Walker Prize, soon to be awarded, Professor Wm. B. Rogers, Professor Goodale, and Colonel Theodore Lyman; on tablets to be placed in the entrance hall of the Museum, commemorative of its great benefactors, Rev. Robert C. Waterston, Edward Burgess, and Alpheus Hyatt.

The Council also voted that the President appoint a committee to consider and report upon a plan for the reception of the American Association for the Advancement of Science, that body having decided to meet in Boston the coming summer.

In November, the Council granted to Mr. L. S. Burbank permission to use the lecture room of the Society for a course of geological lectures, he paying only such expenses as might be incurred for janitor's services, etc.

In December, a vote was passed by the Council authorizing the Committee on Publication to attempt the publication of an illustrated quarto volume of the Memoirs as a part of the Society's celebration of the semi-centennial anniversary of its foundation, by soliciting subscriptions for such memoirs at ten dollars per copy. The committee was also authorized to begin to prepare and arrange for the publication when five hundred dollars were subscribed.

In December, a petition to the Society having been presented for the formation of a section of Microscopy, signed by Messrs. S. P. Sharples, Samuel Wells, R. R. Andrews, Edward Burgess, J. Frank Brown, David Hunt, Jr., Francis A. Osborn, R. C. Greenleaf, A. Hyatt, G. F. Waters, and W. F. Whitney, the consent of the Corporate Members was given at two meetings in accordance with the By-laws, and the section was thus formed.

1880. *Walker Grand Honorary Prize.* In January, the Committee on the award of the Walker Grand Honorary prize, having unanimously recommended Dr. Joseph Leidy, of Philadelphia, as eminently worthy to receive it, for his prolonged investigations and discoveries in Zoölogy and Palaeontology, as presented in publications made by him, it was voted by the Council that the grand prize be given to Dr. Leidy, and that in consequence of the extraordinary merit of his work that the sum awarded be one thousand dollars.

In January, also, the Custodian reported to the Council that the Committee of the department of Comparative Anatomy objected to his proposed re-arrangement of the collection of that department, and asked that the question at issue might be referred to the next meeting for decision. Thus was brought before the Council the very important matter of determining whether the collection of Comparative Anatomy, like the other collections of the Society, should be arranged in subordination to the great plan proposed and adopted at the commencement of the decade for the whole museum, or if the collection of that department should remain an exception, not becoming a part of a series, the full completion of which was essential to illustrate in the best manner the general laws of science.

At the next meeting of the Council, which was held January 21, there was a very full attendance, and a warm discussion took place upon the proposed action of the Custodian in which Dr. Dwight, representing the Committee of the department of Comparative Anatomy, — Professors Hyatt and Shaler, Colonel Lyman and Messrs. Allen and Bouvé took part.

The great work that had been done by members of the committee upon the collection in past years, demanded that all said by them against a change should be thoughtfully and respectfully considered. There was therefore, no disposition to hasten a decision, and accordingly a vote was passed referring the matter to a committee of three to be appointed by the President. Colonel Theodore Lyman and Messrs. S. H. Scudder and Samuel Wells were named as this committee, and instructed to report at a meeting to be held a week later. Upon the Council again coming together a report was presented by the chairman of the committee favoring the proposed re-arrangement, whereupon Dr. Dwight said he would not further oppose the execution of the plan of the Custodian, though he personally believed the collections would be injured by the change.

The Council then passed a vote with but one dissentient voice, approving the proposed action of the Custodian in carrying out the plan of 1870, with regard to the department of Comparative Anatomy.

Thus was settled, not without much feeling, but amicably, a question, the decision of which in favor of the proposed change, was regarded by the great majority as most important for the welfare of the Society, whilst a number of members influential through eminent service in its behalf, thought the proposed action uncalled for and detrimental.

It may be conceded that much worthy of consideration was said in support of their views, but it is believed that all students of nature will finally concur in the opinion that the decision made was a wise one.

Dr. Thomas Mayo Brewer.

At the general meeting of the Society on February the fourth, the President, Mr. T. T. Bouvé said:

Since we last met, the Society has lost one of its oldest and most valued members, Dr. Thomas M. Brewer.

It grieved me as an old personal friend to learn when in a distant state, that the disease, by which as I knew before leaving home he was prostrated, had terminated fatally, and that I should not again receive his pleasant greeting on earth, or even have the sad satisfaction of being present at the funeral services following his departure. The long intercourse between us had always been of the most agreeable character, and I feel that I have reason to mourn that it has so unexpectedly and mournfully terminated. This is not the place, however, for me to indulge in the expression of personal bereavement, but rather to dwell on the great loss the Society and community have met in the death of our beloved associate.

Dr. Brewer was born in Boston, Nov. 21st, 1814. He graduated at Harvard College in 1835, and in the Medical School in 1838. He labored in his profession for several years, but his tastes and inclinations were stronger for other pursuits. He was fond of literary labor, and, having strong political tendencies was early led to write for one of the leading Whig papers of the period, the Boston Atlas, and at length to become one of its editors, in which capacity he manifested marked ability both as a writer and close observer. Subsequently he became interested in the firm of Swan and Tileston, a publishing house which was afterwards changed to that of Brewer and Tileston. He retired from business in 1875 and then visited Europe, where he remained two years. He had become well known by his ornithological labors and received consequently very gratifying attention from many distinguished scientific men whilst abroad.

In the cause of popular education he was very zealous, manifesting at all times great interest in the public schools of the city. He was long a member of the Boston School Committee, and served in this capacity with great devotedness. His last election to this office was in 1879, for the term of three years.

Dr. Brewer was elected a member of this Society October 7th, 1835, and soon became well known by his valuable contributions, mostly upon his favorite subject of ornithology. It is pleasant to recall the fact that his first communication to the Society was in defence of Nuttall and Audubon, the distinguished naturalists, the latter his warm personal friend, against some unjust attempts in a foreign magazine to detract from their well earned and deserved reputation. Not long after he presented a highly interesting paper upon the Birds of Massachusetts, in which he gave an account of over forty species not embraced in the State report of Dr. Hitchcock upon the Geology and Natural History of the State. From that early period, now nearly half a century since, he never ceased to manifest great interest in the welfare of the Society, by frequent communications and in such other ways as his health would admit.

Apart from what he performed for the Society, he accomplished much for scientific knowledge by contributions to several publications of great value, and by articles which he furnished for some of the popular magazines.

As these remarks will be supplemented by particular mention of Dr. Brewer's scientific writings in a sketch furnished by his friend Mr. J. A. Allen, it will not be necessary for me to make further reference to them, and I need only add that, had he lived free from the business cares that until recently absorbed most of his time, much more might have been looked for from him relative to the habits of birds, particularly of such as find a home permanently or temporarily in New England.

We of the Society will greatly miss his efficient labors in striving to complete the collection in the department of New England Ornithology, for the development of which he manifested much and increasing interest.

In the death of Dr. Brewer our Society has lost a most valuable member, and the community, a good and wise citizen, one of whom it may be truly said : He was always faithful to the duties of every position in which he was placed, and ever ready to work where he recognized that his labors would promote the public welfare.

The following notice of Dr. Brewer's scientific labors by Mr. J. A. Allen, was also contributed.

The death of Dr. Brewer removes another of the older American ornithologists, of whom there now remain two only whose period of scientific activity extends back to the time of Audubon and Nuttall. Dr. Brewer's first formal contribution to ornithology, entitled "Some additions to the Catalogue of the Birds of Massachusetts in Prof. Hitchcock's Report, etc.," was published in 1837, in the first volume of the "Journal" of this Society. These additions numbered forty-five species and increased by one-fourth the list of birds previously known as inhabitants of this State. Previously, however, he had furnished valuable notes and rare specimens of birds to Audubon, who in his great work on North American birds, makes frequent mention of his indebtedness to "his young friend, Mr. T. M. Brewer of Boston."

In 1840, he became more generally known as an ornithologist through his edition of Wilson's "American Ornithology," — the only American edition of Wilson's work, except Ord's, published prior to 1871. The "Brewer Edition," from its comparatively small cost, placed this delightful work within the reach of a wide circle of readers, to whom the more expensive original and Ord editions were inaccessible. It was enriched by the addition to the original text of the synonymy and critical commentary of Jardine's edition, and by a very useful and carefully digested synopsis of all the birds at that time known as North American.

In 1857 was published the first part of his "North American Oölogy," which forms part of volume IX of the "Smithsonian Contributions to Knowledge." The full title of the work — "North American Oölogy; being an account of the geographical distribution of the birds of North America during the breeding season, with figures and descriptions of their eggs" — indicates very fairly its scope and character, but in addition to the topics thus indicated, the work gives a pretty full exposition of the breeding habits of the species treated, so far as then known, and also full tables of synonymy. Owing to the great cost of the illustrations, the work was not continued beyond the first part, which treats of the Birds of Prey, the Swifts, Swallows, Goatsuckers and Kingfishers. This work, until within the last year, was the only special treatise extant on the subject to which it relates, and will ever hold the place of a standard work. It is, moreover, a work which brought to its author great credit, and through which he became widely known as an ornithologist of high standing.

In 1874 appeared " A History of North American Birds," under the joint authorship of S. F. Baird, T. M. Brewer, and R. Ridgway, in three quarto volumes devoted to the "Land Birds." To this work the whole of the biographical part, forming probably two-thirds of the letterpress, was contributed by Dr. Brewer, and throughout evinces his thorough familiarity with the literature of the subject, and shows the hand of the master in all that relates to his special department of a work which marks an era in the history of North American ornithology.

Dr. Brewer's minor papers appeared at intervals throughout the long period of forty years, and embrace important contributions to our knowledge of American birds.

He has left the manuscript for the completion of his share of the great work on North American birds already mentioned, the final revision of which he had just completed; also material for the contemplated continuation of his "North American Oölogy." His collection of eggs — the accumulation of a long series of years, — is doubtless one of the best private collections extant.

Dr. Brewer having been engaged during the larger part of his life in absorbing professional or commercial pursuits, his contributions to ornithology must have been largely the work of such limited time as could be spared from his business engagements, and only within the last few years was he able to devote himself wholly to his favorite studies. Although an authority of unsurpassed eminence in his special province, — that of North American Oölogy, — his labors were mainly restricted to this field, taken, however in its broader sense. Removed suddenly, apparently when there were years of activity and leisure before him for scientific research, his loss is one not easily replaced, nor its importance readily appreciated except by those who knew him intimately and were familiar with his conscientious manner of investigation, his warm sympathy, and the thorough loyalty of his friendship.

At a meeting of the Council on the 17th of March, the President called the attention of the members to the fact that the 28th of April would be the semi-centennial anniversary of the formation of the Society, suggesting that a public celebration of the event should take place.

After discussion it was unanimously voted, that the President should appoint a committee, including himself as chairman, to arrange for a proper celebration, with full powers to take such measures as they judged expedient. The committee as formed consisted of the President, Mr. John Cummings, Mr. S. H. Scudder, Mr. Charles W. Scudder, and Mr. Edward Burgess. It will be remembered that the Council in December had passed a vote in view of this year being the semi-centennial one of the foundation of the Society, that there should be published an illustrated quarto volume of its memoirs as a part of the Society's celebration of the event, if subscriptions could be obtained for copies that would yield five hundred dollars. As more than the necessary number of names had already been secured, preparation was made for the issue of such a volume. Subsequently the President was solicited to write for the same volume a sketch of the history of the Society, from its foundation to the close of the fiftieth year of its existence. This, after much hesitation, he consented to do, recognizing the importance of having such a sketch prepared, whilst yet some of the founders of the Society were alive and able to give information concerning their early brother members, and fearing that otherwise it would be left undone.

The committee appointed to take measures for the celebration of the semi-centennial anniversary were faithful to their trust, taking active measures to ensure success. It soon became manifest that the occasion was to be one of great interest, all persons addressed being found ready to coöperate with the committee in carrying out their plans. Cheerfully His Excellency Governor Long, His Honor Mayor Prince, President Eliot of Harvard University, Dr. Samuel Eliot, Superintendent of the Public Schools, Mr. Agassiz, Director of the Museum of Comparative Zoölogy, and the Rev. Robert C. Waterston, responded to calls upon them to take part in the proceedings. The committee's labors were multifarious; they had printed for use at the meeting and for distribution, an introduction to the General Guide to the Museum then in preparation by Prof. Hyatt; they had moved the elephant from his elevated position, and other large animals from their accustomed places, and had erected across the north portion of the main hall a platform to accommodate the speakers and distinguished visitors. This was carpeted and furnished with chairs, the rest of the hall having settees over the floor.

At the general meeting of the Society, April 21st, the Nominating Committee having reported a list of officers for election at the annual meeting, to take place on the 5th of May, in which Mr. Bouvé's name was mentioned for President, he addressed the meeting, referring to his having consented four years previously, at the kind solicitation of members, to withdraw his resignation then tendered, stating that there were several reasons why he should decline re-election at the present time, and urging that the Society would not ask him to reconsider his determination.

Mr. Scudder expressed the hope that the President's withdrawal was not imperative, and dwelt upon the work done under his administration, which had resulted in the final crystallization of the policy of the Society.

Remarks were also made by Mr. Hyatt, Mr. Burgess and Mr. Nathan Appleton, expressive of regret at the contemplated action of the President. He, however, warmly thanking the speakers for their kind expressions, reiterated his resolve to resign. It was therefore voted to recommit the report to the nominating committee for reconsideration. This being done they withdrew, and after consultation re-entered the meeting, and presented an amended report, nominating for President in the place of Mr. Bouvé, Samuel H. Scudder. The report was then accepted.

At this meeting the models of the sun and the earth were presented to the Society by the Boston Scientific Society. These consist of a gilt ball representing the sun, three inches in diameter, and a white plate on which is a black spot three one-hundredths of an inch in diameter, which symbolizes the earth. These were placed one on the centre of each arch at the side of the stairs in the main hall of entrance to the Museum. They

represent approximately the proportionate size of the sun and the earth, and their distance from each other relative to size. The proportionate scale of the models and their distance apart is about a foot to three millions of miles, or about one inch to two hundred and fifty thousand miles.

A vote was passed, that the President appoint at leisure a committee of three to consider the desirability of abolishing the Committees in the departments, and of devising a different plan for organizing the Council, and to propose the necessary change in the Constitution and By-Laws for this purpose. The President subsequently appointed as this committee, S. H. Scudder, Dr. B. Joy Jeffries, and Edward Burgess.

THE SEMI-CENTENNIAL CELEBRATION OF THE FOUNDATION OF THE SOCIETY; APRIL 28.

The anniversary day was pleasant and all things conspired to render the occasion interesting and joyous. The spacious platform which had been erected across the north portion of the main hall was occupied by the President, the speakers, the officers of the Society and a large number of ladies and gentlemen. A large audience, composed of members of the Society and very many prominent men and women of the city and State, filled the floor of the hall and such portions of the galleries as were convenient to use. Amongst the distinguished persons present, were His Excellency Governor Long, President Eliot of Harvard University, Prof. Asa Gray, the illustrious botanist, Alexander Agassiz, Director of the Museum of Comparative Zoölogy, Count Louis François de Pourtalès, Dr. Samuel Eliot, Superintendent of the Public Schools, Miss Lucretia Crocker, Supervisor of the Public Schools, Dr. D. Humphreys Storer, Judge G. W. Warren, Prof. F. W. Putnam, Rev. Robert C. Waterston and Mrs. Waterston, Hon. Josiah Quincy, Prof. E. S. Morse, Colonel Theodore Lyman, Dr. J. C. White, Mr. Justin Winsor, Librarian at Harvard University, and Mr. John Cummings.

At half past three, the time of commencement, the President, Thomas T. Bouvé, after calling the assembly to order, began his address as follows:

Members of the Society, my Associates in its service, my Companions for many years in its labors, its trials and its achievements : — I congratulate you. I think we have reason to congratulate each other that we come here surrounded by a host of sympathizing friends; and ladies and gentlemen, whose names we have not the honor of having recorded on our rolls as members, as a representative of the Society, I bid you a hearty welcome here to commemorate its formation and to rejoice in its success.

With these very few words of greeting, for the time will admit of no more, I proceed at once to present what I have prepared for the occasion. It is an account of the doings of those who took an active part, before the Society was formed, in interesting the public in natural history. I do this because their labors have not been duly appreciated, and because the lessons which their experience is designed to teach certainly require that we should take time to do it. What I hold in my hand is intended as an introductory chapter in the history of the Society of Natural History on which I am engaged, — a memorial volume to be issued this year.

The President then proceeded to present the early steps taken to inculcate a love for the study of nature in this community, particularly dwelling upon the formation of the Linnaean Society, its history and its decline. He then gave a brief account of the movements made towards the formation of a new Society, which culminated in the existence of the Boston Society of Natural History. As nearly the whole address is embraced in the opening pages of this volume, no further mention of it is necessary here.

At the close of the President's remarks a telegram was handed to him from Prof. William B. Rogers dated Washington, D. C., expressing regret that he could not be present, and rejoicing in the prosperity of the Society. His Excellency Governor Long was then introduced.[1]

ADDRESS OF GOVERNOR LONG.

When I was invited to be present at this interesting anniversary, thoroughly grateful for the courtesy, I felt at first that neither personally nor as an official of the State ought I to take any other part in it than that of a looker-on. But I remembered that the seeds of your noble institution, Mr. President, like those of so many of the best fruits of New England, were sown not altogether by the scientists nor by any one profession, but by common men who lifted up their eyes above the ordinary toil of life, and who for themselves and their fellow-men reached out to higher levels of knowledge and usefulness. I remembered too that your first great endowment came from a merchant — type of the unbroken line of the peerless merchants of Boston — who was little known among scientific scholars, yet contributed from the accumulations of his thrift to a higher culture than his own, and that this was only the beginning of a series of generous contributions from citizen after citizen, which culminated at last in ample revenues from your chief benefactor, who was not less distinguished for his wisdom in affairs than for his professional acquirements. And I remembered more than all, that the Commonwealth, which from the days of her founders until now never yet has failed the cause of education among her children, had from the first been the steadfast friend of this Society, giving it incorporation, aiding it in its early years with a modest but saving annual subsidy, and, in 1861, making to it the munificent donation of land on which its foundations now rest secure,— a donation that came not only with the good will and the God-speed of the Commonwealth, but with all the sympathy and inspiration of the soul of Governor Andrew, who, next to his devotion to human rights and hate of human wrongs, cherished the love of that enlarging learning which he knew is from the meanness of wrong to the nobility of right the slow but sure highway.

And so as one of the many citizens of Massachusetts, and also as one in official station representing her, I am emboldened, at your request, Mr. President, to unite my voice in the acclaim that hails this fiftieth anniversary of your existence. Memory and imagination,— those exquisite poets of the human mind,— memory that looks tenderly back over the past, and imagination that idealizes and yet in all its mounting knows that it fails to picture or command the future — are making this occasion not the mere boast of fifty years' success, but a tribute to what man has done, and a stimulus to what man yet a thousand times more shall do in behalf of the happiness, the delight, the knowledge, the ennobling of his fellow-men, unlocking from every nook and corner of the earth, and displaying in every form and motion of life, the beneficence of God. What a stride from those first small days,— that parlor sofa that once held you all,— those modest rooms, to this splendid temple, which I trust is to be your permanent home, where shall not only gather your rare and beautiful collections, but cluster with them also the memories of the

---

[1] The addresses at the Semi-Centennial meeting as presented, with the exception of that of Dr. Waterston, were taken from the reports made of them for the Boston Daily Advertiser.

zeal and devotion that have marked so many of your members. The birds of Bryant, the insects of Harris, the shells of Gould, the fossils from the Sivalik Hills, the contributions of a thousand helpful hands from every quarter of the globe suggest something more than their scientific value. For they are still alive with the generous love of science which prompted their bestowal, and which, clinging to them still like the scent to the vase, wreathes your walls, more beautifully than the chisel of the artist and in more enduring material, with the names and the features of those of whom I have spoken. Yes, and of Greene and Wyman and Jackson and Greenwood and Brewer and a hundred others.

If fifty years have wrought all this from such a slender beginning, what shall not fifty years more achieve? Everything, indeed, for science; everything for the increase of human knowledge. But more than all else, speaking for that Commonwealth which means not a function of government, but means the common weal of the people and of all the people of Massachusetts, her humblest, her weakest, her most dependent, those who sadly and heavily bear the burdens, who hew the wood and draw the water, I love to think that your labors, much as they delight you, will still more bear fruit for them, and that you are fulfilling the time when the student of science, exulting in the treasures that come to his exploring, and touching at his fingers' ends the keys that turn every element of the physical world into an agency of usefulness, not only finds his own cup full, but is the benefactor of the whole human race, alleviating the weight of toil, shortening the hours of the drayage of labor, enlarging the capacities and material of a brighter, happier, more generous life for all alike, and letting every soul go freer and freer in its up-springing and response to God.

The President next introduced Dr. Samuel Eliot, Superintendent of the Boston Public Schools.

Address of Dr. Eliot.

In opening his speech Dr. Eliot observed that he did not understand why he was called upon to represent the city of Boston in the absence of Mayor Prince. The only title, said he, which I can so much as imagine entitling me to speak in behalf of Boston, is that, to some extent, I am, for the time being, a representative of the public education of the city. Boston has no brighter jewel in her crown, Boston has had no higher function in all the long years of its past, than that which has made her the teacher and the mother of so many thousands of her children. Indeed, this education given in the public schools of various grades and names, and the work of such a Society as this, interests me very deeply. I think, as I stand here, of the scenes that I have looked upon in this and the adjoining building, where the teachers of our public schools have gone at the invitation of this Society, and, through individual genius and the contributions of the friends of this Society, have received lessons which they, in their turn, have given to their children. And when I think of all that this involves of nearness to nature, which forms so true an essential of education, and which, without such help as this Society has given, would be to-day little more than a name among our teachers and our pupils, I feel that I have the right, in behalf of the public schools of Boston and of the whole community, to thank the Society of Natural History for the help which they have given us. Nearness to nature, as I said, is one of the great essentials of education, but it has been one of the most difficult essentials to secure even in our comparatively late day. Anything that helps us to secure it; anything that brings nature closer to the schools, and the schools closer to nature, is doing good far beyond the limit of the schools. Think, for a moment, of the homes from which the pupils of our public schools come, of the absolute ignorance of nature, of all the beauties connected with her, or of the mysteries which extend so completely over all. Think of the clouds that may hang heavily over house after house and tenement after tenement within the limits of our city, and think how grateful the people must be, that from this Society as its source, is flowing in streams through the schools sweet and healing water, and is now reaching these homes; that there is no home now so far away but that nature is reaching it, and day by day will take possession of it. That is the inestimable service, Mr. President, which I am here to acknowledge, and I do it with a most glad and most grateful heart. It is not merely of the lessons and teachers of which I have spoken. Here are these collections, whose founders are everywhere generously commended. If the doors are open the light goes out through them and lights the earth, and we may be glad if we can even add a hundredth part to the radiance that is everywhere spreading abroad from them. As gratitude, Mr. President, is always a lively sense of favors to come I want to express my gratitude for the help that is yet to be given by this Society to those who come after us, and the next half-century will be even more fruitful than the last half-century has been, in maintaining the highest interest in the schools and homes which Boston claims as her own.

Address of President Eliot.

President Charles Eliot, of Harvard University, upon being introduced to the audience said:

This Society has two distinct objects — (1) the promotion of natural history by stimulating and aiding advanced study and original research, and (2) the enlightenment of the common people concerning animate and inanimate nature. What I have to say touches each of these two objects.

It would carry us into a discussion too solemn for this occasion to attempt to state the primary reasons which should induce men to study nature devotedly, although no tangible benefits could ever flow from that study; for I have never been able to find any better answer to the question — what is the chief end of studying nature — than the answer which the Westminster catechism gives to the question, what is the chief end of man — namely, "to glorify God, and to enjoy him forever."

I shall ask your attention to a proposition which contains only a secondary, though sufficient, reason for fostering the study of natural history — to the proposition that the human race has more and greater benefits to expect from the successful cultivation of the sciences which deal with living things than from all the other sciences put together. I by no means forget what mechanics and physics have brought to pass within a hundred years. They have already reduced the earth to one-tenth of its former size, as regards the carriage of persons and goods, and for the transmission of thought, will, and fact, they bid fair to make the whole surface of the globe as one room. They have made it easy, on the one hand, to concentrate population in dense masses, and on the other to reach new soils and shores, and to distribute to all countries the peculiar productions of each. These wonderful achievements of mechanics and physics, aided by chemistry, produce indirect effects upon the well-being of man, some good effects and some bad, with a probable preponderance of good; but their direct influence upon human character and happiness is not large. The reduction in size of our earth, our country, or our town, which railways, telegraphs and telephones have brought about is in itself no satisfaction. Rapid locomotion is not an object in itself. Does the average man get any more happiness out of his little span than he did one hundred years ago? or does he have a longer span? And if he does, have the inventions of the past century in mechanics and physics been a direct cause of the improvement? The answers to these questions are not ready and clear. We hesitate to give an affirmative reply. The fact is, that mechanics and physics deal only indirectly with human misery,—namely, climatic influences, not understood, and, therefore, not to be guarded against, violent and unpredictable extremes of heat or cold, wetness or dryness, ravages of noxious plants and animals, diseases both of men and of useful animals and untimely death. All these evils belong to the domain of natural history, and for ultimate deliverance from them we must look to the student of natural science.

It is astonishing how little progress has been made by the race in discovering the means of overcoming these evils. Civilized society to-day would be almost as helpless as Pharnoh was against the plagues which afflicted the Egyptians,—the river water suddenly made so foul that the fish in it died, frogs, lice, flies, a murrain upon cattle, boils, hail, locusts, dark fogs and the dread pestilence which struck one race and spared another upon the same soil. These are evils which, for the most part, we find resistless to-day. Every now and then some city's water supply is rendered unfit for use by an extraordinary production of multitudinous little plants or animals; the plant-louse destroys the vines in a wine-producing country, and brings the whole population to want; pleuro-pneumonia kills the cattle, now in this district, now in that; an obscure fungus causes the potato to rot, and a sudden famine is the result; the Colorado beetle, once a rarity in the collections of entomologists, swarms over a continent, devouring vast crops, and forcing the husbandman to abandon, for a time at least, the cultivation of various useful plants; in some of the Western States the harvest depends, not so much on the foresight and skill of man as on the favorableness or unfavorableness of the season to the development of grasshoppers. Indeed, thus far, any single-minded and prolific worm is more than a match for man. Think, too, of the diseases which afflict humanity, and are the source of by far the greater part of the sufferings and sorrows of men! There are the regular diseases to which we are so accustomed that we consider them normal phenomena, the new diseases, which appear or reappear at considerable intervals, and the occasional pestilences. Man is still so ignorant of the causes and sources of these various disorders, of the conditions which develop them, and of the means of eradicating and resisting them, that he is inclined to regard disease as a part of the order of nature, over which he can win no control.

But in view of all that science has accomplished within the lifetime of this Society, shall we not declare that this idea of nature and of man's relation to his environment is cowardly, stupid and ungrateful? Can we not clearly foresee that by the patient, thorough, cumulative study of natural history in all its branches, men will gradually arrive at a knowledge of plants and animals, and of the favorable and unfavorable conditions of life for all plants and animals, which will give them control over many evils which they now find wholly mysterious and irresistible? I can only touch very briefly upon some of the grounds of this belief.

The physician or surgeon of the last century was hardly wiser than Hippocrates or more successful; but any old physician or surgeon would tell us to-day that the means and methods of observation, diagnosis and treatment have wonderfully improved during his lifetime; that many operations are now successfully performed which were formerly supposed to be impossible; that the whole subject of preventive medicine and public hygiene has been developed in his day; and that he has seen the beginnings of the scientific study of heredity, that most fruitful and promising field of scientific and philanthropic research. Thanks in part to the progress in physics and chemistry, natural history possesses new and powerful implements of research, and new methods of inquiry which are of infinite promise. The morbid anatomist observes, not the gross external appearances, but the abnormal cellular changes which produce, or are, disease; the physiologist studies the processes of living animals; the chemist is constantly making natural organic products by artificial means; the embryologist has become conversant with those slight differentiations in the egg which are the starting points of wide diversities; substantial beginnings of weather knowledge appear; the whole earth has been explored, and now for the first time the fauna of the ocean abysses is made known.

Antiquity had its great students of nature, but they lacked the means of diffusing, preserving and accumulating their discoveries. The past four centuries have had abundant means of recording and transmitting from one generation to another all the scientific truth which they became possessed of. It is in this steady, patient and orderly accumulation of facts concerning living things that the hope of winning for man new powers over the gravest natural evils really lies. This Society has a part in making that pregnant record.

There is another aspect of your work which seems to me very important. You propose to maintain for the public an exhibition of all forms of vegetable and animal life in their wondrous and endless variety. Hither people may come and see their fellow-beings in the widest and truest sense. Moralists tell us that the best development of an individual man is not to be reached through introspection, self-reference and an overweening anxiety about his own salvation. They say to every man — look out and not in. The same exhortation might well be addressed to the human race. Mankind needs to look out, and not in; to realize that it is but one, though a noble one, among countless races and tribes of creatures which inhabit or have inhabited this atom of an earth, and that its welfare is not the sole end of creation, or the one absorbing interest of the Creator. A few years ago all men believed that the whole boundless universe centred upon man. That delusion has lost its hold, except perhaps within the well-protected domain of dogmatic theology. But there are still many people who cling to the kindred conceit that this earth, at least, was made for man. It is a belief which will not survive much acquaintance with the vast solitudes of the earth which teem with other life than man's — the everglades, the jungles, the mountains and seas. It is a belief which a thoughtful man or child will be apt to qualify or resign, as he studiously examines such a collection of natural history as this Society strives to maintain.

Address of Mr. Alexander Agassiz.

Mr. Alexander Agassiz was the next speaker. In the first part of his address he mentioned the difficulties through which the Society had passed. An interesting extract from his remarks is given below:

The scientific man should be without nationality, ready to welcome progress from any quarter. Science is bound neither by country nor creed in its relation to new information. An important publication, a new line of research, a brilliant hypothesis, should appeal to us, not because it is American, German, French or English, nor because it is on the winning side in the questions of the day. It is, of course, natural that a country comparatively young in scientific culture should turn to older institutions for its standards, should be constantly tempted to compare its own learned societies and their doings with those of more ancient date and established influence. But while measuring our progress by theirs with honorable emulation, let us not make the mistake of also measuring our scientific men by a reflected light only, making our own recognition of them wait upon that from the other side of the water. Every nation should be proud of its great men, and may be excused for overrating them, but it should also add to an excusable national vanity an independence capable of recognizing, appreciating and sympathizing with the men who are raising the intellectual standard of their country to that of older ones. The pioneers of science in this country were neither remote imitators nor simply commentators; they have not only laid the foundations of natural science in this country, but they have extended its boundaries on many fields. Nor should we assume that they had need of a kind word of recognition from the other institutions or individuals. Let me not, however, be understood for a moment as disparaging the intelligent criticism of press or colleagues at home or abroad. I only wish to distinguish between that and the notoriety so easily gained by constant appeals to the public either in person or through scientific quacks.

Since, however, the true investigator rarely has either the time or the disposition to become the expounder of his own work, it is not always possible for the public to draw the line between those who speak from their own knowledge and the scientific *litterateur* who forages in any field where booty is to be gained. We have met to-day to honor the pioneers of science in this country by a grateful recognition of what has been accomplished from the small beginnings of fifty years ago. Taking up some of the more prominent names of the early days of the Natural History Society we must award the highest place to men like Wyman, Harris, Bigelow, Gould, Storer and Binney, whose investigations have paved the way for their successors of the present day. They were men of no ordinary stamp. They were men who in any country would have been recognized as leaders in science, and whose fame will live when many of us are forgotten.

The speech closed with a high tribute to the late President Wyman.

ADDRESS OF REV. ROBERT C. WATERSTON.

On a semi-centennial celebration like this, while we have reason to congratulate the members of the Society of Natural History here assembled, on the great success which has crowned our past efforts, and on the cheering prospects of the future, which dawn before us like the morning of a yet brighter day, still we cannot but recall with feelings of sadness and solemnity the many who have labored with us in the earlier history of the Society, no longer here. Largely to their unwearied efforts are we indebted for the prosperity we now enjoy. Constant inspiration comes to us from the remembrance of their quickening zeal, their love of knowledge, and their generous desire to communicate to others, what they so profoundly valued themselves. How heartily do we wish they could be with us, on this eventful day. And yet, as we look around upon these walls, and gaze upon the life-like portraits of the past officers and benefactors of the Society, it seems as if, in very truth, they were actually here, participating with us in the privileges of this occasion.

Before us, is our first President, Dr. B. D. Greene, with his calm expression of blended sweetness and power. A love of nature pervaded his life. Extensively on this continent, in the tropics, and in most of the countries of Europe, he diligently pursued his botanical researches. Blessed with ample means, he was able to make his investigations under every advantage. Years which might have been given to luxurious repose, were by him gladly devoted to earnest study. Thus did he acquire a knowledge seldom surpassed, and while constantly consulted by younger botanists, never did he decline to impart from his abundant resources. We do not forget that his rare herbarium, containing the results of long personal industry, and the fruit of more than a quarter of a century of intercourse and exchange with Sir William Hooker and other distinguished botanists in every section of the globe, including plants gathered during the first Expedition of Sir John Franklin, constituting in all an invaluable collection for quality as well as quantity, we do not forget that this he presented to the Society, together with between one and two thousand volumes of botanical works from his library; and that at the time of his death, he enriched the Society by a munificent bequest.

And here by his side, is " the beloved physician," Dr. Augustus A. Gould, who from his large professional labors, could always find time for the benefit of this Society. In the department of conchology he was an acknowledged authority. The collections here bear testimony to his zeal. I well remember the interest he awakened by one of his lectures to teachers within these walls. Many of his hearers stopped and expressed their wish to visit in his company the sea-shore, that they might gather shells on the sands and listen to his instruction in the midst of Nature. He made arrangements with them on the spot, and within a week they went together to a neighboring beach, and there they passed such a day as they will never forget.

And here is our friend Professor Jeffries Wyman, who shunned popularity, rather than sought it, and who cared always to *be* and never to *seem*. His aim was ever Truth, simple, absolute Truth. Indefatigable in his researches, he would never abandon any investigation until it was thoroughly completed, and would leave nothing for students who should come after, but astonishment at what he had accomplished. While engrossed in his studies

I doubt if he would have been disturbed though an armed force had cannonaded the building. It was said of Constable the artist, that in the fields he would sit so calmly in his contemplation of the landscape, that the field-mice would creep into his pocket. I think they might have done the same with Professor Wyman, though I would not answer for it that they might not become, under his hand, interesting specimens in Comparative Anatomy. Unassuming in manner, and with a mortal aversion to pretentious conceit, no man valued true merit more heartily than he did, or was more earnest to assist struggling endeavor. His name is now honored as widely as science is known.

And here we look upon the face of Agassiz whose benignant smile is to-day, as it ever was, a benediction. How absolutely with him the man of science became the acknowledged Instructor. Whether in the halls of legislation or the popular assembly, or before a convention of teachers, or in his own private lecture-room, he was the Educator. He seemed born for this vocation. His gift of speech, his genial spirit, his sympathetic and magnetic power, made all listen with avidity. He knew not only how to gather, but how to impart. Whether he was discoursing upon glaciers or embryology, upon the structure of animal life, coral-reefs, star-fish, or an oyster, he was alike able to arrest and rivet attention, leading the mind from point to point, wondering and delighted, until rising above the individual it grasped the universal, and seeing the hidden law, it recognized through that, the Divine Intelligence.

With voice, manner, look, he held entranced the hearer, leading him onward from stage to stage in the line of progress. In all he did, he was preëminently the teacher of the individual, the community, the nation. "I have been," he said, "a Teacher ever since I was fifteen years of age. I am so now, and I hope I shall continue to be all my life." He did so continue, and so he still is; through the memory of his life, and through the words he has left us, he is emphatically the Educator; kindling a desire for knowledge and the love of progress. The increasing interest in the study of natural history, seen everywhere, how much he did to awaken !

While we look upon that countenance, do we not all recall those words of Longfellow, addressed to Agassiz on his fiftieth birthday, where Nature is represented as speaking:

> " Come wander with me," she said,
> "Into regions yet untrod ;
> And read, what is still unread,
> In the Manuscripts of God ! "
>
> " So he wandered away and away
> With Nature, the dear old Nurse,
> Who sang to him night and day
> The hymns of the Universe ! "

And even thus, by night and by day, to every true-hearted Naturalist, Nature pours forth her celestial melodies:

> " And whenever the way seems long,
> And our hearts begin to fail,
> She will sing a more wonderful song, —
> Or tell a more marvellous tale ! "

The members of this Society know full well the deep joy that is awakened through that harmony with Nature which comes from the study of her works. The vast collections of wonders treasured up within these walls, are infinitely more to the naturalist than curiosities. They are revelations of eternal laws. They are the condensed history of the ages. They converse, in a mysterious language, of things that were; unfolding the marvellous processes that are ever going on in the hidden laboratories of the earth.

According to our power of observation, the development of our faculties, the extent of our knowledge, and the elevation of our own nature, will be what we shall here find and enjoy. Such collections as are within these walls will help us to ascertain whether the works of the Almighty have a language which we can interpret. Here, according to our susceptibility, will a love of knowledge be stimulated, the intellectual energies quickened, and all that is best and noblest in our nature called into activity.

Not as a place for idle amusement were these walls erected. Not to gratify a vague inquisitiveness were these collections gathered. Not for spinning the gossamer threads of fanciful speculation were these halls and lecture-rooms dedicated. But for the highest culture of which man is capable. For the acquirement of solid information. For the opportunity of studying results gained by scientific explorers all over the globe. We cannot personally accompany Sir Edward Parry and Sir John Richardson to the Arctic regions, or with Humboldt climb Chimborazo, or penetrate the forests with Audubon, or sail in "Her Majesty's ship" the "Beagle" round the world, but we can come here and study the result of such labors. All that is of deepest interest between the equator and the two poles, is here brought together. In books of voyages and travels, in works upon botany, zoölogy, and palæontology; through specimens of rocks, ores, and fossils, gathered from every zone: what branch of the natural sciences may not here be investigated? Here is opportunity for observation and thought, analysis and comparison. Who will affirm that such an institution is not an essential part of our whole educational system, from the elementary School, up to the University; yes, and onward through that continued education which shall extend to the utmost limit of life?

This educational principle was recognized from the very commencement of the Society, its avowed purpose being "the encouragement and promotion of the Science of Natural History," which it was distinctly stated, the friends of the Society not only desired for themselves, but that the interest might be extended far beyond their own circle.

They were, however, few in number, and with limited means; a scanty library and a meagre collection, with as yet but feeble response from the public. This now populous city was then not much more than a village, and the very taste which the founders of this institution sought to direct and foster, had first to be created. We can hardly know how they surmounted the difficulties they had to overcome. Still they persevered until at length they became established in a building of more adequate accommodation in Mason Street. Through every stage, there was a recognition of the same educational principle, and, as their opportunities were enlarged, this purpose became more and more prominent. Not only scientific students and intelligent citizens availed themselves of its advantages, but often entire schools, with their teachers, visited the Museum for a day's study; the curators and officers of the Society giving explanations in their several departments, thus rendering the occasions of real service to both masters and pupils.

As the collections accumulated, and the beneficial influence of the Society became more fully demonstrated, a larger field constantly opened; and an appeal was at length made to the Commonwealth for an appropriation of land upon which a more suitable building might be erected. The motive urged was, that the institution would thus be established "*on a permanent basis of augmented usefulness.*" It was declared that the result of its thirty years' efforts had been a rapid advancement of knowledge, with an almost universal dissemination of a love for the natural sciences, that now there was a general recognition of its claims to an honorable rank in our system of public education, while it was acknowledged that its labors tended to promote both the intellectual and material prosperity of the Commonwealth.

Thus while it was well understood that scientific men and professional students were to have every advantage within command of the Society, still it was also understood that the classification of all the collections, and their entire arrangement, was to be such that the public generally should have opportunity of gaining correct knowledge, and that such practical aid should be rendered to our schools, as might be invaluable in its results.

My recollection of this Society goes back to the time when it had its rooms in the old Atheneum in Pearl Street. The building in Mason Street I often frequented, and at the time when the plea was made for aid from the Commonwealth, I had the privilege of being one of the petitioners, and acted with the committee, addressing the members of the Legislature at the State House. I recall, as if it were yesterday, the interest of that time. I had just returned from Europe, and during an absence of several years had enjoyed opportunities of observing the working of such institutions abroad, and feeling strongly that the educational principle was of the utmost importance, I dwelt upon it in my statements. That this view had weight with the members of the Legislature, I have reason to know, and upon this consideration the generous aid of the Commonwealth was granted.

I well remember an address by Professor Agassiz, at that time, in the House of Representatives, on which occasion he dwelt upon the desirableness of training the young, from their earliest years, to observe and study the works of God in Nature, urging this as among the best means of disciplining the intellectual powers, purifying the taste and exalting the character. He insisted that the study of the phenomena of nature was one of the most potent means of developing the human faculties, and that such education should be introduced into the schools as soon as practicable, and made an indispensable part of all education; he trusted that the time when the importance of this view would be fully recognized was only so far remote as was necessary for the preparation of teachers capable of properly imparting this instruction. The only difficulty, he added, is to find teachers equal to the task, and the task is no small one. The whole force of his argument went to prove that an institution like this, to aid teachers in their preparation, was of inestimable importance. Here, as we may easily understand, those who have an aptitude for such studies, may find materials, examples, illustrations, suggestions, all brought to their hand arranged and classified. With such advantages the study of natural history may be interwoven with the whole system of education, and become one of its most essential features.

After this building was completed, additional funds were requisite, to carry out the work contemplated. The Commonwealth had granted the land. The building was erected by generous contributions. Now, therefore, that forty thousand dollars in addition was to be given by its earnest friends, it was not simply to render it more attractive to citizens and strangers, but it was avowedly to make it "*one of the first Educational Scientific Institutions in the Country.*"

This Society has not rested satisfied with making profession of this purpose. It has lived up to its profession and its purposes have been faithfully carried out. Every promise has been kept, and every reasonable anticipation realized.

Persons who are not thoroughly acquainted with this Society, can hardly understand the amount of talent and labor which has been concentrated in this work. What self-sacrifice on the part of individuals, unremitting perseverance and toil have been necessary to complete every arrangement.

No one knows better than yourself, Mr. President, that no money could pay for the thought and labor which has been freely rendered here by the officers and friends of this institution, while their love for the Society and the cause to which it is devoted, has been in their estimation an ample reward.

After the dedication of the building, the work first inaugurated was a series of lectures and addresses in this hall to the Teachers of the Schools of Boston. Between six and seven hundred teachers availed themselves of the privilege. At the introductory meeting the Governor of the Commonwealth, John A. Andrew; the Mayor of the City, F. W. Lincoln; the President of Harvard University, Thomas Hill; the Secretary of the Board of Education, Joseph White; the Superintendent of Schools, John D. Philbrick; and George B. Emerson, one of the earliest members of the Society, took part, making it a memorable occasion.

After this there were lectures on successive weeks by Professor Jeffries Wyman, Dr. Asa Gray, Dr. Augustus A. Gould, Professor W. B. Rogers and others. These lectures were amply illustrated, covering botany, conchology, and general zoölogy. The instructors of over thirty thousand children were present. The ablest scientific men in the country on those days imparted freely of their knowledge, suggesting the best means of conveying instruction, and giving a fresh impulse to the educators assembled, who, on their part, warmly appreciated the interest thus shown, and hailed it as one of the new instrumentalities for their improvement.

This hope on their part has not been disappointed. The Society has been consistently faithful to its avowed purpose, and whenever their limited funds have been inadequate to meet the necessary expenditure, generous assistance has been liberally furnished by public-spirited friends.

To render the collections of the Society more instructive, a careful rearrangement has been made throughout, involving immense labor. Thus through all the departments the educational requirements have been recognized, and the successive stages in the history of creation are visibly unfolded to the eye, exemplifying the actual results of scientific knowledge and principles. The hasty observer can have but a feeble conception of the sublime meaning embodied in this careful and scholarly arrangement, but the more fully it is comprehended the more profound will be the appreciation.

Teachers and pupils may often be seen together, thoughtfully pursuing their investigations from hall to hall. Some with artistic skill making drawings, others taking notes, and many more lost in astonishment, and filled with admiration and delight.

But added to this, regular classes have been formed to whom systematic instruction has been given. The study of natural history having been definitely introduced into the public schools, a new zeal has been awakened among the teachers. With some teachers, additional knowledge is a necessity, while with all it is evidently a pleasure. The different branches are pursued under the guidance of able professors in connection with this Society. What is known as the "Teachers' School of Science" has acquired positive importance. Professor Hyatt, the Custodian, has been unceasing in his efforts, and has been gratified at the extraordinary success which has followed his labors. This special work has been going on for the last ten years, but never with such marked results as during the past year. The number of applicants for admission to these lectures has been four times larger than in any previous period. Over six hundred persons recorded their names as students, while the average attendance on each pleasant day was five hundred. There have been distributed among these students more than one hundred thousand specimens. Yes, during the present year there has actually been given away — not one thousand, or ten thousand, or fifty thousand, but — though one can hardly credit it — one hundred thousand specimens, all of which may be studied by the teachers at their homes, or used for illustration in their schools.

We talk of the wonders of the telephone; yet here is a still more felicitous method of communication; six hundred intelligent teachers, going forth from this place to convey the knowledge gained to thirty thousand young people, full of life and eager to learn. Thus has this Society become more emphatically than ever before — an educational power in the community.

Still it would be unjust to infer, from the facts which have been considered, that the larger portion of the attention of this Society has been given to teaching even instructors. Accomplished naturalists, through its collections and its library, find ample material to extend their investigations. Many come here to test their theories, or more fully to establish their conclusions. Besides which, many of the members, in the course of the year (on their individual account, and for professional purposes), visit distant parts of the country, or take even a wider circuit. They may be found along the whole coast of New England, searching her rocks and sands, or dredging in the deep-sea, or exploring the Gulf-stream, or among the Florida reefs, or skirting the shores of the Great Lakes, or passing down the Valley of the Mississippi, or climbing the Rocky Mountains and the Sierra Nevada, or descending the Western slope, or threading the Pacific Coast, or penetrating to Alaska, and China, and Japan. And when they return, they come to tell us of their experiences, bringing additions to our collections, and recounting in addresses and lectures the result of their scientific investigations. Has not one spoken of Iceland, and another of Labrador? One of Indian relics and Western mounds? One of Colorado with its extensive parks and prolific mines of silver and gold? One of the Calaveras and Mariposa groves with their colossal trees, the famous *Sequoia gigantea*, and the Yosemite Valley with its unequalled waterfalls and stupendous granite domes? One of Alaska, and another of China and Japan?

It is certainly not claiming too much when we say that at the regular meetings of this Society one may hear as interesting and instructive accounts as can be found recorded in all literature. And thus to members, and to all who have the privilege of being present, such opportunities are exceedingly attractive. These addresses and lectures are not the less entertaining because they are instructive. The stories of the Arabian Nights are not more wonderful than are often these narratives. Travellers' Stories they are, but none the less true because stranger than fiction. Sindbad the sailor saw no greater treasures than are those which at times are added to our collections. Some of these are as of yesterday, while others take the mind back to that early time "when the morning stars sang together and all the sons of God shouted for joy!"

Mr. President, I congratulate you on this interesting anniversary, and I am sure the members will unite with me in saying that the time of your official connection with this Society covers one of the brightest periods of its history.

At the close of the address of the Rev. Mr. Waterston, the President, expressing the great satisfaction felt by the Society at such a large attendance on the part of its friends, invited all present, with the aid of the "Introduction to a General Guide to the Museum," which had been distributed among them, to look over the collections, either then or at a more convenient time. The lateness of the hour prevented more than a very cursory examination of them.

In the evening a reception was given by the President, at his residence in Newbury Street, to the members of the Society and many ladies and gentlemen interested in its work. Thus the day was appropriately closed in the enjoyment of social intercourse, and all parted, feeling that the celebration of the Semi-Centennial Anniversary of the foundation of the Society had been thoroughly successful.

The annual meeting of the Society was held on the fifth day of May, Vice-President S. H. Scudder being in the Chair.

After the reading of the records of previous meetings the report of the Custodian, of the Secretary and of the Treasurer were presented. From these, abstracts will be here given.

The Custodian commenced by stating that in some respects the official year just closed was one of the most important in the history of the Society. It was marked not alone by being the termination of the first half century of its existence, but by the fact that the Museum had begun at last the career for which preparation had been making during the past ten years.

Of the publications he remarked that they were very creditable, but that it should not be forgotten that paucity of resources had caused the frequent refusal of important papers; that this was greatly to be deplored, since properly illustrated publication is often the only reward of scientific labor, and the prompt issue of memoirs is essential to the successful attainment of the chief object of all scientific associations that seek to encourage the spirit of original research.

The material results, as exhibited in the collections, the library, and the publications, were very valuable as credentials of a prudent and economical administration. The Society might rest well satisfied with the position which these had earned for it in the estimation of a community which rightfully demands such guarantees of the proper use of trust funds. These, however, were not the best fruits of its exertions. These seem to lie in the fact that the community is beginning dimly to comprehend that an institution of this kind creates an atmosphere around it which is beneficial to them and to their children, and also that it works directly for their intellectual improvement.

The celebration of the anniversary of the formation of the Society was dwelt upon at some length by the Custodian, but as a full account of this has already been given it is not necessary to repeat his remarks. Much was said by him also relative to the resignation of the President which will be here omitted.

The preparation of the general guide to the Museum, the numbering of the cases, the lettering of the rooms and galleries, and the construction of two new floor cases were mentioned as having been completed during the year. Synoptical collections for the departments of Mineralogy, Geology and Palaeontology had also been made and were or soon would be on exhibition.

In the department of Geology much had been done by Mr. Crosby, assisted by Miss Carter. About 2500 specimens of rocks had been catalogued, and nearly 2000 of these mounted and labelled. These included a collection of specimens illustrating a synopsis of the classification of rocks, a systematic or lithological collection, a collection illustrating structural geology, and one of historical geology.

The important subject of dynamical geology, the Custodian stated, must remain unrepresented until floor cases could be furnished. The lack of means at present prevents this from being done. The principal accession to the department of Geology consisted of four hundred specimens contributed by Mr. Crosby.

The Palaeontological collection had been increased by a small but quite valuable series of Crinoids purchased by the Laboratory fund.

The labelling and cataloguing of the Mollusca had been completed by Mr. Van Vleck, assisted by Miss Washburn. To this department a very valuable addition had been made by the purchase of the Blaschka models. These were made of glass and represented very closely the living animal. There were 74 specimens in all, representing 17 genera and 44 species of the soft bodied Cephalopods and naked Gasteropoda.

The Corals and the Echinoderms had been rearranged, mounted and labelled during the year, this work having also been done by Mr. Van Vleck, assisted by Miss Washburn.

In the department of Entomology, Mr. Henshaw had been engaged in selecting specimens for the formation of a synoptical collection representing the anatomy of insects, and considerable progress had been made by him in identifying and arranging the species of the general systematic collections.

The department of Comparative Anatomy had been entirely rearranged so as to bring it into harmony with the rest of the collections of the Museum. In the wall cases of Room G, a synoptical collection had been placed illustrating the type characteristics and anatomical peculiarities of the different classes of Vertebrates. A similar collection of Invertebrates will occupy the two floor cases which had just been erected in the same room. The osteological portion of the collection in the main hall remained nearly as before, but the special homologies of the limbs and systems of organs, etc., among Vertebrates had been placed in Room F. To Dr. W. F. Whitney, the Society is indebted for the entire rearrangement of these last, and for much assistance in other portions of the work.

The identification and labelling of the New England collection of fishes had been commenced by Mr. Van Vleck. A large number of species obtained at Annisquam by the efforts of the Custodian, had been added to this collection.

Of the Amphibia, 75 species had been identified, arranged and catalogued. Of the New England species, of which there are 25 in all, 23 were reported as in the collection.

In referring to the department of Ornithology, the Custodian alluded to the death of the distinguished ornithologist, Dr. Thomas M. Brewer, and of the great service rendered by him to the Society in this department, whilst in charge of its general collection. To his exertions also the Society owes its fine collection of eggs and nests, and also the New England collection of birds. This last he would have undoubtedly made complete had he lived a year or two longer.

Some work had been done in arranging and labelling several of the groups of birds, by Mr. Henshaw, assisted by Miss Washburn.

The terse remarks made by the Custodian upon the mammals need no abbreviation or variation. They are therefore given verbatim: "The less said about the mammals the better. They are a disgrace to the institution, but there is no way of getting a respectable collection except by buying specimens, and this is impossible for us."

In the department of Botany the Custodian stated that considerable progress had been made towards the formation of a synoptical collection of plants, so that each order and some of the sub-orders shall be represented by one species which will be mounted, framed, and appropriately labelled. Already ninety specimens, representing eighty-five orders and sub-orders had been finished. The arrangements of the general collection according to Bentham and Hooker's Genera Plantarum had progressed under the direction of Mr. Cummings, and much had been done towards supplying deficiencies in this collection.

It had been the habit of the Custodian during the vacation period of the summer months to pass much time in dredging and fishing off the coast, with the purpose of obtaining for the Society specimens necessary for the completion of the New England collections, and in this work he had been aided by assistants in the Museum and others. Of the labors of the previous season he thus speaks: "The summer of 1879 was spent at Annisquam by the Custodian and a party consisting of Mr. Van Vleck, Mr. E. G. Gardiner and Mr. E. R. Warren. The collecting was more successful than during the previous season, but still the need of a large boat and greater facilities is imperative." To supply this need, the Custodian intended to have another and more capacious boat ready for use before another summer.

The Laboratory. In this department there had been much accomplished of satisfying character. Instruction had been given as usual to classes from the Boston University and the Massachusetts Institute of Technology. Besides these another class of twenty-six persons, all teachers except four, had entered upon a course which is to last for two winters, or about one hundred hours, two hours being devoted to it every Saturday morning. A small class of advanced students have been taking a course in biology, given by the assistant, Mr. Van Vleck.

Teachers' School of Science. It will be remembered that at the time of the last annual meeting of the Society, and when the report for the previous year was presented, the very successful course of lectures to the teachers then in progress was not quite completed. Those given by the Custodian were soon after brought to a satisfactory close, and a series of five on mineralogy followed, delivered by Mr. Burbank. These were very instructive, and the interest in them was shown by the average attendance being kept up to the last. A geological excursion by the lecturer and a part of the teachers was made to Marblehead after the course was finished.

The report of the Secretary, Mr. Burgess, was very gratifying, giving as it did statistics showing much activity and progress in the several departments mentioned.

Of members, twenty-six Associate had been elected during the year, but no Corporate,

Corresponding or Honorary. Five Associate or Corporate members had resigned, and four had died. The whole number of Associate and Corporate members was stated to be 451.

There had been an average attendance of thirty-nine persons at the sixteen general meetings of the Society. The largest number present at any one time was eighty-one, the smallest nineteen. Eight meetings of the section of Entomology had been held, the average attendance at which had been eight persons. The meetings of the botanical section had been given up in consequence of the non-attendance of a sufficient number of members to render them interesting.

In December of the past year, by consent of the Society, the section of Microscopy was revived, and monthly meetings had since been held, though without a very promising attendance.

Of the library, the Secretary stated that the additions to it during the year exceeded those of any other in the Society's history. These were summarized thus:

	8vo.	4to.	Fo.	Totals.
Volumes	348	69	2	419
Parts of Volumes	947	156	170	1273
Pamphlets	335	52	2	389
Maps and Charts				99
In all				2180

Besides the constant use made of the books by members and others at the Library, there had been borrowed 1110 volumes during the year, by one hundred and twenty-three persons.

Of the publications two parts of the twentieth volume of the Proceedings, and a third article for the third volume of the Memoirs had been issued, the last being a revision of the Palaeozoic Cockroaches of the world, by Mr. Samuel H. Scudder, 113 pages, 5 plates. Of "Occasional Papers" a volume had been published, being the third of the series, containing Mr. W. O. Crosby's contributions to the Geology of Eastern Massachusetts, 266 pages, with 5 plates and a colored map.

In addition to these, No. 6 of the series of Guides for Science Teaching, by Professor Hyatt, had been printed, also a pamphlet introductory to the general guide to the Museum, also by Professor Hyatt. Copies of this last publication were presented to the audience at the celebration of the semi-centennial anniversary of the Society.

The Committee on Publications having suggested that a special volume should be published commemorative of the fiftieth anniversary of the Society, the Council voted that this should be done provided a sufficient number of subscribers could be obtained for such volume at the rate of ten dollars a copy, to justify the necessary expenditure. To ensure the success of this project the Rev. Robert C. Waterston, with characteristic generosity, had already given one hundred dollars. It was understood that the volume should contain a history of the Society, and a series of scientific papers, and be entitled "Anniversary Memoirs of the Boston Society of Natural History."

Walker Prizes. Relative to the Walker Prizes, the Secretary stated that no essay had been presented on the subject proposed for 1880, viz.:

"The evidences of the extension of the Tertiary deposits seaward along the coast of Massachusetts."

Mention was made of the award of the Grand Walker prize during the year to Dr. Leidy, but as this has been particularly related on a former page, no further statement is required here.

The Treasurer's report showed that there had been an excess of expenditures over the receipts of $698.95. As, however, the payments included the $1000 awarded for the Grand Walker prize, and as such prize is only payable once in five years, the spirit of the determination that expenditures should be kept within the limits of receipts was not violated.

At the election, the officers chosen were as follows. The full list is here presented that it may be seen in whose hands the destiny of the Society was entrusted at the close of the first half century of its existence, and at the commencement of a new era.

PRESIDENT,
SAMUEL H. SCUDDER.

VICE-PRESIDENTS,
JOHN CUMMINGS, F. W. PUTNAM.

CUSTODIAN,
ALPHEUS HYATT.

HONORARY SECRETARY,
S. L. ABBOT.

SECRETARY,
EDWARD BURGESS.

TREASURER,
CHARLES W. SCUDDER.

LIBRARIAN,
EDWARD BURGESS.

Committees on Departments of the Museum.

MINERALS.
THOMAS T. BOUVÉ,
R. H. RICHARDS,
M. E. WADSWORTH.

GEOLOGY.
WILLIAM H. NILES,
G. FREDERIC WRIGHT,
L. S. BURBANK.

PALAEONTOLOGY.
THOMAS T. BOUVÉ,
N. S. SHALER.

BOTANY.
JOHN CUMMINGS,
CHARLES J. SPRAGUE,
J. AMORY LOWELL.

MICROSCOPY.
SAMUEL WELLS,
R. C. GREENLEAF,
B. JOY JEFFRIES.

COMPARATIVE ANATOMY.
THOMAS DWIGHT,
W. F. WHITNEY.

RADIATES, CRUSTACEANS AND WORMS.
H. A. HAGEN,
ALEXANDER AGASSIZ,
L. F. POURTALÈS.

MOLLUSKS.
EDWARD S. MORSE,
J. HENRY BLAKE.

INSECTS.
SAMUEL H. SCUDDER,
EDWARD BURGESS,
A. S. PACKARD, JR.

FISHES AND REPTILES.
F. W. PUTNAM,
THEODORE LYMAN,
S. W. GARMAN.

BIRDS.
J. A. ALLEN,
SAMUEL CABOT.

MAMMALS.
J. A. ALLEN,
E. L. MARK,
GEORGE L. GOODALE.

On the announcement of the ballot the President elect said, "that in occupying the position to which he had been called, he could only express the wish that the choice had fallen elsewhere, for he felt he owed the Society any service he might be able to render. Any one as long acquainted with its government as he had been, must be alive to the responsibilities of its highest office, but knowing the hearty support which would be given to one aiming to carry out the objects of our Society with singleness of purpose, he could not foster such misgivings as naturally arose in undertaking them."

Mr. Scudder then sketched briefly the Society's work, more particularly dwelling upon its chief aim, popular instruction. The highly complimentary remarks towards the writer and compiler of this history which followed, not only made by Mr. Scudder but by many others, and the action taken by the Society, were of too personal a character to admit of his presenting them here. Nothing certainly could have been more grateful to his feelings than such a manifestation at the close of his long official life as President of the Society.

The Standing Committees elected by the Council for the official year 1880–81 were as follows: *Library*, Edward Burgess, W. H. Niles, W. F. Whitney. *Publications*, S. H. Scudder, S. L. Abbot, Edward Burgess, Alpheus Hyatt, J. A. Allen. *Museum*, Alpheus Hyatt, S. H. Scudder, Thomas T. Bouvé, John Cummings. Edward Burgess; *Walker prizes*, William B. Rogers, Alexander Agassiz, F. W. Putnam. *Membership*, S. H. Scudder, M. E. Wadsworth, B. Joy Jeffries, Edward Burgess, George L. Goodale. *Lectures and meetings*, S. H. Scudder, M. E. Wadsworth, Edward Burgess, F. W. Putnam, W. H. Niles. *Bird certificates*, Edward Burgess, J. A. Allen. *Trustees*, Thomas T. Bouvé, John Cummings, C. W. Scudder.

The fifth decade had now passed. If it could be said of the fourth that it was a period of great events in the history of the Society, the same could be said of the fifth, though those of the latter were of a less striking character. During the fourth, large donations and bequests were made, enabling the Society to erect its magnificent museum and to take a position among the leading institutions of the kind in the world, publishing freely its Memoirs and Proceedings, and making exchanges with kindred societies, thus acquiring for itself respect at home and abroad. During the fifth, scarcely a donation or bequest of any amount was received, though the lack of means was felt in every department. This prevented such expansion of the work of the Society as was deemed desirable, and made it dependent on the individual contributions of its members, mainly upon one of them, to accomplish much that it was able to do. What particularly characterized the last decade was the great change effected in its plans and purposes, but more in its modes of action and in the arrangement of its collections; not through revolution but by evolution, the result of advanced views in relation to museums and teaching, growing out of the experience of the Society itself and of kindred institutions at home and abroad. No longer would it suffice that great collections should be made in the different departments of natural history, however well arranged and labelled the specimens might be in each; it was necessary that all should be subordinated to a comprehensive plan, so that they should bear a proper relation to each other, and, moreover, include synoptical series which should furnish to those seeking knowledge a key to the proper understanding of the whole. A further development of thought upon the Museum led to the formation of a separate local New England collection in each department. Now to accomplish this, and to provide for the safety of the fast increasing collections, it was absolutely necessary not only to prepare rooms unfinished at the commencement of the decade, but to reconstruct all the cases first erected in the building because of their defective character, as has been mentioned on an earlier page. This change alone, with the necessary relabelling and other work upon the specimens, was the labor of years, but one of vast importance to the future influence of the Museum as an educational instrumentality. This great work could not have been done in the thorough manner it was, had not the more important change been first made of placing at the head of the Museum a scientific man whose single duty it was to act as a Custodian, and to furnish him with paid assistants to work upon the collections. Fortunately for the Society, Mr. Alpheus Hyatt, a man of large natural endowments and of broad comprehensive views, was elected to this office. To him was due the conception of the plan finally carried out for the arrangement of the whole Museum. It was the good fortune of the writer to be associated with him in this work and to give the influence of his official position as President of the Society in having it fully and faithfully done

The financial resources of the Society were somewhat impaired during the decade by the fitting up of the rooms alluded to and the reconstruction of the cases. It also suffered by the great fire of 1872, having held a considerable amount of stock in insurance companies which became worthless, and by being called upon to pay assessments to mutual companies in which its property was insured. If thus for reasons not arising from any fault or bad management the income of the Society was lessened, the Council may well point with satisfaction to the fact, that the ordinary expenses were not allowed to exceed the income. To prevent this from being the case, however, much was left undone that ought to have been done, and it was only by the pecuniary aid of neighbors and friends that the Society was recently able to enclose the grounds about its Museum with a suitable curbing of stone, and properly grade them.

The Society lost by death during these ten years, many of its most highly valued and honored members, Louis Agassiz, Dr. Jeffries Wyman, Dr. Charles Pickering, Edward Pickering, Dr. John B. S. Jackson and Dr. Thomas M. Brewer, all of whom were conspicuous in its annals. It lost, too, by removal, some who in the early part of the decade were prominent in its proceedings, one of whom was Dr. Sterry Hunt, the eminent geologist, and another, Dr. Samuel Kneeland, who for many years was a very efficient officer and member, and often contributed specimens of considerable value to the collections. It may truly be said of the latter that during his long connection with the Society he seldom, if ever, left home without bringing back with him something for presentation. He was almost a constant attendant too upon the meetings, and frequently took an active part in them.

The members of the Society who took the most prominent part in the proceedings at the general meetings and at those of the sections during the first five years of the decade were S. H. Scudder, Dr. Thomas M. Brewer, Alpheus Hyatt, Dr. H. A. Hagen, F. W. Putnam, N. S. Shaler, Dr. T. Sterry Hunt, Thomas T. Bouvé, Dr. Samuel Kneeland, Dr. Charles T. Jackson, W. H. Niles, E. S. Morse, Dr. Charles Pickering, Edwin Bicknell, F. G. Sanborn, Charles Stodder, Dr. Thomas Dwight, Jr., Dr. W. G. Farlow, Edward Burgess, R. C. Greenleaf, Prof. C. H. Hitchcock, Dr. C. S. Minot, B. P. Mann, Rev. J. B. Perry, L.

S. Burbank and J. A. Allen. Those who took the most prominent part during the last five years were S. H. Scudder, Alpheus Hyatt, F. W. Putnam, M. E. Wadsworth, Edward Burgess, W. H. Niles, W. O. Crosby, E. P. Austin, Dr. H. A. Hagen, Dr. Thomas M. Brewer, Dr. W. G. Farlow, Dr. C. S. Minot, Thomas T. Bouvé, Dr. T. Sterry Hunt, L. S. Burbank, Dr. Samuel Kneeland, Dr. B. Joy Jeffries, Rev. George F. Wright, and Dr. G. L. Goodale.

The average attendance each year during the decade at the general meetings was as follows:

1870–71	18 meetings,	an attendance of	40		1875–76	18 meetings,	an attendance of	33
71–72	18	"	"	32	76–77	19	"	"	33
72–73	18	"	"	26	77–78	16	"	"	35
73–74	16	"	"	54	78–79	16	"	"	31
74–75	18	"	"	57	79–80	16	"	"	40

The average of all these is somewhat larger than during any previous ten years, being thirty-eight. That of the previous ten years was thirty-six. The great increase of attendance in the years 1873–74 and 1874–75 was due largely perhaps to the change made in giving notices of the meetings, the custom being first adopted in the fall of 1873 to designate the subjects that were to be brought before them.

The attendance at the meetings of the sections was as follows:

Of Entomology,

1870–71	5 meetings,	average attendance,	10		1875–76	4 meetings,	average attendance,	8
71–72	7	"	"	"	11	76–77	1	"	"	"	8
72–73	7	"	"	"	9	77–78	6	"	"	"	9
73–74	6	"	"	"	12	78–79	9	"	"	"	10
74–75	5	"	"	"	8	79–80	7	"	"	"	8

Of Microscopy,

1870–71	5 meetings,	average attendance,	11		1873–74	1 meeting,	attendance,	12
71–72	5	"	"	"	12	74–75	2 meetings,	average	"	9
72–73	1 meeting,	attendance,	12				

The little interest manifested in this section led to its dissolution in 1875. Its revival was authorized by the Council in 1879, and one meeting followed with an attendance of nine persons; it was the only one.

Of Botany, section formed in 1876,

1876–77	8 meetings,	average attendance,	27		1878–79	6 meetings,	average attendance,	7
77–78	2	"	"	"	18			

Interest in this section was shown as long as able botanists appeared to address the members. As soon as this ceased to be the case the attendance fell off.

The large and important part of the work of the Society done through the Committees of the Council makes it proper to give the names of all such members as have served upon these during the decade. They are as follows:

On the Library. C. K. Dillaway, J. E. Cabot, Dr. T. M. Brewer, William T. Brigham, Dr. A. S. Packard, Jr., Edward Burgess, William H. Niles, Samuel H. Scudder, Alpheus Hyatt, N. S. Shaler, J. A. Allen and S. W. Garman.

On Walker Prizes. Dr. Jeffries Wyman, C. J. Sprague, Thomas T. Bouvé, Dr. Asa Gray, Alexander Agassiz and William B. Rogers.

On Lectures. Thomas T. Bouvé, Rev. Joshua A. Swan, John Cummings, John D. Runkle, Alpheus Hyatt, Edward Burgess, Dr. James C. White, F. W. Putnam, Dr. B. Joy Jeffries, M. E. Wadsworth and William H. Niles.

On Publications. Thomas T. Bouvé, Dr. Samuel L. Abbot, Dr. Thomas Dwight, Dr. Thomas M. Brewer, Dr. A. S. Packard, Jr., Rev. Joshua A. Swan, Edward Burgess, Samuel H. Scudder, J. A. Allen, Alpheus Hyatt and John D. Runkle.

On the Finance Committee and as Trustees. Charles J. Sprague, Thomas T. Bouvé, Edward Pickering, John Cummings and Charles W. Scudder.

On Meetings. J. A. Allen, Dr. A. S. Packard, Jr., Dr. J. B. S. Jackson, Dr. H. A. Hagen, Edward Burgess, Dr. James C. White, N. S. Shaler, L. S. Burbank.

On Nominations for Membership. Dr. S. L. Abbot, F. W. Putnam, Samuel H. Scudder, Dr. B. Joy Jeffries, Edward Burgess, Dr. Thomas Dwight, Samuel Wells, Alpheus Hyatt, Thomas T. Bouvé.

On the Museum. Alpheus Hyatt, Thomas T. Bouvé, John Cummings, Samuel H. Scudder, Edward Burgess and F. W. Putnam.

The publications of the Society during the decade were, the second volume of its Memoirs in quarto, 560 pages, containing twenty important papers read or presented at its meetings, and three numbers of the third volume; a part of the 13th volume of the Proceedings of the Society, not issued at the time of the annual meeting in 1870, with six full volumes from the 14th to the 19th inclusive, and three parts of the 20th volume; two volumes of its Occasional Papers, one, The Spiders of the United States, a collection of the Arachnological writings of Nicholas Marcellus Hentz, M.D.; the other, Contributions to the Geology of Eastern Massachusetts, by W. O. Crosby; six numbers of a series of Guides for Science Teaching; also a pamphlet introductory to a general guide to the Museum to be hereafter published.

The library had increased largely since 1870, when the whole number of its volumes was given as 9396, and of pamphlets as 2677. . The number of volumes at close of the decade, counting them as bound, whether containing more than one, as was often the case, or not, and estimating the unbound parts in proper proportion, was over 14,000, and that of the pamphlets including maps and charts, was but slightly short of 6000.

Before proceeding to express such general views upon the Society, as press themselves upon the mind after sketching its history, and in view of its present condition, it will not be amiss to refer to the original members yet living, after the lapse of half a century since they took part in its formation. Of these there are four, Theophilus Parsons, Dr. Edward Reynolds, Dr. D. Humphreys Storer and Mr. George B. Emerson, all men who have distinguished themselves in their several walks of life, and whose association would have conferred honor upon any Society. Two of these, Dr. Storer and Mr. Emerson, were active members during many years, and both of them held high offices in it. Of the former and of his services to the Society, a full notice has been given in these pages. It is a pleasant duty to present here some account of the latter.

George B. Emerson.

George B. Emerson was born at Wells, Maine, then a part of Massachusetts, September 12th, 1797. His father was Dr. Emerson, a well known physician, and a man of cultivation and taste. He graduated at Harvard in 1784, and was an excellent Latin scholar, besides being well read in history and English literature. His house was a favorite resort for the judges and lawyers who attended the sessions of the Supreme Court of Massachusetts, held semi-annually at York and at Portland, and young Emerson thus early became acquainted with such men as Judge Jackson and the reporter, Dudley Atkins Tyng, gentlemen distinguished for their ability, as well as the refinement of their manners.

Dr. Emerson was chairman of the School Committee, and always was particular to see that the master was a well educated man, and a proper person to have the charge of children. His sons were sent to school during the winter season, but kept at home during the summer, where the practical education that they received on their father's farm, both in the knowledge which it imparted of common ways of country life, and familiarity with common things, and in the information which they derived from acquaintance with the vegetable and animal life around them in the fields, woods, rivers and sea, is spoken of by the subject of this notice as being of the most valuable character. The father evidently evinced great good judgment in his management of the education of his boys.

Young Emerson early familiarized himself with the trees, shrubs and plants of the neighborhood, reading eagerly all books on botany which came in his way, and learning what he could from his father relating to that science. He also was an interested reader of books of travel and poetry, and at the proper time was led to the study of Latin and Greek, becoming familiar in certain ways with the classics before entering Dummer Academy at Byfield, where he went to prepare for Harvard. He entered college in 1813, being in the class with Caleb Cushing, George Bancroft, S. J. May, Samuel E. Sewall, and other since well-known men. His experience in college was a pleasant and profitable one, varied as it so often was in the case of boys from the remote country districts, by occasional teaching of country schools during the long vacations. While at Harvard he very nearly lost his life by the experiment tried both by himself and his chum, of cutting down the term of sleep from the normal quantity to four hours a day; devoting the time stolen from needed rest to over-study. A severe illness and long consequent sojourn at home were the price of this ill-considered action.

He graduated in 1817, and after recovering from another severe illness, the result of overwork, accepted a position offered him of master of an excellent private school, at Lancaster, Mass. Here continuous trouble with his eyes, brought on by inattention to general health and too much study previously, was a great annoyance to him; still his school was a great success, his ability as a teacher being fully exemplified. He continued at Lancaster for two years, and then accepted an invitation from President Kirkland to become a tutor in the mathematical department at Harvard. Here he was again thrown on terms of intimacy with some of his early college friends, Caleb Cushing, Edward Everett and others, besides meeting most agreeably George Ticknor, then a lecturer on French literature, Professor Farrar, Dr. Bowditch, the great mathematician, Rev. Mr. Norton and other prominent men of the time.

A trip to the White Mountains about this period, with a party of his college friends, is most delightfully described in his little volume of "Reminiscences."

In 1820 was established in Boston the English Classical School, and Mr. Emerson was chosen its first principal. After a remarkably successful experience as teacher in this institution, he in 1823 organized his celebrated school for young ladies, which was for many years regarded as unequalled in the educational advantages to be enjoyed by all who were in it as pupils.

In the formation of the Boston Society of Natural History, Mr. Emerson took an active part, and in 1837 he was chosen President. At that time the scientific survey of the State was determined by the members to be of the utmost desirability, and Mr. Emerson was deputed to memorialize the State government upon the subject. This he did, laying his memorial before Governor Everett, by whom it was most cordially and graciously received. In due time the Governor informed Mr. Emerson that the legislature, both houses of which justly appreciated his memorial, had authorized the executive to appoint six proper persons to conduct the survey of the State, and had passed an appropriation to cover the expenses thereof; and he requested that Mr. Emerson should suggest the names of such scientific men as he thought competent for the work. The result was that the gentlemen appointed were almost entirely those named by him. The Governor desired that he should hold himself responsible for all the reports presented; but his friends in the Society, knowing his ability, were not satisfied except by his taking a more active part in the survey; and he eventually divided the botany with Dr. Dewey, the doctor taking all other plants and Mr. Emerson the trees and shrubs. The report which he subsequently made to the legislature was not only admirable in its scientific features, but was most charming from a literary point of view. It takes one out with the writer into the fields and woods, and makes the reader at once the interested student and the personal friend, so to speak, of the tree or shrub which the writer may be describing at the time. This report was made up from the observations and study of nine successive years, nearly three months of each of which he gave to the work, visiting all parts of the State in its prosecution.

Mr. Emerson published, in 1875, a new edition of his Report on the Trees and Shrubs, superbly illustrated by colored plates, a full set of which, suitably framed, he presented to the Society to be placed in the collection of New England Trees and Shrubs, and which may now be seen in the botanical gallery devoted to that section.

The well-known "Memorial of the American Institute of Instruction to the Massachusetts Legislature," was prepared and placed in the hands of the Governor by the President, Mr. Emerson; and the result of this course was the formation of the Board of Education with Horace Mann, then President of the Senate, as its secretary. The cause of education took a new departure from this time forth, and the good effect of this action, in which Mr. Emerson was prominent, was inestimable.

Mr. Emerson's zeal in the cause of good education sprang very largely from the affection for the young, which has always during his lifetime kept pace with his great love of nature. The influence which he exerted among his pupils through this feeling of personal

interest has been very warmly spoken of by many of them. His religious tendencies were very decided. He had wished in his boyhood to go to West Point, but his mother's earnest desire to the contrary had dissuaded him from this course, and his subsequent tastes led him to study with the intention of entering the ministry, for which profession he would seem to have been particularly fitted by nature. The young ladies of his school always looked to him as a friend and adviser, and have many of them alluded feelingly to the few earnest words spoken by him in the morning service as of more value to them than all the ordinary instruction in the school.

Mr. Emerson's interest in the Society has always been very strong; manifested to a greater or less degree by his presence at meetings and by occasional participation in the proceedings. His last prominent appearance before the Society was in 1874, when he delivered the memorial address upon Louis Agassiz.

The history of the Society has now been traced from its formation to its present proud position as one of the leading scientific institutions of the world. We have dwelt upon the reasons that endangered its continued success in the early period of its existence, and have witnessed the untiring devotion of its members, some of whom gave voluntarily, years of life to its service. We have seen too that only by the large donations and bequests of its great benefactors did it escape the fate of the Linnaean Society which preceded it, and of many other similar societies not sustained by government aid, and depending on the unpaid labor and contributions of their members. That these gifts were mainly due to a recognition of the disinterested devotion of the members of the Society to the work undertaken by them, and of the importance of that work as an educational and elevating influence in the community, is unquestionably true, markedly in the case of the largest benefactor of all, Dr. William J. Walker, who, through Dr. Jeffries Wyman, for whom he had great regard, and others, made himself well acquainted with the leading members of the Society, and with their designs and purposes in the matter of educating the community in natural history, before making it the recipient of his bounty.

It becomes the members of the Society, especially such as have been instrumental in shaping its destiny, to ask whether it has met the reasonable expectations of its founders. Have their hopes for its growth and its influence been fulfilled? As an associate with the original members, and as having been acquainted to a considerable degree with their thoughts and feelings, the writer unhesitatingly answers Yes! far beyond their most sanguine hopes and expectations. Not that they limited in their own minds the possibility of achievement, but they simply had no conception that in the lifetime of any of them the Society would have one of the best structures in the world for exhibition, with collections of great magnitude in all the departments of natural history, unequalled in arrangement for instruction; or that it would carry on such educational work as has been done, and is now doing, through the Teachers' School of Science and other instrumentalities.

Nor does it less become the members to ask, especially in view of the fact that for further progress in the work carried on by them they will yet be obliged to rely on additional aid, whether the Society has faithfully administered the trusts reposed in its care; and whether the wishes of those who endowed it with means by which it has become what it is, have been fully regarded in the use of the property placed at its disposal.

To this the writer also responds unhesitatingly in the affirmative, sustained by the gratifying fact that among the nearest representatives of the great donors may be found those best pleased with all the Society has done.

For the better understanding, on the part of the members of future generations, of the condition of the affairs of the Society at the present period, it may not be amiss to state concisely what are its possessions, just what it is now doing, with what means, its present needs, and what are the hopes and the aspirations of those who are now its active members. First then as to its possessions. It owns the building known as the Museum, its cases, furniture, library and the collections contained therein, free from all incumbrance. The value of the building with cases may be estimated at the cost, $150,334.86, as it certainly could not be erected at the present time without a larger expenditure. The money value of the library and collections cannot be given. The former embraces as before stated, over 14,000 volumes and nearly 6000 pamphlets.

The collections may be said to be of inestimable worth not only to the Society, but to the community, for a considerable portion of unique and type specimens in the several departments could never be replaced. There is not on the part of the public an adequate conception of the extent of these collections and of the great importance that they should be properly cared for, scientifically arranged and fully labelled in order that they may continue in all the future to serve as they now do, to help in the education of those who seek to know something of the works of the Great Creator of all things, and who are not able to attend the scientific schools where this knowledge is specifically taught. The following statement will show the magnitude of the cabinet at this period.

Mineralogical Collection.

General collection	5,660 specimens.
New England collection	679 "
Total	6,339 "

Geological Collection.

Catalogued and on exhibition	3,265 specimens.
Others yet uncatalogued	1,700 "
Total	4,965 "

The New England rocks are all included in the 1700 yet uncatalogued, and they amount, in round numbers, to 1500 specimens.

Palaeontological Collection.

Europe	13,691 specimens.
North America, exclusive of New England	7,678 "
South America	170 "
Asia and Australia	170 "
Africa	14 "
New England	550 "
Mounted and arranged	22,273 "

Unmounted, North America	800 specimens.
" New England	200 "

Anatomical Collection.

Skeletons, preparations and other specimens	4,153 specimens.

Microscopical Collection.

Bailey collection	1,839 specimens.
Burnett "	566 "
R. C. Greenleaf and Dr. A. D. Sinclair collection	480 "
Rogers collection	275 "
Received from Messrs. A. Hyatt and W. O. Crosby	114 "
Received from Mr. E. Samuels	24 "
" " others	62 "
Total	3,860 "

Sponges.

A general collection not yet in a condition to determine number and species; also a large collection of New England specimens not yet examined.

BOSTON SOCIETY OF NATURAL HISTORY.

Radiates.	Species.	Specimens.
Coelenterates.		
General collection including New England species	200	1,000
Echinoderms.	Species.	Specimens.
General collection	120	1,000
New England collection	25	700
Total		1,700
Worms.	Species.	Specimens.
General collection	150	400
New England collection	150	400
Total		800
Crustacea.	Species.	Specimens.
General collection	400	1,000
New England collection	150	1,500
Total		2,500
Insects.	Species.	Specimens.
General collection	10,000	35,000
Harris "	4,364	11,023
New England collection	3,000	7,600
Total		53,623
Mollusks.	Species.	Specimens.
General collection	5,400	32,000
New England collection	100	3,000
Total		35,000
Fishes.[1]	Species.	Specimens.
General collection	700	2,500
New England collection	115	2,000
Total		4,500
Amphibia.	Species.	Specimens.
General collection	70	324
New England collection	14	100
Total		424

Reptiles.	Species.	Specimens.
General collection	200	740
New England collection	23	77
Total		817
Birds.		Specimens.
General collection of mounted birds		11,801
New England collection of mounted birds		527
Total		12,328
Bird skins about		5,000
Eggs of birds about		5,200
Mammals.	Species.	Specimens.
General collection	54	67
New England collection	30	51
Total		118

Besides some alcoholic specimens and skins.

Botanical Department.

Herbarium.

General collection	.	28,885 specimens.
Lowell "	.	20,986 "
New England collection	.	3,277 "
Total	.	53,148

On Exhibition in glass cases.

General collection	.	2,666 specimens.
New England collection	.	406 "
Total	.	3,072 "

The New England specimens on exhibition consist of:

30 framed lithographs presented by Mr. George B. Emerson.

182 mounted specimens of trees and shrubs, presented by Mr. Edward T. Bouvé.

194 specimens of wood and fruit, presented by Mr. Edward T. Bouvé.

Besides the Museum Building, the Library and the collections mentioned, the Society holds property in notes, bonds and stocks, amounting in value to $154,405, estimating the bonds and stocks at their par value, which is below what they would now sell for in the market.

---

[1] It has been stated in this history, and the statement has been repeated, that the specimens of Massachusetts fishes presented by Dr. D. Humphreys Storer were nearly all allowed to perish for want of care and attention. The author is happy to be able to say that a considerable number of these, about one half, have recently been found in the general collection, identified and placed on exhibition.

As to what it is now doing. It is engaged, through the constant and arduous work of the assistants in the Museum, in perfecting the work that has been going on for several years, of rearranging, placing upon tablets, rebottling and relabelling the specimens according to their several needs in all the departments, and in exerting proper means for their preservation. None but those engaged in such work can understand the labor and the watchfulness constantly required to prevent injury through many causes, but more particularly through the destructive action of vermin, and from the evaporation of liquids in which thousands of specimens are immersed. The modern cases, it is true, are generally secure from the admission of pests, but frequent examination of their contents is not less necessary. The opening of a door for a moment may sometimes admit an anthrenus, the progeny of which it may require weeks to eradicate. Constant vigilance can only preserve the perishable portion of natural history collections from ruin.

It is striving constantly to render its collections more educational, not only by such arrangement as will facilitate their study, but by models and anatomical preparations giving the internal structure and showing the habits of animals.

It holds meetings on the first and third Wednesday evenings of each month, except during the warm season, at which scientific communications, either written or verbal, are made by members, followed often by discussions upon the matter presented. All important communications and remarks are published in the Memoirs or Proceedings of the Society, together with any business transacted. Besides the general meetings there are others held of such sections as may be active. There have been three, those of entomology, microscopy and botany, but only one of these, that of entomology, can be said to exist at present, otherwise than nominally.

In its Laboratory it is doing much for those who seek knowledge in natural history. Instruction is given to a class of the students of the Boston University in Biology and Zoölogy; to a class of the students of the Institute of Technology in Zoölogy and Palaeontology; and to a special class of teachers of the Public Schools in Zoölogy. The laboratory room and the working collections therein are used also by other persons engaged in teaching or studying. The accommodations of the room are inadequate for all who give and seek instruction, not affording proper conveniences for either. About seventy persons now make use of it.

Respecting the very important educational work the Society has done through the Teachers' School of Science, it is a matter of great regret that lack of means prevented its continuance through the past winter. The maintenance of this has hitherto entirely depended on contributions from individuals who, recognizing the great benefits arising from the instruction of teachers, have voluntarily proffered aid. Whilst, therefore, it cannot be said that just at the present period the Society is carrying on this work, it may nevertheless, soon be the case, as it stands ready with its unequalled facilities to recommence the courses of instruction whenever it can have the necessary help.[1]

---

[1] Since the period at which the historical sketch closes, two ladies of Boston, to whom the city owes much, Mrs. Quincy A. Shaw and Mrs. Augustus Hemenway, with unsolicited generosity, tendered the necessary means for the continuance of the Teachers' School of Science during the following season. Several courses of lessons to the teachers of the Public Schools are, therefore, being given at the time of the publication of this volume.

In its publications the Society is doing a great work. The issues are of such character as to constantly enhance its reputation at home and abroad, and enable it through exchange with foreign bodies to secure for the use of the members and others engaged in the study of natural history, memoirs and journals indispensable to students, and which the Society could not otherwise obtain. Exchanges are made at the present period with three hundred and sixty societies and proprietors of scientific journals. To meet the call for the various publications of the Society, its Memoirs, Proceedings, and Occasional Papers, an edition of eight hundred of each issue is printed.

In addition to all that has been mentioned, the Society is sustaining its Library, which is not only open to members but to all engaged in scientific investigation, upon proper application, and under reasonable restriction. By an agreement with the Institute of Technology, its students are allowed the privilege of consulting the books and taking them out for study. The use of the Library is now much greater than at any former period, and is constantly increasing.

Now what are the means at the present period upon which the Society can rely to go on with its work? They are manifestly not its ownership in what is visible, its beautiful building, its growing library, and its grand collections. These are of inestimable value, but they are all of them sources of great expense, not of income. To sustain these, to continue publication, without which there can be but little progress, and to do such educational work as is now called for, a much larger funded property is required than that now held by the Society. This amounts, as has been stated, to $154,405 at the par value of the stocks held by it, and from this an income can scarcely be looked for exceeding eight thousand to nine thousand dollars per annum. Assessments on members increase this from one to two thousand dollars more.

Now when it is borne in mind that from this income it is incumbent upon the Society to pay on an average about three hundred dollars yearly for prizes; to have in its employ an accomplished scientific man in general charge of its Museum, with several able assistants; a secretary and librarian, also of scientific attainments, with assistants in the library; and a janitor to look after the building and contents; to say nothing of the necessary repairs, fuel, gas, etc., the question may well be asked how an income that will scarcely meet the living expenses of many individual families in the community, can suffice for such requirements. In truth it has only been by exceeding economy that these absolutely necessary expenses have been kept within the income. All of extraordinary character have been met by help from individual members and others. It has been found almost impossible to spare any reasonable amount for additions to the cabinet, and consequently the New England collections in the several departments which it is very important to complete, are yet very far from being so. What was long since stated by the Custodian of the New England collection of mammals yet remains true: "It is a disgrace to the Society." This is the more unfortunate from the fact that some of the larger animals may ere long become extinct in our borders.

Having now presented a statement of the possessions of the Society at this time, what it is doing and the income upon which it depends to sustain its work, a few words upon its requirements, its hopes and its aspirations, may be added.

As to its requirements, these have partially been given in mentioning its means and their inadequacy; others equally necessary but not so pressing will be here referred to.

It needs to build another gallery in the Museum as originally designed, in order that the New England collections in the various departments may be brought together. It needs means to enable it to bind thousands of volumes in its library, periodicals received by exchanges, and other works which it has hitherto been unable to do. Thanks to the Huntington Frothingham Wolcott fund, it will henceforth be able to take care of books received, but it requires a large sum to bind those obtained in the past and which suffer from want of it.

Of its hopes, they are that it may not only be able to go on with its work, but that it may progress, and that the requirements for this may not long be wanting. Doing what it is in fostering the taste for a study refining and elevating in its tendencies, it feels that its efforts should not be allowed to become futile through lack of necessary means to continue its work without constant struggle.

Of its aspirations for the future, they are such as all will commend who recognize that progress is a duty, viz.: That it may be able to meet the increasing call from a growing community for instruction in natural history, to such as cannot avail themselves of the advantages afforded otherwise, by an expansion of its laboratory and other facilities; that it may, before a long period has elapsed, be able to add an aquarial garden to its collections, both for the study of the habits of a portion of the animal kingdom and as an additional attraction to visitors of the Museum; and that as these desires cannot have full fruition without more extensive accommodations, that the day may not be far distant when it shall possess the ability to enlarge the Museum building so as to best serve its designs and purposes; that it may also be able to publish the increasing researches of its members with the illustrations they require; which it is now by no means able to do, many memoirs being diverted to other channels of publication which would naturally be offered to the Society were it able to do more than at present.

The names of some of the most able naturalists of the country, including several of the most distinguished of the age, are to be found on its roll of active members during the half century, as Louis Agassiz, Jeffries Wyman, Asa Gray, Augustus A. Gould, Wm. B. Rogers, Henry D. Rogers, Thomas Nuttall, Charles Pickering, D. Humphreys Storer, George B. Emerson, Amos Binney, Charles T. Jackson, Thaddeus W. Harris, Count Desor. Others of its members if less illustrious as scientists have been men of such excellence of life and character as to have endeared them to all the community. Who that knew in life Dr. Benj. D. Greene, the Rev. F. W. P. Greenwood, Dr. John Ware, Dr. Martin Gay, Mr. Thomas Bulfinch, and many others worthy of mention with these, will not feel that its annals have indeed been sanctified by a spirit of purity and simplicity throughout all the years of the half century now closed. If anything has made the writing of these pages a pleasing task to the author, it has been the contemplation of such exalted worth as marked the lives and deeds of so many of his associates. This has sometimes impressed him with a feeling that the atmosphere about him was hallowed by their presence.

The writer in his concluding remarks cannot do better than to commend to the government of the Society, the expressive words of its great benefactor, in bequeathing to it the property, without which it could not have continued its work, and to express the hope that the request so touchingly urged may not only be sacredly regarded through coming years, but that the policy indicated may be observed in relation to all property that the generosity of others may hereafter bestow upon the Society; to the end that its means of usefulness be not impaired, and that its elevating and beneficent influences be continued through all generations.

The words referred to are as follows:

"Finally, I request the recipients of the above bequeathed property to realize that no inconsiderable portion thereof has been gathered as the fruits of a laborious vocation, exercised through anxious days and sleepless nights; that it is given to them, *in trust nevertheless*, to be expended so as to inure to the greatest advancement of sound education in the departments as above specified, and the public good. I request that its investment may be safely guarded; that its expenditure may be subject to the strictest economy; yet that it may be appropriated liberally where the objects aimed at justify an open hand, and cannot be afforded the cause of education and the public good at less expense."

With due regard to what is here expressed, the permanence of the Society is at least secure, and it may reasonably be presumed that the means of progress will not forever be wanting.

PAST OFFICERS OF THE SOCIETY.

PRESIDENTS.

	Elected.	Retired.		Elected.	Retired.
Thomas Nuttall,	May, 13, 1830.	Aug. 9, 1830.	John Collins Warren,	May 5, 1847.	May 4, 1856.[1]
Benjamin D. Greene,	Aug. 9, 1830.	May 3, 1837.	Jeffries Wyman,	June 18, 1856.	May 4, 1870.
George B. Emerson,	May 3, 1837.	May 17, 1843.	Thomas T. Bouvé,	June 15, 1870.	May 5, 1880.
Amos Binney,	May 17, 1843.	May 5, 1847.	Samuel H. Scudder,	May 5, 1880.	

FIRST VICE PRESIDENTS.

George Hayward,	May 13, 1830.	May 12, 1832.	Charles T. Jackson,	May 17, 1843.	May 6, 1874.
John Ware,	May 12, 1832.	May 4, 1836.	Samuel H. Scudder,	May 6, 1874.	May 5, 1880.
F. W. P. Greenwood,	May 4, 1836.	May 5, 1841.	John Cummings,	May 5, 1880.	
Amos Binney,	May 5, 1841.	May 17, 1843.			

SECOND VICE PRESIDENTS.

John Ware,	May 13, 1830.	May 12, 1832.	D. Humphreys Storer,	May 17, 1843.	May 2, 1860.
Francis C. Gray,	May 12, 1832.	May 7, 1834.	Augustus A. Gould,	May 2, 1860.	Sept. 15, 1866.[1]
F. W. P. Greenwood,	May 7, 1834.	May 4, 1836.	Thomas T. Bouvé,	Nov. 21, 1866.	June 15, 1870.
Walter Channing,	May 4, 1836.	May 3, 1837.	Richard C. Greenleaf,	May 3, 1871.	May 6, 1874.
Amos Binney,	May 3, 1837.	May 5, 1841.	John Cummings,	May 6, 1874.	May 5, 1880.
C. T. Jackson,	May 5, 1841.	May 17, 1843.	Frederick W. Putnam,	May 5, 1880.	

CORRESPONDING SECRETARIES.

Gamaliel Bradford,	May 13, 1830.	May 7, 1834.	Augustus A. Gould,	May 17, 1843.	May 1, 1850.
Amos Binney,	May 7, 1834.	May 3, 1837.	J. Elliot Cabot,	May 1, 1850.	June 1, 1853.
Epes S. Dixwell,	May 3, 1837.	May 17, 1843.	S. L. Abbot,	Nov. 2, 1853.	May 3, 1876.
		Name of office changed.			

HONORARY SECRETARY.

S. L. Abbot,	May 3, 1876.

RECORDING SECRETARIES.

Theophilus Parsons,	May 12, 1830.	Sept. 2, 1830.	S. L. Abbot,	May 3, 1848.	Oct. 19, 1853.
D. Humphreys Storer,	Sept. 2, 1830.	May 4, 1836.	Benjamin S. Shaw,	Nov. 2, 1853.	June 2, 1858.
Martin Gay,	May 4, 1836.	May 2, 1838.	Samuel Kneeland, Jr.,	June 16, 1858.	May 7, 1862.
Augustus A. Gould,	May 2, 1838.	May 15, 1839.	Samuel H. Scudder,	May 7, 1862.	May 4, 1870.
Jeffries Wyman,	May 15, 1839.	Mar. 17, 1841.	Joshua A. Swan,	May 4, 1870.	Oct. 31, 1871.[1]
Frederick A. Eddy,	May 5, 1841.	April 20, 1842.	Edward Burgess,	Feb. 21, 1872.	May 3, 1876.
T. Bulfinch,	May 4, 1842.	May 3, 1848.			
		Name of office changed.			

SECRETARY.

Edward Burgess,	May 3, 1876.

TREASURERS.

Simon E. Greene,	May 13, 1830.	May 2, 1832.	Nathaniel B. Shurtleff,	May 1, 1850.	May 5, 1858.
Amos Binney,	May 2, 1832.	May 7, 1834.	Amos Binney,	May 5, 1858.	Sept. 4, 1861.
Epes S. Dixwell,	May 7, 1834.	Dec. 7, 1836.	Thomas T. Bouvé,	Sept. 4, 1861.	May 3, 1865.
Ezra Weston, Jr.,	Dec. 7, 1836.	May 1, 1839.	Edward Pickering,	May 3, 1865.	Nov. 21, 1876.[1]
John James Dixwell,	May 1, 1839.	May 14, 1845.	Charles W. Scudder,	Feb. 21, 1877.	
Patrick T. Jackson, Jr.,	May 14, 1845.	May 1, 1850.			

LIBRARIANS.

Seth Bass,	May 13, 1830.	May 2, 1832.	Samuel H. Scudder,	May 4, 1864.	May 4, 1870.
Charles Amory,	May 2, 1832.	May 1, 1833.	Joshua A. Swan,	May 4, 1870.	Oct. 31, 1871.[1]
Charles K. Dillaway,	May 1, 1833.	May 4, 1864.	Edward Burgess,	Feb. 21, 1872.	

[1] By death.

BOSTON SOCIETY OF NATURAL HISTORY.

CABINET-KEEPERS.

	Elected.	Retired.		Elected.	Retired.
Estes Howe,	May 7, 1834.	May 20, 1835.	Henry J. Bigelow,	Dec. 30, 1840.	Mar. 17, 1841.
Nathaniel B. Shurtleff,	May 20, 1835.	May 3, 1837.	Thomas T. Bouvé,	May 5, 1841.	May 4, 1842.
T. M. Brewer,	May 3, 1837.	May 2, 1838.	Henry Bryant,	May 4, 1842.	Oct. 4, 1843.
Jeffries Wyman,	May 2, 1838.	May 1, 1839.	Henry J. Bigelow,	Nov. 1, 1843.	May 5, 1847.
Samuel Cabot, Jr.,	May 1, 1839.	Oct. 2, 1839.	Samuel Kneeland, Jr.,	May 5, 1847.	May 2, 1849.
William I. Bowditch,	Oct. 2, 1839.	Nov. 5, 1839.	C. C. Shcafe,	May 2, 1849.	May 6, 1852.
Samuel L. Abbot,	Nov. 5, 1839.	Dec. 30, 1840.	Charles Stodder,	May 5, 1852.	May 4, 1864.

This office was abolished in 1864.

CUSTODIANS.

Samuel H. Scudder,	May 4, 1864.	May 3, 1865.	Alpheus Hyatt,	May 4, 1870.
Samuel H. Scudder,	Oct. 8, 1866.	May 4, 1870.		

CURATORS.

Benjamin D. Greene,	May 13, 1830.	Sept. 2, 1830.	Winslow Lewis, Jr.,	May 2, 1832.	May 2, 1838.
Francis C. Gray,	May 13, 1830.	May 2, 1832.	William B. Fowle,	May 2, 1832.	May 20, 1835.
Walter Channing,	May 13, 1830.	May 4, 1831.	Clement Durgin,	May 2, 1832.	May 1, 1888.
Edward Brooks,	May 13, 1830.	May 4, 1831.	G. W. Otis,	May 2, 1832.	May 20, 1836.
Amos Binney,	May 13, 1830.	May 2, 1832.	Charles T. Jackson,	May 1, 1833.	May 2, 1888.
Jos. W. McKean,	May 13, 1830.	May 20, 1835.	John B. S. Jackson,	May 7, 1834.	May 2, 1888.
George B. Emerson,	May 13, 1830.	May 3, 1837.	Thaddeus W. Harris,	May 20, 1835.	May 2, 1836.
Francis Alger,	May 13, 1830.	May 7, 1834.	J. E. Teschemacher,	May 20, 1835.	May 2, 1838.
J. S. Copley Greene,	Sept. 2, 1830.	May 2, 1832.	Martin Gay,	May 20, 1835.	May 4, 1836.
Joshua B. Flint,	May 4, 1831.	May 2, 1832.	D. Humphreys Storer,	May 4, 1836.	May 2, 1838.
Augustus A. Gould,	May 4, 1831.	May 2, 1838.	N. B. Shurtleff,	May 3, 1837.	May 2, 1838.

The curatorships were assigned to special departments for the first time in 1838.

CURATOR OF ETHNOLOGY.

Charles Pickering,	Feb. 5, 1862.	May 1, 1867.

The Curatorship of Ethnology founded in 1862, was abolished in 1867.

CURATORS OF MAMMALS.

Winslow Lewis,	May 2, 1838.	May 1, 1839.	Jeffries Wyman,	May 1, 1839.	May 6, 1840.

CURATOR OF COMPARATIVE ANATOMY.

Nathaniel B. Shurtleff,	May 2, 1838.	May 6, 1840.

CURATORS OF COMPARATIVE ANATOMY AND MAMMALS.

Nathaniel B. Shurtleff,	May 6, 1840.	May 2, 1849.	James C. White,	Dec. 1, 1858.	May 6, 1868.
Samuel Kneeland, Jr.,	May 2, 1849.	June 7, 1854.	C. F. Folsom,	Nov. 18, 1808.	Oct. 8, 1869.
Jeffries Wyman,	June 7, 1854.	May 6, 1857.	Thomas Waterman,	Jan. 5, 1870.	May 4, 1870.
John Green,	May 6, 1857.	Nov. 17, 1858.			

The Departments of Mammals and of Comparative Anatomy were united in 1840, and again separated in 1870.

CURATORS OF BIRDS.

Thomas M. Brewer,	May 2, 1838.	May 6, 1840.	Samuel Cabot, Jr.,	May 1, 1844.	May 3, 1854.
Marshall S. Scudder,	May 6, 1840.	Dec. 16, 1840.	Henry Bryant,	May 3, 1854.	Feb. 2, 1867.[1]
S. L. Abbot,	Dec. 16, 1840.	May 1, 1844.	J. Elliot Cabot,	May 1, 1867.	May 4, 1870.

CURATOR OF BIRDS (nests and eggs).

Thomas M. Brewer,	July 2, 1851.	May 4, 1870.

CURATORS OF REPTILES AND FISH.

D. Humphreys Storer,	May 2, 1838.	May 17, 1843.	Jeffries Wyman,	May 17, 1843.	May 3, 1848.

The Curatorship was separated into two divisions in 1848.

CURATORS OF REPTILES.

Jeffries Wyman,	May 3, 1848.	May 7, 1851.	Samuel A. Green,	May 2, 1860.	May 1, 1861.
Horatio R. Storer,	May 7, 1851.	Dec. 21, 1853.	Francis H. Brown,	May 1, 1861.	Oct. 4, 1865.
Jeffries Wyman,	Jan. 4, 1854.	June 7, 1854.	Burt G. Wilder,	Oct. 18, 1865.	Oct. 1, 1868.
J. Nelson Borland,	Dec. 6, 1854.	May 2, 1860.	J. A. Allen,	Nov. 18, 1868.	May 4, 1870.

[1] By death.

HISTORICAL SKETCH OF THE

CURATORS OF FISHES.

	Elected.	Retired.		Elected.	Retired.
W. O. Ayres,	May 3, 1848.	July 16, 1851.	N. E. Atwood,	Dec. 17, 1856.	May 5, 1858.
Silas Durkee,	July 16, 1851.	May 21, 1856.	Samuel Kneeland, Jr.,	May 5, 1858.	May 4, 1859.
Samuel Kneeland, Jr.,	May 21, 1856.	Sept. 3, 1856.	F. W. Putnam,	May 4, 1859.	May 4, 1870.

CURATORS OF INSECTS.

Thaddeus W. Harris,	May 2, 1838.	May 3, 1848.	Silas Durkee,	May 21, 1856.	May 5, 1858.
Waldo I. Burnett,	May 3, 1848.	July 1, 1854.[1]	Alex. E. R. Agassiz,	May 5, 1858.	Mar. 2, 1859.
Henry K. Oliver, Jr.,	May 2, 1855.	Sept. 5, 1855.	Samuel H. Scudder,	Mar. 16, 1859.	May 4, 1870.

CURATORS OF MOLLUSKS.

T. J. Whittemore,	June 5, 1839.	May 5, 1841.	William Stimpson,	Dec. 4, 1850.	May 18, 1853.
Augustus A. Gould,	May 5, 1841.	May 17, 1843.	T. J. Whittemore,	May 18, 1853.	May 2, 1860.
A. E. Belknap,	May 17, 1843.	May 1, 1844.	Arthur T. Lyman,	May 2, 1860.	May 16, 1860.
Augustus A. Gould,	May 1, 1844.	May 14, 1845.	Nathan Farrand,	June 6, 1860.	May 4, 1863.
Edward Tuckerman,	May 14, 1845.	May 6, 1846.	Alpheus Hyatt,	Oct. 21, 1863.	May 1, 1867.
John Bacon, Jr.,	May 6, 1846.	May 3, 1848.	Edward S. Morse,	May 1, 1867.	May 4, 1870.
William Read,	May 3, 1848.	Nov. 20, 1850.			

CURATORS OF CRUSTACEANS AND RADIATES.

Amos Binney,	Feb. 3, 1841.	May 5, 1841.	John P. Reynolds,	May 2, 1855.	May 6, 1857.
William O. Ayres,	July 16, 1851.	May 18, 1853.	Theodore Lyman,	May 6, 1857.	Sept. 2, 1857.
J. B. S. Jackson,	May 18, 1853.	May 2, 1855.			

The Curatorship was separated into two divisions in 1857.

CURATORS OF CRUSTACEANS.

H. R. Storer,	Sept. 2, 1857.	May 4, 1859.	Alpheus S. Packard, Jr.,	Dec. 2, 1863.	May 4, 1870.
Albert Ordway,	May 4, 1859.	Dec 18, 1861.			

CURATORS OF RADIATES.

Theodore Lyman,	Sept. 2, 1857.	May 4, 1864.	Addison E. Verrill,	May 4, 1864.	May 4, 1870.

CURATORS OF BOTANY.

J. E. Teschemacher,	May 2, 1838.	May 5, 1852.	Horace Mann,	May 3, 1865.	Nov. 11, 1868.[1]
Charles James Sprague,	May 5, 1852.	May 3, 1865.			

CURATORS OF MICROSCOPY.

Silas Durkee,	June 8, 1857.	May 2, 1860.	B. Joy Jeffries,	May 2, 1860.	May 4, 1870.

CURATORS OF MINERALS AND GEOLOGY (State collection).

Charles T. Jackson,	May 2, 1838.	May 5, 1841.	T. Bulfinch,	May 5, 1841.	May 4, 1842.

CURATOR OF MINERALS AND GEOLOGY (Society collection).

Martin Gay,	May 2, 1838.	May 4, 1842.

The State Collection was withdrawn from the Society's Museum, and the Curatorship of Mineralogy and Geology divided, in 1842.

CURATORS OF MINERALS.

Martin Gay,	May 4, 1842.	May 2, 1849.	William T. Brigham,	May 4, 1863.	May 3, 1865.
Francis Alger,	May 2, 1849.	May 21, 1856.	Thomas T. Bouvé,	May 3, 1865.	May 4, 1870.
John Bacon,	May 21, 1856.	May 4, 1863.			

CURATORS OF GEOLOGY.

Thomas T. Bouvé,	May 4, 1842.	May 4, 1863.	William T. Brigham,	Jan. 2, 1867.	May 4, 1870.

The department of Palaeontology was added to that of Geology in 1863, and raised to a separate department in 1867.

CURATOR OF GEOLOGY AND PALAEONTOLOGY.

Thomas T. Bouvé,	May 4, 1863.	Jan. 2, 1867.

CURATORS OF PALAEONTOLOGY.

Thomas T. Bouvé,	Jan. 2, 1867.	May 1, 1867.	Alpheus Hyatt,	May 1, 1867.	May 4, 1870.

The office of Curator was abolished May 4, 1870 and Committees on the several departments were elected.

[1] By death.

COMMITTEES ON DEPARTMENTS.

Geology and Minerals.

	Elected.	Retired.		Elected.	Retired.
Thomas T. Bouvé,	1870.	1872.	William T. Brigham,	1870.	1872.
Charles T. Jackson,	1870.	1872.			

The departments of Geology and Minerals, united in 1870, were separated in 1872.

Geology.

William H. Niles,	1872.		T. Sterry Hunt,	1874.	1879.
William T. Brigham,	1872.	1873.	L. S. Burbank,	1874.	
Thomas T. Bouvé,	1872.	1873.	Rev. G. Fred. Wright,	1879.	
John Cummings,	1873.	1874.			

Minerals.

Thomas T. Bouvé,	1872.		R. H. Richards,	1874.	
Charles T. Jackson,	1872.	1874.	M. E. Wadsworth,	1879.	
L. S. Burbank,	1872.	1879.			

Palaeontology.

W. H. Niles,	1870.	1875.	Thomas T. Bouvé,	1870.	
N. S. Shaler,	1870.		Jules Marcou,	1876.	1878.

Botany.

William T. Brigham,	1870.	1874.	J. Amory Lowell,	1870.	
Charles J. Sprague,	1870.		John Cummings,	1874.	

Comparative Anatomy.

Thomas Dwight,	1870.		James C. White,	1870.	1880.
Jeffries Wyman,	1870.	1874.[1]	William F. Whitney,	1879.	

Radiates and Crustaceans [and Worms, added in 1873].

A. S. Packard, Jr.,	1870.	1875.	H. A. Hagen,	1875.	
A. E. Verrill,	1870.	1875.	L. F. de Pourtalès,	1876.	
Alexander Agassiz,	1870.				

Mollusks.

Edward S. Morse,	1870.		J. Henry Blake,	1873.	
John Cummings,	1870.	1873.	C. O. Whitman,	1879.	1880.
Levi L. Thaxter,	1870.	1879.			

Insects.

F. G. Sanborn,	1870.	1873.	Edward Burgess,	1870.	
A. S. Packard, Jr.,	1870.		S. H. Scudder,	1873.	

Fishes and Reptiles.

D. H. Storer,	1870.	1873.	Richard Bliss, Jr.,	1873.	1877.
F. W. Putnam,	1870.		S. W. Garman,	1877.	
J. A. Allen,	1870.	1872.	Theodore Lyman,	1878.	
Samuel Kneeland,	1872.	1878.			

Bird's [nests and eggs. Dropped from title in 1873].

Thomas M. Brewer,	1870.	1880.[1]	J. Elliot Cabot,	1870.	1871.
Samuel Cabot,	1870.		J. A. Allen,	1871.	

Mammals.

J. A. Allen,	1870.		J. H. Emerton,	1873.	1875.
Thomas Waterman, Jr.,	1870.	1873.	E. L. Mark,	1879.	
J. B. S. Jackson,	1870.	1879.	George L. Goodale,	1880.	

Microscopy.

Edwin Bicknell,	1870.	1877.[1]	B. Joy Jeffries,	1870.	
R. C. Greenleaf,	1870.		Samuel Wells,	1877.	

[1] By death.

CONTENTS.

NOTICE OF THE LINNAEAN SOCIETY, pp. 3–14.

Early publications and instruction in natural history, 3.— Organization, Dec. 8, 1814, of the N. E. Society for the promotion of Natural History, 3.— Members and rules, 4.— Change of name in 1815 to Linnaean Society of New England, 6.— Collection of specimens and addresses, 6.— Division of the Museum into departments, 7.— Sea-serpent Stories, 10.— Signs of dissolution, 10.— Attempts to unite with the Athenaeum, 12.— Decision to dispose of the collections, 12.— Lessons taught by the failure of the Linnaean Society, 13.

THE BOSTON SOCIETY OF NATURAL HISTORY, DECADE I, MAY 1830 — MAY 1840, pp. 14–36.

Formation of the new Society and election of officers, 14,— with Thomas Nuttall as President, who declined to serve, and Benjamin D. Greene is chosen, 14.— Lectures arranged, 15.— Attempt to recover the collections of the Linnaean Society, 16.— Character of the meetings, 17.— Quarters taken in Pearl Street, 17.— First Annual Meeting and reports, 18.— Geological survey of the State, 19.— Difficulties before the early students of natural history, 20.— Removal to Tremont Street, 21.— Attempts to raise a permanent fund, 21.— Extent of collections, 23.— Gift from Ambrose S. Courtis, 23.— Publication of a "Journal," 24.— Second Survey of the State, 25.— Death of Ambrose S. Courtis, his bequest and notice of his life, 26.— Purchase of the Hentz Collection, 27.— Resignation of Mr. Greene and election of George B. Emerson, second President, 28.— Financial troubles, 28.— Annual Meeting for 1838–39, 29.— Settlement of the Courtis bequest, 30.— Aid given to naturalists, 30.— Death of Simon E. Greene, 30.— Annual meeting, 1840, 31.— Review of the decade, 31.

DECADE II, MAY 1840 — MAY 1850, pp. 36–56.

Bequest of Simon E. Greene, 36.— Annual meeting, 1841, 37.— Meeting of the American Association of Geologists and Naturalists, 38.— Annual reports for 1842, 38.— Adoption of a Diploma, 39.— Annual reports, 1843, 40.— Election of Dr. Amos Binney as third President, 40.— Death of the Rev. F. W. P. Greenwood, 40.— Annual meeting of 1844, 41,— and of 1845, 43.— Endeavors to raise funds for the Society, 43.— Bequest of John Parker, 33.— The "Sea-Serpent" again, 44.— Annual reports 1846, 45,— Death of Dr. Amos Binney, 46.— Annual meeting, 1847, 48.— Election of Dr. J. C. Warren, fourth President, 48.— Purchase of the Medical College and removal to Mason Street, 49.— Annual reports for 1848, 50,— and for 1849, 51.— Deposit in the Library of the books of "A Republican Institution," 52.— Donation of Jonathan Phillips, 52.— Death of Dr. Martin Gay, 52.— Annual reports for 1850, 53.— Early discoveries of gold in California, 54.— Review of the second decade, 55.

DECADE III, MAY 1850 — MAY 1860, pp. 56–81.

Annual meetings 1851 and 1852, 57,— and of 1853, 58.— Purchase of the fossil foot-prints from the Connecticut Valley, 59.— Death of James E. Teschemacher, 59.— Annual meeting of 1854, 61.— Death of Dr. Waldo I. Burnett, 61.— Annual meeting of 1855, 63.— Death of James Brown, 63.— Death of Dr. Thaddeus W. Harris, 64,— and of the Rev. Zadock Thompson, 65.— Annual meeting, 1856, 66.— Election of Dr. Jeffries Wyman, fifth President, 68.— First and only field meeting of the Society, 68.— Deposit from Dr. Binney's Library, 69.— Deaths of Corresponding Members, J. W. Bailey, W. C. Redfield, and Michael Tuomey, 69.— Annual meeting of 1857, 69.— Formation of a Section of Microscopy, and bequest of the collection of Prof. Bailey, 71.— Donation of the B. D. Greene Herbarium, 71.— Annual meeting, 1858, 72.— Deaths of Dr. James Deane and F. W. Cragin, 73.— Thoughts of a new building, 74.— Annual meeting 1859, 74,— and of 1860, 76.— Sketch of Dr. D. Humphreys Storer, 77.— Review of the third decade, 80.

BOSTON SOCIETY OF NATURAL HISTORY.

DECADE IV, MAY 1860–MAY 1870, pp. 81–138.

Bequest of Jonathan Phillips, 81.—Constant exertions for a grant of land for a new building, 81.— First donation from Dr. William J. Walker, 82.— Grant of land to the Society and the Massachusetts Institute of Technology, 83.— Annual meeting 1861, 83.— Sale of building on Mason Street and temporary removal to Bulfinch Street, 84.— Plans for the new building, 85.— Large osteological additions, 85.— Gift of ethnological collections from the Boston Marine Society, 87.— Successful efforts of the Building Committee, subscriptions of $20,000 obtained and the second gift from Dr. W. J. Walker, 87.— Contracts for the new Building, 88.— Annual reports for 1862, 87.— Death of Dr. B. D. Greene, 88.— Gift of the Megatherium cast, 91.— Annual meeting of 1863, 91.— Deaths of Dr. George Hayward and Francis Alger, 92.— First meeting in the new building, 92.— Financial shadows, 94.— New offer of $20,000 from Dr. Walker on condition of raising an equal amount, 95.— Death of Dr. Edward Hitchcock, 95,— of Dr. John Ware, 95.— Resignation of Mr. Dillaway, the Librarian since 1833, 96.— Annual meeting 1864, 96.— Office of Custodian created, and election of S. H. Scudder, 97.— Dedication of the new Museum, 99.— Death of C. A. Shurtleff, 100.— Subscriptions to its Working Fund completed, 100.— Conditions as to use of the amount received from Dr. Walker, 100.— Establishment of Walker Prizes, 100.— Reorganization of a Section of Microscopy, 102.— First course of lectures to Teachers, 102.— Death of Dr. William J. Walker, and sketch of his life, 103.— Bequests of Dr. Walker, 105.— Annual meeting, 1865, 105.— Cost of the Museum, 106.— Ravages of insects, 106.— Gift of the Lafresnaye Collection of Birds by Dr. Henry Bryant, 108.— Attempt to make Dr. Wyman Director, 109.— Annual meeting, 1866, 109.— Establishment of the "Memoirs" as a new series of the "Journal," 109.— Death of Prof. Henry D. Rogers, 111.— Death of Dr. Augustus A. Gould, 111.— The Custodianship, 116.— Formation of a Section of Entomology, 117.— Bequest of Miss S. P. Pratt, 117.— Death of Dr. Henry Bryant, 117.— Coöperation with explorations of the Smithsonian Institution, 118.— Discussion on the House Sparrow, 118.— Abolition of the Department of Ethnology, 119.— Completion of some unfinished rooms, 119.— Bequest of Paschal P. Pope, 119.— Annual meeting, 1867, 119.— Death of Thomas Bulfinch, 120.— Public lectures, 121.— Annual meeting 1868, 121.— Admission of ladies to meetings, 123.— Death of Horace Mann, 123.— Annual meeting 1869, 124.— Results of the Central American explorations, 125.— Excessive expenditures, 126.— Celebration of the centennial anniversary of Humboldt's birth, 127.— Founding of a Humboldt Scholarship in the Museum of Comparative Zoölogy, 128.— Formation of Committees in charge of the different collections, 129.— Annual meeting 1870, 129.— Resignation of Mr. Scudder from the Custodianship, etc., and of Professor Wyman from the Presidency, 132.— Election of Prof. A. Hyatt, Custodian, and Rev. J. A. Swan, Secretary and Librarian, 133.—.Review of the fourth decade, 133.— Part taken by members of the Society in the war of the rebellion, 133.— Joseph P. Couthouy, 138.— Gift of the H. F. Wolcott Fund, 138.

DECADE V, MAY 1870–MAY 1880, pp. 140–243.

Duties of the salaried officers, 141.— Election of Thomas T. Bouvé, President, 142.— Plan for arranging the Museum proposed by Professor Hyatt, 143.— Skeleton of a Fin-back whale secured, 145.— Arrangement with the Trustee of the Lowell Institute for series of lectures under the Society's auspices, 145.— Establishment through John Cummings of the Teachers' School of Science, 145.— Bequest from Sidney Homer, 146.— Annual meeting 1871, 146.— Death of the Secretary, Rev. J. A. Swan, 148.— Election of Edward Burgess, Secretary and Librarian, 149.— Death of William H. Dale, and his bequest to the Section of Entomology, 149.— Annual meeting 1872, 149.— Annual meeting 1873, 152.— Award of the first Grand Walker Prize to Alexander Agassiz, 154.— Death of Prof. Louis Agassiz, 154.— Precautions against fire, and progress of the re-arrangement of the Museum, 164.— Attempt to induce the Legislature to authorize a new survey of the State, 165.— Annual meeting 1874, 165.— Gift of the Eser Palæontological Collection by Mr. John Cummings, 166.— Dr. Charles T. Jackson, 167.— Thoughts of the establishment of a Zoölogical Garden and Aquarium, 160.— Death of Dr. Jeffries Wyman, 169.— Purchase of the Wyman Collection of Comparative Anatomy, 177.— Annual meeting, 1875, 177.— Bequest of the C. S. Hale Collection of Fossils, 179.— President Bouvé wishes to resign, but is lead to reconsider it, 180.— Alterations in the Constitution,— Corporate and Associate membership, 181.— Annual meeting 1876, 181.— Death of Dr. Walter Channing, 183.— Death of Edward Pickering, 184.— Death of Prof. F. B. Meek, 185.— Consideration of opening the Museum on Sundays, 185.— Annual meeting 1877, 186.— Death of Dr. Charles Pickering, 189.— Death of Prof. C. F. Hartt, 192.— Annual meeting 1878, 194.— Death of Gurdon Saltonstall, 197.— Death of Prof. Joseph Henry, 198.— Remarkable work of the Teachers' School of Science, 199.— Death of Dr. J. B. S. Jackson, 199.— Annual meeting 1879, 202.— Teachers' School of Science, 204.— Vote to publish an Anniversary volume, 207.— Award of the second Grand Walker Prize to Prof. Joseph Leidy, 208.— Discussion relating to the Collection of Comparative Anatomy, 208.— Death of Dr. T. M. Brewer, 209.— Plans for a fiftieth anniversary celebration, 211.— Resignation of Mr. Bouvé from the Presidency, 212.— Fiftieth anniversary celebration, April 28, 1880, 213.— Address of Mr. Bouvé, 213,— of Governor Long, 214,— of Dr. Samuel Eliot, 215,— of President Eliot, 216,— of Mr. Alex. Agassiz, 219,— of Rev. R. C. Waterston, 220.— Close of the celebration, 226.— Annual meeting 1880, 226.— Election of officers, with Samuel H. Scudder as President, 230.— Review of the fifth decade, 231.— Original members yet living, 234.— Sketch of George B..Emerson, 235.— Present condition of the Society and the hopes of its founders, 237.— Statistics of the Library and Museum, 238.— Funded property, 239.— Present work, 240.— Inadequacy of means, 241.— Aspirations, 242.— Wishes expressed in Dr. W. J. Walker's will, 243.

List of past officers of the Society, 244.
Contents, 248.
List of portraits, 250.

PORTRAITS IN THIS VOLUME.

BENJAMIN D. GREENE, M.D., First President of the Society. Heliotype from a life-size crayon portrait in the possession of the Society. Opposite page 80.

GEORGE B. EMERSON, LL.D., Second President. Heliotype from an enlarged photograph. Opposite page 236.

AMOS BINNEY, M.D., Third President. Heliotype from a portrait in oil in possession of the Society. Opposite page 40.

JOHN COLLINS WARREN, M.D., Fourth President. Steel engraving from a daguerreotype by J. A. Whipple. Opposite page 66.

JEFFRIES WYMAN, M.D., Fifth President. Heliotype from an enlarged photograph finished in crayon, in the possession of the Society. Opposite page 169.

THOMAS T. BOUVÉ, Sixth President. Heliotype from a crayon portrait in possession of his family. Opposite page 212.

WILLIAM J. WALKER, M.D. Heliotype from a crayon in possession of the Society. Opposite page 105.

AUGUSTUS A. GOULD, M.D. Engraving by H. Wright Smith, from a daguerreotype by Southworth & Hawes, originally published in the Annual of Scientific Discovery for 1861. Opposite page 112.

D. HUMPHREYS STORER, M.D. Steel engraving, prepared for the "Biographical Encyclopedia of Massachusetts of the Nineteenth Century," published in New York in 1879. Opposite page 80.

www.ingramcontent.com/pod-product-compliance
Lightning Source LLC
Chambersburg PA
CBHW031932230426
43672CB00010B/1898